Recent Researches in

Sanskrit Computational Linguistics

Recent Researches in Sanskrit Computational Linguistics

Fifth International Symposium Proceedings

4-6 January 2013, IIT Bombay, India

Edited by

MALHAR KULKARNI

CHAITALI DANGARIKAR

PRINTWORLD

Publishers of Indian Traditions

Cataloging in Publication Data — DK
[Courtesy: D.K. Agencies (P) Ltd. <docinfo@dkagencies.com>]

Recent researches in Sanskrit computational linguistics : fifth international symposium proceedings, January 4-6, 2013, IIT, Mumbai, India / edited by Malhar Kulkarni, Chaitali Dangarikar.
p. cm.
English and Sanskrit.
Includes index.
ISBN 9788124606988

1. Sanskrit language – Data processing – Congresses. 2. Computational linguistics – Congresses. I. Kulkarni, Malhar. II. Dangarikar, Chaitali.

DDC 491.2 23

First published in India, 2013
ISBN 13: 978-81-246-0698-8

Printed and published by:
D.K. Printworld (P) Ltd.
Regd. Office: 'Vedaśrī', F-395, Sudarshan Park
(Metro Station: Ramesh Nagar)
New Delhi – 110 015-11
Phones: (011) 2545 3975; 2546 6019; *Fax*: (011) 2546 5926
E-mail: indology@dkprintworld.com

To

Gérard Huet

A modern

Lakṣyaikacakṣuṣka

Organization

The 5th SCLS was organized at IIT Bombay together by the Cell for Indian Sciences and Technology in Sanskrit (CISTS), the Department of Humanities and Social Sciences (HSS), and the Centre for Indian Language Technology (CFILT), Department of Computer Science and Engineering (CSE).

Programme Chair

Malhar Kulkarni	Department of Humanities and Social Sciences, Indian Institute of Technology Bombay, India

Steering Committee

Brendan Gillon	McGill University, Montreal, Quebec, Canada
Gérard Huet	INRIA, Rocquencourt, Paris, France
Girish Nath Jha	Jawaharlal Nehru University, New Delhi, India
Amba Kulkarni	Department of Sanskrit Studies, University of Hyderabad, India
Malhar Kulkarni	Department of Humanities and Social Sciences, Indian Institute of Technology, Bombay, India
Peter Scharf	Université Paris Diderot, Laboratoire d'Histoire des Théories Linguistiques, Paris, France

Programme Committee

Pushpak Bhattacharyya	Department of Computer Science and Engineering, IIT Bombay, India
Brendan Gillon	Department of Linguistics, McGill University, Montreal, Quebec, Canada
Oliver Hellwig	University of Berlin, Germany
Gérard Huet	INRIA, Rocquencourt, Paris, France
Girish Nath Jha	Jawaharlal Nehru University, New Delhi, India
Amba Kulkarni	Department of Sanskrit Studies, University of Hyderabad, India
K.V. Ramkrishnam-acharyulu	Rashtriya Sanskrit Vidyapeeth, Tirupati, India
Peter Scharf	Université Paris Diderot, Laboratoire d'Histoire des Theories Linguistiques, Paris, France
Lalit Kumar Tripathi	Rashtriya Sanskrit Sansthan, Allahabad, India
Srinivasa Varakhedi	State Sanskrit Education, Karnataka Samskrit University, Bengaluru, India

Sponsoring Institutions

Rashtriya Sanskrit Sansthan, New Delhi, India

Indian Institute of Technology Bombay

Foreword

IT gives us great pleasure to place before the scholarly world this volume containing selected and invited papers for the 5th International Sanskrit Computational Linguistics Symposium held at IIT Bombay (IITB) during 4-6 January 2013. This Symposium took place after two years since the 4th Symposium was held in December 2010 at Jawaharlal Nehru University (JNU), New Delhi.

In a meeting of Steering Committee held during the 4th Symposium at JNU, New Delhi, we proposed to host the 5th Symposium and presented a tentative schedule of programme that we would carry out towards organizing the Symposium. Accordingly, we first created a Symposium site as early as May 2011 and started displaying information regarding the Symposium there. We also immediately announced for submissions for the Symposium ensuring that scholars who wish to submit their contribution get enough time (one year) to prepare and submit.

We adopted Easy Chair as a medium to handle the submissions and their reviews (by the reviewers) and based on the criteria mentioned in the Easy Chair (with the help of members of the Programme Committee and Steering Committee) selected fourteen papers out of total 20 submissions. Below we present a topic-wise summary of all these papers and the way they have been thematically arranged. Before that we would like to mention a few words about the invited speakers and their topics. It was decided in the virtual Steering Committee meetings that no previously invited speakers should be invited again. We followed suit and still were fortunate enough to find three most distinguished scholars who have worked in different fields whom we decided to invite to deliver special lectures at the Symposium.

We invited V.P. Bhatta, Director, Deccan College Post-Graduate and Research Institute, Pune and Former General Editor of the *Encyclopaedic Dictionary of Sanskrit on Historical Principles* (*EDSHP*) and requested him to deliver a lecture on the methodology of *EDSHP* and the process of digitization of the resources of *EDSHP* which he readily obliged to. Such a lecture at this Symposium here at IITB is the most appropriate, as we, at IITB are involved in building a Sanskrit Wordnet (an online multipurpose Thesaurus of Sanskrit) and would like to learn many things from *EDSHP*. Eivind Kahrs, through his publications and lectures, has displayed a wide range of authority on Semantic aspect of Indian grammatical theory which is another important theme of this Symposium. Peter Scharf through this work on developing computational tools of Sanskrit as well as Pāṇinian grammar has served the cause of Sanskrit Computational Linguistics in a unique way and therefore he was invited to deliver a talk on the computational database of Pāṇini's grammar. We would like to express our gratitude to all these three distinguished scholars for accepting our invitation.

The fourteen papers classified under three broad themes are arranged as presented below:

The first group of papers deals with modelling of *Aṣṭādhyāyī* and its supplementary texts. There are four papers in this section. A paper by Amba Kulkarni and Anil Kumar deals with the problem — is it possible to decide the type/sub-type of a compound merely on the basis of its components? The paper analyses the compound formation rules in *Aṣṭādhyāyī* and reports interesting issues in the development of a tool called Compound Type Identifier. The paper by Wiebke Petersen and Simone Soubusta aims to present an approach towards creating a digital, web-based edition of the *Aṣṭādhyāyī* on the basis of a database scheme which provides the core of the digital edition. Another paper in this section is by N. Shailaja and Amba Kulkarni which records findings of the study of various *dhātupāṭha*s and also provides a quantitative measure of differences in various *dhātupāṭha*s along with postulation of the canonical form of a verbal root and its meaning, thereby facilitating an electronic linkage. The paper by Shridhar Subbanna and Shrinivas Varakhedi aims to show that the structure of *Aṣṭādhyāyī* is similar to any computer program and this can be established in various ways.

The second group of papers broadly deals with different Computational Tools for Sanskrit Language. Goyal and Huet discuss various features of the system developed by Gérard Huet and assess it in terms of incompleteness measure in comparison with Pāṇinian framework and try to assess their statistical relevance. A paper by Oliver Hellwig presents quantitative approaches for automatically constructing citation networks from lexically and POS tagged Sanskrit texts, and proposes numeric measures for filtering out "interesting" citations. It also discusses how the resulting data can be evaluated in philological research. A paper by Amba Kulkarni and K.V. Ramakrishnamacharyulu examines the *śābdabodha* theories present in Sanskrit texts from the point of view of extracting a set of relations essential to build a rule-based dependency parser. Mishra, Bali and Jha describe a system to develop Text Normalizer (which is a step towards building a TTS system from Sanskrit) which recognizes a few types of non-standard words and converts them into standard Sanskrit word sequence. The system applies lexical approach for short forms of words and rule-base approach for different formats of numbers. Shivaja S. Nair, Shrinivas Varakhedi and V. Sheeba present a few representative examples of the concept clusters from *Amarakośa* KnowledgeNet (A-KN) where the extended *Nyāya-Vaiśeṣika* (NV) ontology is applied. It also shows how the knowledge base of *Amarakośa* requires an extension for developing the NV ontology. Srigowri and Karunakar describe *Gaveṣikā*, a Sanskrit search engine that extends the functionality of Lucene search engine by plugging in a morphological generator and a spelling variation module.

Application of various computational tools in the traditional Sanskrit concerns is an important theme to which are devoted four papers. These form the third groups Tirumala Kulkarni describes how computational tools are useful for teaching and learning of Vedānta. Varalakshmi describes the use of these tools in better understanding and interpreting the *alaṁkāra*s. Ryali and Scharf describe various applications of a newly-developed software called Sanskrit Image-Text Alignment (SITA) software in recording variants in different manuscripts. Sven Sellmer proposes a quantification method for the phenomenon that many textual elements have a tendency to appear at the same metrical positions. This paper also explains how to build a metrical concordance.

We would like to thank all the contributors for their co-operation and patience in submitting their contribution in the format we wanted.

We would like to express our gratitude to a number of people who were instrumental in preparing this volume. We would like to first of all thank all the Programme Committee members who reviewd the papers and gave invaluable comments. Next our thanks go to the printer and publisher, Shri Sushil Mittal of the D.K. Printworld to have carried out the job of printing these proceedings in a neat and time-bound manner. Our heartfelt thanks are due to the staff of D.K. Printworld as well.

Mention must be made of two important scholars who have been inspirational throughout, Eivind Kahrs and Pushpak Bhattacharyya. Eivind has helped us during the process of review immensely and also kindly obliged us by accepting our invitation to deliver an invited talk. Pushpak Bhattacharyya has been our guiding light at IITB. In fact, all our activities related to computation of Sanskrit at IITB are fortunate enough to have Pushpak's supporting supervision. We would also like to thank authorities of IIT Bombay for having facilitated the smooth Symposium programme.

Finally we would like to say that we wish to express our gratitude to Gérard Huet who initiated this series of Symposia and who has trodden an independent path of a *Lakṣyaikacakṣuṣka*. We see that Pāṇinian grammatical tradition of today needs scholars who think along the lines of a *Lakṣyaikacakṣuṣka* and for them Gérard is a unique example to follow and that's why we dedicate this volume to him.

January 2013 **Malhar Kulkarni**

Chaitali Dangarikar

Contents

Organization vii

Foreword ix

1. Lexicography and Computerization 1
   – *V.P. Bhatta*

2. Meaning: Some Aspects of Semantics in Early India 22
   – *Eivind Kahrs*

3. An Analytic Database of the Aṣṭādhyāyī 40
   – *Peter M. Scharf*

4. Clues from Aṣṭādhyāyī for Compound Type Identification 62
   – *Amba Kulkarni* and *Anil Kumar*

5. Structure and Implementation of a Digital Edition of the Aṣṭādhyāyī 84
   – *Wiebke Petersen* and *Simone Soubusta*

6. Comparison of Pāṇinīya Dhātuvṛttis 103
   – *N Shailaja* and *Amba Kulkarni*

7. अष्टाध्याय्यामुपसामग्रि निष्पादनयन्त्रपरिकल्पनं च 115
   – *Sridhar Subbanna* and *Shrinivasa Varakhedi*

8. Completeness Analysis of a Sanskrit Reader 130
   – *Pawan Goyal* and *Gérard Huet*

9. Googling the Ṛṣi 172
– *Oliver Hellwig*

10. Parsing Sanskrit Texts: Some Relation-specific Issues 191
– *Amba Kulkarni* and *K.V. Ramakrishnamacharyulu*

11. Text Normalizer for Sanskrit 213
– *Diwakar Mishra, Kalika Bali* and *Girish Nath Jha*

12. Extended Nyāya-Vaiśeṣika Ontology as Applied to Amarakośa KnowledgeNet 223
– *Sivaja S. Nair, Shrinivasa Varakhedi* and *V. Sheeba*

13. Gaveṣikā: A Search Engine for Sanskrit 243
– *Srigowri* and *Karunakar*

14. वेदान्तसंस्कृतम् 253
– *तिरुमल पि कुलकर्णी*

15. श्लेषालङ्कारः – संस्कृतविश्लेषणसाधनानां परीक्षणाय एकः समाह्वयः 262
– *वरलक्ष्मीः*

16. Variations in Manuscripts with Reference to the Indic Collections at Brown University and the University of Pennsylvania 286
– *Anupama Ryali* and *Peter M. Scharf*

17. Words in Metrical Milieux: A Computational Approach to a Neglected Field 301
– *Sven Sellmer*

Lexicography and Computerization

(with special reference to *An Encyclopaedic Dictionary of Sanskrit on Historical Principles*)

V.P. Bhatta

Deccan College Post Graduate and Research Institute, Pune

1 Introduction

Lexicography, as Bo Svensen (2009) states, is an activity, which consists in observing, collecting, analysing and describing in a dictionary a number of lexical items (such as words, word elements and word combinations) and includes examination and development of theories concerning the compilation, characteristics, purposes and use of dictionaries. Sanskrit lexicography (*kośaśāstra*) is no exception; and it too consists in observing, collecting, analysing and describing Sanskrit words, and Sanskrit word elements; and includes examination and development of theories concerning the compilation, characteristics, purpose and use of Sanskrit Dictionaries.

Lexicon or dictionary (*kośa*) is the vocabulary of a language, which involves the study of the form, meaning and behaviour of words. To put it in another way, dictionary is a book that lists the words of a language in alphabetical order and gives their grammatical categories, meanings and usages in a systematic way. Thus, lexicon or dictionary (C.C. Berg, Repoart, P.U.) is a systematically arranged list of socialized linguistic forms compiled from the speech habit of a given community. The main purpose of a dictionary, thus, is to give information about words of a language arranged in alphabetical order and that about the development of their meanings in a systematic way.

The *Encyclopaedic Dictionary of Sanskrit on Historical Principles*, which is being compiled at the department of Sanskrit and Lexicography, Deccan College, Post Graduate and Research Institute, Pune, is the only encyclopaedic dictionary of Sanskrit ever planned anywhere in the world at present, which aims at giving exhaustive information about the words of Sanskrit (including their historical and cultural background) in alphabetical order and about the development of their meanings on historical principles.

1.1 Objective

An Encyclopaedic Dictionary of Sanskrit on Historical Principles, being first ever encyclopaedic dictionary of Sanskrit, needs to be compiled according to lexicographical principles strictly; further, since the Encyclopaedic Dictionary of Sanskrit is based on over twelve million data references or slips, extracted from Sanskrit sourcebooks, computerization of the data references/slips is a necessity. The present article, therefore, is meant to describe the various aspects of lexicography and computerization of slips with reference to *An Encyclopaedic Dictionary of Sanskrit on Historical Principles.*

2 Types of Dictionary

Different types of dictionaries are used for different functions with different linguistic activities. Dictionary can be classified mainly into two types as Linguistic Dictionary and Encyclopaedic Dictionary. While linguistic dictionary is primarily concerned with lexical units and other linguistic properties, encyclopaedic dictionary, like *Encyclopaedia Britanica* or *An Encyclopaedic Dictionary of Sanskrit*, is concerned with the denotation of linguistic units.

Linguistic dictionary is either diachronic or synchronic. Diachronic dictionary is basically concerned with the development of lexical units (words) of language regarding both word forms and word meanings throughout the time period of a language. For instance, *Oxford English Dictionary*, being a diachronic dictionary, is concerned with the development of the lexical units of English language regarding both English word-forms and English word-meanings. On the other hand, synchronic dictionary is concerned with the language, as it exists at a particular time period. For instance, Grassman's *Dictionary of the Ṛgvedic Sanskrit* deals with the Vedic Sanskrit language as it existed in the Ṛgvedic period.

Further, diachronic dictionary is either etymological or historical. While etymological dictionary focuses on the prehistory of words and is concerned with the origin and development of words, historical dictionary focuses on the development of word-meanings throughout the history of a language and is concerned with various extra-linguistic-cultural aspects of a language. Thus, the etymological dictionary of Sanskrit such as the *Etymological Sanskrit Dictionary* by Mayrhofer focuses on the prehistory of Sanskrit words and is concerned with the origin and development of Sanskrit words. On the other hand, the historical dictionary of Sanskrit such as *An Encyclopaedic Dictionary of Sanskrit on Historical Principles* focuses its attention on the development of Sanskrit word meanings throughout the history of Sanskrit language and is concerned with the extra-linguistic cultural aspects of Sanskrit.

2.1 Data Collection from the Primary Source

Lexicography demands that collection of data references/slips and their selection must precede the actual compilation of dictionary. It is necessary that entire data references from both primary and secondary sources are made available to the lexicographer for effective and scientific editing of any dictionary.

Prof. S.M. Katre (P.M. Pingale, 2007), a pioneering lexicographer, who nurtured the dream of compiling *An Encyclopaedic Dictionary of Sanskrit on Historical Principles* at the Deccan College, realized the importance of data collection and embarked upon the data collection from primary and secondary sources and established the Department of Sanskrit at the Deccan College with himself as the general editor and Dr. M.A. Mehendale and Dr. S.B. Deo as research assistants.

It must be observed here that there existed a number of Sanskrit Dictionaries published in Europe and India. The noteworthy among them, are: (i) The Dictionary of Böhtlingk and Roth, i.e. *Petersburg's Wörterbuch* (P.W. hereafter) and (ii) *Sanskrit – English Dictionary* by M. Monier Williams,. and (iii) *The Practical Sanskrit English Dictionary* by V.S. Apte. However, the amount of literature available to them was limited in its extent and they used around 500 works as corpus. A large number of works were published after P.W. ; and several important branches of Sanskrit literature such as *Arthaśāstra, Nāṭyaśāstra*, Architecture, *Tantra*, and *Āyurveda* were missing in the earlier dictionaries. Also extensive Vedic word concordance VVRI, by Viśveśvarānanda Institute, the critical editions of the *Rāmāyaṇa* and the *Mahābhārata* by BORI, and D.B.H.S. etc. were published after P.W. Considering these later publications and the Lacuna in the earlier Sanskrit dictionaries, Prof. S. M. Katre, along with Professors. L. Renou, Sunitikumar Chatterjee and P.V. Kane, chalked out a 'Minimum Programme' for the proposed Sanskrit dictionary at the Deccan College, which consisted of roughly 1,500 Sanskrit texts, out of five thousands Sanskrit texts, representing various fields.

Once the corpus was fixed, Prof. Katre appointed a number of editors, two assistant editors and fifteen traditional pandits (Shastris) in the Sanskrit Department for the efficient extraction of data references from the primary and secondary source books. The editors and other staff were trained in the modern linguistics so that they can incorporate both traditional Sanskrit viewpoints and modern scientific linguistic methodology into the extraction and preparation of data references. The actual extraction thus started in 1948 and continued for 25 long years upto 1973 culminating into the preparation of over twelve million data reference. Each data/reference slip records six fields, namely exact lemmata, approximate grammatical category, approximate meaning or shastric gloss or paraphrase, citation to attest the vocable, abbreviation of the texts and exact reference.

2.2 Data Collection from the Secondary Sources

Besides collection of data references from the primary source books, collection of data references from the secondary source is also necessary for the effective compilation of any dictionary. Secondary sources consist of lexica such as *Amarakośa*, indices such as VVRI, dictionaries such as P.W.and special studies such as *Nyāyakośa*.

The use of secondary sources for collection of data references has the advantage that the information appears in an organized form; however, it has its own drawback, namely the linguistic description, forming the basis of the organization of the source, may represent a passed stage of linguistic development.

2.3 Data Selection

Data selection, which is either outer, i.e. selection of lemmas or inner, i.e. information about lemmas, should be authentic. That is to say that the lexicographer must ensure that the selection of data represents the authentic usage of the language in the dictionary. Prof. Katre, thus, took care of the fact that the selection of lemmas and the information about the lemmas are authentic and the Deccan College dictionary provides the authentic description of usages of Sanskrit beginning from the early *Ṛgveda* to the latest *Hāsyārṇava*.

3 Main Components of Dictionary

Dictionary consists of several components such as lemma, spelling (or orthography), morphology, part of speech, meaning description or analysis and reference.

3.1 Lemma

Lemma functions as the representative of linguistic sign. Lemma equals to a word in ordinary language and a dictionary can be described as a list of lemmas or words in an alphabetical order.

In '*An Encyclopaedic Dictionary of Sanskrit on Historical Principles*', compiled at the Deccan College, lemmas are listed in their stem forms and not in nominative singular forms. For instance, the lemma '*apekṣāva*(*n*)*t*' is listed in its stem form and not in its nominative singular form, which may be either '*apekṣāvān*' or '*apekṣāvatī*'. It should be noted here that selection or choosing of lemma in *An Encyclopaedic Dictionary of Sanskrit* is an art and is possible only through experience. While basic lemmas or words are automatic, compound and technical lemmas or words need careful consideration on the part of the lexicographer. For instance, while the basic lemmas or words such as अथ (*atha*) are automatic and are selected in the Dictionary, the compound and technical lemmas such as विभावानुभावव्यभिचारिसंयोग (*vibhāvānubhāvavyabhicāri-saṁyoga*) and अपूर्व विधि (*apūrva-vidhi*) are selected and chosen on careful consideration of the information they provide.

3.2 Spelling or Orthography

Spelling or orthography is another important information given in a dictionary. Information about spelling or orthography is conveyed by the lemma in any dictionary. The basic rule about spelling or orthography is that the lemmas should be present in graphic form normally used in a language.

In a Sanskrit dictionary, meant for both national and international scholars and students, lemma should be spelled preferably in the Devanāgarī script. The Devanāgarī spelling of lemma facilitates all the Sanskrit scholars alike. Consider for instance, the lemma

अपेक्षाकारण(apekṣā-kāraṇa). Here the Devanāgarī spelling provides all the information required for understanding the lemma. The orthography of Sanskrit is mostly fixed and variations pertain to only *v* and *b* etc. Free variations such as *ś* and *ṣ*, as suggested by Śikṣās, should be recorded in the Sanskrit ictionary.

The Devanāgarī orthography demonstrates not only traditional accent, but also marks the formal features of vocables of Sanskrit. However, it must be noted that only transliterations, which are provided in the bracket, show the grave and acute accents, besides immediate constituents or I.C. cuts as in *apekṣā-kāraṇa*.

3.3 Morphology

Morphology is generally divided into two categories: (a) inflection and (b) word-formation or etymology. This helps the user to find the irregular inflected forms of the word on the basis of the lemma and provides the etymology of the word. The users are expected to be familiar with the regular features of inflections; and only irregular features of words are separately listed.

The *An Encyclopaedic Dictionary of Sanskrit on Historical Principles*, however, does not directly list the irregular inflected forms of all the words; however, it provides for the irregularinflected forms indirectly by way of citations which invariably incorporate the irregular inflected forms.

However, the *Encyclopaedic Dictionary* provides the etymology of all the words. It does so by directly listing the classes (*gaṇa*) and *pada*s of all the verbs and also preverbs. In the case of nouns, adjectives, adverbs, etc. it provides etymology by giving required etymology in the form of scholia.

3.4 Part of Speech

Indication of part of speech is to provide information about the grammatical properties of the lemma. Indication of part of speech or information about grammatical status of a word helps the user to identify the lemma word and its function in a sentence. Consider, for instance, the lemmas '*anvartha-nāman*', adj. (having significant name) and '*anvartha-nāman*' n. (significant name). Here the notations adj. and n. stand for adjective and noun status, respectively, of the lemma word *anvar-*

tha-nāman; and the information about the grammatical properties helps the user to understand different functions of anvartha-nāman.

3.4.1 Classification of Words: Nominals and Verbal Roots .

Scientific classification of Sanskrit words is provided by Yāska in his *Nirukta*. Yāska has ruled (*Nirukta* 1.2) that words are classified mainly into four catergores: (1) nominals (*nāman*), (2) verbal roots (*ākhyāta*), (3) affixes (*upasarga*) and (4) particles (*nipāta*). Consider, for instance, the nominal '*go*' (*gaús*) f. (cow), the verbal root '*i*'- II. P. (to go), the affix '*ápa*' adv. (away) and the particle '*ca*' ind. (also). This classification of Sanskrit words is the most scientific classification ever attempted and helps the user giving the basic grammatical categories of Sanskrit words and their use.

However, Pāṇini provides twofold classification of derived words (*pada*) as nominal word-forms (subanta) and finite verbal-forms (*tiṅanta*) (A.M. Ghatage, 1976). The nominal-word-forms are further classified as adnominals (*karmapravacanīya*) (P.1.4.58), which are included in the larger group of preverbs (*upasarga*). The next larger group, which includes both adnominals and preverbs, consists of adverbials (*gati*) such as *alam* -producing complex verbal forms such as '*alam karoti*'. And the largest group, which includes all the four earliar groups, consists of indeclinables (*avyaya*), and they have lost declensional terminations after them (P.2.4.82).

3.4.2 Adjectives

Adjectives are generally the words which give additional information about nouns. Sanskrit does not have regular adjectives. What Sanskrit has are only qualifiers or modifiers (*guṇavacana*) such as 'handsome' or 'beautiful' (*sundara*) which qualify. Consider for instance the expression 'Handsome man has arrived' (*sundaraḥ puruṣaḥ āgataḥ*), here the qualifier *sundara* qualifies the man. However, indication about adjectives can be extended by indication about constructions. Consider for instance, 'A person is handsome', (*puruṣaḥ sundaraḥ*) and 'Woman is beautiful' (*strī sundarī*). Here the adjective *sundara* is used only predicatively.

3.4.3 Adverbs

The adverbs (*kriyāviśeṣaṇa*), which qualify the verbal action, are generally the words that speak about the way or manner in which action takes place. Consider, for instance, the expression,.'One should pronounce the word loudly' (*uccaiḥ uccaritavyam*). Here the adverb 'loudly' (*uccaiḥ*) speaks about the manner in which the action of pronunciation takes place and hence constitutes adverb. However, it should be borne in mind that affixes and other categories, which are other than *svarādi nipātas*, are also adverbs.

3.4.4 Verbal Roots or Finite Verbal Forms

The verbal roots or finite verbal forms (*tiṅanta*) are classified into ten different classes (*gaṇa*) and belong to either *Parasmaipada* or *Ātmanepada*. Information about verbal roots can be provided by stating about the class and *pada* of the verbal root concerned. For instance consider the roots इ (*i*-) II.P. and एध् (*edh*)- I.A. Here II.P. stands for the second class and *parasmaipada* of the root '*i*' and I.A. stands for the first class and *ātmanepada* of the root '*edh*'.

4 Homonymy, Synonymy and Poslysemy

4.1 Homonyms

In the compilation of dictionary, uniform principles must be applied in deciding the lemma and what are homonyms (*sabhaṅgaśleṣa*), synonyms (*samānārtha*) and polysemous words (*anekārtha*). Homonyms have identical base; but they belong to different lemmas, and hence they need to be separated and two or more lemmas need to be established. The base forms of homonyms or two different lexical items may have same spelling, but they have a relationship of homonymy between them. Consider, for instance;

1. Lead (led) 'metal', and
2. Lead (li:d) 'to go in front'.

In other words, homonyms (*sabhaṅgaśleṣa*) are two or more words that have the same sounds; but have the different lexical sources and different meanings. Homonyms, therefore, have the same phonetic forms, but have unrelated meanings (Nalini Sādhale, 2007). Consider for instance, the homonyms:

(1) अक्ष (*akṣa)* m. axle,

(2) अक्ष (*akṣa)* m. dice and

(3) अक्ष (*akṣa)* m. soul or self. Here the words '*akṣa*' (axle), '*akṣa*' (dice) and '*akṣa*' (soul) have identical phonetic forms, but have different lexical sources and hence are homonyms.

4.2 Synonyms

Whereas, synonyms (*samānārtha*) are the words which have the semantic relations that hold between two or more words expressing the same meaning. Synonymy is the relation between two or more words or the equivalence of meaning of different words. Consider for instance, the words: (i) *jala, udaka* and *pānīya.* All the three words hold semantic relation among them, denote the same meaning of water; but have different phonetic forms. Thus, while homonyms are words of identical forms and of different meanings, synonyms are words of different forms but of identical or same meaning. Lexicographer needs to set up different synonyms or near synonyms separately though they denote same meaning. In other words, different synonyms need to be set up as separate entries, while listing the same meaning (of water) under all the synonyms.

4.3 Polysemous words

Another linguistic category, which is closely connected with homonymy and synonymy, is polysemy (*anekārthatva*). Sanskrit, due to the different uses of words under different contexts, has developed a large number of polysemous words and the Sanskrit lexicographer needs to list all the different meanings of polysemous words under the same entry. Consider for instance the word '*hari*' in (i) '*haraye namaḥ*', (salutation to Viṣṇu) and in (ii) '*hariḥ caṅkramyate*' (monkey jumps). Here the word '*hari*' means the lord Viṣṇu in the first instance; whereas it means monkey in the second instance. Thus, the word '*hari*' in Sanskrit is polysemous (*anekārtha*)[1]. The lexicographer therefore needs to study different contexts as well as historical and cultural backgrounds of

[1] [Editor's note: For a detailed list of twenty-four meanings of the word Hari, please refer to an online multipurpose multilingual Thesaurus, Sanskrit Wordnet on the site: http://www.cfilt.iitb.ac.in/wordnet/webswn/]

the polysemous words before assigning different meanings of polysemous words.

5 Designation, Connotation and Range of Application

Lexical meanings stand in the centre of lexicographer's attention; and words are used to refer to the parts of extr-linguistic world as understood by the speaker (Zgusta, 1971).

The lexicographer must clearly distinguish different components of lexical meaning such as designations (denotation) or expressive power (*abhidhā* or *śakti*), connotation and range of application. The designation or expressive power of the lexical item (word) 'cow' (*go*) in the sentence 'Bring the cow' (*gām ānaya*), for instance, is the conventional relation between the lexical item 'cow' (*go*) and the extra-linguistic world meaning of cow; and the lexical item (world) 'cow' (*go*) expresses the extra-linguistic world of cow through the designation (denotation) or expressive power.

Connotation of a lexical item is the signification which adds extra-linguistic value to the basic designative function. For instance, consider the connotations of the lexical items '*mṛtaḥ*' (dead) and '*divam gataḥ*' (gone to the heaven) in '*saḥ mṛtaḥ*' (he is dead) and '*saḥ divam gataḥ*' (he has gone to the heaven), respectively. Here while the connotation of the lexical item '*mṛtaḥ*' as 'dead' is colourless, the connotation of the lexical item '*divam gataḥ*' as 'gone to the heaven' is vulgar and adds extra-linguistic value to the designative function.

The range of application of a word delimits the exact range to which a word is applied. For instance, consider the range of applications of the words '*manuṣyaḥ*' and '*naraḥ*.' They have the same designation and denote human beings. The word '*manuṣyaḥ*' has a limited range of application and applies to the one descended from Manu, and the word '*naraḥ*' has a larger range of application and applies to human being in general.

6 Significations and Meanings

Before we embark upon the meaning description or meaning analysis in a dictionary, it is obligatory that we explain significations (*vṛtti*), as words convey their lexical meanings through significations. Words do not have an abstract existence as derived from their lexical bases according to grammar in any language. They are used in language only to convey particular meanings and conveying of meanings is possible only through significations. Thus, a lexicographer must have a thorough grasp of all the significations for effective description of meaning and analysis. The primary signification (*vṛtti*), that is necessary for the conveying of primary meaning, is the expressive power or denotation (*śakti* or *abhidhā*) (Śakti vā.1.1). The most common primary meanings of any word are the generality or generic property (*jāti*), form (*ākṛti*) and individual (*vyakti*). For instance, the signification of expressive power of the word *go* (cow) in a sentence *gām ānaya* (Bring the cow) convey the generality of cow or cowness, the form of cow (*ākṛti*) and the individual of cow (*govyakti*).

However, lexical meanings are diverse and many. Besides expressed primary meanings, words convey secondary meanings (*gauṇa*). The secondary significations such as indication (*lakṣaṇā*) help the words convey secondary indicatory meanings. For instance, the signification of indication of the word *gaṅgā* (Ganges) in the expression *gaṅgāyām ghoṣaḥ* (the village exists on the bank of the ganges) helps the word *gaṅgā* to convey the secondary indicated meaning of the bank of the Ganges, as the primary signification of expressive power or denotation of the word *gaṅgā* cannot help it to convey the secondary meaning of the bank of the Ganges. Thus the lexicographer must have thorough knowledge of secondary significations as well.

Further, it must be noted that words convey, besides lexical meanings (both primary and secondary), even non-lexical meanings. The signification of suggestion (*vyañjanā*) helps the words convey non-lexical meanings. For instance, the words or expressions *gato 'stam arkaḥ* (the sun has set) convey the non-lexical meaning of appropriate time for robbery, the meeting of lover, etc., besides the lexical meaning of the setting of sun. Here the signification of suggestion helps the words or expressions *gato 'stam arkaḥ* to convey the non-lexical suggested meaning of appropriate time.

Lastly, the words convey different meanings when uttered in different contexts due to the difference in speaker's intention (*tātparya*). Thus, like signification, even speaker's intentionshelps words convey context specific meanings. For instance, the expression *saindhavam ānaya* (bring *saindhava*), uttered in different contexts of eating and setting out on a journey, conveys different meanings of salt and the Sindhu-horse. Here the speaker's intention helps the words or expressions to convey different contextual meanings of salt and the Sindhu-horse. Thus, thorough knowledge of significations has a direct impact on the meaning description or meaning analysis.

7 Distinction of Meanings

The main purpose of any dictionary is to distinguish and analyse the meanings of lexical items in a language. As stated above, meanings of words are specified by significations and contexts.

However, besides signification, lexicographer has to adapt morphological, syntagmatic, semantic, paradigmatic and pragmatic criteria for the distinction of meanings. One must note that meanings are mostly based on corpus data/references. Lexicographer has to largely depend on the corpus data/references available to him for the various shades of meanings of words.

The lexicographer should study all the available citations thoroughly to ascertain different meanings of words. It is necessary to decide how many meanings are to be set up and how many shades of meanings are called for a particular word. While morphological meanings, literal meanings, syntactic and paradigmatic meanings are conventional and based on uses (*rūḍha*), pragmatic meanings are contextual meanings and are based on contexts.

Now, for instance, consider the contextual meanings of the word or expression अपूर्व (*a–pūrva*), which is an adjectival term in Sanskrit. One of the important situational features which is contextually relevant to the word *a-pūrva* is non-precedence or absence of precedence. Based on such a non-precedence, the term *a-pūrva* may be stated to convey the following contextual meanings:

3. '*a-pūrva*'
   - (a) not preceded by any thing, i.e. first in creation in *yad apūrvam yakṣam antaḥ prajānām tanme manaḥ*
   - (b) _ not having any one before in *apūrrvenoṣitā vācaḥ*
   - (c)
     - (i) not having archetype in *apūrvo yajñakratuḥ*
     - (ii) original in *apurva evāyam dhātuḥ*
   - (d) cause in *tad etat brahmā pūrvam*
   - (e) not existing before, i.e. new, fresh in *idam adyā pūrvam kriyate*
   - (f) not preceded by any grammatical element in *pade anudāttapūrve pūrve vā nityaḥ*

4. Situational features, which influence contextual meanings, consist of acts involved. Thus, on the basis of different acts involved, various acts may constitute contextual meanings of the term *a-pūrva*. Consider for instance, the following meanings of *a-pūrva*:
   (a) not stated or prescribed before in *tatrāpūrvo vidhiḥ*
   (b)
      (i) not acquainted with before, stranger in *bāhyam janam sañjighṛkṣad apūrvam*
      (ii) not known before in *apūrvam praśnam anuttamam*
      (iii) not experienced before in *apūrvoyam vikāraḥ*
   (c) not seen before in *rūpam prabhāvam …apūrvam*
   (d) not heard before in *tam sa śusrāva kākusthaḥ …apūrvam*
   (e) not given before in *sva dravya dānam apūrvam*
   (f) not ruled before in *rājā yathāpnoti hi gām apūrvām*
   (g) not practiced before in *ayam tvapūrvaḥ kramaḥ*
5. One of the situational features that changes the meanings of the term *a-pūrva* is the unprecedentedness or excellence. Based on the unprecedentedness, the term *a-pūrva* betrays the following contextual meanings:
   (a) unprecedented, i.e. excessive (emotions etc.) in *apūrvo' yam sambhramaḥ*
   (b) extraordinary, excellent in *apūrvam tanum āśritaḥ*
   (c) unique, unparalleled in *icchāmyaham apūrvam vāhanam*
   (d) strange in *apūrveṇa veśeṇa dṛṣṭvā*
   (e) wonderful in '*vibhudha śreṣtham apūrvam amitaujasam*
6. The word *apūrva* itself also can constitute the meaning of the word. For instance, consider *apūrvam ityetad anuvartate*
7. Other meanings are also possible in the case of the term *a-pūrva*. For instance, 'subsequent', 'transcendental' and 'not connected with the east' are some of the other meanings of the term.

The above meaning analysis amply testifies the fact that the lexicographer has to adapt morphological, syntactic, semantic and pragmatic criteria for the distinction of meanings of Sanskrit words.

7.1 Role of Accent in Meaning Distinction

Now as regard the role of accent in the meaning distinction: Besides signification, morphology and contexts, Vedic accent plays an important role in the meaning distinction. Consider for instance, the word अपस् (*ápas*) n. with an initial accent and the word अपस् (*apás*) n. (= āp, Dvirū K. (Ha.) 100) with middle accent. Here while the word *ápas* with the initial accent (RV. 1. 2.9) means power of working, the word apás with middle accent (Tai Bṛā. II.vii.17 3) means water. Also consider, for instance, the word ब्रह्मन् (*bráhman*) n. with initial accent and the word ब्रह्मन् (*brahmán*) m. with last accent. Here while the word *bráhman* n. with initial accent means growth or expansion, the word *brahmán* m. with last accent means one who prays or a priest. Thus, like signification and morphology etc, even Vedic accent plays a crucial role in the distinction of meanings.

8 Meaning Analysis

8.1 Chronological Approach

The lexicographer of a historical dictionary, like *An Encyclopaedic Dictionary of Sanskrit on Historical Principles*, needs to have a chronological approach in the analysis of meanings of words. That is to say that all the different meanings of a word need to be listed chronologically. Consider for instance, the meanings of the verbal root अन्वि (anv-i) II. P. viz.

8. to go along, to travel along, RV. I. 113.8;
9. to obtain, to attain, RV. I. 163.8;
10. to fall to one's share, RV. IV. 4 .11;
11. to act according to, to conform to RV. IV. 26.2;
12. to imitate, to equate, *Tai S.* v.v.1.2;
13. to search, *Tai. Brā.* III.vii. 4.12;
14. to reappear, to occur again, *Tai Ā.* I.10.4;
15. to seek after, *Kaṭh U.* 4.2;
16. to express, to convey, *Kauṣī Brā. U.* 88; 336;
17. to become related or connected with, *Nidā Sū.* 135.12;

18. to know, to realize, Mahạ̄ Bhā. II. 53.4;
19. to lead to, to effect, Mahā Bhā. III.181.6;
20. the root *anv-i*, *Kāvyāda*.2.64.

The above listing of the meanings of the verbal root अन्वि (*anv-i*) in the Dictionary of Sanskrit amply demonstrates the chronological approach of the lexicographer and the chronological listing of the meanings which help the user to understand the historical development of the word and the meanings.

8.2 Logical Approach

Besides chronological approach, a lexicographer must also have a logical approach to the analysis of meanings so that various meanings can be logically related. Further, single senses in a historical dictionary cannot be listed individually, as it would be chaotic rather, they need to be grouped together and semantically related.

Consider, for instance, the meaning analysis of the word अन्तिक (*antika*) adj. The word *antika* has developed different meanings such as: to, towards, proximity, gap, immediate neighbourhood, side, close, presence, privacy, and type of construction. Here, while the meanings 'to' and 'towards' need to be listed separately under one head, as they constitute different meanings from the rest of the meanings, the other meanings - 'proximity', 'gap', 'immediate neighbourhood' and 'side' need to be grouped together and listed under different head as they can be logically connected with each other. Again, the meanings - 'close presence' and 'privacy' - can be grouped together under yet another head, as they are semantically related. Whereas the last meaning - 'type of construction' - needs to be given a separate individual status as it cannot be logically connectable with any other meaning.

8.3 Other Criteria

The meanings of words may also be analysed as expressed common things and denoted proper names. For example, consider the meanings of the word अन्त्य (*antya*). While the variety of Ruby constitutes an expressed meaning of the word, name of Rudra constitutes the denoted proper name.

Further, meanings of words may also be analysed as technical and non-technical. While the technical meanings are to be listed chronologically, the non-technical meanings need to be related and listed logically and semantically. Consider, for instance, the meanings of the word अनुवाद (*anuvāda*). While one of the six types of *vāda*s and one of the four types of cognitions constitute the technical meanings of the word and hence are listed chronologically, recitation and restatement have been developed as the non-technical meanings and hence need to be related and listed logically and semantically together.

Another important aspect in the meaning analysis of a historical dictionary is the analysis of current and obsolete meanings. The lexicographer must show the vital difference between the current and obsolete meanings by citing the citations that illustrate the current status of meanings form all periods of time and by citing the citations that illustrate the obsolete status of meanings from only that period of time in which they were present. For instance, the lexicographer can show the current meaning of food and the obsolete meaning of grassy bank or ground of the word अंधस् (*andhas*) (n.) by citing the citations that illustrate the sense of food from all the periods and by citing the citations that illustrate the sense of grassy bank or ground from only that period of time in which it was present. Thus the current and obsolete meanings constitute an important aspect of meaning analysis.

It should be noted, however, that the criterion of frequency, which is used in the analysis of meanings in the descriptive dictionary, cannot be adopted in a historical dictionary. Frequency of meaning has no role to play in the analysis of meanings in this kind of dictionary.

Lastly, the lexicographer needs to deal with the meanings, which are both attested and non- attested in the literature. While the attested meanings are naturally supported by the relevant citations, the non-attested meanings are required to be supported by the statement of lexicons. For instance, food and cloud are the attested and non-attested meanings of the word अन्न (*anna*) n. While the attested meaning of food is supported by number of citations, the non-attested meaning of cloud needs to be supported by the statement of lexica.

Use of chronological arrangement of lexical material in other Languages

We have seen earlier that the chronological arrangement of lexical materials or references is quite useful in understanding the development of words and their meanings in a historical Sanskrit dictionary. Likewise, the chronological arrangement of lexical materials in other languages such as Marathi is quite useful. The reason for the usefulness is threefold: First, the chronological listing of the materials allows the user to understand the first occurrence of the word concerned and its meaning; second, it demonstrates the chronological or historical development of the word and changes in the meaning if any; and third it tells the current or obsolete status of the word in the language. Thus, chronological arrangement of lexical material is desirable in other languages as well.

9 References

Any historical dictionary that arranges its citations or lexical materials chronologically must necessarily provide exact references to materials. Actual reference of the lexical materials constitutes the very essence of historical dictionary. The historical development of words and meanings is possible to be shown only when its materials are provided with exact references. The names of the source books should be abbreviated with exact dates and details of references like maṇḍala, sūkta and mantra listed at the end of each citation. The Deccan College dictionary has adapted the most scientific methodology of references by providing the names of the source books in their abbreviated forms and also the details such as page and line or chapter, section and verse numbers. The reference helps the user to trace the lexical materials in the literature and study the contexts concerned whenever necessary.

10 Computerization

We shall now deal with the computerization, rather scanning and digitization, of the data/references or slips in the scriptorium of the Deccan College and its impact on the lexicography or the science of dictionary making in the light of *An Encyclopaedic Dictionary of Sanskrit on Historical Principles*. At the very outset, it must be stated that the computerization or scanning and digitization of over twelve million data/references, collected from both primary and secondary sources, is the primary need of dictionary making. Computerization of the data/ references facilitates the compilation of the *Encyclopaedic Dictionary* in a big way. The Sanskrit lexicographer at the Deccan College can select and choose the computerized data/references available in the scriptorium in a matter of second and computerization, therefore, expedites the dictionary making substantially and also most importantly it can help the compilation of subject wise Sanskrit dictionaries if and when the authorities decide to do so.

The lexicographer or editor of *An Encyclopaedic Dictionary of Sanskrit on Historical Principles* at the Deccan College handles, at present, over twelve million data/references or slips stored at the scriptorium manually for the compilation of the Dictionary. He has to study each of the twelve million data/references which contain six fields:. (i) lemmata, spelling/orthography/transliteration, (ii) grammatical category, (iii) etymology/scholia , (iv) meaning/Sanskrit paraphrase, (v) actual citation and

(vi) exact reference/abbreviation. He does so at present by accessing the particular sourcebook wherefrom the data/references are extracted manually. Since the sourcebooks number thousands for certain entries like *a- pūrva*, the lexicographer /editor needs to access thousands of books from the departmental library and study all the six fields which is quite time-consuming.

Further, the data/references, which are scripted on the paper slips are getting brittle, (they were extracted way long back during 1948-72) and hence need to be preserved properly, as they constitute the very heart of *An Encyclopaedic Dictionary of Sanskrit on Historical Principles*. In view of this necessity, Prof. S.D. Joshi, the then general editor (in-charge) and the head of the Department of Sanskrit and Prof. V.N. Mishra, the then director of the Deccan College, considered various options for the preservation of the data references/slips; but eventually agreed upon the computerization/scanning and digitization of data references or slips as the preferred solution for the preservation. I must also mention that during this time, Joshi and Mishra came into contact with the Māhārājā of Drangdhara. Gujarat, and held several meetings with the Heads of CDAC and NIC which led to a proposal for the central government for the computerization of data references.

However, there was a lull in the effort for the computerization of the scriptorium between 1995 and 2003 as Joshi and Mishra, retired from service and a caretaker was appointed for the running of the Deccan College. The efforts for the computerization of the scriptorium picked up once again when Prof. K. Paddaya was appointed as the director of the College and I was appointed as the general editor of the Department of Sanskrit. Around the same time Smt. Rashmi Chaudhari, director of languages, Ministry of Human Resources and Development (MHRD), visited the Department of Sanskrit and sanctioned Rs. 62 lakh towards the computerization of the data reference in the scriptoriums. Nevertheless computerization gathered momentum in the years 2008-09 when Dr Narendra Jadhav, the then vice-chancellor of the University of Pune, helped the Deccan College in obtaining Rs. 5 crore from the MHRD. through University Grants Commission (UGC). for the computerization of the data references.

When half of the sanctioned amount was released by the MHRD. through UGC. in 2009, the Deccan College authorities set up a Scanning and Digitization Committee as me as the chairman, the Director and two senior editors, Prof. J.D. Sathe and Prof. V.M. Kshirsagar to plan and oversee the actual scanning and digitization programme. The committee held several meetings and resolved to scan all the twelve million data references/slips but to digitize only the lemmata and the actual reference out of the six fields, (i) lemmata, (ii) grammatical category, (iii) etymology, (iv) approximate meaning, (v) citation, and (vi) actual reference. The Committee resolved so to minimize the cost involved in the computerization/scanning and digitization programme. However, it took care of the fact that all the six fields contained in the data references/slips are available for the lexicographers at the Deccan College and planned the inter linking of the digitized and scanned fields with the actual sourcebooks. Thus, the Committee sanctioned the development of special software by which all the digitized and scanned fields are interlinked to the scanned images of the sourcebooks on the computer.

Once the details of computerization/scanning and digitization of data references were finalized by the Committee, the Deccan College authorities awarded the computerization/scanning and digitization project to Modular InfoTech and actual work is fast-nearing completion. It is hoped that the computerization/scanning and digitization of data references will definitely help in the preservation of the same data references and also help in the reduction of physical/manual labour involved in the compilation of the dictionary.

However, it must be noted here that computerization, despite being complimentary to the compilation of the dictionary, does not reduce the lexicographical or editorial work in any way. A lexicographer in the Department of Sanskrit and Lexicography is expected to be a thorough scholar and knowing all the sixty two branches of Sanskrit literature. Despite computerization facilitating ready reference on the computer, he has to study the lemmata, the grammatical category, the meaning, the citation and the reference, and correct and change the six fields and prepare the dictionary articles. He has to plan each entry according to the needs and provide extralinguistic information which are not available in the computerized data references. The only help the computerization provides for the lexicographer at the Deccan College is the saving of the manual labour in the form of bringing of the sourcebooks to the editor's table.

11 Conclusion

Lexicography or science of dictionary making needs to be strictly followed in the compilation of any dictionary so that the dictionary becomes authentic.

Though different types of dictionaries are used for different functions, encyclopaedic dictionary needs to utilize all the lexical materials in a language and provide all the denotations of its linguistic units.

Data collection must necessarily precede the actual compilation of any dictionary; and Prof. S.M. Katre made available over twelve million data references from over 1500 sourcetexts of Sanskrit; and this enables the lexicographers at the Deccan College to study the lexical material scientifically and provide the authentic information.

Lemmas, which equal words in a dictionary, must necessarily be chosen with due care as the linguistic and extralinguistic information depend upon the lemmas selected.

Correct spelling or orthography of lemmas is crucial to any dictionary, as the user depends totally on the spelling/ orthography of lemmas and wrong spelling or orthography leads to grave information about the words in a dictionary.

Now as regards the morphology, it is crucial to the grasping of grammatical information about words; and *the Encyclopaedic Dictionary of Sanskrit* provides morphological information by listing grammatical categories and giving citations with irregular forms.

Yāska has provided the most scientific grammatical categories or parts of speech as nominals, verbal roots, affixes and particles and Pāṇini provided further classifications of grammatical categories as adnominal, and these need to be shown after the dictionary entries strictly.

In any dictionary, homonyms, synonyms and polysemous words must be set up according to the principles of homonymy, synonymy and polysemy; and they should be distinguished accordingly.

A lexicographer must have a clear understanding of designation, connotation and range of application; and also he must know different significations such as expressive power or denotation, indication and suggestion for understanding of various types of meanings of words.

Meaning description or meaning analysis constitutes the very essence of any dictionary and a lexicographer must describe or analyse meanings of words by using all his knowledge of significations and contexts. Also he must adopt chronological, logical and other approaches for his meaning description/analysis.

Computerization of data references/slips in the scriptorium is essential for both the preservation of the same data references/slips and saving of the manual labour of lexicographers/editors. However, it is not a substitute for the lexicography/editorial work, which constitutes a totally different science and requires thorough understanding of all the branches of Sanskrit literature and application of mind.

References

1. Ali, M. Al-Kasimi. *Linguistics and Bilingual Dictionaries*, Leiden, E.J. Brill. 1977.
2. Bhatta, V.P. Significance of Historical Dictionary, *Research Trends in Lexicography, Sanskrit and Linguistics*, Deccan College, Pune. 2007.
3. Bo, Svensen. *Handbook of Lexicography*, Cambridge University Press, Cambridge. 2009.
4. Ghatage, A.M. *An Encyclopaedic Dictionary of Sanskrit on Historical Principles*, Vol. I, Deccan College, Pune. 1976.
5. Katre, S.M. *Lexicography*, Annamalai University, Annamalainagar. 1965.
6. Kipfer, Barbara Ann. Work book on Lexicography, *Linguistic Studies*, University of Exeter. 1984.
7. Pingle, P.M. Collection of the Data for the Encyclopaedic Dictionary on Historical Principles, *Research Trends in Lexicography*, Deccan College, Pune. 2007.
8. Sadhale, Nalini. Synonyms, Homonyms and Taxonyms in Sanskrit and in History of Agriculture, *Research Trends in Lexicography*, Deccan College, Pune. 2007.
9. Singh, Ram Adhar. *An Introduction to Lexicography*, CIIL, Mysore. 1982.
10. Zugusta, L. *Manual of Lexicography*, Academia, Prague. 1971.

Meaning

Some Aspects of Semantics in Early India

Eivind Kahrs

University of Cambridge
egk1000@cam.ac.uk

vāgarthāviva saṃpṛktau vāgarthapratipattaye |
jagataḥ pitarau vande pārvatīparameśvarau ||

'To fully comprehend [the relation between] word and meaning, I praise those who are as inseparably united as word and meaning are, the parents of the universe: Pārvatī and the Supreme Lord (Śiva).'

This is how Kālidāsa, by many considered the greatest of Sanskrit poets, chooses to praise the God Śiva and his consort Pārvatī in the opening verse of his *Raghuvaṃśa*. This is how he describes the divine embrace that results in the creation of the universe. That a poet of Kālidāsa's caliber includes the relation between word and meaning in a poetic image indicates the position linguistics and philosophy of language held in Indian cultural history.

Now, there are two primary traditions in Indian linguistic theory: *Vyākaraṇa* and *Nirukta* or *Nirvacanaśāstra*. That is, of course, not to shut out the linguistic deliberations of the Mimaṃsakas, the Naiyāyikas, the Buddhists, and others. But these two are at the core. The *Vyākaraṇa* tradition is well known to us through a number of treatises, mainly in the form of commentaries and elaborations on the works of three grammarians: Pāṇini, Kātyāyana, and Patañjali. Pāṇini is the author or compiler of the *Aṣṭādhyāyī*, a grammar of Sanskrit that consists of about 4,000 rules in eight chapters (*adhyāya*s), each chapter containing four sections (*pādas*). To this work, pivotal to the later tradition, Kātyāyana added 5,000 critical remarks (*vārttika*s). Finally, Patañjali commented on Kātyāyana and Pāṇini in his *Mahābhāṣya*, the 'Great Commentary'. This monumental work is more concerned with interpretation than with the *construction* of a grammar which had been Pāṇini's task a few centuries earlier, and constitutes the basis for virtually all subsequent discussions on philosophy of language and difficult points of grammar in the *Vyākaraṇa* tradition. Patañjali can with some certainty be placed in the second century BCE but there is no conclusive evidence for the dating of either Pāṇini or Kātyāyana. An opinion that is commonly held is that at least one century separated Patañjali from Kātyāyana and that at least another separated Kātyāyana from Pāṇini. In stark contrast to the situation in *Vyākaraṇa*, only one basic work of *Nirvacanaśāstra* has survived. This is the *Nirukta* of Yāska. Apart from this basic text, all we have is three commentaries on it and a commentary on the *Nighaṇṭu*, the lexicographical work upon which the *Nirukta* itself is a kind of commentary. Yāska's *Nirukta* is primarily concerned with semantic analysis, that is to say, the meaning of Vedic words.

Meaning is a property by virtue of which a sentence such as 'Devadatta cooked the rice' can be used to communicate the information that Devadatta cooked the rice. The Sanskrit term for 'meaning' in this sense is *artha*, as met with in Kālidāsa's verse. The term *artha* requires a few remarks, but, first of all, one should be reminded that 'meaning' is itself a slippery term. We may, for example, say 'what's the meaning of all this?', 'I did not mean it', 'the meaning of this word is …', etc. As pointed out by W.V. Quine (1953) there is also a gulf between 'meaning' and 'naming' even in the case of a singular term that is genuinely the name of an object. He takes from Frege the example of 'Evening Star' and 'Morning Star'. Both of these terms name the same thing but they cannot be said to have the same meaning. There is, however, no reason to assume that the Indians worked within a modern framework that distinguishes clearly between meaning and reference. Indeed, the term *artha* frequently refers to that which is designated by a term, to the thing meant.

It is also clear that it is possible to claim that 'purpose' is a constant basis for the rendering of the term *artha*. Indeed, 'purpose' is often the rendering resorted to by Sanskrit authors. For example, Kaiyaṭa, the eleventh-century commentator on the *Mahābhāṣya*, glosses *anarthaka* by *niṣprayojanam* 'without purpose' (MbhP I:32b). In the context of *nirvacana* analysis this is important in as much as a *nirvacana* analysis is an analysis of *words* with regard to how they are related to *things*, and this is where the semantic range of the term *artha* becomes crucial. With the above background, let me turn to some indigenous discussions of the term *artha*.

An easy entry into the indigenous discussions of *padārtha*, the *artha* of a word (*pada*), is provided by Patañjali in the *Paspaśāhnika*. In the introductory section of Patañjali's *Mahābhāṣya* Patañjali presents the problem as follows (Mbh I:6,8–11):[1]

> *Now, what is the artha of a word: a class (ākṛti) or rather an individual thing (dravya)?*[2] *Both, he (= Patañjali) says. How do we know? The Teacher (= Pāṇini) has formulated rules in both ways. Considering a class (ākṛti) to be the artha of a word, it is stated [by A 1.2.58] that when there is designation of a class (jāti 'class; genus; species') the plural may optionally be used with regard to one single thing. [And] considering an individual thing (dravya) to be the artha of a word, the [fact that there should be a] single remainder is taught by [A 1.2.64 which begins] sarūpāṇām 'of elements showing the same form'.*[3]

Kaiyaṭa remarks on this as follows (MbhP I:56b):[4]

---

1 *kiṃ punar ākṛtiḥ padārtha āhosvid dravyam | ubhayam ity āha | kathaṃ jñāyate | ubhayathā hy ācāryeṇa sūtrāṇi paṭhitāni | ākṛtiṃ padārthaṃ matvā jātyākhyāyām ekasmin bahuvacanam anyatarasyām ity ucyate | dravyaṃ padārthaṃ matvā sarūpāṇām ity ekaśeṣa ārabhyate||*

2 A word of caution seems necessary here. In Nyāya-Vaiśeṣika *padārtha* is a technical term commonly translated 'category', and *dravya* and *sāmānya* 'universality' or *jāti* 'class; genus' figure among these. It could therefore be the case that Patañjali is playing around with words here in order to point out various possibilities: we are dealing with *something* (*padārtha*) which could be *dravya* as well as *jāti* and not the one excluding the other.

3 A 1.2.64 *sarūpāṇām ekaśeṣa ekavibhaktau* is the rule which teaches that out of a series of stems showing the same form, only one is retained before one single case ending. In other words, this is the rule that accounts for the fact that we say *vṛkṣāḥ* 'trees', and not *vṛkṣaś ca vṛkṣaś ca vṛkṣaś ca*, 'a tree and a tree and a tree'.

4 *tatra jātivādina āhuḥ — jātir eva śabdena pratipādyate, vyaktīnām ānantyāt saṃbandhagrahaṇāsaṃbhavāt | sā ca jātiḥ sarvavyaktiṣv ekākārapratyaya-darśanād astīty avasīyate | tatra gavādayaḥ śabdā bhinnadravyasamavetāṃ jātim abhidadhati | tasyāṃ pratītāyāṃ tadāveśāt tadavacchinnaṃ dravyaṃ pratīyate | śuklādayaḥ śabdā guṇasamavetāṃ jātim ācakṣate | guṇe tu tatsaṃbandhāt pratyayaḥ, dravye saṃbandhisaṃbandhāt | saṃjñāśabdānām apy utpattiprabhṛtyā vināśāt piṇḍasya kaumārayauvanādyavasthābhede 'pi sa evāyam ity abhinnapratyayanimittā ḍitthatvādikā jātir vācyā | kriyāsv api jātir vidyate, saiva dhātuvācyā | paṭhati – paṭhataḥ – paṭhanti – ityāder ab-*

This being so,[5] *those who hold the view that a jāti 'class; genus' [is the artha of a word] state: it is only a class that is conveyed by a word, for [otherwise] it is not possible to grasp the relation [between a word and its artha] because there is an endless number of individual things. And it is established that there is such a thing as a jāti since we perceive the cognition of a single shape (ākāra) with regard to all individuals [of the same class]. This being so, words such as gauḥ 'cow' denote a jāti which is inherent in different individuals. When this [jāti] has been understood [as the artha of a given word], we understand an individual thing (dravya) limited by that [jāti] since it possesses that [individual]. Words such as śukla 'white' signify a jāti which is inherent in a quality. And in the case of such a quality, cognition takes place because of [its] relation to it [= to the jāti], [while] in the case of an individual thing (dravya), cognition takes place because of [its] relation with the relatum.*[6] *Even words which are proper names express a jāti such as ḍitthatva 'Ḍittha-hood', [a property] grounded on an unchanging cognition so that one says 'this is that very same [person]', although there is change of [his] body in the stages of youth, adulthood, etc. from birth to death. With regard to actions too we find a jāti; indeed, it is expressed by a verbal root. Because an unchanging cognition is present from such [verbal forms] as paṭhati 'he recites', paṭhataḥ 'the two of them recite', [and] paṭhanti 'they recite', a jāti is accepted [in the case of verbal forms] as the cause of that [unchanging cognition]. Those, however, who hold the view that a vyakti 'individual thing' [is the artha of a word] say that it is only an individual manifestation (vyakti) that is denoted by a word. But*

---

hinnasya pratyayasya sadbhāvāt ‖ *tannimittajātyabhyupagamaḥ* ‖ *vyaktivādinas tv āhuḥ — śabdasya vyaktir evābhidheyā, jātes tūpalakṣaṇabhāvenāśrayaṇād ānantyādidoṣānavakāśaḥ* ‖

5 The context concerns the application of the two views with regard to two *paribhāṣās*, general rules of interpretation. This need not concern us here.

6 The *jāti* 'class; genus' (such as *śuklatva* 'white-ness', the property of being white) is inherent in the *guṇa* 'quality' which is inherent in the *dravya* 'individual thing'. In this way the *jāti* is indirectly related to the *dravya* through the *guṇa*.

> *since the jāti is resorted to by implication, there is no occasion for such error as [having to assume] innumerable [relations].*

Patañjali's initial discussion concerns directly only the context of the *Aṣṭādhyāyī*, although Kaiyaṭa places it within a larger framework. Later on, however, Patañjali puts his initial statement to good use in his discussion of the compound *śabdārthasambandhe* in the phrase *siddhe śabdārthasaṃbandhe*, traditionally considered the first part of the first *vārttika* of the *Mahābhāṣya*.

Patañjali states (Mbh 7,8–10)[7]

> *Now, with what artha of the word [siddha] in mind have we analysed [the compound] as siddhe śabde 'rthe sambandhe ca, 'when the word-form, [its] artha, and the relation [between them] are permanently established'? He (= Patañjali) says: the ākṛti 'class'. How come? Because the ākṛti is permanent (nitya), [while] the dravya 'individual thing' is non-permanent. Now, if the artha of a word is the dravya, how do we then analyse [the compound]? [As:] siddhe śabde 'rtha-sambandhe ca, 'when the word-form and the relation with [its] artha is permanently established'. For the relation between things that possess an artha and the arthas is permanent.*

If the *artha* of the word *siddha* 'permanently established' is an *ākṛti* 'class', Patañjali interprets the compound entirely as a *dvandva*. If, however, the *artha* is a *dravya* 'an individual thing', he keeps the last two members of the compound as a unit, itself now a *tatpuruṣa* compound: *arthasaṃbandha*, 'the relation with the *artha*'. Kaiyaṭa elaborates on this as follows (MbhP I:62b):[8]

> *On the view [that a word signifies] a dravya 'individual thing', because the dravya is non-permanent, the [word] artha has*

---

7 *atha kaṃ punaḥ padārthaṃ matvaiṣa vigrahaḥ kriyate siddhe śabde 'rthe saṃbandhe ceti | ākṛtim ity āha | kuta etat | ākṛtir hi nityā dravyam anityam || atha dravye padārthe kathaṃ vigrahaḥ kartavyaḥ | siddhe śabde 'rthasambandhe ceti | nityo hy arthavatām arthair abhisaṃbandhaḥ ||*

8 *dravyapakṣe dravyasyānityatvād arthagrahaṇaṃ saṃbandhaviśeṣaṇārtham upāttam | anitye 'rthe kathaṃ saṃbandhasya nityatā – iti cet, yogyatālakṣaṇatvāt saṃbandhasya | tasyāś ca śabdāśrayatvāt – śabdasya ca nityatvād adoṣaḥ ||*

> *been mentioned for the purpose (artha) of qualifying [the word] saṃbandha 'relation'. [But] if [someone asks:] when the artha is non-permanent, how can the relation [with the artha] be permanent, [we answer that this is] because the relation is defined as yogyatā 'suitability'.*[9] *And because the word-form is the substratum of that [relation], there is no fault since the word-form is permanent.*

Patañjali continues his discussion as follows (Mbh 7,11–12; 18–20):[10]

> *Or rather, this analysis [of the compound] as siddhe śabde 'rthe saṃbandhe ca, 'when the word-form, [its] artha, and the relation [between them] are permanently established', is proper only when the artha of the word [siddha] is the dravya 'material substance'. For the dravya 'material substance' is permanent, [whereas] the ākṛti 'shape' is non-permanent. How do we know? Because so it is seen in daily life. ... [But] this analysis [of the compound] as siddhe śabde 'rthe saṃbandhe ca, 'when the word-form, [its] artha, and the relation [between them] are permanently established', is proper also when the artha of the word [siddha] is the ākṛti 'shape'. Well, but it was said that the ākṛti is non-permanent. That is not so; the ākṛti is permanent. How? By making out that when it has come to an end in a certain place, it has not come to an end everywhere, but is [on the contrary] observed as remaining in other individual things (dravyāḥ).*

Here Patañjali considers other meanings of the terms *dravya* and *ākṛti*, taking them in the completely different senses of 'material substance' and 'shape; form' respectively. He goes on to offer examples of how a material substance (*dravya*) such as clay or gold is permanent

---

9 That is to say, words are assumed to be permanently suited to signify, that is, refer to the things meant.

10 *atha vā dravya eva padārtha eṣa vigraho nyāyyaḥ siddhe śabde 'rthe saṃbandhe ceti | dravyaṃ hi nityam ākṛtir anityā | kathaṃ jñāyate | evaṃ hi dṛśyate loke | ... | ākṛtāv api padārtha eṣa vigraho nyāyyaḥ siddhe śabde 'rthe saṃbandhe ceti | nanu coktam ākṛtir anityeti | naitad asti | nityākṛtiḥ | katham | na kvacid uparateti kṛtvā sarvatroparatā bhavati dravyāntarasthā tūpalabhyate |*

(*nitya*), while the shape (*ākṛti*) of things made from them may vary and is therefore non-permanent (*anitya*). Taking *ākṛti* in the sense of 'shape; form' he then turns the argument around, claiming that the *ākṛti* is indeed permanent in the sense that although it comes to an end somewhere, it will still remain in other *dravyas*, thus incidentally resorting to the previous sense of *dravya* as 'individual thing'.

Tired of the discussion, Patañjali concludes (Mbh I:7, 23–25):[11]

> *Or rather, what is the use of our saying 'this is permanent', 'this is non-permanent'? Thinking that whatever is permanent (nitya), that is the artha of the word, this analysis [of the compound] is made: 'when the word-form, [its] artha, and the relation [between them] are permanently established'.*

Kaiyaṭa remarks on this in the following, illuminating manner (MbhP I:64b):[12]

> *'Whatever is permanent.' The artha of a word is the appearance of a cognition. Whenever a word is pronounced, then a cognition appears with the shape of the artha; that is to say, the artha is permanent because it is permanent in the form of a continuous flux.*

Nāgeśa, the late seventeenth to eighteenth century author of the *Mahābhāṣyapradīpoddyota*, or *Uddyota* for short, elaborates on Kaiyaṭa's statement as follows (MbhU I:64b):[13]

---

[11] *atha vā kiṃ na etenedaṃ nityam idam anityam iti | yan nityaṃ taṃ padārthaṃ matvaiṣa vigrahaḥ kriyate siddhe śabde 'rthe saṃbandhe ceti |*

[12] *yan nityam iti | buddhipratibhāsaḥ śabdārthaḥ, yadā yadā śabda uccāritas tadārthakārā buddhir upajāyate — iti pravāhanityatvād arthasya nityatvam ity arthaḥ ||*

[13] *yan nityam iti | vyaktijātyākṛtīnāṃ madhye yan nityam ity arthaḥ || nanu śaśaśṛṅgādipadārthānāṃ kathaṃ nityatvaṃ, teṣāṃ svarūpasyaivābhāvād ata āha — buddhipratibhāsa iti | bāhyaḥ padārtho na śābdabodhe viṣayaḥ, kiṃ tu bauddhaḥ | sa ca pravāhanitya iti bhāvaḥ || etac ca mañjūṣāyāṃ vistareṇa nirūpitam ||*

> *'Whatever is permanent'. That is to say, whatever is permanent among the vyakti 'individual thing', the jāti 'class' or the ākṛti 'generic shape'. Well, but how can the artha of words such as śaśaśṛṅga 'the hare's horn' be permanent, since these have no form of their own? Therefore he (= Kaiyaṭa) states: 'whatever appears in the mind'. In linguistically based cognition the object (viṣaya) is not the external artha of a word, but a mental one. And that is permanent in the form of a continuous flux. This is what Kaiyaṭa means to say. And this [topic] has been discussed at length in the Mañjūṣā.*[14]

From Nāgeśa's last remark it is evident that this brief presentation is not in any way an exhaustive discussion of the indigenous elaborations on the term *artha*. But it has sufficiently established that the distinction between meaning and thing meant is extremely blurred, and that the discussion revolves around three possibilities: the *artha* of a word is a class (*jāti*, *ākṛti*); a shape or form that appears in the mind (*ākṛti*, *ākāra*); and an individual thing (*dravya*, *vyakti*). It is also clear that in *Vyākaraṇa* questions of meaning become questions of reference. The gulf between 'meaning' and 'naming' has narrowed considerably, and this is one of the reasons why it is possible to arrive at the *artha* or 'meaning' of a term though that term itself by means of the very method of *nirvacana* analysis as presented in Yāska's *Nirukta*.

Now, it is also clear that the term *artha* is used in a more abstract way than simply referring to the thing meant. As far as I know, it is in the *Nirukta* itself (Nir 1.3) that we find the earliest extant discussion on whether certain linguistic elements express an *artha* 'meaning' or 'purpose' (*arthān nirāhuḥ*). The context is the meaningfulness of *upasargas* — preverbs or prepositions. This serves to demonstrate that the term *artha* implies more than just 'thing' or 'referent', since the meaning of preverbs surely is rather abstract.

The term *artha* is also used to denote meaning in a broader sense, more specifically with regard to the meaning of a corpus of texts. For example, Sāyaṇa, the fourteenth-century Vijayanagara commentator of Vedic texts, concludes his exposition of *Nirvacanaśāstra* in his introduction to his commentary on the *Ṛgveda* as follows (Sāy p. 29):

---

[14] For example in Nāgeśa's *Vaiyākaraṇasiddhāntalaghumañjūṣā* (*bauddhārthanirūpaṇa*).

tasmāt vedārthāvabodhāyopayuktaṃ niruktam, 'therefore *nirukta* is useful for grasping the meaning (*artha*) of the Veda'.

Similarly, the *Nirukta* commentator Durga remarks with regard to the *Nighaṇṭu* (D I:30, 3–4):

> *sa ca ṛṣibhir mantrārthaparijñānāyodāharaṇabhūtaḥ pañcādhyāyīśāstrasaṃgrahabhāvenaikasminn āmnāye granthīkṛta ity arthaḥ,*
> *'that is to say, in order that [we shall get] knowledge of the meaning (artha) of the Vedic verses, the Ṛṣis have also made it [= the sam-āmnāya] into a text that serves as an example in the form of a compendium of a Śāstra which consists of five parts in one single [ekasmin = sam, cf. Nir 1.3] āmnāyaḥ (repetition within certain limits)'.*

Clearly it is the meaning of the Veda Yāska has in mind when he quotes the following verse (Nir 1.18):

yad gṛhītam avijñātaṃ nigadenaiva śabdyate |
anagnāv iva śuṣkaidho na taj jvalati karhicit ||

> *What has been taken [from the teacher's mouth] but not understood [and] is uttered by mere recitation, that never flares up, like dry firewood on a non-fire.*

The verse is quoted also by Patañjali in the Paspaśāhnika of the *Mahābhāṣya* (Mbh I:2,15–16),[15] a clear example of how Patañjali shows Yāska respect in this introductory chapter.

Yāska also comments on a Vedic verse (ṚV 10.71.4) that makes his attitude quite clear (Nir 1.19):

utá tvaḥ páśyan ná dadarśa vā́cam utá tvaḥ śṛṇván ná śṛṇoty enām |
utó tvasmai tanvàṃ ví sasre jāyéva pátya uśatī́ suvā́sāḥ ||

> *And many a one, [although] seeing, does not see Speech; and many a one, [although] hearing, does not hear Her; and to*

[15] Reading *adhītam* 'studied' for *gṛhītam*.

> *many a one She spreads out [Her] body, like a wife wearing clean clothes, having desire for [her] husband.*

This verse too is quoted by Patañjali (Mbh I:4, 2–3). His interpretation agrees more or less with Yāska's, except for one significant point: to Yāska the wife who uncovers herself uncovers knowledge, the illumination of meaning (*artha*) (*svam ātmānaṃ vivṛṇute jñānaṃ prakāśanam arthasya*), and the verse is a praise of one who knows the meaning (*arthajñapraśaṃsā*); to Patañjali the verse says that speech uncovers itself to someone who knows speech (*vāg vāgvide svātmānaṃ vivṛṇute*), that is to say, to the grammarian. Yāska (Nir 1.20) goes on to quote the subsequent verse (ṚV 10.71.5), and remarks: *arthaṃ vācaḥ puṣpaphalam āha*, 'he declares the meaning of speech to be its fruit and flower'.

Finally, the following passage from the *Mahābhāṣya* may serve to illustrate the intricacies of the term *artha* (Mbh I:363, 24–28):[16]

> *There will, in fact, be no attempt at instruction in meaning (artha). For there are many words whose meanings are unknown, such as jarbhárī turphárītū.*[17] *In fact, many meanings are understood without the use of words, by closing the eyes or by doing things with the hands. Indeed, there is no purpose whatsoever in explaining meaning which has [already] been understood. For he who says that the sun rises in the east and sets in the west, that sugar is sweet, [or] that ginger is pungent, what is accomplished by him?*

Let these considerations suffice to establish that the term *artha* is as complex an entity as its English counterpart 'meaning' which I have used to translate it. Let it also be clear that I am first and foremost dealing with linguistic meaning in the sense that we deal with the mean-

---

16 *apravṛttiḥ khalv apy arthādeśanasya* | *bahavo hi śabdā yeṣām arthā na vijñāyante* | *jarbhárī turphárītū* || *antareṇa khalv api śabdaprayogaṃ bahavo 'rthā gamyante 'kṣinikocaiḥ pāṇivihāraiś ca* || *na khalv api nirjñātasyārthasyānvākhyāne kiṃ cid api prayojanam asti* | *yo hi brūyāt purastād āditya udeti paścād astam eti madhuro guḍaḥ kaṭukaṃ śṛṅgaberam iti kiṃ tena kṛtaṃ syāt* ||

17 ṚV 10.106.6.

ing of singular and general terms. In that context questions of meaning are primarily questions of reference. In order to account also for the broader and the more abstract senses of *artha*, however, I shall confine myself to saying that words signify.

Yāska's *Nirukta* deals directly with meaning, but semantics do play an important part in Pāṇini's *Aṣṭādhyāyī* as well. For example, you do not add a suffix unless there is meaning involved. Moreover, in Pāṇinian grammar the term *kāraka* (lit.: 'doer; accomplisher') applies to direct participants in actions. Such a participant is a *sādhana*,[18] a means of realising the action, and every participant is assigned to one of a set of six *kāraka* categories.[19] The abstract syntactic level at which *kāraka*s are introduced in the grammar serves to mediate between the levels of semantics and morphology. By this device Pāṇini is able to account for the relationship between possible semantic choices on the side of the speaker and some basic features of Sanskrit syntax and morphology. Such participants in actions are, at the abstract level of *kāraka* syntax, assigned to particular *kāraka*-categories. In a similar way the set of *lakāra*s, a set of ten suffixes marked with an *L*, are introduced after verbal roots at the same abstract level. At this level all verbal endings, except for the ones that denote *bhāva* (lit.: 'being; state of action'), can be said to signify agents and objects in relation to activities. By A 3.4.69 *laḥ karmaṇi ca bhāve cākarmakebhyaḥ* an L-suffix is added to a verbal root to denote — in addition to the agent (*kartari*, A 3.4.67) — the object, or, in the case of verbal roots which are objectless (*akarmaka*, that is, intransitive verbs), the mere activity expressed by the verbal root (*bhāva*). When the relevant semantic choices have been considered on the side of the speaker, the abstract syntactic level of *kāraka*s and *lakāra*s is sorted out. The correct distribution of case endings and finite verbal endings is then accounted for in the syntax of a Sanskrit sentence by means of operational rules.

However, *kāraka*s do not pertain to the derivation of sentences alone. Any verbal noun derived by a *kṛt*-suffix (a primary suffix) is

---

18 I analyse this term as *sādhyate 'nena*, '[something] is realised/accomplished through it'.

19 In the *Aṣṭādhyāyī* these are defined in the following order: *apādāna* 'stable point when there is movement away', *saṃpradāna* 'recipient; indirect goal', *karaṇa* 'instrument', *adhikaraṇa* 'locus', *karman* 'object; goal', and *kartṛ* 'agent'. Moreover, a subcategory of agent is defined, namely *hetu*, the causal agent.

considered to denote either a participant in an action, in which case it is assigned to one or the other of the six *kāraka* categories, or it is considered to denote the mere activity (*bhāva*) expressed by the verbal root. By way of example, the suffix *LyuṬ* (*-ana* with *guṇa* and presuffixal accent) is introduced to form neuter action nouns (*bhāve*), by A 3.3.115 *lyuṬ ca*, and also to form nouns expressing the instrument or the locus of the action expressed by the root, by A 3.3.117 *karaṇādhikaraṇayoś ca*. This means that when analysing a particular word, alternative interpretations are often possible. Accordingly, a word such as *utpāda*, to which I shall return further on, can be interpreted as *bhāvasādhana*, that is to say, as an action noun (with *LyuṬ* by A 3.3.115 *lyuṭ ca*) denoting the mere activity of uttering or pronouncing, or, alternatively, as either *adhikaraṇasādhana*, that is to say, as a noun denoting a locus, 'place of utterance', or *karaṇasādhana*, as a noun denoting a means of uttering (the latter two formed with *LyuṬ* by A 3.3.117 *karaṇādhikaraṇayoś ca* which teaches that this suffix is added also to denote the instrument and the locus). These rules do not permit its analysis as *karmasādhana*, that is, as denoting the object of the action.

All this has implications for the interpretation of Sanskrit nouns and thus ultimately for lexicography. In Yāska's *Nirukta*, more than a hundred words are analysed by a construction that involves the ablative form of a neuter verbal noun in *-ana*, to be interpreted as a *nomen actionis* or *bhāvasādhana* if one adheres to Sanskrit terminology. A representative example of this type of construction is (Nir 9.26): *sindhuḥ syandanāt*. I suggest the following interpretation: '*sindhu*' (the river Indus) [is so called] on account of the streaming (*syandanam*)'. The name '*sindhu*' is related to the verbal noun by an ablative construction which explains why '*sindhu*' came to signify the river of that name, or any river, and the construction is thus a natural reply to the question *kasmāt* 'why?'. The most commonly used Sanskrit dictionaries record that the verbal nouns in *-ana* employed in this type of construction quite frequently are attested only in the *Nirukta*, a fact that indicates that these forms are in principle derived by Yāska himself for the technical purpose of *nirvacana* analysis.

In his article 'Sur quelques formations sanskrites en *-ti-*' Louis Renou (1951) drew attention to the fact that much as nouns in *-ti* are, in principle, 'regular' formations, a number of them are nevertheless listed in the *uṇādisūtra*s, or, more precisely, in the commentaries on the *uṇādisūtra*s. As Renou points out (1951: 1), Hemacandra's

Dhātupārāyaṇa, for example, presents a large number of forms in *-ti* that are lacking in standard Sanskrit dictionaries. However, some formations in *-ti* raise questions of a similar nature, as did the neuter verbal nouns in *-ana* above. That forms met with in the epigraphical record should be included in dictionaries is obvious. As examples, Renou (*ibid.*: 2) mentions *aṃhati* (variant *aṃhiti*) in the sense of 'gift', and *jñāti* in the sense of 'information, knowledge', among others.

Consider now the analysis of some forms in *-ti* and *-ana* met with in the *Prasannapadā*, Candrakīrti's commentary on Nāgārjuna's *Mūlamadhyamakakārikā* (ed. L. de La Vallée Poussin 1903–13: 4, 5–6):

> *tatra niruddhir nirodhaḥ kṣaṇabhaṅgo nirodha ity ucyate* |
> *utpādanam utpādaḥ ātmabhāvonmajjana[m ity arthaḥ]* |[20]
> *ucchittir ucchedaḥ prabandhavicchittir ity arthaḥ* |

The first line one could render: 'In this respect,[21] *nirodha* is *niruddhi*: it is *kṣaṇabhaṅga* that is called *nirodha*.' In other words, *nirodha* is explained by *niruddhi*, a verbal noun in *-ti* formed from the same root with the same preverb. The form *niruddhi* is not met with in extant lexica. It seems therefore likely that it was derived by Candrakīrti for the particular purpose of interpreting *nirodha* as *bhāvasādhana* by glossing it with a form in *-ti*, that is to say as meaning 'a ceasing'. Candrakīrti goes on to say that *nirodha* is *kṣaṇabhaṅga*. Now, it is not easy to provide an elegant translation for the Buddhist term *kṣaṇabhaṅga*, nor is it unambiguous how best to analyse the compound. Suffice it to say that the term refers to the fact that all phenomena are of momentary existence, hence a *vigraha* of the compound could be *kṣaṇād bhaṅgaḥ*, the ceasing to exist after only one moment, or, perhaps, *kṣaṇena bhaṅgaḥ* or *kṣaṇe bhaṅgaḥ*, the ceasing to exist every moment, that is to say, 'continuous instant ceasing'.

The second line of the passage is a little more problematic, but brings out the point I wish to make, namely that it is possible for the purpose of interpretation to form verbal nouns in *-ti* or *-ana* from any verb or verbal noun. The line could be rendered: '*utpāda* is *utpādana*,

---

[20] J.W. de Jong (1978: 29) prefers the reading *ātmabhāvonmajjanam* met with in a manuscript acquired by G. Tucci which was not available to La Vallée Poussin.

[21] The passage is introduced by the words *avayavārthas tu vibhajyate*, 'but the meaning of the various parts is explained in detail [as follows]'.

[that is to say,] the emerging of a bodily form'. Here *utpāda* is glossed *utpādana*, which, as a causative formation, is somewhat difficult to reconcile with the fact that the verb *un-majj* 'to emerge' is intransitive. Turning to standard lexica, we meet with further problems. For *utpādana* as a neuter noun, Monier-Williams has 'the act of producing or causing, generating, begetting'. *A Dictionary of Pāli* (M. Cone 2001) has 'uppādana, *n.*, ~ā, *f.* [*S.* utpādana], *producing, generating*'. Should we emend to *utpadana*, that is to say, to a non-causative form? Edgerton lists the form *utpadyana* in BHSD: 'utpadyana (nt.; = Pali uppajjana: MIndic -ana formation to utpadyate), *production*, *origination*: Gv 48.5 (prose), read: harṣa-utpadyana-saṃtānāni (see s.v. saṃtāna 2)'. 'Production' and 'origination' are unlikely synonyms, since they are based on transitive and intransitive verbs, respectively. Under *utpadyati*, however, BHSD has '(2) in mg. of Skt. caus. utpādayati, *produces*, *causes*'. Turning to the entry for *saṃtāna* that Edgerton referred to above, one finds that he translates *harṣa-utpadyana-saṃtānāni* 'their mental conditions productive of joy'. Here he seems to take *utpadyana* as transitive.

In any case, *utpādana* remains problematic. A form *utpadana* is not met with in lexica. To emend to *utpādyana* is problematic. The solution that emerges as the most plausible is therefore to conclude that Candrakīrti formed *utpādana* directly on *utpāda*, again to make it clear that he interprets *utpāda* as *bhāvasādhana*, 'an emerging'. This conclusion is supported by the continuation of the explanation: *ātmabhāvonmajjana*, 'the emerging of a bodily form', where *unmajjana* is a neuter action noun in *-ana*.

Finally, *ucchitir ucchedaḥ prabandhavicchittir ity arthaḥ* could be rendered: '*uccheda* is *ucchitti*, that is to say, the ceasing of continuity'. Once again, Candrakīrti makes it clear that he takes *uccheda* 'cutting off, destruction, annihilation' to be *bhāvasādhana* by forming a feminine verbal noun in *-ti*, *ucchitti*, 'a cutting off, a destroying'. Again the gloss is formed from the same root with the same preverb. The form *ucchitti* is not met with in lexica either, nor is the further gloss °*vichitti*, another formation in *-ti*. Now, one may argue that forms such as *niruddhi*, *utpādana*, *ucchitti*, and *vichitti* do not merit the distinction of being of lexicographical interest, but what they convey about the terms they are used to interpret certainly does.

Fully aware that I have only been able to touch upon a few aspects of early Indian semantic theory, I shall end by contrasting two passages, one from the *Saddanīti*, a twelfth-century grammar of Pāli written by the Burmese monk Aggavaṃsa, and the other from Patañjali's *Mahābhāṣya*. Both passages deal with the relationship between words and meanings, and illustrate two very different approaches to semantics.

Aggavaṃsa's task is to derive meaning from the usage encountered in a corpus of texts, the Theravāda Pāli canon, by analysing constructions on the basis of *sādhana*s (= *kāraka*s) (Sadd 69, 2–11).[22]

Here the term *sādhana* has been promulgated for the sake of the skill of the learned with regard to usages as well as meanings. For it is the case that linguistic usages have meanings that are hard to understand when they are constructed with words whose *sādhana*s are badly laid down, while they have meanings that are easy to understand when they are constructed with words whose *sādhana*s are neatly laid down. Therefore usages are rooted in *sādhana*s, and meaning is rooted in usage. For those [learned] who are in the habit of analysing the meaning in that they make [it] adequate according to usage — only those learned, whose intellect is very sharp with regard to meanings that can be grasped by means of *sādhana*[-analysis] such as in 'only he who is invited receives a robe often, he who is not invited, rarely'[23] and even

---

[22] *idha payogesv atthesu ca viññūnaṃ pāṭavatthaṃ sādhananāmaṃ pakāsitaṃ; tathā hi dunnikkhittasādhanehi padehi yojitā saddappayogā dubbodhatthā honti, sunikkhittasādhanehi pana padehi yojitā subodhatthā honti. Tasmā payogā sādhanamūlakā; attho ca payogamūlako. Payogānurūpaṃ hi aviparītaṃ katvā atthaṃ kathanasīlā "yācito va bahulaṃ cīvaraṃ paribhuñjati appaṃ ayācito" ti evamādisu sādhanavasena gahetabbesu atthesu aññesu c'atthesu paṭutarabuddhino paṇḍitā yeva ekantena Bhagavato pariyattisāsanadharā nāma hontī ti veditabbaṃ.*

[23] This seems to be the sense, *bahulaṃ* going either with *cīvaraṃ* in the sense of 'plenty of' or as an adverb with *paribhuñjati*, and so the *sādhana* expressed would be *kamma*, that is, *yācito* is to be interpreted as the object of the action denoted by the verb *yācati*, although he appears as the agent of the action expressed by the finite verb *paribhuñjati* with regard to the rest of the sentence. The idea seems to be that only someone asked or invited enjoys or accepts something, whereas someone who is not invited or asked does not. The rather odd example — odd in the sense that *kamma* would be the interpretation of *yācito* which certainly comes to mind first — is probably chosen by Aggavaṃsa either because he simply wants to say that past participles are to be interpreted as *kammasādhana* in general, or because *yācito* is *kammasādhano* but seems to have no bearing on the rest of the sentence in as much as it appears as *kattar* with regard to *paribhuñjati*, or because past par-

with regard to other meanings,[24] [only those] are completely in possession of the teaching of the doctrine of the Blessed One; thus one should know.

Here Aggavaṃsa makes it quite clear that he has a canon to account for and for him there is an opposition between the science of grammar and the canon. The sole authority is the canon and the Aṭṭhakathās. Compare this with the following passage from Patañjali's *Mahābhāṣya* (Mbh I:464,15–21):[25]

> *But now this need not be like that.[26] For meaning should indeed not be fashioned by words, words should indeed be fashioned by meaning.[27] Let it be viewed like this: The very nature of meaning[28] is of such a kind that even without usage of*

---

ticiples often have to be interpreted as active in late Pāli and hence as *kattusādhana*.

24 That is, the meanings of words which are not susceptible of *sādhana* analysis. The *nissaya* as quoted by Helmer Smith (Sadd 69, n. 2) gives the example *yevāpana* 'whatever else', an adjective formed as a syntactical or irregular compound from the phrase *ye vā pana* (*ye* as Māghadism for *yaṃ*), that is, 'those who go around saying *ye vā pana*'.

25 *nanu ca naitenaivaṃ bhavitavyam | na hi śabdakṛtena nāmārthena bhavitavyam | arthakṛtena nāma śabdena bhavitavyam | tad etad evaṃ dṛśyatām artharūpam evaitad evaṃjātīyakaṃ yenātrāntareṇāpi puruṣaśabdaprayogaṃ rājani so 'rtho gamyate | kiṃ punas tat | svāmitvam | kiṃkṛtaṃ punas tat | svakṛtam | tad yathā | prātipadikārthānāṃ kriyākṛtā viśeṣā upajāyante tatkṛtāś cākhyāḥ prādurbhavanti karma karaṇam apādānaṃ saṃpradānam adhikaraṇam iti | tāś ca punar vibhaktīnām utpattau kadā cin nimittatvenopādīyante kadā cin na |*

26 The specific context is the claim that in the phrase *rājñaḥ puruṣaḥ*, 'the king's man', one should add a genitive ending also after the word *puruṣa* 'man' just as it is added to *rājan* 'king'. The genitive case suffix indicates that *rājan* is the *viśeṣaṇa* 'qualifier' in a 'qualifier–qualified' relationship. Details need not concern us here.

27 Cf. also Mbh I:362, 17–19. In that context Kaiyaṭa remarks (MbhP II:510): *pratyāyayiṣitārthapratipādanāya śabdaprayogāt*, '["words should be due to meaning":] because words are used to communicate the meaning which is desired to be conveyed'.

28 The word *artharūpa*, lit. 'the form of meaning' is glossed *arthasvabhāva* 'the nature of meaning' by Kaiyaṭa (MbhP II:510).

> *the word puruṣa 'man', that meaning [namely, rajñaḥ 'of the king'] is understood with regard to [the word] rājan 'king'. What, then, is that [meaning]? Ownership. [And] what, then, is that fashioned by? [It is] fashioned by sva 'itself'. The reason is that special qualities of the meanings of nominal stems come into being fashioned by actions, and fashioned by those [qualities] designations arise, [namely,] karman, karaṇa, apādāna, sampradāna, and adhikaraṇa. And these, again, are sometimes offered as the cause for the arising of case suffixes, [and] sometimes not.*

For the Sanskrit grammarian Patañjali meaning determines usage, grammar deals not with ontology but with things as they are spoken about. This, to me at least, represents a very healthy approach to semantics.

Abbreviations and Primary Sources

A	*Aṣṭādhyāyī* of Pāṇini. Ref. to O. Böhtlingk (ed.): Pāṇini's Grammatik, herausgegeben, übersetzt, erläutert und mit verschiedene Indices versehen, Leipzig: Haessel, 1887.
Mbh	*Vyākaraṇa-mahābhāṣya of Patañjali*, ed. Franz Kielhorn, 3 vols., Bombay, 1880–85. 3rd ed., revised etc. by K.V. Abhyankar, Poona: BORI, 1962–72.
MbhP	*Mahābhāṣyapradīpa of Kaiyaṭa*, 5 vols., ed. by Bhārgavaśāstrī Bhikājī Jośī 1951 (vol. I, 5th ed.), 1942 (vol. IV), 1945 (vol. V), Śivadatta Kudāla 1912 (vol. II), and Raghunāth Śarmā – Śivadatta Kudāla 1937 (vol. III).
MbhU	*Mahābhāṣyapradīpoddyota of Nāgeśabhaṭṭa*, ed. as MbhP.
Nir	*Nirukta* of Yāska. Ref. to L. Sarup (ed.): The Nighaṇṭu and the Nirukta, the oldest Indian treatise on etymology, philology, and semantics. Sanskrit text, Lahore: University of the Panjab, 1927.
ṚV	*Ṛgveda*. Ref. to Ṛgveda-saṃhitā śrīmatsāyaṇācārya-viracita-bhāṣyasametā [Ṛgveda-saṃhitā with the commentary of Sāyaṇa], ed. N.S. Sontakke et al., 5 vols., Poona: Vaidika Saṃśodhana Maṇḍala, 1933–51. [Vol. 1 repr. 1972.]

Sadd	*Saddanīti* of Aggavaṃsa. Ref. to H. Smith, (ed.): Saddanīti: la grammaire palie d'Aggavaṃsa: I Padamālā, II Dhātumālā, III Suttamālā, Lund: Gleerup, 1928–30.
Sāy	Sāyaṇa's introduction to his commentary on the *Ṛgveda*; see ṚV.

References

1. Franklin Edgerton, Buddhist Hybrid Sanskrit Dictionary, New Haven: Yale University Press, 1953. [Repr. Delhi: Motilal Banarsidass, 1970.]
2. Cone, M.: 2001, A Dictionary of Pāli: Part I, Oxford: Pali Text Society.
3. Durga's commentary (Ṛjvartha) on the Nirukta: The Nirukta of Yāska (with Nighaṇṭu) edited with Durga's commentary, vol. I (BSS 73) ed. by H.M. Bhadkamkar assited by R.G. Bhadkamkar, Bombay 1918.
4. de Jong, J.W.: 1978, 'Textcritical notes on the Prasannapadā', Indo-Iranian Journal 20: 25–59.
5. La Vallée Poussin, L. de (ed.): 1903–13, Mūlamadhyamakakārikās (Mādhyamikasūtras) de Nāgārjuna avec la Prasannapadā commentaire de Candrakīrti (Bibliotheca Buddhica IV), St.-Pétersbourg.
6. Quine, Willard Van Orman: 1951, "Two dogmas of empiricism", Philosophical Review 60: 20–43.
7. Renou, L.: 1951, 'Sur quelques formations sanskrites en -ti-', Vāk 1: 1–4.

An Analytic Database of the Aṣṭādhyāyī

Peter M. Scharf

Université Paris Diderot

Abstract. A database of Pāṇini's *Aṣṭādhyāyī* was created in 1991. The database analyzes *sandhi* in *sūtras*, provides morphological identification of each word, analyzes compounds, indicates recurrence of terms, indicates the type of each *sūtra* and the significance of the case used in each word. It likewise provides extensive classification of grammatical elements including roots, *gaṇa*-elements, affixes, augments, markers, and *pratyāhāras* and other technical terms.

Keywords: Pāṇini, Aṣṭādhyayī, database, grammar, Indian linguistics, computational linguistics, Sanskrit

1 Introduction

Valuable analyses of the *Aṣṭādhyāyī* have been created in printed form since Böhtlingk published his second volume of *Pāṇini's Grammatik* in 1840. Katre (1967–69) undertook a detailed analysis with Sanskrit text in Romanization and with English translation. Editions of the *Aṣṭādhyāyī*, *Kāśikā* and *Siddhāntakaumudī* include analytic appendices. Shastri and Sarma (1976) and Sri Ramachandrudu and Sarma (1985) created analytic indices for the *Kāśikā*, as Pansikar (1985) did in his edition of the *Siddhāntakaumudī*. Yet a digital database affords benefits in the ease and flexibility of use not possible in a printed edition. A digital database, for instance, allows dynamic indexing in accordance with multiple parameters in order to produce specially focused indices meeting the specific research needs of a particular scholarly question. It would be tedious and expensive to produce numerous such indices in print even if one could anticipate all the desired combinations of search criteria. Moreover, inevitably due to the highly technical and complicated nature of the material, the available printed analyses contain numerous errors in substance and production. Subsequent reprints of these analyses reproduce errors in the originals and reattach lists of corrigenda. Integrating such corrigenda adds an additional impediment to an already opaque subject. A digital database can be corrected, revised, and extended iteratively. It is for these reasons that the production of a database of the *Aṣṭādhyāyī* was recognized as a desideratum. The current paper describes such a database and discusses issues related to its design and implementation.

In a project headed by George Cardona to create a relational database of Sanskrit grammatical texts under a grant from the National Endowment for the Humanities in 1991, I created a database for Pāṇini's *Aṣṭādhyāyī* using Fourth Dimension on the Macintosh. This *Aṣṭādhyāyī* database consists of four files: a *sūtra* file, a *pada* file, an *anuvṛtti* file, and a prātipadika file. The *sūtra* file contains one record for each *sūtra* of the *Aṣṭādhyāyī*, the *pada* file contains one record for each *pada* of the *Aṣṭādhyāyī*, the *anuvṛtti* file contains one record for each *pada* each time it is understood to recur in a *sūtra* other than the one in which it is explicitly stated. Finally, the *prātipadika* file contains one record for the base of each *pada* explicitly stated in the *sūtra* and one for each compound constituent. Compounds are analyzed down to their finest relevant stem.

The categories used to classify various types of entities in the *Aṣṭādhyāyī* are the original Pāṇinian terms themselves or traditional Sanskrit terms commonly used for them. The choice to use the Sanskrit grammatical terminology was deliberate in spite of the lack of transparency of such terminology to someone not already very familiar with Sanskrit grammar. The terminology and the distinctions it designates are precise. Equivalent terminology is not necessarily readily available in a European language, and, even where it is, the terms are different in different languages. Where equivalent terminology is not available, the use of European categories is likely to obscure and confuse Pāṇinian categories more than it will elucidate them. The invention of new artificial terminology of precise scope would likely be as opaque in its application to Sanskrit grammar as the original Sanskrit terminology itself. In any case, the communication of categorization is separable from implementing a correct and precise categorization. Mapping to equivalent terminology with explanations of differences in scope can be added subsequently.

2 The *Sūtra* File

Each record of the *sūtra* file contains fields indicating the number of the *sūtra* in the *Aṣṭādhyāyī*, the number of the *sūtra* in the *Siddhāntakaumudī*, the *sūtra*, the *sūtra*-type, and a comment field. The first field contains a five digit long integer in the range 11001-84068 which is a unique reference to each *sūtra* in the *Aṣṭādhyāyī* corresponding to the traditional numbering of the *Aṣṭādhyāyī*. The first digit in the number designates the *adhyāya*, the second the pāda, and the last three digits the *sūtra*; this number serves as a key linking the *sūtra*, *pada*, *anuvr̥tti*, and *prātipadika* files. Transcoding software allows an interface to display all Sanskrit content in either Romanization or Devanāgarī depending upon the preferences selected by the user. The *sūtra*-type field contains one of six *sūtra*-type designations: *saṁjñā*, *paribhāṣā*, *vidhi*, *niyama*, *pratiṣedha*, and *atideśa*. In addition, the *sūtra*-type field in the record for 1.2.32 *tasyādita udāttamardhahrasvam* contains the designation *ākhyāna*, being the only one that is a description rather than any of these types.

The comment field contains miscellaneous information relevant to the *sūtra*. This information may concern any one of the fields in the *sūtra*, *pada*, *anuvr̥tti* or *prātipadika* files, or may be independent. At present, most independent comments concern the scope of application of a *sūtra*, particularly what general rule is blocked by the rule in question.

3 The *Pada* File

The *pada* file contains two numeric fields that uniquely refer to each word in the *Aṣṭādhyāyī*. The first is the composite *sūtra* number that links the file with the *sūtra* file. The second is the number of the word in the *sūtra*. Next are fields that designate the gender, case and number of each nominal, and the person, number, voice and tense/mood of each inflected verb form. The next field designates the significance of the use of the case of nominals. The last field designates the number of the last *sūtra* in which the term recurs, if it recurs; this number was used to generate the *anuvṛtti* file.

The number and case will always be indicated if the word is a nominal form with a *vibhakti*. However, the gender is indicated only if usage of a word in the *Aṣṭādhyāyī* shows its gender, or its gender is well known to be exclusively masculine, feminine or neuter. If the *vibhakti* used at the end of a word leaves it vague whether a word is masculine or neuter, masculine or feminine or any gender, the gender is not indicated. In fact, since the data has not yet been correlated, the gender may remain un-indicated in one record even if its gender is known from usage in another record. A nominal is indicated as indeclinable if a declinable stem is given without a *vibhakti*, that is, if the nominal is what is termed an *avibhaktikanirdeśa*, as well as if it is a particle, adverb or other recognized indeclinable.

The use of the case is designated by a term in one of seven hierarchical lists. One list for each case lists the possible case-use designations for that case as shown in Table 1. The seventh case (locative) has a sublist of five types of adhikaraṇa.

The few occurrences of vocative forms (in 6.1.118 and 8.2.67) are designated 1 (nominative) and described as vocative in the com-

Table 1: Case-use

1	*ādeśa, karman, prathamārtha, prātipadikārtha, pratipādya, saṁjñā, saṁjñin, uddeśya, upasarjana, vidheya*
2	*dvitīyārtha, kāla, karman, kriyāviśeṣaṇa, nirvartya, prāpya, vikārya*
3	*adhvan, apradhāna, hetu, itthambhūtalakṣaṇa, kāla, karaṇa, kartṛ, tulyārthayoga, tṛtīyārtha*
4	*caturthyartha, kriyārthopapadakarman, tadartha*
5	*apādāna, avadhi, hetu, pūrvapañcamī, pañcamyartha,* 2.3.29 *anyayukte,* 2.3.29 *dikśabdayukte, dūrāntika* 2.3.35.
6	*āgamin, avayavin, karman, kartṛ, kāryin, nirdhāraṇa, sambandha, saṁjñin, sthānin, ṣaṣṭhyartha, atasarthapratyayena*
7	*adhikaraṇa* [*samīpa, upaśleṣa, viṣaya, vyāpaka, dūrāntika* 2.3.36], *abhidheya, nimitta, nirdhāraṇa, parasaptamī, satsaptamī, saptamyartha, upapada*

ment field. I was liberal in designating consonant stems as ending in the first *vibhakti* (nominative) even when Pāṇini does not apply changes usual for stems ending in *c*, *j*, *ś*, etc. Although such stems are not actually legitimate Sanskrit nominative forms, their syntactic role in the *sūtras* in which they occur is that of a nominative. For example, 3.1.83 *halaḥ śnaḥ śānajjhau* provides that the affix *śānac* replaces the *vikaraṇa śnā* if followed by the second-person singular imperative termination *hi*. Interword *sandhi* is shown at the junction of *śānac* and *hau*, namely, replacement of initial *h* by the voiced aspirated stop produced at the same place of articulation of the preceding stop ($h \rightarrow jh$), and voiding of the preceding stop ($c \rightarrow j$). Yet the replacement of the final palatal stop by its corresponding velar by 8.2.30 *coḥ kuḥ*, by which one would obtain *śānag ghau* instead of *śānaj jhau* is not undertaken. Such a change is imperative in ordinary Sanskrit but frequently not implemented for elements in grammatical rules. The reason is obvious: it would obscure the nature of the elements, particularly the final markers (*anubandha*) attached to affixes. In this case, the marker attached is *c* not *k*. Nevertheless, I identify the case of such items as nominative because they are the items provided by the rule (*ādeśa*) in place of the substituend (*sthānin*) taught in the genitive. On the other hand, *an*-stems that appear unchanged in their original form, I have called *avibhaktikanirdeśa* 'a form devoid of a nominal termination'. All *nipātanas* and anything provided by a *vidhi* are given the designation *vidheya*.

When a sixth *vibhakti* occurs in syntactic connection with the words *lopa*, *luk*, *lup* or *ślu* used to indicate various modes of deletion, I designate the case use *kāryin* 'operand'. This is a compromise between calling it a *sthānin* 'substituend' and *karman* 'direct object'. If the words *lopa*, etc. are *kriyāśabdas*, then that which is not seen (1.1.60 *adarśanam lopaḥ*) is the karman as it is in 6.1.68 where the conjugated verb in the passive *lupyate* '...is deleted' is supplied. Moreover the *Kāśikā* does not refer to *lopa* as an *ādeśa* or to that which is designated by a form in the genitive in a *sūtra* that provides deletion as a *sthānin*. The commentaries often refer to that upon which operations take place as the *kāryin*.

The designations *viṣaya* 'domain' and *nimitta* 'condition' for the use of the locative (seventh *vibhakti*) have been used sparingly while the designation *abhidheya* 'to be denoted' has been applied liberally to anything referred to in the commentaries by the locative of words indicating a semantic object including *artha* 'meaning', *dyotya* 'to be co-signified', *gamyamāna* 'being understood' as well as *abhidheya* and *vācya* 'to be denoted'. The importance of such semantic designations in the generation of speech forms in the Pāṇinian linguistic system has been discussed at length by Scharf (2009a, 2009b, 2011).

4 The *Anuvr̥tti* File

The *anuvr̥tti* file gives each recurring *pada* under the *sūtra* in which it recurs. Where only one item in a compound *pada* recurs, just the recurring part is shown in the *anuvr̥tti* file entry. The termination is adjusted to reflect relevant changes in number, and in a single instance the case is adjusted: The term *ādeśe* in 1.1.48 recurs terminating in the first *vibhakti* in 1.1.49-55. The adaptation of the case of a recurring item to the context in which it recurs is approved under the name *vibhaktivipariṇāma* by the grammatical tradition. The file was generated using the information entered in the range field of the *pada* file. That field relied almost exclusively upon the numerical margin notes designating the extent of *anuvr̥tti* in Gopāla Śāstrī's edition of the *Aṣṭādhyāyī*. Occasional adjustments on an ad hoc basis were made based upon statements in the *Kāśikā*. Most of these adjustments are made where more than two terms in a *sūtra* pass to following *sūtra*s and one or more continue further than others.

Besides the *anuvr̥tti* field, the *anuvr̥tti* file contains the five-digit key by which the records of the *anuvr̥tti* file are related to the record in the *sūtra* file concerned with the *sūtra* in which the *pada*s recur (see description under *sūtra* above). Similarly an integer identifies the sequence of each *pada* that recurs in the *sūtra*. These two numbers together uniquely designate each record in the *anuvr̥tti* file. Two additional numbers identify the original location in which the recurring *pada* was explicitly stated. They specify the number of the *sūtra* of origin and the number of the *pada* in that *sūtra*. These two numbers together uniquely identify each *pada* in its position in the *pada* file in the order in which it recurs in the *sūtra* in which it is explicitly stated in the *Aṣṭādhyāyī*.

5 The *Prātipadika* File

The *prātipadika* file contains records with ten fields referencing, listing, and describing each stem and compound element in the *Aṣṭādhyāyī.* The first three fields identify the number of the *sūtra*, the number of the *pada* in that *sūtra*, and the number of the *prātipadika* in the *pada.* Together they uniquely designate each *prātipadika* file record. The third of these fields contains a number that shows the hierarchy of constituents in compounds. A zero in the field indicates that the *prātipadika* in this record is the stem to which the *vibhakti* is added to form a *pada* in the *pada* file. If that *prātipadika* is a compound containing grammatically relevant elements, the immediately following records contain the constituents of the compound. The first two digits of a number which is greater than zero in the *prātipadika* number field indicates the number of the immediate constituent of the compound. The third and fourth digits indicate the second-level compound components and so on.

The fourth field in the *prātipadika* file contains the *prātipadika* itself in the Sanskrit Library Phonetic basic encoding (SLP1) documented in Scharf and Hyman (2011: 151-158). Entries range from single characters, where a single sound is referred to by its own form, to a compound of 145 characters.

The fifth field designates the type of compound. The entries include the names of the well-known classes of compounds, the names of their subclasses, and a couple of categories for the leftovers. These entries are organized into a list including the well-known compound types: *avyayībhāva*, *bahuvrīhi*, *dvandva*, and *tatpuruṣa* along with the leftover categories *asamartha* and *supsupā.* Two subordinate lists under *dvandva* and *tatpuruṣa* include subclasses. In the included list under *dvandva* are listed *itaretaradvandva* and *samāhāradvandva.* Whenever possible, one of these two more specific terms is used. If a *dvandva* is the subordinate member of another compound, it may be impossible to determine whether it is an *itaretara* or *samāhāra.* In these cases, and only these cases, is the term *dvandva* entered.

The following entries for the compound field are found in an included list under *tatpuruṣa*: *dvitīyātatpuruṣa*, *tr̥tīyātatpuruṣa*, *caturthītatpuruṣa*, *pañcamītatpuruṣa*, *ṣaṣṭhītatpuruṣa*, *saptamītatpuruṣa*, *ekadeśatatpuruṣa*, *nañtatpuruṣa*, *kutatpuruṣa*, *gatitatpuruṣa*, *prāditatpuruṣa*, *upapadatatpuruṣa*, *kālatatpuruṣa.*

The terms *dvigu* and *karmadhāraya*, being subclasses of *tatpuruṣa*, are also listed in the *tatpuruṣa* included list. Most of these terms are well known, and Scharf (2002) provides further explanation of compound types with examples. Nevertheless, I make a few comments concerning the more obscure compound types here. The terms *kutatpuruṣa*, *gatitatpuruṣa*, and *prāditatpuruṣa* are used for compounds formed by 2.2.18.

The term *upapadatatpuruṣa* refers to compounds formed by 2.2.19. By 3.1.92, terms ending in the seventh *vibhakti* in *sūtras* 3.1.106 through the end of the third adhyāya are termed *upapada*. These *sūtras* provide a *kṛt* suffix after a verbal root on the condition that the root is syntactically connected with the mentioned *upapada*. The *upapadas* in these *sūtras* are obligatorily compounded with the resulting *kṛt*-final *prātipadikas* before nominal terminations are added; the *kṛt*-final *prātipadikas* never stand alone uncompounded. Details concerning the derivational process are discussed at length by Scharf (2011).

I use the term *ekadeśatatpuruṣa* for compounds formed by 2.2.1 and the term *kālatatpuruṣa* for those formed by 2.2.5. The term *supsupā* designates compounds formed by 2.1.4 which do not fall within more specific categories Pāṇini specifies. Finally, the term *asamartha* designates compounds formed of constituent *padas* which separately bear syntactical relations to *padas* not included in the compound.

It is essential to note the following distinction in the usage of terms in the *Aṣṭādhyāyī*: (a) terms used to refer to items as objects of grammatical rules, and (b) terms used to convey their meaning whether it be ordinary or technical. The *prātipadika* of any term of type (a) has been entered in the *prātipadika* field of an independent record isolated from any compound in which it may occur. Complete information concerning such an element has been entered in the remaining fields of the *prātipadika* file. Words cited as *nipātana* and their compound constituents have also been treated in this manner. Terms of type (b), on the contrary, have deliberately been left unanalyzed and unidentified when such analysis would hinder the ability of a database user to select terms of type (a). For example, in 1.3.19, *viparābhyāṁ jeḥ*, which states that the *ātmanepada* terminations occur after the verbal root *ji* preceded by the prefixes *vi* or *parā*, *vi* is given in a separate record and identified as a *gaṇa* element and member of the *prādi gaṇa*. In 1.3.20, *āṅo do 'nāsyaviharaṇe*, however, the prefix *vi* in *viharaṇa* is not even given a separate record, much less identified. The compound *anāsyaviharaṇa* 'not using the mouth, i.e. not speaking', states a meaning condition for the occurrence of the *ātmanepada* terminations after the root *dā* preceded by the prefix *āṅ*. It is analyzed as a *nañtatpuruṣa* compound consisting of the elements *an* and *āsyaviharaṇa*. The former is not given in its original form *nañ* to prevent interference with the grammatically significant *nañ* which occurs for instance in 2.2.6 *nañ*, the rule that provides for the formation of *nañtatpuruṣa* compounds. The latter, *āsyaviharaṇa*, is analyzed as a *ṣaṣṭhītatpuruṣa* compound consisting of the elements *āsya* 'mouth' and *viharaṇa* 'opening, exercising'. The element *viharaṇa*, however, is used in its conventional sense so remains unanalyzed.

Two additional fields, ID1 and ID2, contain entries identifying the general and specific grammatical categories into which a *prātipadika* may fall. These fields contain categories which apply only to grammatically significant elements, so not every *prātipadika* used in the *Aṣṭādhyāyī* contains entries in these fields. The entries are organized in hierarchical lists to show the relationship of the general to the specific categories. The ID1 field contains one of the following entries designating nine mutually exclusive categories: *āgama*, *dhātu*, *gaṇa* element, *it*, *pratyāhāra*, *pratyaya*, *saṁjñā*, *sarvanāmādeśa*, and *śabda*. If *āgama*, *it*, *pratyāhāra*, *sarvanāmādeśa* or *śabda* is entered in the ID1 field, the ID2 field is left blank. If the ID1 field contains one of the four entries: *dhātu*, *pratyaya*, *saṁjñā* or *gaṇa* element, an entry designating a more specific category appears in the ID2 field. These entries designating more specific categories are listed in four included lists named accordingly *dhātu*, *pratyaya*, *saṁjñā* and *gaṇa*.

The *dhātu*-included list of entries for the ID2 field contains the following entries distinguishing the manner used to refer to a dhātu: *a-anta*, *ik-anta*, *sa-anubandhaka*, *sa-vikaraṇa*, *śtip-anta*, and *sanādi-anta*. Simple roots such as are listed in the *dhātupāṭha* may be referred to by citing the *dhātupāṭha* entry with *anubandha*s attached. *Dhātu*s may also be referred to by citing the *dhātu* alone without its *anubandha*s. If the *dhātu* ends in a consonant, however, Pāṇini usually attaches either a final *a* or *i*. Kātyāyana attached the *anubandha k* to the latter (*ik*) to show that it does not condition *guṇa*. In these cases the ID2 field contains the entry *a-anta* and *ik-anta*, respectively. Roots cited in this manner are declined as *a*- or *i*-stem nouns. Just as often, however, a consonant-final *dhātu* is declined as a consonant stem without any additions. When either a vowel-final or consonant-final root is referred to by citing just the root itself, the ID1 field contains the entry *dhātu* and the ID2 field is left blank. Often Pāṇini cites roots by citing a form which looks much like the third-person singular present indicative active of the root. Since roots which do not take *parasmaipada* terminations are also cited in this manner, such forms are not considered to be actual third-person singular present indicative active forms; rather, Kātyāyana derives the citation form with the special suffix *śtip*. The term *śtip-anta* is entered into the ID2 field in these cases. Occasionally, when referring to a root listed in more than one of the ten principal verb classes of the *dhātupāṭha* (*bhvādi*, *adādi*, etc.), Pāṇini wishes to single out the root as listed in just one of them. In such cases he cites the root with the *vikaraṇa* of the intended class added. Here the entry *sa-vikaraṇa* appears in the ID2 field. Finally, to refer to complex roots, i.e. those formed by the provision of one of the suffixes *san*, etc. (3.1.5-31) Pāṇini cites a form with the suffix in question added. In these cases, most of which are causatives formed with the addition of the suffix *ṇic*, the entry *sanādi-anta* appears in the ID2 field. The labeling of such elements is not exhaustive. Although 7.1.100 mentions *dhātu* explicitly, I have not labeled all *dhātus* which are aṅgas before *sup-pratyayas dhātu*. For example, *ac* in 6.4.138, *bhū* in 6.4.85, *dr̥ś* in 7.1.83, *div* in 7.1.84 bear no such label. Moreover, some roots altered in form may not have been restored to their original form. For example, some occurrences of *kir* before a *vibhakti* in the *pada* file may not have been restored to *kr̥̄* in the *prātipadika* file.

The *pratyaya*-included list contains the following entries: *ādeśa*, *apatya*, *kr̥t*, *kr̥t-ādeśa*, *kr̥tya*, *l*-affix, *samāsānta*, *sanādi*, *strī*, *sup*, *sup-ādeśa*, *taddhita*, *taddhita-ādeśa*, *tiṅ*, *tiṅ-ādeśa*, *uṇādi*, *vibhakti*, and *vikaraṇa*. Most of these entries designate subclasses of *pratyayas*. However, *tiṅ-ādeśa* designates substitutes for an entire *tiṅ-pratyaya* (substitutes for part of a *pratyaya* are designated *śabda*); likewise, *sup-ādeśa* designates substitutes for an entire *sup-pratyaya*, *kr̥t-ādeśa* for an entire kr̥t-pratyaya, and *taddhita-ādeśa* for an entire *taddhita-pratyaya*. *Ādeśa* designates a substitute for some other class of *pratyaya*. (substitutes for *pratyayas* are termed *pratyaya* by 1.1.56.) The subclasses of *pratyaya* listed here are not mutually exclusive. If an entry in the *prātipadika* field of a record falls into a category included within a larger category, the term designating the narrower category is entered in the ID2 field. For example, the suffixes listed in 4.1.2 are labelled *sup* rather than *vibhakti*, the suffix *tavyat* is designated *kṛtya* rather than *kṛt* and the suffix *ṭac samāsānta* rather than *taddhita*. In order to select all taddhita suffixes one must search for records in which ID2 is *apatya*, *samāsānta*, *vibhakti*, or *taddhita*. Conversely, if one searches for records in which ID2 is *vibhakti*, the records in which ID2 is *sup* will not be selected. Only those suffixes provided in *sūtras* 4.1.4-75 are given the designation *strī*. Feminine suffixes provided after 4.1.76 are designated *taddhita* and those provided in 3.3.94-112 are designated *kṛt*. No ambiguity should arise concerning the remaining subclasses of *pratyayas*.

The saṁjñā-included list contains the following entries: *anvartha*, *ekākṣara*, *grammarian*, *laukikī*, *laukikī anvartha*, *nakṣatra*, *pūrvācārya*, and *geographic*. Only the designations *ekākṣara* and *grammarian* have been entered consistently wherever a super-short Pāṇinian term or the name of a grammarian appears as the entry in the *prātipadika* field. The others have been entered occasionally when I noticed explicit mention in the *Kāśikā*, *Padamañjarī*, or *Nyāsa*. In refining our database, we should select all records in which ID1 is *saṁjñā* and determine where an entry is required in the ID2 field. In fact, perhaps many more entries in the *prātipadika* field should be labeled *saṁjñā*. The label *saṁjñā* has been entered consistently in the ID1 field only where Pāṇini introduces the saṁjñā. Hence, *pūrvapada*, *uttarapada*, *pūraṇī*, *pūraṇa*, *caraṇa*, *anukaraṇa*, *prathamā*, *dvitīyā*, *tṛtīyā...saptamī*, *strī*, *napuṁsaka*, *puṁsa*, *varṇa*, *svara*, and *oṣṭhya* have not been labeled *saṁjñā*.

The *gaṇa*-included list is far from complete. After 4.1.4, I quit adding new *gaṇas* to the *gaṇa* list and applied only the term *prādi* consistently whenever a member of this *gaṇa* was referred to as the condition for the application of a rule. I deliberately do not enter *prādi* in the ID2 field and do not enter *gaṇa* element in the ID1 field every time an *upasarga* occurs in the *Aṣṭādhyāyī*. I make such entries only when the *upasarga* is intended as a factor in a grammatical rule or occurs in a *nipātana*. I was fairly complete with *sarvādi*, *svarādi* and *cādi* too. To be thorough about labeling all *gaṇa*s we can write a program to select all occurrences labeled *gaṇa* element, then decide which are intended as factors in a grammatical rule.

The next field in the *prātipadika* file is a text field in which are entered *anubandha*s attached to *pratyaya*s, *āgama*s, *dhātu*s, *prātipadika*s or other speech forms. As few as none and as many as three *anubandha*s are attached to single-speech forms. If two or more *anubandha*s are entered in the field, they are separated by a comma followed by a space. Only one speech form, the *pratyaya ḍmatup*, has three *anubandha*s. Sounds added to a speech form just to enable pronunciation are entered in a separate field rather than in the *anubandha* field. For example, the *i* in the affix *sic* is present between the suffix *s* and the *anubandha c*, just to enable pronunciation; it is not an *anubandha*. An *anubandha* referred to explicitly in a *sūtra* providing an operation conditioned by that *anubandha*, such as the *k* and *ṅ* in *kṅit* in 1.1.5 *khṅiti ca*, is not entered in the *anubandha* field. Rather such an *anubandha* is entered in the *prātipadika* field of a separate record; the entry *it* in the ID1 field of that record identifies the *prātipadika* field entry as an *anubandha*. Thus *kṅit* is analyzed as a *bahuvrīhi* compound and the elements *k* and *ṅ* are each entered as *prātipadika*s as is the technical term *it*. However, an *anubandha* referred to as a sound followed by *t* (*tapara*) is identified as *śabda* rather than *it* in the ID1 field. For example, the *u* in the *bahuvrīhi* compound *ud-it* in 1.1.69 is an *anubandha*; however, it is referred to simply as a sound in this *sūtra* and marked with *t* to indicate that just the short *u* is intended. Such *anubandha*s may be selected by searching for all *pada* or *sūtra* file records containing the entry *it* in the *prātipadika* field (and 'TRUE' in the *tapara* field) of their associated *prātipadika* file records. In fact, the term *it* appears in the same *pada* as an *anubandha* referred to explicitly in every case. Hence one may select all *pada*s or *sūtra*s in which explicitly referred to *anubandha*s occur as compound constituents by searching in the *pada* or *sūtra* file for all related *prātipadika* file records in which the entry in the *prātipadika* field is *it*.

Each *l*-affix (*lakāra*) contains one of the *anubandha*s *ṭ* or *ṅ* which are referred to explicitly in *sūtra*s providing operations (3.4.79 *ṭita* *ātmanepadānāṁ ṭere*, 3.4.99 *nityaṁ ṅitaḥ*). In addition, each *l*-affix contains a sound *a*, *i*, *u*, *r̥*, *e*, *o* which serves to distinguish it from other *l*-affixes (*viśeṣaṇārtha*). Haradattamiśra makes clear that these are also termed *anubandha* in his comment on 3.4.77 *lasya*, 'The *a* in *lasya* is just for pronunciation; it is not an *anubandha*. Otherwise (if the *a* in *lasya* were an *anubandha*), *la* would refer only to *laṭ* and *laṅ* (not to *liṭ*, *luṭ*, etc). (*lasya*: *akāra uccāraṇārtha iti*: *nānubandhaḥ*, *anyathā laṅlaṭoreva grahaṇaṁ syāt*.)' The *a* in *lasya*, if it were an *anubandha*, would refer to the *a* in *laṭ* and *laṅ* because they are *anubandhas* too. At the same time, Haradatta's statement here shows that sounds attached for pronunciation are not termed *anubandha* in spite of the reference to them as *anubandhas* in the following statement in the *Kāśikā* under 4.1.2:

> The sounds *u*, etc. (attached to the nominal terminations *s*, etc. in *su*, etc.) are *anubandhas* whose purpose is either to enable pronunciation or to distinguish (the terminations from each other) whichever is appropriate (*ukārādayo 'nubandhā yathāyogam uccāraṇaviśeṣaṇārthāḥ*).

Throughout, the sounds *a*, *i*, *u*, etc. in the *lakāras* are entered in the *anubandha* field. In addition a comment appears pointing out that they are *viśeṣaṇārtha*.

The next field in the *prātipadika* file contains the sounds attached to significant speech forms just to enable pronunciation. There is never more than one such sound and they are always simple vowels. Finally, the last field indicates wherever a *t* is attached to a sound (*tapara*), regardless of whether commentaries argue that it is not *t* or that it is just to ease pronunciation. Remarks addressing such points may be found in the comment field of the *sūtra* file. Part of the purpose of the *tapara* field is to allow one to locate just such arguments.

6 Database Layouts

A number of layouts were prepared to view the data contained in the four data files described above in Fourth Dimension. The expense of the Fourth Dimension database software has proven to render these layouts all but obsolete. The files, however, are easily imported into widely available spreadsheet software such as Microsoft Excel where they can be made into lists, one on each sheet. The built-in functions of the spreadsheet prove to be quite useful in locating, collecting, summarizing, and representing the data. Figure 1 shows the first twenty *sūtras* in the *sūtra* file displayed as a list on one sheet in Microsoft Excel. Figure 2 shows the first ten *sūtras* of the *pada* file, Figure 3, the first fifteen *sūtras* of the *anuvṛtti* file, and Figure 4, the first five *sūtras* of the *prātipadika* file.

	A	B	C	D	E	F	G	
1	SuNı			SN	SKN	Sutra	SutraTy	Comment
2	11001	1	1	1	16	vfdDirAdEc	saYjYA	{s AdEc} in
3	11002	1	1	2	17	adeNguRaH	saYjYA	{s vfdDi} n
4	11003	1	1	3	34	iko guRavfdDI	pariBAzA	Effect of {s
5	11004	1	1	4	2656	na DAtulopa ArDaDAtuke	pariBAzA	{se pratizel
6	11005	1	1	5	2217	kNiti ca	pariBAzA	{se pratizel
7	11006	1	1	6	2190	dIDIvevIwAm	pariBAzA	{se pratizel
8	11007	1	1	7	30	halo 'nantarAH saMyogaH	saYjYA	
9	11008	1	1	8	9	muKanAsikAvacano 'nunAsikaH	saYjYA	
10	11009	1	1	9	10	tulyAsyaprayatnaM savarRam	saYjYA	{s Asya} m
11	11010	1	1	10	13	nAjJalO	saYjYA	{se pratizel
12	11011	1	1	11	100	IdUdeddvivacanaM pragfhyam	saYjYA	
13	11012	1	1	12	101	adaso mAt	saYjYA	
14	11013	1	1	13	102	Se	saYjYA	
15	11014	1	1	14	103	nipAta ekAjanAN	saYjYA	
16	11015	1	1	15	104	ot	saYjYA	
17	11016	1	1	16	105	sambudDO SAkalyasyetAvanArze	saYjYA	
18	11017	1	1	17	106	uYaH	saYjYA	1.1.17-18 c
19	11018	1	1	18	107	U~	saYjYA	also a {se v
20	11019	1	1	19	109	IdUtO ca saptamyarTe	saYjYA	
21	11020	1	1	20	2373	dADA GvadAp	saYjYA	

Fig. 1: The sūtra file

	A	B	C	D	E	F	G	H	I
1	SuNı	V	Pada	(			VerbId	CaseUse	Anuv
2	11001	1	vfdDiH	f	s	1		saYjYA	11003
3	11001	2	At		s	1		saYjYin	0
4	11001	3	Ec		s	1		saYjYin	0
5	11002	1	at		s	1		saYjYin	0
6	11002	2	eN		s	1		saYjYin	0
7	11002	3	guRaH	m	s	1		saYjYA	11003
8	11003	1	ikaH		s	6		sTAnin	11005
9	11003	2	guRavfdDI	m	d	1		AdeSa	11006
10	11004	1	na						11006
11	11004	2	DAtulope	m	s	7		parasaptamI	0
12	11004	3	ArDaDAtuke	n	s	7		parasaptamI	0
13	11005	1	kNiti		s	7		parasaptamI	0
14	11005	2	ca						0
15	11006	1	dIDIvevIwAm		p	6		sambanDa	0
16	11007	1	halaH		p	1		saYjYin	0
17	11007	2	anantarAH		p	1		saYjYin	0
18	11007	3	saMyogaH	m	s	1		saYjYA	0
19	11008	1	muKanAsikAvacanaH	m	s	1		saYjYin	0
20	11008	2	anunAsikaH	m	s	1		saYjYA	0
21	11009	1	tulyAsyaprayatnam	n	s	1		saYjYin	0
22	11009	2	savarRam	n	s	1		saYjYA	11010
23	11010	1	na						0
24	11010	2	ajJalO		d	1		saYjYin	0

Fig. 2: The pada file

It may be helpful to explain an example of the references in the *anuvṛtti* file with reference to these figures. The words *ikaḥ* and *guṇavṛddhī* recur in 1.1.5 from 1.1.3. The *sūtras* are shown on lines 4 and 6 of the *sūtra* file in Figure 1. The words in 1.1.3 are shown on lines 8 and 9 in the *pada* file in Figure 2. Rows 7-8 in

	A	B	C	D	E
1	SuNı	F	Pada	Origi	
2	11002	1	vfdDiH	11001	1
3	11003	1	vfdDiH	11001	1
4	11003	2	guRaH	11002	3
5	11004	1	ikaH	11003	1
6	11004	2	guRavfdDI	11003	2
7	11005	1	ikaH	11003	1
8	11005	2	guRavfdDI	11003	2
9	11005	3	na	11004	1
10	11006	1	guRavfdDI	11003	2
11	11006	2	na	11004	1
12	11010	1	savarRam	11009	2
13	11012	1	IdUdet	11011	1
14	11012	2	pragfhyam	11011	3
15	11013	1	pragfhyam	11011	3
16	11014	1	pragfhyam	11011	3
17	11015	1	pragfhyam	11011	3
18	11015	2	nipAtaH	11014	1

Fig. 3:The *anuvṛtti* file

	A	B	C	D	E	F	G	H	I	J
1	SuNı	F	PratN	Pratipadika	Compound	LexId	SubLexId	Mark	F	Tap
2	11001	1	0	vfdDi		saYjYA				FALSE
3	11001	2	0	At		Sabda				TRUE
4	11001	3	0	Ec		pratyAhAra		c		FALSE
5	11002	1	0	at		Sabda				TRUE
6	11002	2	0	eN		pratyAhAra		N		FALSE
7	11002	3	0	guRa		saYjYA				FALSE
8	11003	1	0	ik		pratyAhAra		k		FALSE
9	11003	2	0	guRavfdDi	itaretaradvandva					FALSE
10	11003	2	1	guRa		saYjYA				FALSE
11	11003	2	2	vfdDi		saYjYA				FALSE
12	11004	1	0	na						FALSE
13	11004	2	0	DAtulopa	bahuvrIhi					FALSE
14	11004	2	1	DAtu		saYjYA				FALSE
15	11004	2	2	lopa		saYjYA				FALSE
16	11004	3	0	ArDaDAtuka		saYjYA				FALSE
17	11005	1	0	kNit	bahuvrIhi					FALSE
18	11005	1	1	kN	dvandva					FALSE
19	11005	1	101	g		it				FALSE
20	11005	1	102	k		it				FALSE
21	11005	1	103	N		it				FALSE
22	11005	1	2	it		saYjYA	ekAkzara			FALSE
23	11005	2	0	ca						FALSE

Fig. 4:The *prātipadika* file

Figure 3 show the words *ikaḥ* and *guṇavr̥ddhi* with 11005 in the SuNum column and 1 and 2, respectively, in the PNum column. In the OriginSuNum column is 11003 and in the OriginPN column are 1 and 2, respectively. These last numbers refer to numbers in the *pada* file. The number 11003 in the OriginSuNum field in the *anuvr̥tti* file refers to 11003 in the SuNum field in the *pada* file in column 1 on lines 8 and 9 in Figure 2, and the numbers 1 and 2 in the OriginPN field in the *anuvr̥tti* file refer to the numbers 1 and 2 in the WN column in the *pada* file in column 2 on lines 8 and 9 in Figure 2.

7 Web Availability

Besides creating database layouts, we also converted the data into forms that can be displayed on the web at `http://sanskritlibrary.org`. The continuous text and *padapāṭha* are displayed in our general text display and additional data is displayed in the *kramapāṭha* web-based reader and index interface. As shown in Figure 5, the reader display shows the *sūtra* in Devanāgarī script and Roman transcription, followed by the words with *sandhi* analyzed (*padapāṭha*). Information in the comment field and several other fields from the *sūtra* and *pada* files is displayed below these. Two additional rows are reserved for a presentation of a comprehensive paraphrase of the *sūtra* and translation, yet to be composed. Mousing over the Devanāgarī text marks word boundaries with a short vertical red stroke. Clicking a word there or in the *padapāṭha* displays its inflectional information, stem, and lexical tag in a box beneath the word, as shown in Figure 6. Finally, pressing the p-key plays a recording of the *sūtra* in the recitation of the *sūtras* by Raghunātha Śarman. Figure 7 shows his picture displayed on the title page of the book in the *kramapāṭha* reader. A menu displays the possible commands, one of which allows configuring the display to suit one's preferences. Another opens a table of contents that allows one to navigate the text easily.

The dynamic index to the reader allows focused access to various sorts of information as shown in Figure 8. An alphabetic list of stems is displayed at the left. Selecting an item in the list displays the *sūtras* in which the term occurs in the tall box in the middle and the lexical category of the stem in the box at the lower right.

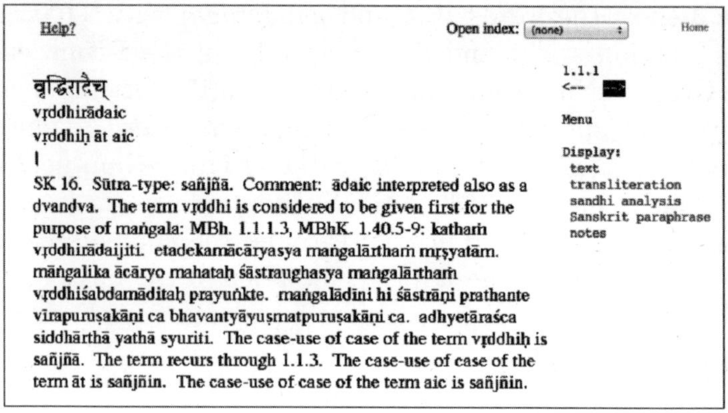

Fig. 5:The Kramapāṭha reader*Aṣṭādhyāyī* 1.1.1

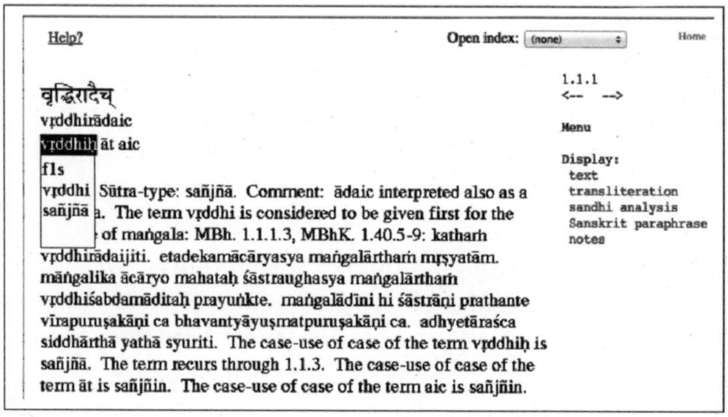

Fig. 6:The Kramapāṭha reader*Aṣṭādhyāyī* 1.1.1 morphological analysis

Fig. 7:The Kramapāṭha reader*Aṣṭādhyāyī* title page

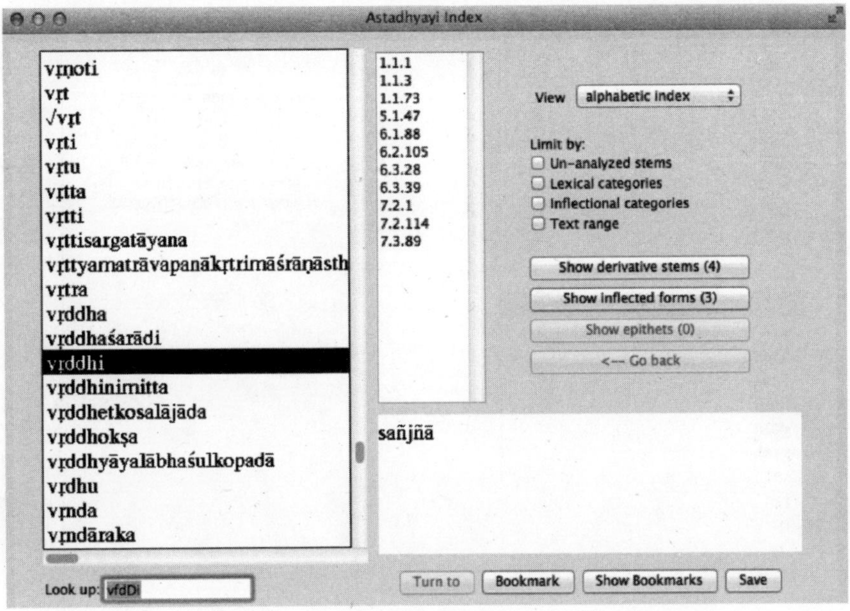

Fig. 8:The Kramapāṭha reader *Aṣṭādhyāyī* index

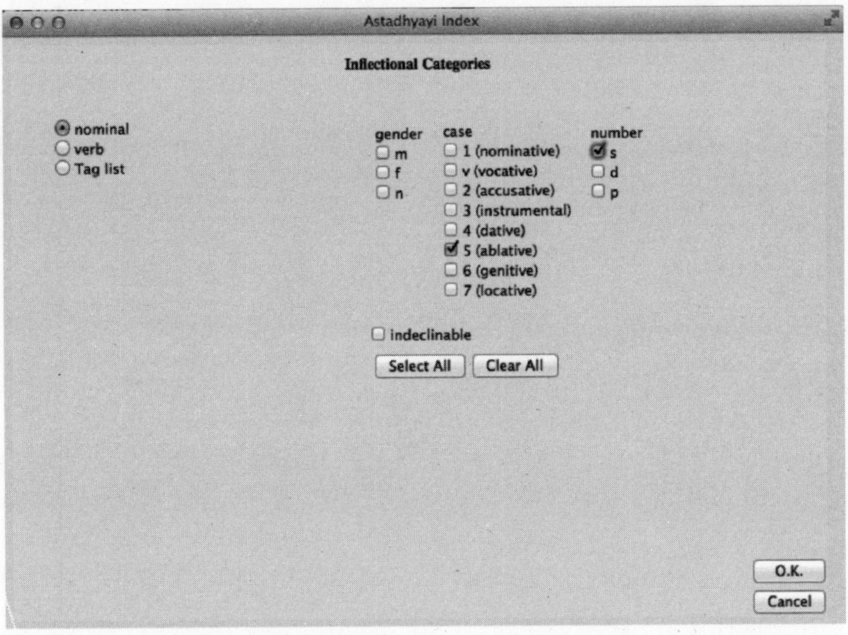

Fig. 9:The Kramapāṭha reader index inflectional categories

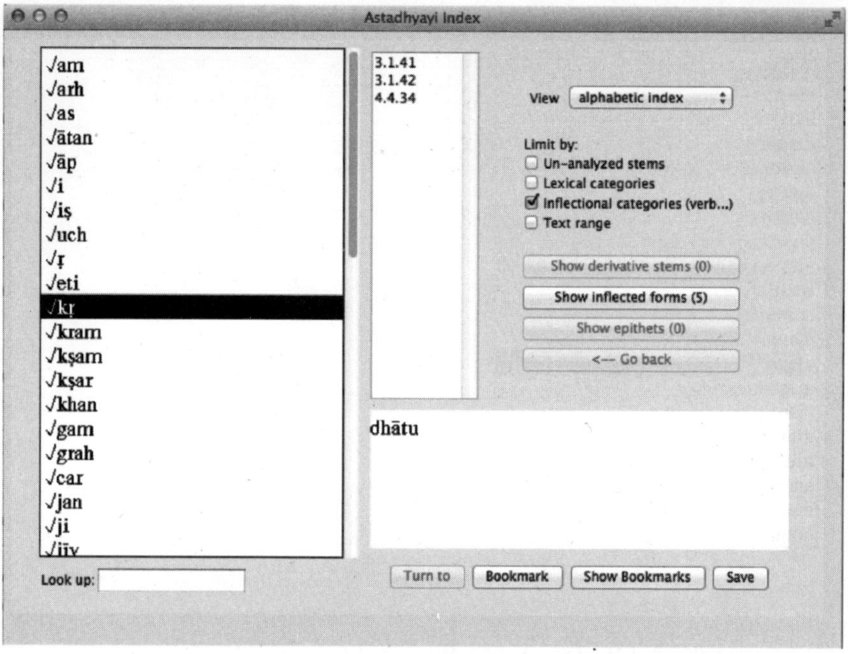

Fig. 10:The Kramapāṭha reader *Aṣṭādhyāyī* verb index

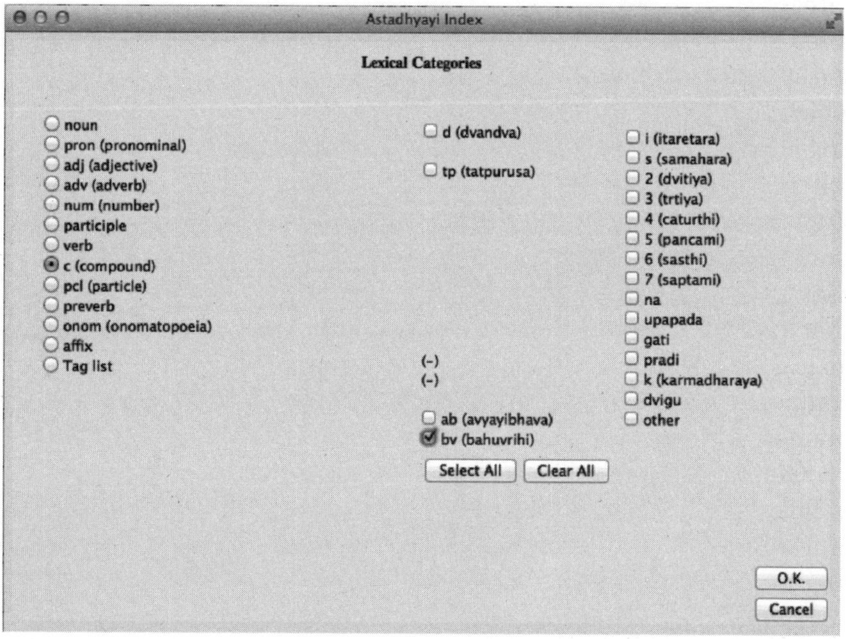

Fig. 11:The Kramapāṭha reader index lexical categories: compounds

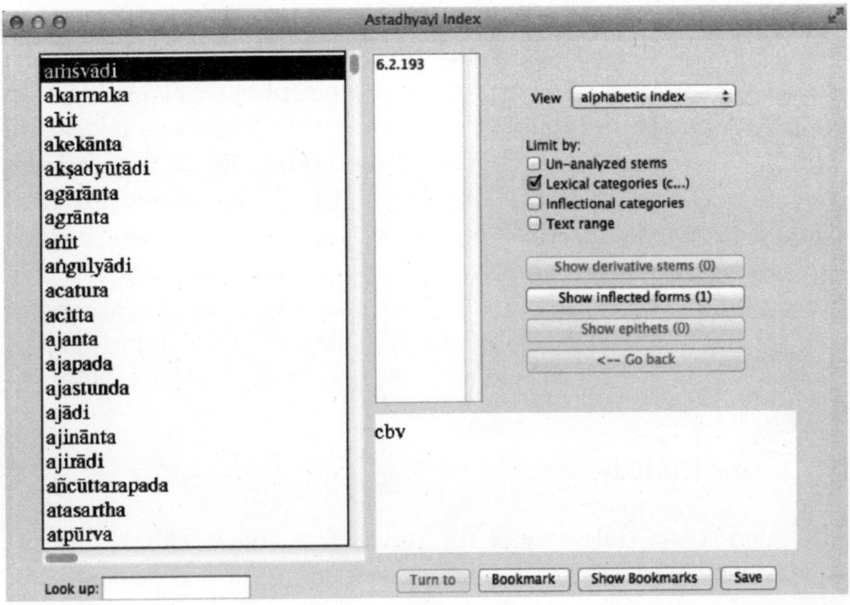

Fig. 12:The Kramapāṭha reader *Aṣṭādhyāyī* bahuvrīhi compound index

The upper right of the window shows various modes of limiting the list at the far left. One can limit by lexical and inflectional categories and text range, and one can limit the list to unanalyzed stems. One can also display inflected forms and derivates of the stem; the derivates displayed include exclusively compounds of which the stem is a constituent. Clicking the inflectional categories box allows one to limit the list to items with the selected inflectional criteria. Figure 9 shows the nominal panel with ablative case and singular number selected. Figure 10 shows the list of verbal roots that results from selecting all verbal inflectional categories. The root *kr̥* is selected so that the tall middle box shows the *sūtras* that contain conjugated forms of that root. Figure 11 shows the lexical categories compound panel with the check box for *bahuvrīhi* compounds selected. Figure 12 shows the list of all *bahuvrīhi* compounds in the *Aṣṭādhyāyī* that results from the search.

Our general text display includes two modes. Continuous text is linked to the Sanskrit Heritage site parser. Where a *padapāṭha* is available, each word is linked to the Sanskrit Library morphological analyzer. In the case of a highly technical *sūtra* text like the *Aṣṭādhyāyī*, which in any case we have already fully analyzed in the database, linkage to a parser cannot be expected to provide interesting results; nor can linkage of each word in its *padapāṭha* to a general morphological analyzer, where we have already undertaken a morphological analysis of the text. Instead, in our *Aṣṭādhyāyī padapāṭha*, each word is linked to the morphological analysis we undertook in the database. The stem is then linked to lexical resources. At present the link is to Monier-Williams' *A Sanskrit English Dictionary* (1899). In due course the stem will be linked to a multi-dictionary interface under development which will include Renou's *Terminologie grammaticale du sanskrit* and Katre's *Dictionary of Pāṇini*. Likewise the continuous text will be accompanied by Katre's translation of the *Aṣṭādhyāyī* in his *Aṣṭādhyāyī of Pāṇini*.

8 Conclusion

The *Aṣṭādhyāyī* database is the product of considerable work involving engagement directly with the grammatical commentaries. It therefore provides a source of knowledge of the elements and structure of the *Aṣṭādhyāyī* independent of the work of Böhtlingk and Katre. As discussed in the course of this paper, the database needs additional editing and there is room for additional work to enrich it and extend it further. Comparison of this database with the analyses of Böhtlingk, Katre, and others would also be interesting. In any case, the database as it is, is presented here to encourage its use in the hope that it may prove beneficial for those engaged in research on ancient Indian linguistic treatises and in Sanskrit computational linguistics.

References

1. Böhtlingk, Otto. 1839-40. *Pāṇini's acht Bücher grammatischer Regeln: herausgegeben und erläutert.* Band I *Pāṇini's Sūtra's mit Indischen Scholien.* Band II. *Einleitung, Commentar, erklärender Index der grammatichen Kunstausdrücke, alphabetisches Verszeichniss der Sūtra's, Gaṇapātha.* Bonn: H.B. König.
2. Böhtlingk, Otto. 1887. *Pāṇini's Grammatik: herausgegeben, übersetzt, erläutert und mit verschiedenen Indices versehen.* Leipzig. Reprint: 2 vols. Olms: Hildesheim, 1964.
3. Katre, Sumitra Mangesh. 1968-69. *Dictionary of Pāṇini.* Deccan College Building Centenary and Silver Jubilee Series 53. 3 Parts. Pune: Deccan College Postgraduate and Research Institute.

4. Katre, Sumitra Mangesh. 1987. *Aṣṭādhyāyī of Pāṇini: Roman Transliteration and English Translation.* Austin: University of Texas Press. Reprint: Delhi: Motilal Banarsidass, 1989.
5. Pansikar, Vasudev Lakshman Shastri, ed. 1985. *The Siddhāntakaumudī with Tattvabodhinī commentary of Jñānendrasarasvatī and Subodhinī commentary of Jayakṛṣṇa.* [*Tattvabodhinī-samākhya-vyākhyā-saṁvalitā śiddhāntakaumudī nāma Bhaṭṭojidīkṣita-praṇītā pāṇinīya-vyākaraṇa-sūtra-vṛttiḥ. Jñānendrasarasvatī-viracitottarakṛdantāntaṁ Tattvabodhinī-vyākhyā, svara-vaidikyoḥ Jayakṛṣṇakṛtā Subodhinī. Vāsudevaśarmaṇā ṭippaṇyādibhiḥ pariṣkṛtā saṁśodhitā ca.*] New Delhi: Meharcand Lachhmandass Publications.
6. Renou, Louis. 1942. *Terminologie grammaticale du sanskrit.* Bibliothèque de l'École des hautes études, IVe Section des Sciences historiques et philologiques, 280-82 fasc. Paris: É. Champion.
7. Shastri, B.R. and V. Sundara Sarma. 1976. *Kāśikā*: Part 3, Indices, Volume 1. Sanskrit Academy Series no. 23. Hyderabad: Sanskrit Academy, Osmania University.
8. Scharf, Peter M. 2009a. 'Modeling Pāṇinian Grammar.' In *Sanskrit Computational Linguistics: First and Second International Symposia, Rocquencourt, France, October 2007; Providence, RI, USA, May 2008; Revised Selected and Invited Papers*, eds. Gérard Huet, Amba Kulkarni, and Peter Scharf, pp. 95-126. Lecture Notes in Artificial Intelligence 5402. Berlin; Heidelberg: Springer-Verlag, 2009. `http://sanskrit.inria.fr/Symposium/Program.html`.
9. Scharf, Peter M. 2009b. "Levels in Pāṇinis *Aṣṭādhyāyī*." In *Sanskrit Computational Linguistics: Third International Symposium, Hyderabad, India, January 2009, Proceedings*, ed. Gérard Huet, and Amba Kulkarni, pp. 66-77. Lecture Notes in Artificial Intelligence 5406. Berlin; Heidelberg: Springer-Verlag, 2009. `http://sanskrit.inria.fr/Symposium/Program.html`.
10. Scharf, Peter M. 2011. 'On the Semantic Foundation of Pāṇinian Derivational Procedure: the Derivation of *Kumbhakāra*.' *Journal of the American Oriental Society* 131.1 (2011): 39-72.
11. Sharma, Aryendra, Khanderao Deshpande, and D.G. Padhye, eds. 1969, 1970. *Kāśikā: A Commentary on Pāṇini's Grammar by Vāmana and Jayāditya.* Part 1 (adhyāyas 1-4) and part 2 (adhyāyas 5-8). Sanskrit Academy Series nos. 17, 20. Hyderabad: Sanskrit Academy, Osmania University.
12. Sri Ramachandrudu, P. and V. Sundara Sarma. 1985. *Kāśikā*: Part 3, *Indices*, Volume 2. Sanskrit Academy Series no. 32. Hyderabad: Sanskrit Academy, Osmania University.

Clues from Aṣṭādhyāyī for Compound Type Identification

Amba Kulkarni and Anil Kumar

Department of Sanskrit Studies,
University of Hyderabad,
Hyderabad
apksh@uohyd.ernet.in, anil.lalit22@gmail.com

Abstract. *Aṣṭādhyāyī* has a section of rules which provides conditions for compound formation. These rules are presented from generation point of view. We study these conditions from the point of view of compound-type identification. A rule-based classifier, based on these rules, is developed whose performance on some of the compound types is encouraging. These conditions also suggest the type of information lexical databases should contain for automatic language analysis, including a compound classifier.

Keywords: Sanskrit Compound Type Identifier, Sanskrit Compounds, classifier, semantic features

1 Introduction

Sanskrit is very rich in compound formation. On an average[1] every fifth or sixth word in a Sanskrit sentence is a compound. The compound formation being productive it forms an open set and as such it is also not possible to list all the compounds in a dictionary. The compound formation involves a mandatory *sandhi.* But mere *sandhi* splitting does not help a reader in identifying the meaning of a compound. Typically a compound does not code the relation between its components explicitly. To understand the meaning of a compound, it is necessary to identify its components

[1] This estimate is based on the manually tagged corpus available with Sanskrit Consortium.

and discover the relation between them.

A worth-noting contribution in the field of Sanskrit compounds is by the Department of Indology of French Institute, Pondichery. It has developed a searchable electronic version of *Pāṇinīya Udāharaṇakośa* (Grimal et al., 2008) providing generation of approximately 4,400 compounds from *Mahābhāṣya, Kāśikā* and *Kaumudī*. This database is very much useful in understanding the process of compound formation. Gillon (2009) suggests tagging of compounds by enriching the context free rules. The idea here is to mark the missing case marker and the head, and specify the enriched category of the compound. The Sanskrit Consortium, a Government of India-sponsored project, has developed a tagset for Sanskrit compounds (Ramakrishnamacharyulu et al. 2012). This tagset has fifty-six tags (Appendix A), which are subclassifications of the major four types *avyayībhāva, tatpuruṣa, bahuvrīhi* and *dvandva.* The subclassification is guided by the paraphrase of compounds. For example, the paraphrase in *tatpuruṣa* is a function of the *vibhakti.* Thus there are seven sub-types under the major type *tatpuruṣa.*

The question we are addressing in this paper is, is it possible to decide the type and sub-type of a compound in the form of string of phonemes without accents, merely on the basis of its components? The famous example of *rāmeśvaraḥ* as illustrated below tells us that mere components do not help us in deciding the type of a compound. *rāmeśvaraḥ*, depending on the context, may mean

a. rāmaḥ ca asau īśvaraḥ ca,
b. rāmaḥ īśvaraḥ yasya saḥ, and
c. rāmasya īśvaraḥ.

In the first case it is *karmadhāraya*, in the second case it is *bahuvrīhi* and in the third case it is *ṣaṣṭhī-tatpuruṣa*! Though the components are the same in all the three cases, relation among these components is determined from the wider context or possibly through an accent.

It is also important to note the level of semantics, the compound types deal with. Consider the compounds *rājapuruṣaḥ, daśarathaputraḥ* and *vṛkṣaśākhā*. In the first case the relation between *rājan* and *puruṣa* is that of servant-master (*sevya-sevaka*), in the second the relation between *daśaratha* and *putraḥ* is of father-son (*pitā-putra*) and in the third case the relation between *vṛkṣa* and *śākhā* is part of (*avayava-avayavi*). However, in all the three cases instead of specifying these deeper relations, relation among the components is expressed through the genitive case suffix in the paraphrase of these compounds as *rājñaḥ puruṣaḥ, daśarathasya putraḥ* and *vṛkṣasya śākhā*, and thus these are classified as *ṣaṣṭhī-tatpuruṣa*. In other words, the classification is not guided by the deeper semantics but by the paraphrase of a given compound, or by what the language expresses.

Thus, on the one hand, to decide the meaning of a compound, we need a fine-grain tagset, at the same time, it cannot be as fine-grained as to distinguish between the meaning of genitive cases in *rājñaḥ puruṣaḥ, daśarathasya putraḥ* and *vṛkṣasya śākhā*. Assuming that we follow the fine-grained classification of compounds as given in Appendix A, the question is, to what extent is it possible to decide the relation between the words only on the basis of components involved? Anil Kumar et al. (2010) have reported that the components do provide an information that is useful for classifying the compounds. For classification, a manually tagged corpus was used as a training data. The results were encouraging, but it was observed that use of rule-based classifier along with the statistical data should provide better results. In this paper we study the relevant *sūtra*s from *Aṣṭādhyāyī* for clues.

2 Clues from Pāṇini's Aṣṭādhyāyī

Pāṇini describes the process of compound formation starting from the paraphrase of a compound. The process starts with an *alaukika vigraha*. It involves deciding the type, the order of the components, the elision of the *vibhakti* of intermediate components, assignment of *svara*s, addition of certain suffixes to change the gender if necessary.

The *sūtra*s dealing with compounds then can be broadly classified into two types:

a. *sūtras* providing semantic conditions for compound formation, and

b. *sūtras* dealing with the process of compound formation involving

  i. decision of word order,

  ii. *vibhakti* deletion,

  iii. *svara* assignment, and

  iv. changes in gender and number

The second type of *sūtras* are useful from generation point of view. They deal with the morphology and phonology. A close look at the Pāṇini's *sūtras* of first type provides us a lot of semantic clues. For example, look at the following *sūtras*.
dvitīyā śrītātītapatitagatātyastaprāptāpannaiḥ (2.1.24)
tr̥tīyā tatkr̥tārthena guṇavacanena (2.1.30)
annena vyañjanam (2.1.33)
pañcamī bhayena (2.1.36)

Each of these *sūtras* gives a criterion for formation of a compound of a particular type either in terms of semantics of the components involved or as a list of words as the first or the second component. Applied reversely, given the components of a compound, these semantic conditions/list provide a clue for deciding the possibility of a compound to be of a particular type. To make the point clear, *pañcamī bhayena*(2.1.36) states that a word ending in fifth case may optionally get compounded with a word indicating fear. For example, *corāt bhayam* is compounded optionally as *corabhayam.* Now, when we analyse this compound, based on the fact that *bhaya* is the second component, we guess that this compound might have been formed by *pañcamī bhayena*(2.1.36), and a Pāṇinian scholar would typically verify that this is so. Verification rules out false positives. In the absence of a compound generator, we skip the verification part and do only guess. We examine below the relevant *sūtras* from the Aṣṭādhyāyī to decide whether the clues they provide are sufficient enough for decision making. It is necessary to keep one deviation from Pāṇini in mind. When a compound W is split as W_1-W_2, the morphological features associated with W are accessible through the analysis of W_2. So when we specify the conditions, the gender and number information corresponding to w_2 actually corresponds to the compound W. Most of the *sūtras* specify a pattern or a condition on either or both the *pūrvapada* as well as *uttarapada.* The *sūtras* we discuss are from *avyayībhāvaḥ* (2.1.5) to *cārthe dvandvaḥ* (2.2.29). Of these, *sūtras* which do not employ any condition but serve only as an *adhikāra sūtra* such as *avyayībhāvaḥ* (2.1.5) and *tatpuruṣaḥ* (2.1.21), etc. will not be discussed.

2.1 Avyayībhāva

The *sūtras* from *avyayaṃ vibhakti-samīpa-samr̥ddhi-vyr̥ddhyarthābhāvātyaya-asaṃprati-śabdaprādurbhāva-paścādyathānupūrvya-yaugapadya-sādr̥śya-sampatti-sākalya-antavacaneṣu* (2.1.6) to *anyapadārthe ca saṁjñāyām* (2.1.21) provide conditions for the formation of an *avyayībhāva* compound. Table 1 summarizes the conditions on the *samāsa pūrvapada* and *uttarapada* described in these rules. Due to *avyayībhāvaśca*(2.4.18), every *Avyayībhāva* compound is in neuter gender. During analysis process, since we split W as W_1, W_2, W_2 will be in neuter gender. Thus a necessary condition for any compound to be an *avyayībhāva* is that W_2 should be in neuter gender.

Sūtra tiṣṭhadguprabhr̥tīni ca (2.1.17) provides an exceptional list of *avyayībhāva* compounds. In order to use the sūtras *saṁkhyā vaṁśyena* (2.1.19) and *nadībhiśca* (2.1.20) for deciding the type of a compound, one needs a list of family names and a list of names of rivers.

Sūtra *yathā 'sādr̥śye* (2.1.7) deals with a broader context. The word *yathā* has four different senses (i) *yogyatā* 'ability', (ii) *vīpsā,* (iii) *padārthānativr̥tti,* and (iv) *sādr̥śya* 'similarity'. *Yathā'sādr̥śye* (2.1.7) states that *yathā* is invariably compounded with a case-inflected word in a meaning other than *sādr̥śya* 'similarity' as in *yathāvr̥ddham* 'every old person'. Since *yathā* in other meanings also gets compounded, as in *yathāśakti,* given a compound with *yathā* as the first component, it is not possible to decide the meaning of *yathā* only on the basis of the following component, without looking at the complete context. Hence it is not possible to decide the meaning of this compound. Nevertheless we can always mark this as an *avyayībhāva.*

Anyapadārthe ca saṁjñāyām (2.1.21) puts a condition that a river name may get compounded with another noun referring to *anyapadārtha* 'a totally new thing', and one needs a broader context to decide whether such a compound is an *avyayībhāva* or not.

Table 1: Conditions for the compound *avyayībhāva*

S.No.	Sūtra Number	First Component	Second Component	Type
1	2.1.6[2]	Any of the prefixes or indeclinables such as *pra, parā, apa,* and *yathā*	Neuter gender in first case	A1
2	2.1.7[3]	*yathā*	Neuter gender in first case	A1
3	2.1.8[4]	*yāvat*	Neuter gender in first case	A1
4	2.1.9[5]	-	*prati*	A2
5	2.1.10[6]	*akṣa, śalākā* or a numeral such as *eka, dvi* etc.	*pari*	A2
6	2.1.12[7]	*apa, pari, bahis* or word ending with *añc*	Neuter gender in fifth case	A1
7	2.1.13[8]	*āṅ*	Neuter gender in fifth case	A1

Continued on next page

[2] *avyayaṃ vibhaktisamīpasamr̥ddhivyr̥ddhyarthābhāvātyayāsamprati-śabdaprādurbhāva-paścādyathā-ānupūrvya-yaugapadya-sādr̥śya-sampatti-sākalya-antavacaneṣu*

[3] *yathā 'sādr̥śye*

[4] *yāvadavadhāraṇe*

[5] *suppratinā mātrārthe*

[6] *akṣaśalākāsaṁkhyāḥ pariṇā*

[7] *apaparibahirañcavaḥ pañcamyā*

[8] *āṅ maryādā 'bhividhyoḥ*

Table 1: Continued from previous page

S.No.	Sūtra Number	First Component	Second Component	Type
8	2.1.14[9]	*abhi, prati*	Neuter gender in first case	A1
9	2.1.15[10]	*anu*	Neuter gender in first case	A1
10	2.1.16[11]	*anu*	Neuter gender in first case	A1
11	2.1.17[12]	*list of tiṣṭhadgu-prabhr̥tī*		A3
12	2.1.18[13]	*pāre, madhye*	Neuter gender in fifth-case	A7
12.1	2.1.18[14]	-	*pārāt, madhyāt*	A7
13	2.1.19[15]	Numerals such as *eka* and *dvi*	family name	A6
14	2.1.20[16]	Numerals such as *eka* and *dvi*	name of a river	A6
15	2.4.83[17]	Any of the prefix or indeclinables such as *pra, parā*, etc.	*prātipadika* ending in '*a*' in third, fifth and seventh	A7

2.2 Tatpuruṣaḥ

The *sūtras* from *dvitīyā śritātītapatitagatātyastaprāptāpannaiḥ* (2.1.24) to *ktvā ca* (2.2.22) provide conditions for the formation of *tatpuruṣa-samāsa*. We treat *karmadhāraya*, which is a special

[9] *lakṣaṇenā 'bhipratī ābhimukhye*
[10] *anuryatsamayā*
[11] *yasya cāyāmaḥ*
[12] *tiṣṭhadgu-prabhr̥tīni ca*
[13] *pāre madhye ṣaṣṭhyā vā*
[14] *pāre madhye ṣaṣṭhyā vā*
[15] *saṁkhyā vaṁśyena*
[16] *nadībhiśca*
[17] *nāvyayībhāvādato 'mtvapañcamyāḥ*

case of *tatpuruṣa* compound, separately. Hence, *sūtras* from *pūrvakālaikasarvajaratpurāṇanavakevalāḥ samānādhikaraṇena* (2.1.49) to *pūrvāparādharottaramekadeśinaikādhikaraṇe* (2.2.1) are dealt with in the next section. Majority of *sūtras* have a requirement of a *kr̥danta* ending in *kta* suffix (a past participle form of a verb). Out of the thirty-eight *sūtras* dealing with *tatpuruṣa*, only twenty-eight can be used to decide the compound type automatically. The remaining ten *sūtras* require extralinguistic information. For example, the sūtra *atyantasaṁyoge ca* (2.1.29) states, if there is an invariable uninterrupted connection (*atyantasaṁyoga*) between the meaning of the two components, then the resulting compound is of type *tatpuruṣa*. It is not possible to decide whether the connection is invariable and uninterrupted or not, only on the basis of its components. On similar reasoning to classify a compound *śaṅkulākhaṇḍaḥ* 'cut by knife' or *dhānyārthaḥ* 'wealth acquired by grain' on the basis of *tr̥tīyātatkr̥tārthena guṇavacanena* (2.1.30) as a *tr̥tīyā tatpuruṣa*, one needs an information that *śaṅkulā* is an instrument used for cutting or wealth can be acquired by grains. Few other *sūtras* that require semantic information are:-

a. *kartr̥karaṇe kr̥tā bahulam* (2.1.32)
b. *kr̥tyairadhikārthavacane* (2.1.33)
c. *annena vyañjanam* (2.1.34)
d. *bhakṣyeṇa miśrikaraṇam* (2.1.35)
e. *kr̥tyairr̥ṇe* (2.1.43)
f. *saṁjñayām* (2.1.44)
g. *kṣepe* (2.1.47)

Sūtra nañ (2.2.6) for *nañ tatpuruṣa* poses a special problem with respect to splitting. While the initial *an* may provide a useful clue for the split, initial *a* may lead to over-generation during *sandhi* splitting. Once split, of course, it is easy to mark such compounds as *nañ tatpuruṣaḥ*.

Sūtras from *ṣaṣṭhī* (2.2.8) to *nityaṃ krīḍājīvikayoḥ* (2.2.17) deal with the *ṣaṣṭhī tatpuruṣa* compounds. Among these only one *sūtra yājakādibhiśca* (2.2.9) is assertive providing a condition for the formation of a compound. *Nityaṃ krīḍājīvikayoḥ* (2.2.17) requires a specific semantics that the resulting compound should indicate a game or a means for livelihood. If the lexicon provides explicitly this information, then only automatic detection of such a compound as a *ṣaṣṭhī tatpuruṣaḥ* is possible. All other *sūtras* prohibit the formation of this compound.

Kugatiprādayaḥ (2.2.18) provides conditions on the first component that it can be either a *ku* or a word which may be termed as *gati* or a list of indeclinables *pra*, etc.. *Upapadamatiṅ* (2.2.19) states a condition in terms of an *upapada*. An *upapada* is a word referring to the word in seventh case in the *sūtras* that prescribe a *kr̥danta* suffix.[18] Thus this condition refers to an internal stage during the derivational process. Then, given a compound, a generated word, how can we decide whether its *pūrvapada* is an *upapada* or not? It is not possible to decide whether the *pūrvapada* is an *upapada* or not, unless we look at the involved process. If *uttarapada* is analysed with these *kr̥danta* suffixes, the derivation of which involves a notion of *upapada*, we may guess the compound to be of type *upapada tatpuruṣa*. Further, since these *kr̥t* suffixes produce words that are bound morphemes, a morphological analyser handling these bound morphemes should help in deciding whether the given compound is an *upapada tatpuruṣa* or not.

Next *sūtra amaivāvyayena* (2.2.20) also puts a condition on *upapada tatpuruṣa* compounds, where the requirement is that the *uttarapada* is an indeclinable derived from an *am* ending *kr̥t* suffix. *Tr̥tīyāprabhr̥tīnyanyatarasyām* (2.2.21) extends this condition on *pūrvapada* to other *upapadas* due to the *sūtras upadaśastr̥tīyāyām* (3.4.47), *anvacyānulomye* (3.4.64) as well. *Ktvā ca* (2.2.22) further extends it to a *kr̥t* suffix *ktvā*. As stated earlier, it is not possible to decide whether the *pūrvapada* is an *upapada* or not. But in this particular case, we have another clue. Due to *samāse anañpūrve ktvo lyap* (7.1.37), the second component is in *lyap*, and the *pūrvapada* is not a prefix. This provides a clue for guessing the *upapada tatpuruṣa* correctly. *Alaṁkr̥tya* is an exception.

Table 2 lists the *sūtras* where it is possible to identify the compound type as *tatpuruṣa* based on the components and their morphological features mentioned in the *sūtras*. The *sūtra pātresamitādayaśca* (2.1.48) provides a list of exceptional *tatpuruṣa*

[18] *tatra-upapadam saptamīsthānam* 3.1.92

compounds. In *caturthī tadarthārthabalihitasukharakṣitaiḥ* (2.1.36), to decide whether the relation between the two components is of *tadartha*[19] or not is difficult. The other conditions of *caturthī tadarthārthabalihitasukharakṣitaiḥ* (2.1.36) which lists various words for the possible candidate are easy to implement mechanically. For automatic detection of a compound type, as is evident from the following conditions, we also require a list of words denoting time, time indicating words which can be used as a measure, parts of a day and night, list of names of river, list of family names, words denoting numbers, etc.

Table 2: Conditions for the compound *tatpuruṣa*

S.No.	Sūtra Number	First Component	Second Component	Type
1	2.1.24[20]	-	*śrita, atīta, patita, gata, atysta, prāpta, āpanna*	T2
2	2.1.25[21]	*svayam* or *svāyam*	*kr̥danta* with *kta pratyaya*	T2
3	2.1.26[22]	*khaṭvā*	*kr̥danta* with *kta pratyaya*	T2
4	2.1.27[23]	sāmi	*tkr̥danta* with *kta pratyaya*	T2
5	2.1.28[24]	a word denoting time	*kr̥danta* with *kta pratyaya*	T2

Continued on next page

[19] *tadarthena prakr̥tivikr̥tibhāva samāsaḥ ayam iṣyate.* Kāśikā (2.1.36)

[20] *dvitīyā śritātītapatitagatātyastaprāptāpannaiḥ*

[21] *svayaṃ ktena*

[22] *khaṭvā kṣepe*

[23] *sāmi*

[24] *kālāḥ*

Table 2 : Continued from previous page

S.No.	Sūtra Number	First Component	Second Component	Type
6	2.1.31[25]	-	*pūrva, sadṛśa, sama, ūnārtha, kalaha, nipuṇa, miśra, ślakṣṇa*	T3
7	2.1.36[26]	-	*artha, bali, hita, sukha, rakṣita*	T4
8	2.1.37[27]	-	*bhaya, bhīti, bhī*	T5
9	2.1.38[28]	-	*apeta, apoḍha, mukta, patita, apatra*	T5
10	2.1.39[29]	*stoka, antika, dūrārtha, kṛcchra*	*krdanta* with *kta pratyaya*	T5
11	2.1.40[30]	-	from the list of *śauṇḍa gaṇa*	T7
12	2.1.41[31]	-	*siddha, śuṣka, pakva, bandha*	T7
13	2.1.42[32]	-	dhvāṅkṣa	T7
14	2.1.45[33]	words denoting part of a day or night	*kṛdanta* with *kta pratyaya*	T7
15	2.1.46[34]	*tatra*	*kṛdanta* with *kta pratyaya*	T7

Continued on next page

[25] *pūrvasadṛśasamonārthakalahanipuṇamiśraślakṣṇaiḥ*
[26] *caturthī tadarthārthabalihitasukharakṣitaiḥ*
[27] *pañcamī bhayena*
[28] *apetāpoḍhamuktapatitāpatrastairalpaśaḥ*
[29] *stokāntikadūrārthakṛcchrāṇi ktena*
[30] *saptamī śōṇḍaiḥ*
[31] *siddhaśuṣkapakvabandhaiśca*
[32] *dhvāṅkṣeṇa kṣepe*
[33] *ktenāhorātrāvayavāḥ*
[34] *tatra*

Table 2 : Continued from previous page

S.No.	Sūtra Number	First Component	Second Component	Type
16	2.1.48[35]	list of exceptional compounds *pātresamitā...*		T7
17	2.2.2[36]	*ardha*	-	T1
18	2.2.6[37]	*a, an*	-	Tn
19	2.2.7[38]	īṣat	-	T
20	2.2.9[39]	-	list of words from *yājaka gaṇa*	T6
21	2.2.18[40]	*ku, kā, pra* etc., may be termed as *gati*	list of words from *yājaka gaṇa*	T6
22	2-2.19[41]	-	a bound morpheme with special *kr̥t* suffix(es)	U
23	2.2.20[42]	word ends with Ṇamul and khamuṅ suffix	a *kr̥t* suffix ending in *am*	U
24	2.2.21[43]	word ends with third case	a *kr̥t* suffix ending in *am*	U
25	2.2.22[44]	word ends with third case	word ends with *kr̥t* suffix *kr̥tvā* or *lyap*	U

35 *pātresamitādayaśca*
36 *ardhaṃ napuṁsakam*
37 *nañ*
38 *īṣadakr̥tā*
39 *yājakādibhiśca*
40 *kugatiprādayaḥ*
41 *upapadamatiṅ*
42 *amaivāvyayena*
43 *tr̥tīyāprabhr̥tīnyanyatarasyām*
44 *ktvā ca*

2.3 Karmadhāraya

Twenty seven *sūtras* from *pūrvakālaikasarvajaratpurāṇa-navakevalāḥ samānādhikaraṇena* (2.1.49) to *mayūravyaṁsakādayaśca* (2.1.72) and *pūrvāparādharottaramekadeśinaikādhikaraṇe* (2.2.1), except *saṁkhyāpūrvo dviguḥ* (2.1.52) indicating a *dvigu*, provide conditions for marking a compound as a *karmadhāraya*. Out of these 23, 15 *sūtras* provide conditions which involve a controlled semantics that can be handled by a computer. Other 8 *sūtras* either deal with open lists or involve deeper semantics. For example, words which share common properties and thus can be compared or compounds with abusing words as one of the components or words indicating a part whole relation form a *karmadhāraya* compound. Sanskrit Wordnet(Kulkarni et al. 2010) and also *Amarakośa* which is tagged for semantic information (Nair et al. 2010) are some of the resources where one can get the pairs with part whole relation. With the availability of this information, *pūrvāparādharottaramekadeśinaikādhikaraṇe*(2.2.1) may be implemented. However, to get an information about the words sharing common properties is not within the reach with the available e-lexicon. Table 3 shows various conditions on the components of *karmadhāraya* compounds as stated in the above range of *sūtras*. As we note, *poṭāyuvatistokakatipayagṛṣṭidhenu-vaśāvehadbaṣkayaṇīpravaktṛśrotriyaadhyāpakadhūrtairjātiḥ* (2.1.65) requires the *pūrvapada* to be a word indicating a class. *Praśaṁsāvacanaiśca* (2.1.66) puts a semantic constraint on the second component demanding it to be a praising word. Similarly *varṇo varṇena* (2.1.69) requires both the components from a list of colour words, while *catuṣpādo garbhiṇyā* (2.1.71) needs the first component to be a four-legged animal. So only if the lexicon is rich with this information, one can use these *sūtras* for compound-type identification. *Mayūravyaṁsakādayaśca* (2.1.72) provides an enumeration of special compounds which otherwise do not have any common semantic condition.

Table 3: Conditions for the compound *Karmadhāraya*

S.No.	Sūtra Number	First Component	Second Component	Type
1	2.1.49[45]	*pūrva, kāla, eka, sarva, jarat, purāṇa, nava, kevala*	-	K1
2	2.1.50[46]	Words indicating a number or direction	-	K3
3	2.1.56[47]	-	A word from *vyāghra gaṇa*	K5
4	2.1.58[48]	*pūrva, apara, prathama, carama, jaghanya, samāna, madhya, madhyama, vīra*	-	K1
5	2.1.59[49]	A word from *śreṇyādi gaṇa*	A word from *kṛt gaṇa*	K
6	2.1.60[50]	A word ending in *kta pratyaya*	Negation of the first component	K2
7	2.1.61[51]	*sat, mahat, parama, uttama, utkṛṣṭa*	-	K1

Continued on next page

45 *pūrvakālaikasarvajaratpurāṇanavakevalāḥ samānādhikaraṇena*
46 *diksaṁkhye saṁjñāyām*
47 *upamitaṃ vyāghrādibhiḥ sāmānyāprayoge*
48 *pūrvāparaprathamacaramajaghanyasamānamadhyamadhyamavīrāśca*
49 *śreṇyādayaḥ kṛtādibhiḥ*
50 *ktena nañviśiṣṭenānañ*
51 *sanmahatparamottamotkṛṣṭāḥ pūjyamānaiḥ*

Table 3 :Continued from previous page

S.No.	Sūtra Number	First Component	Second Component	Type
8	2.1.62[52]	-	*vṛndāraka, nāga, kuñjara*	K2
9	2.1.63[53]	*katara, katama*	-	K1
10	2.1.64[54]	*kim*	-	K1
11	2.1.65[55]	A class denoting word	*poṭā, yuvati, stoka, katipaya, gṛṣṭi, dhenu, vaśā, vehat, baṣkayaṇī, pravaktṛ, śrotriya, adhyāpaka, dhūrta*	K2
12	2.1.66[56]	A class indicating word	words signifying praise such as *matallikā, macarcikā, uddha, tallaja*	K2
13	2.1.67[57]	*yuvan*	*khalati, palita, valina, jarati*	K2
14	2.1.69[58]	a color denoting word	a color denoting word	K3

Continued on next page

---

[52] *vṛndārakanāgakuñjaraiḥ pūjyamānam*

[53] *katarakatamō jātiparipraśne*

[54] *kiṁ kṣepe*

[55] *potāyuvatistokakatipayagṛṣṭidhenuvaśāvehadbaṣkayaṇīpravaktṛ-śrotriyaadhyāpakadhūrtairjātiḥ*

[56] *praśaṁsāvacanaiśca*

[57] *yuvā khalatipalitavalinajaratībhiḥ*

[58] *varṇo varṇena*

Table 3 :Continued from previous page

S.No.	Sūtra Number	First Component	Second Component	Type
15	2.1.70[59]	*kumāra*	a word from *śramaṇa gaṇa*	K2
16	2.1.71[60]	name of a 4-legged animal	*garbhiṇī*	K2
17	2.1.72[61]	Exceptional compounds belonging to *mayūravyaṁsaka* list		K
18	2.2.1[62]	*pūrva, para, adhara, uttara*	a word indicating an object having parts	K
19	2.2.3[63]	*pūraṇa saṁkhyā*	-	K
20	2.2.4[64]	*prāpta, āpanna*	*jīvikā*	K
21	2.2.4[65]	*jīvikā*	*prāpta, āpanna*	K
22	2.2.5[66]	words indicating time used as a measure	words used for measuring	K

2.4 Bahuvrīhi

Among the six *sūtras* from *śeṣo bahuvrīhiḥ* (2.2.23) to *tena saheti tulyayoge* (2.2.28) dealing with *bahuvrīhi*, *śeṣo bahuvrīhiḥ*

[59] *kumāraḥ śramaṇādibhiḥ*
[60] *catuṣpādo garbhiṇyā*
[61] *mayūravyaṁsakādayaśca*
[62] *pūrvāparādharottaramekadeśinaikādhikaraṇe*
[63] *dvitīyatṛtīyacaturthaturyāṇyanyatarasyām*
[64] *prāptāpanne ca dvitīyayā*
[65] *prāptāpanne ca dvitīyayā*
[66] *kālāḥ parimāṇinā*

(2.2.23) is an *adhikāra sūtra* and *anekamanyapadārthe* (2.2.24) lays down the general condition for the formation of *bahuvrīhi.* Conditions stated in *saṁkhyayāvyayāsannādūrādhikasaṁkhyāḥ saṁkhyeye*(2.2.25) and *diṅnāmānyantarāle* (2.2.26) may be used for the detection of *bahuvrīhi. tatra tenedamiti sarūpe* (2.2.27) states that two similar/homophonous words in locative or instrumental case are compounded in the sense of 'this happens with it/there' e.g. *muṣṭīmuṣṭi* and *keśākeśi.* Such compounds are very rare and hence may be treated as exceptions. Table 4 gives a list of possible conditions for detecting a few type of *bahuvrīhi* compounds.

Table 4: Conditions for the compound *Bahuvrīhi*

S.No.	Sūtra Number	Conditions		Type
		First Component	**Second Component**	
1	2.2.25[67]	*saṁkhyeya*	Indeclinable, *āsanna, adūra, adhika, saṁkhyā*	Bvs
2	2.2.26[68]	Name of a direction	Name of a direction	Bsd
3	2.2.28[69]	*sa*	-	BvS

3 Observations

After going through the relevant *sūtras*, we observe that the conditions stated by Pāṇini fall under the following categories.

[67] *saṁkhyayāvyayāsannadūrādhikasaṁkhyāḥ saṁkhyeye*
[68] *diṅnāmānyantarāle*
[69] *tena saheti tulyayoge*

1. A restricted list of words is provided.
2. A restriction in terms of special inflectional suffix/derivational suffix/category is mentioned.
3. A restriction is stated in terms of special technical terms, which are theory internal.
4. A restriction in terms of semantic relations between the components is mentioned.
5. Semantic property of the component is stated as a condition.

Out of these, the fourth and fifth category are important from the point of view of e-lexicon building. The fourth category provides us clues for the important types of relations. Efforts such as Sanskrit Wordnet or on marking semantic information in various *kośa*s such as *Amarakośa* are concerned about lexical as well as semantic relations. In the *sūtra*s related to compounds, we found the mention of following semantic relations.

i. *viśeṣaṇa-viśeṣya-bhāva*
ii. *upamāna-upameya-bhāva*
iii. *avayava-avayavī-bhāva*
iv. instrument-action relation

The fifth category of conditions mentions certain semantic properties such as

a. a number
b. name of a river
c. a family name
d. a direction
e. an abusing word
f. a praising word
g. a four-legged animal
h. a colour word
i. a class (*jāti*)
j. an adjective.

4 Evaluation

We implemented a rule-based classifier, based on the above conditions. Manually tagged corpus of size 600 K is available with the Sanskrit Consortium. It contains around 64 K compounds of two components tagged in context using the tagset specified in Appendix A. Table 5 gives the distribution of high frequent five tags.

Table 5: Distribution of Fine-grain Tags

Tag	# of words	% of words
T6	26,097	40.56
K1	7,909	12.29
Bs6	4,113	06.39
Tn	3,801	05.90
U	2,782	04.32

We observe that out of the 64K compounds, around 30K compounds were either of type T6 or Bs6. Pāṇini's *sūtras* covering these compounds are too general.[70] It is the remaining type of compounds for which Pāṇini's *sūtras* provide semantic criterion; and it has been reported in Anil Kumar et al. (2010) that the performance of statistical parsers on these type of compounds is very poor due to scarcity of the data. We test these compounds for rule-based tagger. We tested our classifier for 11 tags, and their performance is reported in Table 6. The poor performance corresponding to *tatpuruṣa* compounds is due to the non-availability of semantic information. For example, *tṛtīyā-tatpuruṣa* compound needed an information that the first component be a possible instrument for an action denoted by a verb in the second component. In the absence of such information, these compounds cannot be classified.

5 Conclusion

Classification of compounds is a major task in deciding the meaning of a compound. Anil et al. (2010) reported that the precision of a statistical classifier with fifty-five tags is 63.0%, if we consider only the first rank. If we allow the first three ranks, the performance goes up to 81.1%. Statistical taggers perform well provided the training data is sufficient. So their performance goes down on compounds of rare type. On the other hand, a rule-based classifier can perform well on rare type of compounds as well. As we note above, the performance of the rule-based classifier is reasonably good for the tags which are less frequent. If a semantically tagged lexicon is made available, the performance of this classifier may increase further. And a proper combination of the two methods should produce better results.

[70] *ṣaṣṭhī* (2.2.8) and *anekamanyapadārthe* (2.2.24)

Table 5: Performance of rule based tagger on less frequent compounds

Sr. No.	Tag	Manually Tagged	Tagged by m/c	Correct Instances	Precision	Recall	F-measure
1	Tn	3,801	3,770	3,760	99.73	98.92	99.32
2	Tk	47	47	46	97.87	97.87	97.87
3	A1	1,004	1,045	954	91.29	95.01	93.11
4	T4	1,033	1,033	902	87.31	87.31	87.31
5	K1	7,436	2,733	2,365	86.53	31.80	46.50
6	T5	335	100	48	48.00	14.32	22.05
7	T1	132	67	29	43.28	21.96	29.13
8	T2	264	106	37	34.90	14.01	19.99
9	T3	2,334	251	65	25.89	2.78	5.02
10	T7	1,234	31	7	22.58	0.56	1.09
11	A7	13	70	13	18.57	100.00	31.32
		17,633	**9,253**	**8,226**	**88.9**	**46.65**	**61.19**

6 Acknowledgment

We thank the anonymous reviewers for their suggestions and feedback. This work is a part of the Sanskrit Consortium project entitled 'Development of Sanskrit Computational Tools and Sanskrit-Hindi Machine Translation system' sponsored by TDIL Programme, DIT, Government of India.

References

1. Bhat, G.M., 2006: *Samāsaḥ*. Samskrita Bharati, Bangalore, Karnataka.
2. Gillon, B.S., 2007: Exocentric Compounds in Classical Sanskrit, In, *Proceeding of the First International Symposium on Sanskrit Computational Linguistics* (SCLS-2007), Paris, France.
3. Gillon, B.S., 2009: Tagging Classical Sanskrit Compounds, In, *Sanskrit Computational Linguistics* 3, 98-105, Springer-Verlag LNAI 5406.
4. Grimal, F., Sarma, V.V. and Lakshminarasimham, S., 2008: *Pāṇiniyavyākaraṇodāharaṇakoṣaḥ* (Vol. 2: Samāsaprakaraṇam. The book of compound words), French Institute of Pondicherry, Pondicherry.
5. Jha, B.G., 1990: *Samāsa-sandarśikā*. Chowkhamba Surabharati Prakashan, Varanasi, UP.
6. Joshi, S.D. and Roodbergen, J.A.F., 1969: *The Vaiyākaraṇa-mahābhāṣya* (Avyayībhāvatatpuruṣāhnika). University of Poona, Poona, Maharastra.

7. Joshi, S.D. and Roodbergen, J.A.F., 1973: *The Vaiyākaraṇa-mahābhāṣya* (Tatpuruṣāhnika). University of Poona, Poona, Maharastra.
8. Joshi, S.D., Roodbergen, J.A.F., 1996: *The Aṣṭādhyāyī of Pāṇini*, vols. V and VI, Sahitya Academy, New-Delhi.
9. Kulkarni, A.P., A. Kumar, V. Sheeba, 2009: Sanskrit Compound Paraphrase Generator, In: Proceedings of ICON-2009: 7th International Conference on Natural Language Processing, Macmillan Publishers, India.
10. Kulkarni, M., Dangarikar, C., Kulkarni, I., Nanda, A. and Bhattacharya, P., 2010: Introducing Sanskrit WordNet. In *Principles, Construction and Application of Multilingual Wordnets: Proceedings of the 5th Global Wordnet Conference*, Narosa Publishers, India.
11. Kumar, A., V. Mittal, A.P.Kulkarni, 2010: Sanskrit Compound Processor, In *Proceedings of 4i-SCLS 2010: 4th International Sanskrit Computational Linguistics Symposium*, Springer-Verlag LNAI 6465.
12. Mahavira, June 1978: *Pāṇini as Grammarian (With special reference to compound formation)*. Bharatiya Vidya Prakashan, Delhi-Varanasi.
13. Mimamsaka, Yudhisthir: *Mahābhāṣyam (with Hindi commentory)*, Parts I, II and III. Ramlal Kapur Trust, Sonepat, Haryana.
14. Murty, M.S., 1974: *Sanskrit Compounds A Philosophical Study*. Chowkhamba Sanskrit Series Office, Varanasi.
15. Nair, S.S. and Kulkarni, A.P., 2010: The Knowledge Structure in Amarakośa. In *Proceedings of the International Sanskrit Computational Linguistics Symposium*, Springer.
16. Pande, G.D.: *Aṣṭādhyāyī of Pāṇini*. Chowkhamba Surabharati Prakashan, Varanasi.
17. Pandit Ishvarachandra, 2004: *Aṣṭādhyāyī*. Chaukhamba Sanskrit Pratisthan, Delhi.
18. Ramakrishnamacharyulu, K.V., A.P. Kulkarni, , T. Kulkarni, A. Kumar, :*Guidelines for Tagging of Sanskrit Compounds Prepared for Sanskrit Consortium dated 12.03.2012* (unpublished).
19. Sharma, Vasudeva L.S.P., 1908: *The Siddhānta Kaumudī (With Tattvabodinī commentory)*. Nirṇayasāgar Press, Bombay.
20. Shastri, Pt. Guru Prasad, 2006: *Vyākaraṇa-mahābhāṣyam (Only Samāsaprakaraṇam)*. Rashtriya Sanskrit Sansthan, New Delhi.
21. Tarkavachaspati, Taranatha, 1812-85: *Vācaspatyam*. Chowkhamba Sanskrit Series, Varanasi, UP.
22. Tripathi, V.P., 1991: *Samāsa-vr̥tti-vimarśaḥ*. Sampurnananda Sanskrit Vishvavidyalaya, Varanasi.
23. Vasu, S.C., 1891: *The Aṣṭādhyāyī of Pāṇini* (Translated into English). Indian Press, Allahabad.
24. Vasu, S.C.,: *The Siddhānta Kaumudī of Bhaṭṭoji Dīkṣita*. Motilal Banarsidass, New Delhi.

A Compound Tagset

Semantic Classifications of Sanskrit Compounds					
Avyayībhāva			**Tatpuruṣa**		
1	*avyaya-pūrvapada*	A1	1	*prathamā*	T1
2	*avyaya-uttarapada*	A2	2	*dvitīyā*	T2
3	*tiṣṭhadguprabhṛti*	A3	3	*tṛtīyā*	T3
4	*saṁkhyāpūrvapada-nadyuttarapada*	A4	4	*caturthī*	T4
5	*nadyuttarapada-anyapadārthasaṁjñāyām*	A5	5	*pañcamī*	T5
6	*saṁkhyāpūrvapada-vaṃśyottarapada*	A6	6	*ṣaṣṭhī*	T6
7	*pāre-madhye-pūrvapadaṣaṣṭhyuttarapada*	A7	7	*saptamī*	T7
Bahuvrīhi			8	*nañ*	Tn
1	*dvitīyārtha*	Bs2	9	*prādi*	Tp
2	*tṛtīyārtha*	Bs3	10	*ku*	Tk
3	*caturthyarthabahuvrīhi*	Bs4	11	*gati*	Tg
4	*pañcamyartha*	Bs5	12	*taddhitārthadvigu*	Td
5	*ṣaṣṭhyartha*	Bs6	13	*uttarapadadvigu*	Tdu
6	*saptamyartha*	Bs7	14	*samāhāradvigu*	Tds
7	*digvācaka*	Bsd	15	*upapada*	U
8	*saṁkhyobhayapada*	Bss	16	*dvitīyopapada*	U2
9	*upamānapūrvapada*	Bsu	17	*tṛtīyopapada*	U3
10	*praharaṇaviṣayaka*	Bsp	18	*caturthyopapada*	U4
11	*grahaṇaviṣayaka*	Bsg	19	*pañcamyopapada*	U5
12	*saṅkhyottarapada-vyadhikaraṇa*	Bvs	20	*saptamyopapada*	U7
13	*sahapūrvapada-vyadhikaraṇa*	BvS	21	*mayūravyaṁskādi*	Tm
14	*prādi-vyadhikaraṇa*	Bvp	22	*bahupada*	Tb
15	*upamānapūrvapada-vyadhikaraṇa*	BvU	**Karmadhāraya**		
16	*nañ*	Bsmn	1	*viśeṣaṇa-pūrvapada*	K1
17	*bahupada*	Bb	2	*viśeṣaṇa-uttarapada*	K2
Dvandva			3	*viśeṣaṇa-ubhayapada*	K3
1	*itaretara*	Di	4	*upamāna-pūrvapada*	K4
2	*samāhāra*	Ds	5	*upamāna-uttarapada*	K5
3	*ekaśeṣa*	E	6	*avadhāraṇāpūrvapada*	K6
Anya (others)			7	*sambhāvanāpūrvapada*	K7
1	*dvirukti*	d	8	*madhyamapadalopi*	Km
2	*kevala-samāsa*	S		-	

Structure and Implementation of a Digital Edition of the Aṣṭādhyāyī

Wiebke Petersen and Simone Soubusta

Heinrich-Heine-Universität Düsseldorf
wiebke.petersen@phil.uni-duesseldorf.de
simone.soubusta@uni-duesseldorf.de

Abstract. The *Aṣṭādhyāyī*, Pāṇini's grammar of Sanskrit, exhibits an unparalleled structure which to this day has not been fully understood. It encodes the grammar rules in a very concise manner, making use of inheritance and a sophisticated metalanguage. Modern linguistics could benefit from a deep study of its precise description methods. Unfortunately, due to the fact that they have little to no knowledge of Sanskrit and Indian grammatical theory and are unable to read *Devanāgarī*, many (Western) linguists lack the necessary skills to understand the *Aṣṭādhyāyī*. In this paper, we present an approach towards a digital, web-based edition of the *Aṣṭādhyāyī* developed in order to unlock it for broader scientific research. We focus on the database scheme which provides the core of the digital edition.

Keywords: Pāṇini, *Aṣṭādhyayī*, database, grammar, representation

1 Introduction

Sanskrit is the oldest Indo-European language that is still spoken. It distinguishes itself through a rich morphology and phonology. The *Aṣṭādhyāyī*, Pāṇini's approximately 2,500-year old grammar, developed into the standard grammar of Sanskrit. In the process, it shifted from a descriptive into a prescriptive grammar. The main reasons for its still outstanding position are its completeness and its compactness. With respect to its completeness, Bloomfield (1933, p.11) writes:

> "It describes, with the minutest detail, every inflection, derivation, and composition, and every syntactic usage of its author's speech. No other language, to this day, has been so perfectly described."

Consisting in its core of nearly 4.000 very short *sūtra*s (aphorisms), the *Aṣṭādhyāyī* is extremely compact for a grammar of its range. Pāṇini reaches this level of conciseness by developing sophisticated description methods which are based on inheritance and a metalanguage on which Staal (1995, p.107) comments:

> "I believe that Pāṇini reached here a level of artificiality that neither the logicians nor the mathematicians attained. [...] He created artificial constituents and a mechanism through which these constituents could be integrated into a new language, the metalanguage of his grammar."

Modern linguistics could benefit from a deep study of its precise description methods and of the way it is structured. However, most linguists lack the necessary education to study the *Aṣṭādhyāyī* in the way it is usually presented. They do not understand Sanskrit, are not familiar with the traditional Indian grammar terminology and cannot read *Devanāgarī*.

In this paper we present an approach towards a new digital edition of the *Aṣṭādhyāyī* with the aim to unlock it for nonprofessionals. The key idea is to develop an edition that preserves the structure of the *Aṣṭādhyāyī* and does not offer a mere collection of interpreted and translated *sūtra*s. The remainder of this paper is structured as follows: Section 2 elaborates in greater detail the question of why such a new structure-focused edition is useful. In Section 3 an outline of the technical and structural properties of our edition is given. The edition consists of a user interface (Subsection 3.1) and an underlying database (Subsection 3.2). The paper is concluded by an outlook in Section 4.

2 On the Need of a Structure-based Edition of the *Aṣṭādhyāyī*

2.1 The Non-linear Structure of the *Aṣṭādhyāyī*

It is clear that neither the language described in the *Aṣṭādhyāyī* (i.e. Sanskrit), nor Pāṇini's description of it has an inherently linear structure. Pāṇini was confronted with the usual problem of any grammarian of how to present his language description in a linear text. Being situated in an oral tradition, his problem was even more severe, since he could not make use of explicit cross-references, indices or non-linguistic elements like tables and symbols and also because conciseness is especially desirable in a grammar which is meant to be learned by heart and recited regularly. Thus, the question arises of what determines the specific linear order of the *sūtra*s in the *Aṣṭādhyāyī*.

The *Aṣṭādhyāyī* is not ordered according to the ordering principles commonly used in other grammars. The order reflects neither the conventional discrimination between linguistic subdisciplines (e.g. phonology, syntax, semantics,...), nor does it follow any didactic considerations like school grammars (e.g., starting with easier and more frequently used structures). Moreover, no strict order based on treated phenomena like vowel *sandhi* is recognizable. Although Pāṇini's grammar covers not only classical Sanskrit but also aspects of Vedic and of some dialectal and socio-linguistic variants, it is not ordered according to those subjects. Furthermore, the order does not follow any classification based on the descriptive or the operational structure of the grammar. A descriptive classification would distinguish between the tasks which are fulfilled by a *sūtra* (e.g. stating a rule of Sanskrit, stating a meta rule, and stating a definition). An operational structure would present the *sūtra*s in the order in which they are applied in language processing, for example, grammatical derivations.

As the *Aṣṭādhyāyī* follows none of the mentioned ordering principles, the question arises of what determines its structure. It is commonly assumed that the structure of the *Aṣṭādhyāyī* is governed by economical principles, referred to as *lāghava*. However, it is not clear what *lāghava* means with respect to the *Aṣṭādhyāyī*. Gérard Huet (p.c.) proposes an interesting analogy. He compares the way the *Aṣṭādhyāyī* is presented to compiled program code that does not explicitly express the logical structure of the program anymore, but follows efficiency considerations. In our opinion this is a very appropriate analogy. Thus, one should distinguish between Pāṇini's grammar itself as a description of Sanskrit (i.e. Pāṇini's system of grammatical rules which corresponds to the logically structured program source code) and the compiled code in the form of the actual text of the *Aṣṭādhyāyī*, which encodes the grammar in a compact manner by making use of inheritance, a metalanguage, markers and so forth.

All the possible orders discussed above are determined by aspects of the grammar and not by its encoding. Previous studies support the thesis that *lāghava* governs not only Pāṇini's description of Sanskrit but even more its textual encoding. One example for this is Pāṇini's treatment of the phonological and morphophonemic aspects of Sanskrit. With respect to the grammatical description, the question is which phonological rules and which sound classes are assumed. With respect to the encoding of this description, the question is: in what form the rules are presented and how the sound classes are defined and named? For the former, Pāṇini uses natural language case suffixes as metalinguistic markers in order to indicate the role of a sound class in a rule. For the latter, he developed the *pratyāhāra*-technique: it is a generative method to construct maximally short, namely monosyllabic, metalinguistic names for phonological classes. The class names refer to intervals in a marker-interrupted list of Sanskrit sounds listed in the *Śivasūtra*s. In Peterson (2009) it was mathematically proven that there is no shorter solution than this list to the problem of ordering the sounds and placing the markers such that all the desired sound classes form intervals which end immediately before a marker. Thus one could say that Pāṇini compiled the set of sound classes into an interval-based code of minimal length.

It is generally assumed that the compilation of the rest of the grammar is guided by similar principles, i.e. that Pāṇini uses inheritance and rule-blocking mechanisms such that the text of the *Aṣṭādhyāyī* represents his Sanskrit grammar in the shortest possible form. However, a formal proof of this hypothesis is still missing. This thesis is more difficult to prove than the minimality of the *Śivasūtra*s, as for the latter only 14 and not all of the nearly 4.000 *sūtra*s have to be investigated. One of the main motivations for our digital *Aṣṭādhyāyī* edition is to support the verification of such general hypotheses about the structure of the *Aṣṭādhyāyī*.

2.2 Why Traditional Editions Do Not Suffice

The structure of the *Aṣṭādhyāyī* as a compiled grammar makes it very difficult to use. Traditional editions try to support users of the *Aṣṭādhyāyī* in this task. If humans want to apply the grammar in the production of correct Sanskrit sentences, they first have to recompile it. A long line of commentaries on the *Aṣṭādhyāyī* tackle this problem. They explain how the *Aṣṭādhyāyī* encodes individual derivation procedures. Traditionally, the encoded text of the *Aṣṭādhyāyī* is learned by heart and the trained grammarian will jump through the *sūtra*s while generating Sanskrit expressions. Due to its non-linear structure, it is necessary to have access to all of the nearly 4,000 *sūtra*s at once, because *sūtra*s from all 32 *pāda*s (roughly: 'chapters') can be involved in the derivation of a single word. In order to support the reader, a written edition of the *Aṣṭādhyāyī* usually contains several indices (e.g. of the technical terms and the *anubandha*s,) and enriches each *sūtra* with references to other *sūtra*s in order to aid in its comprehension (Vasu, 1891; Katre, 1987; Sharma, 1987-2003; Joshi and Roodbergen, 1991-). Nevertheless, everybody working with the *Aṣṭādhyāyī* without remembering it by heart knows the problem of having an insufficient amount of fingers or bookmarks to mark all the other *sūtra*s influencing the analysis of the *sūtra* that is currently being studied.

By establishing an appropriate digital edition of the *Aṣṭādhyāyī* these difficulties can be minimized. A digital edition allows the modeling of the dependencies between the individual *sūtra*s through active hyperlinks. Additionally, the same *sūtra* data can be reordered according to different ordering principles. Hence, users can easily switch between, for example, the didactically motivated *sūtra*-order given in the *Siddhāntakaumudī* and the original order of the *Aṣṭādhyāyī*. The electronic edition by Shivamurthy Swamiji implements some of these possibilities (`http://www.taralabalu.org/panini/`). It allows users to search for expressions in the *Aṣṭādhyāyī*, uses hyperlinks to navigate through the *anuvṛtti*-inheritance and enables a reordering of the *sūtra*s. However, Swamiji's digital edition follows the traditional line in that it focusses on the question of how the *Aṣṭādhyāyī* are to be applied in language production and not on its structure and how it is encoded in the plain text. Although providing much less functionality than Swamiji's, Peter Scharf's digital edition (`http://sanskritlibrary.org/`) is much closer to our aim. It provides the user with detailed grammatical and metalinguistic information on the *sūtra* components and a link to the Monier

Williams Sanskrit-English Dictionary.

Traditional editions focus on the translations of and comments on the individual *sūtra*s. However, a translation of a Pāṇinian *sūtra* is nearly never a mere literal, word-for-word translation, but also invariably includes an interpretation of its function in the context of the *Aṣṭādhyāyī*. The reason for this is that the *sūtra*s do not form meaningful sentences in Sanskrit. They lack information that has to be inherited from other *sūtra*s and they make use of metalinguistic elements not only as terminological expressions but also as simple markers. If someone who has not mastered Sanskrit tries to investigate the structure of the *Aṣṭādhyāyī* with a traditional edition, he or she will be confronted with interpretations that disambiguate the *sūtra*s. The reader thus loses control over possible alternative interpretations and over the function of the single components of a *sūtra*.

2.3 Requirements of a Structure-based Digital Edition

Our aim is to develop a digital edition that enables linguists with no special training to study the *Aṣṭādhyāyī*. Such a digital edition would not only support the application of the grammar and thereby contribute to the traditional question of the commentators of *how the* Aṣṭādhyāyī *works* but also to the modern question of *how it is structured* (cf. Kiparsky, 2009; Bhate and Kak, 1993). It could be a useful tool to decode Pāṇini's encoding, to recompile the source grammar and to investigate the description techniques used. The aim is not to explain the way the grammar functions, but to provide the means to investigate the principles governing the organization of the *Aṣṭādhyāyī*.

Our target users include those who have no or only insufficient command of Sanskrit. They are not familiar with the traditional Indian grammar terminology and they do not know the traditional commentaries. Instead, they have had basic training in modern linguistics. We therefore transcribe the *Aṣṭādhyāyī* in Latin script and use standard English linguistic terminology.

In order to enable users to follow their own research questions concerning the structure of the *Aṣṭādhyāyī* independent of former interpretations, we follow a text-immanent approach as much as possible and stick to the wording of Pāṇini. Thus, we provide a grammatical analysis and a translation of each word and each element of a compound. *Sūtra* translations and commentaries are provided as an additional help for the user, but not as the main source of information. However, although the text of the *Aṣṭādhyāyī* is very well preserved considering its age, some information has been lost over the millennia. By writing down the *Aṣṭādhyāyī*, accents and nazalization have been lost. As a result, the scope of *anuvr̥tti*-inheritance and the identification of metalinguistic markers cannot be read off the *Aṣṭādhyāyī* text anymore, but must be intellectually reconstructed by referring to knowledge of the object language being described (Sanskrit) and the way it is described (cf.Joshi and Bhate, 1984). As some of our target users will not be able to do this reconstruction themselves, we provide them with this information taken from the classical commentaries.

Another important requirement for a new digital edition is to be flexible. Different users want to research different aspects of the grammar and are thus interested in different parts of the *Aṣṭādhyāyī*. We would thus like to provide different *views* on the same information, allowing users to *zoom in* on different aspects, e.g. see a detailed grammatical analysis of a *sūtra* or an uncluttered overview over all *sūtra*s pertaining to 'phonology'. Being able to combine the existing data in numerous ways to provide these *views* is thus another important consideration.

Lastly, a very important advantage of a digital edition over a non-digital one is that it is generally easier to extend through additional data. Thus, already in the planning process of a new digital edition, one should try to design it such that it can be flexibly extended. For example, since the *Aṣṭādhyāyī* is still being investigated, new, more appropriate translations could be provided and added to the edition. Furthermore, since language is ambiguous, the grammatical analyses of the *sūtra*s are not uncontroversial and it is desirable to represent the conflicting views in a digital edition, so that interested parties can access them. Due to ongoing research, the information about the *Aṣṭādhyāyī* is not static, but changes over time, an aspect that should be taken into consideration. Even beyond this evolving corpus of information, we might want to add further facets to our implementation in the future and should thus provide the technical means to do so.

To sum up, four requirements govern the development of our

structure-based, digital edition of the *Aṣṭādhyāyī* which will be presented in the next section:
(1) require as little prior knowledge as possible, (2) stay as close as possible to the text of the *Aṣṭādhyāyī*, (3) flexible, and (4) extendable.

3 Implementation

3.1 User Interface

In principle, the data of our edition can be approached in two different ways: either by browsing through the *sūtra*s or by searching for occurrences of special patterns within *sūtra*s or among groups of *sūtra*s.

3.1.1 Browsing

One way of accessing the data in our digital edition is by browsing through the *sūtra*s. Figure 1 shows the prototype of our Pāṇini browser developed in the research project '*Pratyāhāra*s or features?' at the University of Düsseldorf[1] and implemented by Oliver Hellwig. The browser is realized as a Hypertext-preprocessor (PHP) application that accepts user input and dynamically changes the display accordingly. The figure shows the default view on the data. The prototype already demonstrates how the four requirements identified in the last section knowledge-independency, literality, flexibility, and extendability are implemented in the user interface.

The interface is flexible and easily extendable. Users can determine which *sūtra*s they want to see by setting the appropriate interval of *sūtra*s within one *pāda* of the *Aṣṭādhyāyī*. Furthermore, they can decide what kind of information they are interested in by selecting the appropriate checkboxes. The set of checkboxes offered depends on previous choices such that, for example, someone who is not interested in 'Grammatical analysis' does not see the boxes for '*Sandhi* form', 'Grammatical information' and 'Semantic information'. Having a decision-dependent menu enables us to extend

[1] Project webpage: `http://panini.phil.uni-duesseldorf.de/`

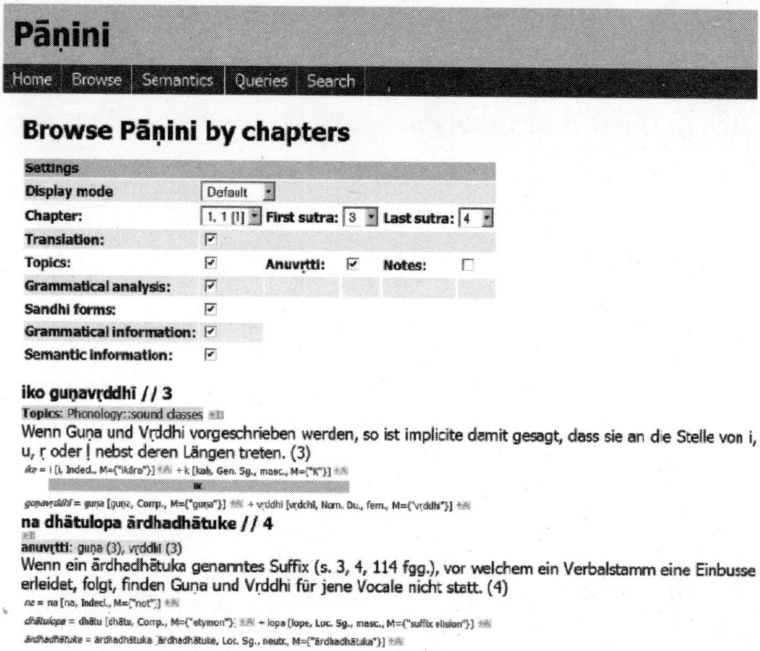

Fig. 1:Pāṇini Browser

the database with additional information (e.g. translations, commentaries, notes) without being forced to overload the user with a confusing menu.

Currently, in the prototype, all the information is presented in Latin script and we use standard modern linguistic terminology such as ‘singular’ (‘Sg.’) instead of *ekavacana*. Furthermore, we provide a translation as well as grammatical information such as part-of-speech, inflectional information and the corresponding lexeme for each expression. Compounds and technical terms like *pratyāhāras* are decomposed into their subparts. On the *sūtra*-level, a translation, the expressions inherited by *anuvṛtti* and keywords (Topics) are provided. Furthermore, the user has the possibility of adding personal notes to the *sūtras*. As our primary focus lies on a detailed analysis of the *sūtra* elements, we currently only provide the German translation from Böhtlingk (1887) which is not protected by copyright. However, our database design is flexible enough to add additional translations to other languages as well (cf. Section 3.2).

Using hyperlinks, it is possible to navigate through the non-linear structure of the *Aṣṭādhyāyī* by jumping to those *sūtras* that provide additional information through *anuvṛtti* or to *sūtras* in which a lexeme co-occurs or which are classified by the same keywords. As our data is stored in a relational database, additional hyperlinks can be added with no effort (cf. Section 3.2).

The figure shows the current default view of the data. Additionally, we provide the possibility of implementing personalized views to aid the users' research. Such a view could, for example, present the *sūtras* in a more compact tabular form containing only the data needed to work on a specific research question. At the moment, we have predefined two tabular views for members of our research group. We plan to develop more predefined views according to the needs of the users of our browser as soon as our Graphical User Interface (GUI) goes online and we hopefully receive valuable feedback.

3.1.2 Searching

One of the primary aims of this digital edition of the *Aṣṭādhyāyī* is searchability – allowing both those already familiar with the *Aṣṭādhyāyī* and those who are new to them to search for specific passages, grammatical features or certain topics. Because this search functionality should not be limited to content-based search (i.e., fulltext search), we also provide concept-based retrieval options (e.g. search for the marker 'L' or for all *sūtras* dealing with 'phonology'). Furthermore, we enable the formulation of complex queries using boolean operators (AND, OR, AND NOT).

For reasons explained below, our implementation uses a relational database for data storage. This offers professional users the advantage of being able to formulate queries directly in Structured Query Language (SQL), provided such inputs are sanitized to avoid SQL injection vulnerabilities. There are virtually no boundaries to the complexity of such queries, allowing experts to make full use of the available data. We are, however, conscious of the fact that not all researchers interested in the *Aṣṭādhyāyī* are familiar with SQL. Furthermore, users would have to familiarize themselves with our database design in order to utilize SQL queries. For this reason, we also offer an alternative, slightly reduced, search interface, a prototype version of which is shown in Figure 2 . The interface requires no expert knowledge to use (although familiarity with boolean logic is recommended for more complex queries). In com-

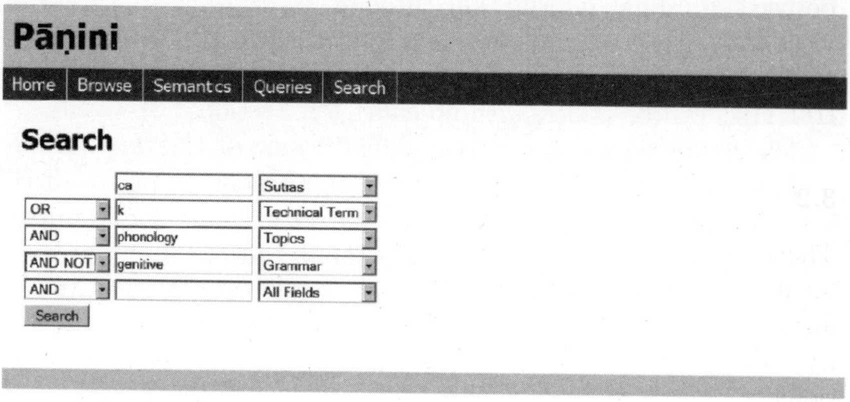

Fig. 2: Pāṇini Browser – search function

parison to the possibilities offered by SQL, the interface is slightly restricted. However, it should still be more than enough for most information needs.

Figure 2 shows an (artificial) example for a complex query. It would return all *sūtra*s that contain either *ca* or the technical term *k* or both, but only if these deal with the topic of 'phonology' and do not contain any words in the genitive case. Searching for the technical term *k*, the topic of 'phonology' and words in the genitive case in this query are examples of concept-based retrieval. Even though this prototype version of the search interface already contains a lot of the desired functionality, we plan to extend the functions of the simplified interface further to include options like searching within a certain *pāda* or phenomena that occur within a certain range of *sūtra*s, among other things.

3.1.3 Personalizing

Another important feature of our digital edition of the *Aṣṭādhyāyī* is that users can personalize the application for their needs by adding notes to *sūtra*s. Users will also have the ability to share not only these notes, but also saved searches and personalized *views* with other users (e.g. members of the same research group). A possible future expansion of this personalization would be to allow users to tag *sūtra*s, to make it easier to re-find passages of interest to them. These tags could also be used as a further index by other users, as is done in many other web applications. The *views* could be used to establish links with other *Aṣṭādhyāyī*-related web services on the level of single *sūtra*s like, the *Aṣṭādhyāyī*-specific Wiki currently being developed under the guidance of Navjyoti Singh at IIIT Hyderabad and similar projects.

3.2 Database

The requirements of a digital edition of the *Aṣṭādhyāyī* that we mentioned above the ability to access different *views* of the information, searchability of the data, extensibility and the flexibility to adapt to changing data have led us to the use of a relational database as the backbone of our implementation. A relational database stores data in so-called *relations* or *tables*, which are sets of tuples that share the same attributes (Codd, 1990, p. 3ff). Databases are an obvious solution for our needs, since they were designed to provide these different *views* that we stipulated above. They are furthermore designed to be adaptable, allow for data control and allow concurrent access. Relational databases also feature flexible authority, i.e. users can be granted access to some parts of the database, while being denied access to others (Codd, 1990). Not to mention that relational databases come with their own powerful query language in the form of SQL, facilitating the above-mentioned searchability. All of these considerations make a relational database most suited for our application in comparison to alternative storage technologies like XML, which features no inbuilt technique to provide different *views*, does not allow concurrent access, and features no access and data integrity control.

Moreover, our database adheres to the third normal form as specified by Codd (1971), which states that all attributes must be atomic, there must be no repeating groups, no partial functional dependencies and no transitive functional dependencies. The objectives of this normalization are to free the database from 'undesirable insertion, update and deletion dependencies' by removing redundancies and to 'reduce the need for restructuring the [database] as new types of data are introduced and thus increase the lifespan of application programs' (Codd, 1971, p. 34).

Despite the fact that databases are most suited for our digital edition of the *Aṣṭādhyāyī*, one implementation detail that requires special attention is the fact that instead of considering each *sūtra* as a whole, we want to attach information to different parts of a *sūtra* (e.g. a word, affix) on a flexible basis. Databases, however, do not provide this sort of relation, necessitating that we develop a way to enable this feature in our implementation, which shall be explained in detail in the next section. Section 3.2.2 then presents the database design as a whole.

3.2.1 Defining the Atomic Units

One important design consideration is that we want to provide analyses and commentaries for all (sub)parts of the *sūtras*: i.e. for word forms, words, compound segments, and affixes as well as metalinguistic units and compounds. This is non-trivial as the object-language and the metalanguage are intermixed in the *Aṣṭādhyāyī*: metalinguistic compounds, i.e. expressions composed of two or more metalinguistic expressions, form new technical terms which are inflected according to the object-language rules; case markers of the object-language serve as metalinguistic markers on object-language expressions and so forth. For example, if we have a *sūtra* like *īdūdeddvivacanaṃ pragṛhyam*, we have inflectional information on the word form level, i.e., *īdūdeddvivacanaṃ* and *pragṛhyam*. On the word level, i.e., *īdūdeddvivacana* and *pragṛhya*, we have, for example, the semantic information that *īdūdeddvivacana* is a determinative compound. One level deeper we find the two segments *īdūdet* and *dvivacana*, the former of which is a copulative compound. On the next level we get the expressions *īt*, *ūt*, and *et*. Here, the deepest level of the object-language is reached. However, *īt*, *ūt*, and *et* are not atomic units in the metalanguage. They are metalinguistic compounds that can be decomposed into *ī+T*, *ū+T*, and *e+T*. Each of those compounds consists of a vowel sound in the object-language and the metalinguistic marker *T*.

The example demonstrates that there is no general fixed number for the levels of analysis and that at each level segments from the object-language and from the metalanguage get intermixed. Therefore, we discarded the idea to build up a general lexicon of all language units such that each *sūtra* can be analyzed as a composition of those units. In order to keep our approach as flexible as possible, we decided to index the *sūtras* *by character* in the *padapāṭha* form and use this index to form intervals on the basis of which an analysis will be allocated and retrieved. Thus, in our previous example the *sūtra* in *padapāṭha* form is *īdūdeddvivacanaṁ pragr̥hyam* and the component *pragr̥hyam* would be addressed by the interval [18,26] (counting the blank as a character) and would be linked to the indices 18 and 26 in the database. Similarly, *ūt* forms an interval from 3 to 4. The rule is that segments that are changed by internal *sandhi* get the indices of the *sandhi*-fied form. Counting the blanks offers the possibility of identifying even empty declension morphemes by intervals. In some rare cases of elision, dummy indices have to be added in order to enable the addressing of each desirable segment by its interval boundaries. Since intervals can overlap, we can identify arbitrary components of a *sūtra* as long as they correspond to a continuous interval in the *padapāṭha* form. Indexing by character allows us to attach information on various levels and to easily add new information (and levels) in the future.

Please note that encoding the *Aṣṭādhyāyī* in Latin script with diacritics simplifies our interval method. The alternative script, *Devanāgarī*, is an alphasyllabic script which expresses complex segments like consonant-vowel pairs and consonant clusters using single graphemes. The transcription in Latin script with diacritics shows a stronger correspondence between sounds and graphemes, although it uses several digraphs (e.g. for aspirated sounds, diphthongs, and *sh*). The relation between sounds and graphemes in *Devanāgarī* is many-to-one while in Latin script it is one-to-many. Thus, using Latin script we tend to get more indices than necessary, which is harmless, while using *Devanāgarī* script, sounds belonging to different segments would often be clustered in a single grapheme and thus in a single index which would be very problematic for our indexing-by-character method. This does not, however, prevent us from being able to display the *sūtras* in *Devanāgarī* in the browser by converting the Latin script to *Devanāgarī* on the fly, should this be desired in a future version.

3.2.2 Database Design

When planning an application with a database backbone, the database design is especially important. While a good design ensures that the database is adaptable and extendable, a badly designed database will likely soon outlive its usefulness. Having to redesign a database, however, also means that the surrounding program code has to be rewritten and the existing data has to be painstakingly migrated from the old database to the new one.

Furthermore, if the old database was not normalized properly (see Section 2), the existing data may already have been corrupted. For this reason, we have designed our database to conform to the third normal form and with a view to future extensions.

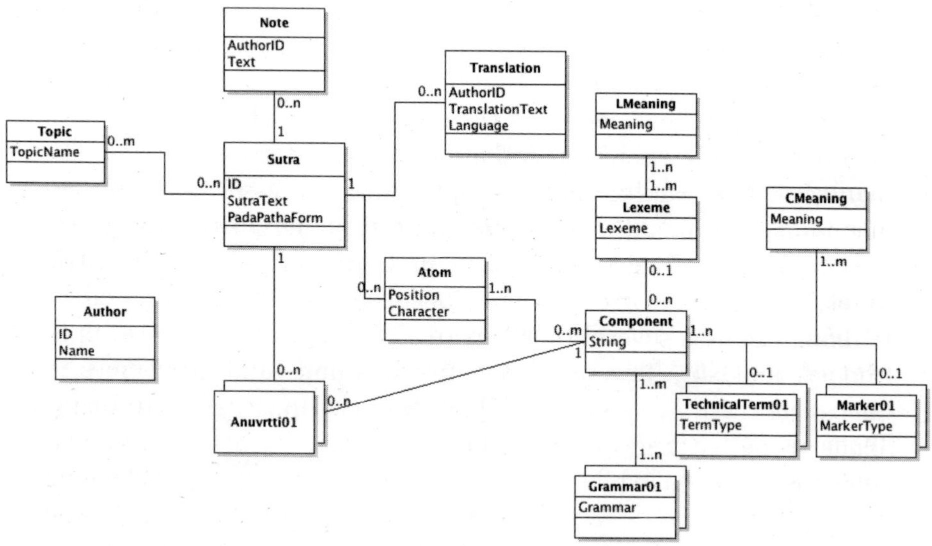

Fig. 3: The database scheme

Figure 3 shows the Unified Modeling Language (UML) diagram of our database. The Sutra table is the central point of the database. It stores all *sūtras* in normal form and *padapāṭha* form with their numbers for easy reference. The connected table Translation contains a variable number of translations for each *sūtra*, referenceable by language and author (through an author ID). Note allows users to comment on *sūtras*, again referenceable by author ID. Topic assigns different categories (e.g. phonology) to *sūtras*. The Atom table contains the character-based index which we described above. Every row in this table contains a *sūtra* ID from the Sutra table, a position (e.g. 1 for the first character) and the character itself. The Component table then takes two atoms from the same *sūtra* (upper and lower bound of the interval) to form a component to which information can be attached.

Each component can be assigned grammatical features from a number of grammar categories (e.g. number, gender) in the Grammar table, as well as up to one lexeme and a variable number of meanings. Linking comments directly to components via its own ComponentNote table could be a useful extension. The Anuvrtti table represents a relation between the Sutra table and the Component table, listing the *sūtra* that inherits via *anuvr̥tti* on one side and specifying which part of another *sūtra* it inherits on the other. TechnicalTerm and Marker are subclasses of Component, i.e. they contain those components that are technical terms and markers, respectively, attaching additional relevant information like term type and marker type. Lexeme also has an n-to-m relation to its own meaning table LMeaning, allowing a meaning to belong to several lexemes and a lexeme to have several meanings. Our existing data has already been stored in the tables Sutra, Atom, Component, Grammar, Translation, and Note. The Anuvrtti table is in the process of being filled, with Topic, TechnicalTerm, and Marker to follow shortly. All the data will of course be proof-read for errors.

Due to the ambiguity of the *Aṣṭādhyāyī*, the database will not contain a finished product so much as an ongoing discussion with conflicting views. Thus the tables Anuvrtti and Grammar as well as Marker and TechnicalTerm will exists not just once, but in different 'versions', so to speak, representing the views and opinions of contributors to the database. These tables Anuvrtti01, Anuvrtti02, etc. will exist in parallel, fulfilling the same functions and users will be able to choose between those different Pāṇini 'interpretations'. Besides choosing a specific view, users will also be able to view all interpretations or only the commonly shared ones. The 01 in Anuvrtti01 represents the author ID, which identifies the author whose views are stored in the table. The table Author lists all authors and their IDs, which are also in the tables Note and Translation, as mentioned above. Please note that we regard classical commentators and editors of existing editions as potential contributors or data 'authors'. After finishing the prototype version of the database and an intensive test period for debugging and receiving user feedback, we intend to ask for permission to integrate existing *Aṣṭādhyāyī* data and to make it available through our web-based GUI. Note that the aim of this paper is not to present the actual data in our database, which will hopefully be extended through other contributors anyway, but to discuss the database design, which needs to be flexible enough to smoothly integrate data from different sources. For the future, it would be great to agree upon one standard database scheme which could provide the basis for a database which integrates all the *Aṣṭādhyāyī*-related information. With SQL as a powerful query language, researchers could compare different analyses by asking questions like "where do author A and author B differ in their grammatical or *anuvṛtti* analysis?" or they could stick to a single-author analysis and use SQL queries to investigate, for example, Pāṇini's use of negation particles.

4 Outlook

The digital edition presented here is being developed by the research group '*Pratyāhāras* or features?' at the University of Düsseldorf as a tool to support the task of uncovering the underlying structure of the *Aṣṭādhyāyī*. One of our central research questions is that if we allow all techniques which Pāṇini uses for the description of phonological classes, is it still true that he uses them in the most economical way possible? And what does 'in the most economical way' mean? If we could succeed in fully understanding the structural principles underlying the *Aṣṭādhyāyī*, i.e. the methods by which it is compiled from a source grammar, we should be able to (semi)-automatically compute a grammatical description in the style of the *Aṣṭādhyāyī*. In analogy to our previous work on the *Śivasūtras*, the hypothesis that the *Aṣṭādhyāyī* is maximally economic could be tested by comparing the computed description to the original one. In order to reduce the difficulty of the task, we start by restricting ourselves to phonological descriptions.

1.1.1 vr̥ddhir ādaic	⇒ vr̥ddhi | (āT ∘ aiC)
$N^1_{sg,fem,nom} \mid (N^2 \circ N^3)_{sg,msc,nom}$	$\Rightarrow N^1 := N^2 \sqcup N^3$
1.1.2 adeṅ guṇaḥ	⇒ (aT ∘ eN) | guṇa
$(N^1 \circ N^2)_{sg,msc,nom} \mid N^3_{sg,msc,nom}$	$\Rightarrow N^3 := N^1 \sqcup N^2$
1.1.3 iko guṇavr̥ddhī	⇒ iK | (guṇa ∘ vr̥ddhi)
$N^1_{sg,fem,gen} \mid (N^2 \circ N^3)_{du,fem,nom}$	$\Rightarrow N^1 \rightarrow (N^2 \sqcup N^3)$

Fig. 4: Formal analysis of the first three *sūtras*

As a first step towards this goal we are currently developing a formal language to decode the *sūtras*, which shall be integrated into our database as well. A first impression of this language can be found in Figure 4. The first *sūtra* consists of a binary compound ($N^1 \circ N^2$) in singular case and a simple noun (N^1) in singular case. The *sūtra* is interpreted as a definition of N^1 by the union of N^2 and N^3. *Sūtra* 1.1.2 follows the same pattern. *Sūtra* 1.1.3 states an operational rule in which the case markers are metalinguistic markers for the rule components. The other *sūtras* will be analyzed in an analogous manner. Please note that the formal *sūtra* language is still under development and that it is presented here only for illustrative purposes. Our assumption is that a full-fledged formal representation will reveal *sūtra* patterns which correspond systematically to interpretations. We hope that such a representation will help us to decode Pāṇini's compilation principles and to reveal the structure underlying the *Aṣṭādhyāyī*.

4.1 Acknowledgments

Research of this paper was conducted in the research project '*Pratyāhāras* or features?' which is funded by a strategic research fund from the University of Düsseldorf. We are grateful to our project colleagues, in particular Silke Hamann, Oliver Hellwig, Norbert Endres, and Anil Kumar for their collaboration. Moreover, we would like to thank, among others, Jan Houben, Gérard Huet, Amba Kulkarni, Anand Mishra, Peter Scharf, and Navjyoti Singh, for inspiring discussions on the research project. Finally, thanks to the anonymous reviewers for their valuable comments.

References

1. Bhate, S., and Kak, S. Pāṇini's Grammar and Computer Science, *Annals of the Bhandarkar Oriental Research Institute, Poona 72* (1993), 79–94.
2. Bloomfield, L. *Language*, Holt, Rinehart and Winston, New York, 1933.
3. Böhtlingk, O. *Pāṇinis Grammatik,* Leipzig, 1887. Reprinted: Hildesheim 1964.
4. Codd, E.F. Further Normalization of the Database Relational Model, *IBM Research Report, San Jose, California RJ909* (1971).
5. Codd, E.F. *The Relational Model for Database Management: Version 2,* Addison-Wesley Longman Publishing Co., Inc., Boston, MA, USA, 1990.
6. Joshi, S., and Bhate, S. *The Fundamentals of Anuvr̥tti*, Publication of the Centre of Advanced Study of Sanskrit, University of Poona, 1984.
7. Joshi, S.D., and Roodbergen, J.A.F. *The Aṣṭādhyāyī of Pāṇini*, Sahitya Akademi, 1991-. So far up to volume 14/2011.
8. Katre, S.M. *Aṣṭādhyāyī of Pāṇini*, University of Texas Press, Austin TX, 1987.
9. Kiparsky, P. On the Architecture of Pāṇini's Grammar, In *Sanskrit Computational Linguistics*, G. Huet, A. Kulkarni, and P. Scharf, Eds., vol. 5402 of *Lecture Notes in Computer Science.* Springer, Berlin, Heidelberg, 2009, pp. 33–94.
10. Petersen, W. On the Construction of Sivasutras-alphabets, In *Sanskrit Computational Linguistics* (2009), A. P. Kulkarni and G.Huet, Eds., vol. 5406 of *Lecture Notes in Computer Science*, Springer, pp. 78–97.
11. Sharma, R.N. *The Aṣṭādhyāyī of Pāṇini,* Munshiram Manoharlal Publishers, New Delhi, 1987-2003. 6 volumes.
12. Staal, F.J. The Sanskrit of Science, *Journal of Indian Philosophy 23*, 1 (1995), 73–127.
13. Vasu, S.C. *The Aṣṭādhyāyī of Pāṇini,* Allahabad, 1891. 2 vols.

Comparison of Pāṇinīya Dhātuvr̥ttis

N Shailaja and Amba Kulkarni

Department of Sanskrit Studies,
University of Hyderabad,
Hyderabad
shailajanakkawar@gmail.com, apksh@uohyd.ernet.in

Abstract. In this paper we note the importance of positing a canonical form for verbal root and its meaning to facilitate the comparison of various *dhātuvr̥ttis*. We also provide some quantitative measure of the differences in the *dhātuvr̥ttis* after correlating four *dhātuvr̥ttis* using canonical forms of roots and meanings.

Keywords: Pāṇinīya Dhātupāṭha, canonical form, quantitative analysis

1 Introduction

Dhātupāṭha is an integral part of the *Aṣṭādhyāyī*. It consists of a list of verbal roots divided into ten sets called *gaṇas*. Classification into *gaṇas* is dictated by the transformations a verbal root undergoes (due to the insertion of a *vikaraṇa pratyaya*) during the formation of verb conjugations in certain tense/mood known as *sārvadhātuka lakāras*. For example, the verbs from *divādi gaṇa* take *śyan* suffix before a *tiṅ* suffix indicating a number and a person. Each verbal root (*dhātu*) is marked with an accent, meaning and optionally some special markers. Special markers associated with the verbal roots in the *dhātupāṭha* either create an environment for application of *sūtras* or trigger certain morphophonemic changes in the verbal roots under special conditions. For example, the *sūtra ḍvitaḥ ktriḥ* (P 3.3.88) allows a *ktri* suffix only in case of verbs with *ḍu* as a marker, such as *ḍukr̥ñ* and *ḍupacaṣ*. The accents as well as the marker *ṅ*[1] indicate a set of terminal suffixes (viz. *ātmanepadī* or

[1] *anudāttaṅita ātmanepadam* (P 1.3.12).

parasmaipadī suffixes) a verb will take. Sometimes the meaning associated with a verbal root also plays an important role in deciding the forms of a verb. For example, the*sūtra nāñceḥ pūjāyām* (P 6.4.30) prohibits the elision of penultimate '*n*' generated in the process of derivation of verbal conjugations of the root *añc*, if the verb is used in the sense of *pūjā* 'worship'. Thus a *dhātupāṭha* is not just a list of verbal roots, but each verbal root carries a bundle of information which is essential for the generation of correct forms. Markers in the form of phonemes, accent and the meaning provide scope for the application of certain *sūtras* during the generation process. In other words, there is a tight coupling between the information coded with the verb roots in a *dhātupāṭha* and the *Aṣṭādhyāyī sūtra pāṭha*. Thus even a slight variation in the *dhātupāṭha* would result in wrong conjugation of a verb.

Therefore we expect that the *dhātupāṭha* is preserved with special efforts, as is true with the Vedas. Ironically we see that there is no consensus regarding the entries of *dhātupāṭha*. There are several versions of *dhātupāṭhas* and they differ from each other significantly. The accent, which carries an important information for the formation of conjugations, and also the nasalization have been lost over the years. It is surprising that the same tradition which has meticulously preserved the Vedas for several centuries devising special methods of recitation, providing enough information for error detection and correction so as to avoid any fault in the transmission, has not paid any attention to preserve the *dhātupāṭha*!

There have been efforts to simulate Pāṇinian system by Goyal et al.(2009), Mishra(2009) and Sridhar(2009), and on Modelling Pāṇini by Scharf (2009). These researchers intend to follow the *Aṣṭādhyāyī* preserving its spirit. For them, therefore, it is crucial to have a *dhātupāṭha* with all its variations as reported in various *vr̥ttis* in electronic form, to note the effect of variation in the generation.

2 Earlier Work

The concordance of the verbal root was first compiled by Liebich (1928). It contained five *dhātupāṭhas*, including three commentaries on *Pāṇinīya Dhātupāṭha*. Palsule (1955) added four more non-Pāṇinian *dhātupāṭhas* to this work making this work more-or-less complete. The highlights of Palsule's concordance are

1. It lists all the verbal roots in an alphabetic order and not in the order of *Dhātupāṭha*.
2. For every root, its *gaṇa* and *padī* as noted in various *Dhātupāṭhas* is provided.
3. The list of verbal roots also contains roots picked up from:
   (a) The St Petersburg Dictionary,
   (b) Sanskrit-English Dictionary by Monier-Williams,
   (c) the roots by Whitney, and
   (d) the roots posited by modern scholars.
   Thus his attempt was to make the list of verb roots as complete as possible.
4. In addition to the concordance of verbal roots, his work also consists of an index of meanings. Against each meaning this index provides a list of verbs and the *dhātupāṭhas* to which they belong to.

This work is very comprehensive but it suffers from two drawbacks if one wants to use it for computational purpose mentioned earlier.

1. The verb roots do not contain any *anubandhas* whereas for Pāṇini the starting point of derivation of conjugates is a verbal root with *anubandhas*. This makes Palsule's concordance unfit for direct use for generation of verbal conjugates following Pāṇini.
2. The index to meanings is arranged alphabetically according to the meanings. For any work on Word Sense Disambiguation in Computational Linguistics, one needs the reverse index, viz. a verbal root mapped to the associated meanings.

Further, there is a tight coupling between the *dhātupāṭha* and the *sūtras* used for generation of verbal conjugations. Hence the purpose of having a concordance of *dhātupāṭhas* in isolation across different grammar systems makes sense only from the meaning point of view and not from the point of view of verb morphology.

3 E-Linked *Dhātuvṛtti*s

Advances in technology makes the comparison of *dhātuvṛtti*s easier. Technology further facilitates one to study these *dhātuvṛtti*s from different perspectives. With an aim to link various *dhātuvṛtti*s electronically and to provide various search facilities over them, we chose the following Pāṇinian *Dhātuvṛitti*s.

1. *Mādhavīya* (Gupta, 1991),
2. *Kṣīrataraṅgiṇī* (Mīmāṁsakaḥ, 2005),
3. *Dhātupradīpa* (Mīmāṁsakaḥ, 1986), and
4. *Śābdikābharaṇam* (Śukla, 2010).

Roughly all these *vṛtti*s belong to twelfth to fourteenth century. *Mādhavīya Dhātuvṛtti* is written by Sāyaṇa, who belonged to late fourteenth century and was with the Vijayanagara emperors Harihara and Bukka. Kṣīrasvāmin of *Kṣīrataraṅgiṇī* is considered to be from the early twelfth century from Kashmir region. *Dhātupradīpa* is written by Maitreyarakṣitaḥ, a Bengali scholar from the late twelfth century. *Śābdikābharaṇam*, by Hariyogī, is also probably from the late twelfth century.

Scholars are aware that the *dhātu*s listed in various *dhātuvṛtti*s differ from each other and also from what Pāṇini had taught. For example, Brahmadatta Jijñāsu (1979) under the commentary on the *sūtra upadeśe'ajanunāsika it* (P 1.3.2) reports that Pāṇini had taught the verbal roots with nasalized sounds, which were lost over a period of time. Observation by Scharf (2009) that 'The unusual prosody inherent in the canonical form of roots became normalized through the natural adaptation of sequences of sounds to those of ordinary Sanskrit' provides an useful insight into the possible cause for the variations. The differences may be attributed to the unnatural combinations of phonemes which required special efforts to pronounce and thus to preserve them.

*Dhātu*s listed in the above *dhātuvṛtti*s differ in following respects:

1. phonemic constituents of the verbal roots,
2. markers attached to them,
3. meaning associated with them,
4. *gaṇa* they belong to, and
5. the accent.

4 Canonical Forms

In order to link these *dhātuvṝttis*, all of them should follow some uniform naming convention for the verbal root and its meaning.

4.1 Canonical Form of the Roots

Scharf (2009) in his digital edition of *Mādhavīya Dhātuvṛtti* proposed the use of canonical form for verb-roots. A canonical form of a verb-root is a sequence of phonemes that conforms to the requirements of rules stated in the *Aṣṭādhyāyī*. These requirements are:

1. The *anubandhas* are marked.
2. Root vowel accents are marked.
3. Roots retain the following impossible/difficult phonetic combinations:
   a. an initial *ṣ* and ṇ as in ṣvada.
   b. dental stops following initial retroflex *s* as in *ṣtak*.
   c. dental *n* instead of homo-organic nasal as in *anc*.
   d. dental *n* instead of *anunāsika* as in *danśa*.
   e. penultimate dental sibilant *s* as in *vrasc*.
   f. penultimate dental *d* as in *adḍ*.
   g. No penultimate *c* before *ch* as opposed to *pracch*.

There are rules in *Aṣṭādhyāyī* which when applied to the roots in canonical form normalize them in due course of generation process. The canonical form is required in order to ensure the correct derivation. In some of the cases *dhātuvṛttis* do not mention these roots in their canonical form, but the commentary does mention the canonical form and refers to *sūtras* which change them to normal form. If the *vṛttikāras* did not believe in the canonical form of the roots, they would not have commented about it in the commentaries. So from the very fact that the commentaries support the canonical forms, we may infer that when the *dhātuvṛttis* mention the roots in their normal form, it is only from the ease of pronunciation/recitation point of view. So in order to link various *dhātuvṛttis*, it is appropriate to map the roots to their canonical forms.

4.2 Canonical Forms of Meanings

The normal convention of specifying the meaning is using an activity specifying word in the seventh case, such as *pūjane.* Sometimes the word *artha* is used as in *gatyārthe.* Similarly we found variations among *vr̥ttikāras* in the use of *kr̥t* suffix to indicate an activity. Some *vr̥ttis* used *ghañ* suffix while others used *lyut* suffix to indicate an activity. To make the linking possible, for each of the root, we chose the form that is used by majority of them as the canonical one.

Following information was marked in all the *dhātuvr̥ttis*.

1. *dhātu* with the *it* marker,
2. meaning,
3. meaning analysis,
4. name of the *gaṇa* the verb belongs to,
5. accent information,
6. *pada* information,
7. *set-anit* information,
8. Pāṇinian *sūtras*, and
9. *kārikās*.

In addition, the canonical form for each verb and meaning in seventh case singular form were provided as an extra mark up for the purpose of linking. These marked-up files were then used for the linking.

5 Comparison of *Dhātuvr̥ttis*

Each entry in the *dhātuvr̥tti* contains one or more roots with one or more meanings associated with it. Since the *dhātuvr̥ttis* differ in both the root entries as well as the meaning associated with them, each single entry was expanded into multiple entries with single root, single meaning per entry while comparing them. Thus if there is an entry in a *dhātuvr̥tti* with m roots v_1, v_2, ..., v_m with n possible meanings m_1, m_2, ..., m_n then the entry is expanded into $m * n$ distinct (verb, meaning) pairs.

For example, an entry such as:*gādhr̥ pratiṣṭhālipsāyoḥ granthe ca* is expanded into three entries, viz.

1. *gādhr̥ pratiṣṭhāyām,*

2. *gādhṛ lipsāyām*, and
3. *gādhṛ granthe.*

Table 1 shows the number of entries in each *dhātuvṛtti* before

Table 1: Number of *dhātus* in each *dhātuvṛtti*

Dhātuvṛtti	**Distinct roots**	**Distinct root-meaning pairs**
Mādhavīya (MD)	1,890	2,227
Kṣīrataraṅgiṇī (KT)	1,885	2,215
Dhātupradīpa (DP)	1,952	2,322
Śābdikābharaṇam (SB)	1,157	1,407

and after this expansion. *Śābdikābharaṇam* (SB) does not have any commentary on the verbs from the tenth *gaṇa*, except for the root *cur*. This explains the low figure against SB in Table 1.

The distribution of roots in various *vṛttis* among various *gaṇas* is shown in Table 2. Some of the roots have multiple meanings.

Table 2: Distribution of roots in different *gaṇas*

Gaṇa	**MD**	**KT**	**DP**	**SB**
bhvādi	978	995	1031	689
adādi	72	69	72	71
juhotyādi	24	25	26	18
divādi	136	134	139	127
svādi	29	29	31	25
tudādi	157	159	168	132
rudhādi	25	25	25	26
tanādi	10	9	10	9
kryādi	60	60	64	59
curādi	399	381	386	1

Since not every *vṛtti* accepts all the meanings, we also compared the *vṛttis* on the basis of root-meaning pairs. There were 3,203 distinct root-meaning pairs found in these four *dhātuvṛttis*. The

Table 3: Distribution of root-meaning pairs in different *gaṇas*

Gaṇa	MD	KT	DP	SB	Matched Entries
bhvādi	1207	1210	1269	865	512
adādi	84	79	72	81	69
juhotyādi	34	36	36	25	20
divādi	157	151	161	152	102
svādi	39	36	41	28	19
tudādi	175	176	189	148	92
rudhādi	32	31	32	26	19
tanādi	10	9	11	10	7
kryādi	69	70	71	66	38
curādi	418	419	426	1	260

distribution of the root-meaning pairs into various *gaṇas* in various *vṛttis* is shown in Table 3. It also shows the common root-meaning pairs across all the *vṛttis* in every *gaṇa*.

Only 1,138 (35%) entries from the four *Dhātuvṛttis* matched with respect to three fields viz. the root, its meaning and *gaṇa* it belongs to. This includes 260 roots from *curādi gaṇa* which are common to three *Dhātuvṛittis* excluding *Śābdikābharaṇam*. The low percentage of common elements is a serious concern and thus it is further necessary to probe for the nature of differences. 2065 entries differed in one or more aspects, such as

1. Different root forms
   Most of the differences in root form are due to short-long vowel variation, or similarity in the sound of phonemes or orthographic similarity. For example *pṛci; pṛcī, vṛji; vṛjī, muṣa; mūṣa, gu; gū, kṛ; kṝ, nṛ; nṝ* show short-long vowel variations. Examples of similar sounding phonems and/or orthographic similarities are *ruśa; ruṣa, hlāda; hrāda, blī; vlī, valha; balha, khaca; khava, sphur; sphul, jehū; jehṛ, ṣvṛ; ṣebṛ*.
   Palsule treats all these verb entries as separate.
2. Different meanings
   Majority of differences in the meaning attribute to the similar sounding phonems and/or orthographic similarity. Some of the examples are *āpravaṇe; āplavane, sevane; secane, bhaṣaṇe; bhāṣaṇe, mrakṣaṇe; mlakṣaṇe*.

3. Different *gaṇa*s
   Approximately 10% differences are due to *gaṇa* differences.

Tables 4 to 7 give some example entries of various differences.

Table 4: Roots not present in all the *vṛttis*

Gaṇa	**Root**	**Meaning**	**MD**	**KT**	**DP**	**SB**
adādi	*aji*	*varjane*	-	-	-	✓
adādi	*śāsti*	*śāsane*	-	-	-	✓
adādi	*ṇisi*	*gatau*	-	-	✓	-
adādi	*ṇisi*	*niśāne*	-	-	✓	-
kryādi	*puṣu/pluṣu*	*pūraṇe/snehane*	-	-	-	✓
juhotyādi	gṛ	*kṣaraṇe/dīptau*	-	-	✓	-
tanādi	*ṛṇu*	*dīptau*	-	-	✓	-
svādi	*ri*	*hiṁsāyām*	✓	-	✓	-

Table 5: Variations in the phonological form of root as well as meaning

Gaṇa	**MD**	**KT**	**DP**	**SB**
adādi	*pṛcī*, ***samparcane***	*pṛcī*, *samparke*	***pṛjī***, *samparke*	***pṛci***, *samparke*
adādi	*ṣasa*, *svapne*	*ṣasa*, *svapne*	*ṣasa*, *ṣvapne*	***sasa***, *svapne*

Table 6: Variations in meaning

Gaṇa	**MD**	**KT**	**DP**	**SB**
adādi	*kasi*, *śāsane*	*kasi*, *śāsane*	*kasi*, ***niśāne***	*kasi*, *śāsane*
adādi	*diha*, *upacaye*	*diha*, *upacaye*	*diha*, ***upatāpe***	*diha*, *upacaye*
kryādi	*bhrī*, ***bhaye***	*bhrī*, *bharaṇe*	*bhrī*, *bharaṇe*	*bhrī*, ***bhaye***

Table 7: Verbs classified into different *gaṇas* by different *vṛttikāras*

Root	Meaning	MD	KT	DP	SB
īṣa	*gatau*	*bhvādi*	*bhvādi*	*bhvādi*	***divādi***
garda	*śabde*	*bhvādi*	*bhvādi/* ***curādi***	*bhvādi*	-

6 Conclusion

Earlier efforts of preparing the concordances of *dhātuvṛitti*s have brought to the surface the differences among them. However, no quantitative account of these differences was available so far. In this paper we tried to give a quantitative measure of various differences and also enumerated the nature of various differences. In addition, by postulating a canonical form for verbal root and its meaning, we could accomplish electronic linking of these resources. Our purpose here is not to reconstruct Pāṇinian *dhātupāṭha*, but to provide a sound database for research. What concerns us here is the large variations among different versions. The overlap is only 35 percent. Such a linking will help one to study the variations from linguistic perspective. With the availability of electronic corpus classified chronologically and the search engine, now it should be possible to study the distribution of possible root forms. However, to comment on the associated meanings, one needs semantically tagged corpus. E-linked *dhātuvṛtti*s are available with a suitable interface at `http://sanskrit.uohyd.ernet.in/scl/dhaatupaatha`.

Dhātupāṭha contains only basic roots, and not the roots derived by adding prefixes. Occurrence of prefixed verbs is very common in Sanskrit literature and *dhātuvṛtti*s do not talk about them. Addition of prefixes not only change the verbal root but also its meaning and the *pada* information. And therefore in addition to linking the *dhātuvṛtti*s it is also necessary to prepare an exhaustive index of verbal roots with all possible prefixes for each one of these roots.

7 Acknowledgement

Scharf's work on *Mādhavīya Dhātuvṛtti* provided the basic insight for this work. Authors thank Karunakar for the programming assistance, Devanand Shukl for helping in designing the mark up, and Ramakrishnamacharyulu and Acharya Anand Prakash for valuable discussions on the Pāṇinian process of generation of verb conjugations.

References

1. Caināni, Māyā. *Dhātupāṭhoṃ meṃ arthanirdeśa*, Vidyanidhi Prakashan, Delhi, 1995.
2. Govindacharyah. *Vaiyākaraṇa-siddhānta-kaumudī*, Chaukha- mba, Surabharati Prakashan, Varanasi, 2010.
3. Gupta, Jayakṛṣṇadāsa Haridāsa. *Mādhavīyādhātuvṛttiḥ sāyaṇācāryaḥ*, Chaukhamba Sanskrit Series, Banaras, 1991.
4. Jijñāsu, Brahmadatta. *Aṣṭādhyāyī (Bhāṣya) Prathamāvṛtti*, 3vols. , Ramlal Kapoor Trust Bahalgadh, Sonepat, Haryana, India, 1979 (In Hindi).
5. *Kāśikā.* Vāmana-Jayāditya-viracitā Pāṇinīyāṣṭādhyāyīsūtra vṛttiḥ, Sanskrit Academy, Osmania University, Hyderabad, 2008.
6. Liebich, Bruno. *Konkordanz Pāṇini: Chandra*, Indische Forschungen 6, Breslau: Marcus, 1928.
7. Misra, Anand. Simulating the Pāṇinian System of Sanskrit Grammar. In, *Sanskrit Computational Linguistics* 1 & 2, pp. 127-138, Springer-Verlag LNAI 5402, 2009.
8. Mīmaṃsakaḥ, Yudhiṣṭhira. *Daivam*, Śrīkṛṣṇalīlāśukamuni-viracita-puruṣakārākhyāvārtikopetam, Bharatiya Pracya Vidya Pratisthanam, 1971.
9. Mīmāṃsakaḥ, Yudhiṣṭhira. *Kāśakṛtsna-dhātuvyākhyānam*, Śrīcannavīrakavikṛtakarṇāṭakaṭīkāyāḥ, Bharatiya Pracya Vidya Pratisthanam, 1974.
10. Mīmāṃsakaḥ, Yudhiṣṭhira. *Dhātu-pradīpaḥ*, Maitreya-rakṣita-viracitaḥ, Śrīśacandracakravartī Bhaṭṭācāryaḥ, Ramlal Kapoor Trust, Sonepat, Hariyana, 1986.
11. Mīmāṃsakaḥ, Yudhiṣṭhira. *Mahābhāṣyam, Patañjali-muni-viracitam*, Ramlal Kapoor Trust, Sonepat, Hariyana, 1993.
12. Mīmāṃsakaḥ, Yudhiṣṭhira. *Kṣīra-taraṅgiṇī, kṣīrasvāmi- viracitā*, Ramlal Kapoor Trust, Sonepat, Hariyana, 2005.
13. Palsule, G.B. *Concordance of Sanskrit Dhatupathas*, Bhadarkar Oriental Research Institute, Pune, 1955.

14. Scharf, Peter. Modelling Pāṇinian Grammar. In, *Sanskrit Computational Linguistics 1 & 2*, pp. 95-126, Springer-Verlag LNAI 5402, 2009.
15. Scharf, Peter. *Mādhavīya Dhātuvṛttisaidhāntikānukramaṇī*, Providence, RI: The Sanskrit Library, 2009.
16. Śukla, Devananda. *Śābdikābharaṇam*, Harayogikṛtam, Rashtriya Sanskrit Sansthan, New Delhi, 2010.
17. Tārānāthatarkavācaspatibhaṭṭa. *Vācaspatyam*, Rashtriya Sanskrit Sansthan, Delhi, 2006.
18. Tripāṭhī, Bhāgīrathaprasāda. *Dhātvarthavijñānam*, Vārāṇasī, 1902.
19. Tripāṭhī, Bhāgīrathaprasāda. *Pāṇinīyadhātupāṭhasamīkṣā* Prathamo bhāgaḥ, Vārāṇasī, 1906.
20. Tripāṭhī, Bhāgīrathaprasāda. *Pāṇinīyadhātupāṭhasamīkṣā* Dvitiyo bhāgaḥ, Vārāṇasī, 1906.
21. Vāgīśaḥ, Satyānandaveda. *Dhātupāṭha-prayogadīpikā*, Jodha-pur, Rajasthan, 2010.

अष्टाध्याय्यामुपसामग्रि निष्पादनयन्त्रपरिकल्पनं च

Sridhar Subbanna[1] and Shrinivasa Varakhedi[2]

[1] Rashtriya Sanskrit Vidyapeetha, Tirupati, India,
sridharsy@gmail.com

[2] Karnataka Samskrit University, Bengaluru, India,
shrivara@gmail.com

Abstract. शब्दनिष्पत्तिकरणे तथा वाक्यरचनायाञ्च अष्टाध्यायी किञ्चित् स्वयंचलद्यन्त्रमिव कल्पयितुं शक्यते। तत्रत्यसूत्राणां क्रमश्च सुव्यवस्थितः। एतादृशी च व्यवस्था सङ्गणकतन्त्रे वरीवर्ति। अत एवाष्टाध्यायी सङ्गणकप्रतिमानरूपेणानुचिन्तयितुं शक्यते। तस्यां च अष्टाध्याय्यां विद्यमानाः प्रमुखाः कल्पनाः संज्ञा, परिभाषा, अनुबन्धः, प्रक्रिया, असिद्धं, विरोधपरिहारः चेत्यादयः। ताश्च सङ्गणकशास्त्रस्य समुचित-कल्पनाभिः उपसामग्रि (metadata) , कार्यकल्पः (function), निष्पादनयन्त्रपरि-कल्पनं (concept of production system), विधिकल्पः (algorithm) इत्यदिभिः सह योजयितुं शक्यन्ते। तासु च उपसामग्रि निष्पादनयन्त्रपरिकल्पनं चाधिकृत्येदं शोधपत्रम्। अष्टाध्यायीनिरूपितशब्दनिष्पत्तौ प्रायः परिणामितया न साक्षादुपयुज्यमानाः प्रक्रियायामेव उपक्षीणप्रयोजनाः वर्णरूपाः संज्ञारूपा वा सूचकाः उपसामग्रितया, तथा अष्टाध्यायीमेकां निष्पादनयन्त्रम् (production system), इति कल्पयित्वा, तद्यन्त्रगतनियमा ((production rules) इव अष्टाध्यायीस्थविधिसूत्राणि, यन्त्रस्याङ्गानीव अग्रतआवर्तकविधिकल्पादीनि (forward chaining algorithm etc.) इति परस्परं योजनादिकमस्मिन् पत्रे प्रदर्श्यते।

Keywords : अष्टाध्यायी, उपसामग्रि, सङ्गणकतत्त्वम्, निष्पादनयन्त्रम्, नियमः, Aṣṭādhyāyī, metadata, computation, production system, algorithm, forward chaining, rules.

शब्दनिष्पत्तिकरणे तथा वाक्यरचनायाञ्च अष्टाध्यायी किञ्चित् स्वयंचलद्यन्त्रमिव कल्पयितुं शक्यते। तत्रत्यसूत्राणां क्रमश्च सुव्यवस्थितः। शब्दनिष्पत्तिः प्रकृतिप्रत्ययानां संयोजनेन भवति। तच्च संयोजनं सूत्रप्रवृत्तिनिमित्तकं कार्यम्। सा च प्रवृत्तिः व्यवस्थितां प्रक्रियामनुसरति। एतादृशी च व्यवस्था सङ्गणकतन्त्रे विद्यते, आवश्यकी अनिवार्या उपजीव्या च। अत एवाष्टाध्यायी सङ्गणकप्रतिमानरूपेणानुचिन्तयितुमनुरूपा भवति। अस्मिंस्तु पत्रे सङ्गणकशास्त्रप्रमेयानाश्रित्य अष्टाध्याय्यां विद्यमाने तत्त्वे उपसामग्रि निष्पादनयन्त्रपरिकल्पनं च प्रदर्श्येते।

1 उपसामग्रि (Metadata)

सामग्र्याः उपरि समीपे वा वर्तमानं यत् तत् उपसामग्रि ।[3] सामग्री एव निर्दिष्टव्यवस्थाश्रयेण दत्तांश इत्युच्यते । तस्मात् दत्तांशः सामग्री इति च अनर्थान्तरम् । सामग्रीमधिकृत्य योजितकार्यार्थमुपयुक्ताः सङ्केताः उपसामग्रिपदेन उच्यन्ते । यथा ग्रन्थालयस्य ग्रन्थसूचीनिर्माणे ग्रन्थसम्बन्धिसूचनाः व्यवस्थापयितुमुपयुक्तानि सङ्केताक्षराणि, यैः ग्रन्थकर्ता, शीर्षकं, विषयः, स्थानं, मूलं, भाषामाध्यमं, प्रकाशनवर्षं चेत्यादिसूचनाः प्राप्यन्ते ।

अष्टाध्यायीसूत्रसूचितासु शब्दवाक्यनिष्पत्तिप्रक्रियासु ये वर्णाः वर्णसमूहा वा साक्षादुपयुज्यन्ते ता सामग्र्य (data) इत्युच्यन्ते । यथा रामेण इत्यत्र 'राम' इति प्रातिपदिकं सामग्री इत्युच्यते । ताभिः सह वर्तमानाः किन्तु निष्पत्तौ प्रायः परिणामितया न साक्षादुपयुज्यमानाः प्रक्रियायामेव उपक्षीणप्रयोजनाः वर्णरूपाः संज्ञारूपा वा सूचकाः उपसामग्रि (metadata) इत्युच्यन्ते । यथा रामेण इति शब्दनिष्पत्तौ 'राम' इत्यस्य सामग्र्याः कर्तृकारकसंज्ञा उपसामग्रि भवति । तच्च उपसामग्रि क्वचित् चिह्नत्वेन, क्वचित् समानपरिणामार्हाणां समूहीकरणार्थमित्यादिप्रयोजनमुद्दिश्य पाणिनिना कल्पितम् ।[2] उपसामग्रिविभागप्रयोजनादिकं विस्तरेण पश्यामः ।

1.1 उपसामग्रिविभागः

उपसामग्रि त्रिविधं प्रयोजनानुसारेण । आद्यं चिह्नत्वेन प्रत्याहारेषु उपयुज्यमाना इतः । द्वितीयं समानपरिणामार्हाणां समूहीकरणत्वेन व्यापारप्रकारसूचकादिप्रयोजनार्थं प्रक्रियासु उपयुज्यमानम् इद्रूपम् तदन्यसूत्रैः विधीयमानसामग्रीसहभूतम् । तृतीयमपि तदर्थमेव, किन्तु प्रक्रियासु उपयुज्यमानं संज्ञारूपं तदन्यसूत्रैः विधीयमानम् ।

1.1.1 सूचकरूपमुपसामग्रि

चतुर्दशप्रत्याहारसूत्रेषु निर्दिष्टमन्त्यं हल् सूचकरूपमुपसामग्रि भवति । प्रत्याहारगुच्छनिर्माणे अस्योपयोगः । 'अक्' इति एकं प्रत्याहारगुच्छम् । तत्र व्यक्तिभूताः 'अ', 'इ', 'उ','ऋ', 'ऌ' इति वर्णाः सामग्र्यः, प्रक्रियायां साक्षादुपयुज्यमानत्वात् । णकारः अत्र अप्रयोजकः, सामग्र्यपि न भवति इत्त्वात् । ककारस्तु 'अक्' नामकगुच्छनिर्माणे उपयुक्तमुपसामग्रि । अष्टाध्याय्यां उपयुज्यमानानामेकचत्वारिंशत्प्रत्याहाराणां निर्माणे एतत् त्रयोदशसङ्ख्याकमुपसामग्रि उपयुक्तम् ।

तेषु च प्रत्याहारसूत्रेषु निर्दिष्टमुपसामग्रि अधोनिर्दिष्टयां सूच्यां स्थूलाक्षरैः लिखितं वर्तते ।

[3] उपकृष्णं भक्ताः इत्यत्र कृष्णसमीपवन्तः भक्ताः इत्यर्थः । यथार्थं प्रमाणमित्यत्र अर्थम् अनतिक्रम्य वर्तमानं प्रमाणं यथार्थमिति अभियुक्तानां प्रयोगः । अव्ययीभावसमासोऽयम् ।

[2] एतेषामुदाहरणानि अग्रे द्रष्टव्यानि ।

अ इ उ ण् । ऋ ऌ क् । ए ओ ङ् । ऐ औ च् । ह य व र ट् । ल ण् । ञ म ङ ण न म् । झ भ ञ् । घ ढ ध ष् । ज ब ग ड द श् । ख फ छ ठ थ च ट त व् । क प य् । श ष स र् । ह ल् ।

1.1.2 निबन्धरूपमुपसामग्रि

शब्दनिष्पत्तिप्रक्रियायां सोपानानि नैकानि भवन्ति । तेषां मध्ये कानिचित् विविधानां शब्दानां निष्पत्तौ साधारणानि भवन्ति । तत्साधारण्यं कुशलतरमार्गेणोपयोक्तुम् अल्पाक्षरसम्पादनार्थञ्च पाणिनिः कानिचित् सूचकानि कल्पयामास । इद्रूपाण्येव सूचकत्वेन प्रायुङ्क्त । तान्येव निबन्धरूपमुपसामग्रि । तद्यथा - 'हरये', 'हरेः', 'हरेः', 'हरौ' इति चत्वारि रूपाणि हरिशब्दस्य । तथैव 'शम्भवे', 'शम्भोः', 'शम्भोः', 'शम्भौ' इति च रूपाणि शम्भुशब्दस्य । तेषां द्विविधानामपि शब्दानां चतुर्णामपि रूपाणां निष्पत्तौ उपयुज्यमानायां प्रक्रियायामिदं साधारणं सोपानं यत् प्रातिपदिकस्य गुणादेश इति । तं विधातुमयं क्रमः अनुसृतः पाणिनिना । तयोः प्रातिपदिकयोः विधीयमानेषु प्रत्ययेषु एकमेव सूचकं 'ङ'काररूपमुपसामग्रित्वेन कल्पयामास । ते च प्रत्ययाः 'ङे', 'ङसि', 'ङस् ', 'ङि' इति । तेषामुपयोगञ्च आदिष्टवान् 'घेर्ङिति' (७.३.१११) इति सूत्रेण गुणादेशविधायकेन । अपि च ङिद्रूपोपसामग्रिविधानस्य अन्यत्रापि प्रयोजनानि भवन्ति । यथा- 'ङेर्यः' (७.१.१३), 'आण् नद्याः' (७.३.११२), 'सर्वनाम्नः स्मै' (७.१.१४), 'ङिति ह्रस्वश् 'च (१.४.६), 'याडापः' (७.३.११३), 'सर्वनाम्नः स्याड्ढ्रस्वश्च' (७.३. ११४) इत्यादिषु ।

तेषां सूचकानाम् 'इत् ' इति संज्ञा व्यवहृता पाणिनिना । इत्संज्ञाविधायकानि चेमानि सूत्राणि[3] ।

1. उपदेशेऽजनुनासिक इत् (१.३.२)
2. हलन्त्यम् (१.३.३)
3. न विभक्तौ तुस्माः (१.३.४) (इत्-निषेधकसूत्रम्)
4. आदिः ञिटुडवः (१.३.५)
5. षः प्रत्ययस्य (१.३.६)
6. चुटू (१.३.७)
7. लशक्वतद्धिते (१.३.८)

1.1.3 संज्ञारूपमुपसामग्रि

अन्यविधमुपसामग्रि संज्ञारूपम् । तत् प्रक्रियासु उपयुज्यमानमन्यसूत्रैः विधीयमानञ्च । संज्ञाज्ञापकानि निमित्तानि सूत्रेषु विहितानि । अपि च एतत्संज्ञानिमित्तकानि कार्याणि इतरत्र सूत्रेषु लक्षितानि । तद्यथा 'स्वतन्त्रः कर्ता'(१.४.५४) इति सूत्रेण क्रियायां स्वातन्त्र्येण विवक्षितः प्रातिपदिकार्थः कर्तृसंज्ञकः भवतीति व्यधायि । सत्याञ्च कर्तृसंज्ञायां 'कर्तृकरणयोस्तृतीया' (२.३.१८) इति सूत्रेण तृतीयाविभक्तिविधानरूपं कार्यं लक्षितम् । ततश्च कर्तृवाचकं 'राम' इति प्रातिपदिकं स्वातन्त्र्यविवक्षायां 'रामेण' इति रूपं प्राप्नोति ।

2 निष्पादनयन्त्रम् (Production System)

निष्पादनयन्त्रं (Bullinaria 2005) नाम नियमगणगर्भितः गणकविधिकल्पः (computational algorithm), येन परिवर्तनशीलानि विभिन्नरूपाणि परीक्ष्य साधारणी प्रक्रिया काचित् निरूप्यते। एते च नियमाः प्रक्रियायां यान्त्रिकयोजनायां कार्यचयने उपयुज्यन्ते। एषः विधिकल्पः अन्त्यमुद्दिष्टं रूपं सम्पादयितुं यान्त्रिकप्रक्रियां निर्वहति। अस्य द्वौ अंशौ। आगामिक्रियायाः पूर्वभाविनिमित्तनिर्धारणम्, एवं क्रियमाणः व्यापारश्च। दत्तांशस्थाने कार्यस्य निमित्तानि लभ्यन्ते चेत् तन्निमित्तकः विधिः प्रवर्तते। तथा च कार्यं सम्पद्यते। तदा विधिप्रवृत्तिः सफला। ततश्च निमित्तान्तरं क्रियान्तरञ्च।

निष्पादनयन्त्रे दत्तांशसङ्ग्रहः नियमविवृतिश्च घटकीभूतौ। नियमविवृतिश्च प्रसङ्गविशेषे नैकनियमप्राप्तौ अन्यतमस्वीकारे प्रक्रियाक्रमनिर्धारणे वा सूत्रं कल्पयति। अत्र निर्दिष्टरूपसाधनाय कार्यचयनार्थम् 'अग्रतआवर्तकविधिकल्पः'(forward chaining algorithm) उपयुज्यते।

अष्टाध्यायी निष्पादनयन्त्रम् (production system) इति रूपेण कल्पयितुं शक्यते, निष्पादनयन्त्रम् तु गणकतन्त्रज्ञाने कृतकमेधा (artificial intelligence) नामके क्षेत्रे एकं कल्पनमिति विदितम्। तद्गतनियमाः (production rules) इव अत्रत्यानि विधिसूत्राणि। तद्गतं rule engine इव विधिप्रणयनयन्त्रम्। यन्त्रस्याङ्गानि अग्रतआवर्तकविधिकल्पादीन्यपि rule engine मध्ये वर्तन्ते इति तु विव्रियते।

2.1 विधिप्रणयनयन्त्रम् (Rule Engine)

अष्टाध्यायीसूत्राणि कयाचित् काल्पनिकभाषया (Kalpan 1994) रचितानि न तु व्यवहारभाषया। सूत्रेषु सामग्रीभिः सह ये विभक्तिप्रत्ययाः सहोद्दिष्टाः तैः सा भाषा रचिता। तान् प्रत्ययान् व्याख्यातुं नियमाः परिभाषासूत्रैः (metarules) लक्षिताः। परिभाषासूत्रैः अन्यसूत्रगतप्रत्ययानां प्रत्यायनप्रकारः सूचित इत्यर्थः। यथा 'इको यण् अचि' (६.१.७७) इति सूत्रे, इकः = इक् + ङस् (षष्ठीविभक्तिः), यण् = यण् + सु (प्रथमाविभक्तिः), अचि = अच् + ङि (सप्तमीविभक्तिः) इति पदानि सन्ति। तत्र 'ङस्' इति स्थान्यर्थकं, 'षष्ठी स्थाने योगा' (१.१.४९) इति सूत्रात्। 'ङि' इति साक्षात्परत्वनिमित्तं सूचयति, 'तस्मिन्निति निर्दिष्टे पूर्वस्य' (१.१.६६) इति सूत्रात्। तथैव अन्यान्यपि सूत्राणि अन्यविभक्तिप्रत्ययानां व्याख्यानं परिभाषयन्ति। यथा 'तस्मादित्युत्तरस्य' (१.१.६७), 'प्रथमानिर्दिष्टं समास उपसर्जनम्' (१.२.४३), 'तत्रोपपदं सप्तमीस्थम्' (३.१.९२) इत्यादयः।

विधिसूत्रेभ्यश्च प्रक्रिया विहिता भवति। इमे प्रश्नाः उपजायन्ते। कदा विधिसूत्राणि प्रवर्तन्ते? सूत्राणां परस्परं विरोधे क उपायः? किञ्च एषां विधीनां स्वरूपम्? कथञ्च उपसामग्रि व्याख्येयम्? इत्यादि। इमे सर्वे प्रश्नाः कैश्चित् परिभाषासूत्रैः अष्टाध्याय्यामेव परिहृताः। इतरे व्याख्यानपरम्परया परिहृताः। तान्यधीत्य कश्चित् वैयाकरणः प्रक्रियाः प्रवर्तयितुं समर्थः भवति। तस्य स्थाने विधिप्रणयनयन्त्रमिति नाम्ना यन्त्रमेकमत्र कल्प्यते। तद्यन्त्रं परिभाषाणां ज्ञानवत् तदनुसारेण विधिप्रणायकञ्चेति कल्पनम्।

2.1.1 यन्त्रप्रणयनपद्धतिः - (Rule Engine Algorithm)

यन्त्रकर्तृकप्रणयनस्य पद्धतिः इत्थं निष्कर्षयितुं शक्यते। यन्त्रं तु साक्षात् अग्रतआवर्तकविधिकल्पम् (Forward Chaining Aslgorithm) अनुसृत्य वर्तते। स च विधिकल्पः शब्दनिष्पत्तिपर्यन्तं क्रमशः सूत्राणां प्रवर्तकः। तदर्थं यन्त्रस्य द्वे निविष्टे (input) आवश्यके भवतः। प्रसङ्गः अष्टाध्यायी च।

प्रसङ्गो नाम निष्पत्तिप्रक्रियायामुपयुक्तानां सोपानानां समुदायः। आदौ विवक्षातः प्रथमसोपानं प्रसङ्गे प्राप्नोति। तदनन्तरं सूत्रप्रवृत्त्यनन्तरं द्वितीयसोपानमुत्पद्यते। तदा प्रथमसोपानमात्रयुक्तः प्रसङ्गः द्वितीयसोपानेन उपचितो भवति। तथैव सूत्रप्रवृत्त्यनुसारेण प्रसङ्गे सोपानानि संयुज्यन्ते। एकैकस्मिन्नपि सोपाने सामग्रीणां तत्सहकृतोपसामग्रीणाञ्च समूहाः, तत्सोपानकारणीभूतसूत्राणि च भवन्ति। तदिदं चित्रे (Fig.1), अधो निर्दिष्टायामुत्पीठिकायाञ्च दर्शितम्।

प्रसङ्गः				
सोपानं	उपसामग्रिसहिताः सामग्र्यः सूत्रञ्च			
१	उप-सामग्रि	धातुः, कर्तरि, वर्तमानः, प्रथमपुरुषः, एकवचनं		
	सामग्री	भू		
	सूत्रम्	-		
२	उप-सामग्रि	धातुः, कर्तरि, वर्तमानः, प्रथमपुरुषः, एकवचनं	लकार, टित्	
	सामग्री	भू	ल्	
	सूत्रम्	वर्तमाने लट् (३.२.१२३)		
३	उप-सामग्रि	धातुः, कर्तरि, वर्तमानः, प्रथमपुरुषः, एकवचनं	पित्, प्रत्ययः, सार्वधातुकः, तिङ्	
	सामग्री	भू	ति	
	सूत्रम्	तिप्तस्झिसिप्थस्थमिब्वस्मस् तातांझथसाथांध्वमिड्वहिमहिङ् (३.४.७८)		
४	उप-सामग्रि	धातुः, कर्तरि, वर्तमानः, प्रथमपुरुषः, एकवचनं	शित्, पित्, प्रत्ययः	पित्, प्रत्ययः, सार्वधातुकः, तिङ्
	सामग्री	भू	अ	ति
	सूत्रम्	कर्तरि शप् (३.४.१००)		

५	उप-सामग्रि	धातुः, कर्तरि, वर्तमानः, प्रथमपुरुषः, एकवचनं	शित्, पित्, प्रत्ययः	पित्, प्रत्ययः, सार्वधातुकः, तिङ्
	सामग्री	भो	अ	ति
	सूत्रम्	सार्वधातुकार्धधातुकयोः (७.३.८४)		
६	उप-सामग्रि	धातुः, कर्तरि, वर्तमानः, प्रथमपुरुषः, एकवचनं	शित्, पित्, प्रत्ययः	पित्, प्रत्ययः, सार्वधातुकः, तिङ्
	सामग्री	भव्	अ	ति
	सूत्रम्	एचोऽयवायावः (६.१.७८)		

अत्र प्रसङ्गाष्टाध्यायीरूपनिविष्टयोः (input) मध्ये अष्टाध्यायी नाम तद्गतानि सर्वाणि विधिसूत्राणि, नान्यानि सूत्राणि। तानि तु विधिसूत्रविचारसमये (sec. 3) विव्रियन्ते।

यन्त्रं तु आदौ तावत् तत्तत्प्रसङ्गेषु सूत्रस्यौचित्यं निश्चिनोति। तदर्थमेकं विधिकल्पमनुसरति यस्य नाम निश्चायकविधिकल्पः (Applicability Algorithm) इति। उचितत्वेन चितं सूत्रमस्मान् निष्क्रान्तं भवति। एकैकस्मिन्नपि प्रसङ्गे तथाभूतानां सूत्राणां समूहं तु यन्त्रं सङ्गृह्णाति, न तु पूर्वप्रसङ्गे चितानाम्। तेषां पूर्वप्रसङ्गोचितत्वात्। सङ्ग्रहे अनेकसूत्राणां सत्त्वे तेषां मध्ये परस्परं विरोधो भवतीति हेतोः सङ्गृहीतसूत्राणां मध्ये एकमेव सूत्रं प्रवर्तनाय निर्णेतव्यम्। एकस्मिन्प्रसङ्गे एकेनैव सूत्रेण प्रवर्तनीयत्वात्। एकस्मिन्काले एकस्मिन्वस्तुनि एकेनैव कार्येण भाव्यत्वात्। तदर्थं सूत्राणां विरोधपरिहारं कृत्वा एकं सूत्रं निर्णेतव्यम्। तदर्थं विरोधपरिहारविधिकल्पः (Conflict Resolution Algorithm) कल्पितः। निर्णीतं सूत्रं प्रसङ्गे प्रवर्तयति। यन्त्रे तदर्थं प्रवर्तकविधिकल्पः (Operation Algorithm) नाम अन्यः विधिकल्पः कल्पितः। अयमस्मिन् चित्रे (Fig. 2) दर्शितः।

एतेषु विधिकल्पेषु मध्ये अग्रतआवर्तकविधिकल्पं, निश्चायकविधिकल्पं, प्रवर्तकविधिकल्पञ्च सूचीकटाहन्यायेन अत्रैव पश्यामः। विरोधपरिहारविधिकल्पस्तु विस्तरेणान्यत्र (Subanna & Varkhedi 2009) अस्माभिः विवृतः।

2.1.2 अग्रतआवर्तकविधिकल्पः (Forward Chaining Algorithm)

अग्रतआवर्तकविधिकल्पः अनुमितिमालम्ब्य प्रवर्तते। प्रसङ्गे रूपपरिवर्तनकार्याणि यावन्निमित्तोपलम्भं सम्पादयति। विधिकल्पे घटकीभूतानां निमित्तदर्शनाभावे इष्टरूपसिद्धौ आत्मानं विरमयति। एषः विधिकल्पः प्रसङ्गाश्रयेण निमित्तानुसारेण नियमचयनं कृत्वा अग्रतः कार्यं निष्पादयति। अग्रतआवर्तकविधिकल्पस्य यादृच्छिकपरिवर्तनशीलेषु प्रसङ्गेषु अधिकः उपयोगः।

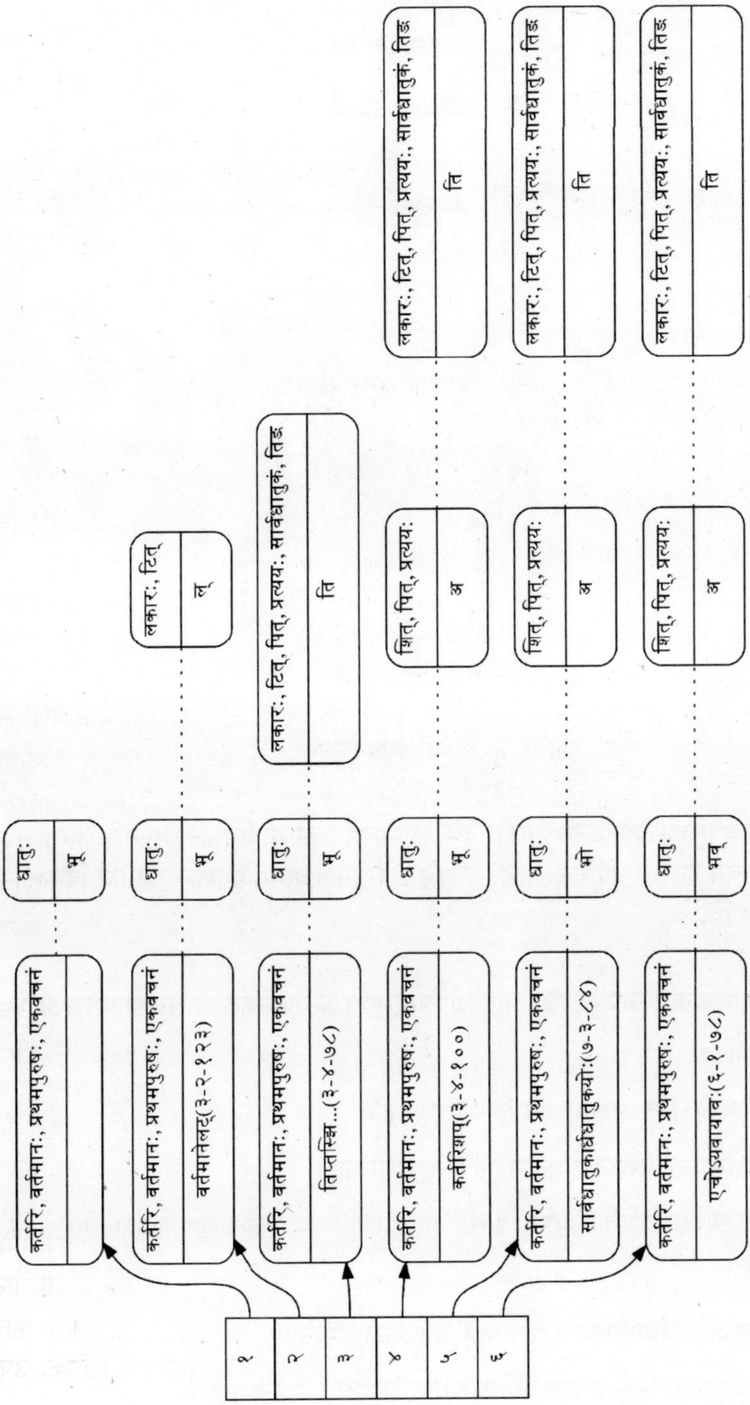
१
२
३
४
५
६
कर्तरि, वर्तमानः, प्रथमपुरुषः, एकवचनं
धातुः
भू
कर्तरि, वर्तमानः, प्रथमपुरुषः, एकवचनं
वर्तमानेलट्(३-२-१२३)
धातुः
भू
लकारः, टित्
ल्
कर्तरि, वर्तमानः, प्रथमपुरुषः, एकवचनं
तिप्तस्झि...(३-४-७८)
धातुः
भू
लकारः, टित्, पित्, प्रत्ययः, सार्वधातुकं, तिङ
ति
कर्तरि, वर्तमानः, प्रथमपुरुषः, एकवचनं
कर्तरिशप्(३-४-१००)
धातुः
भू
शित्, पित्, प्रत्ययः
अ
लकारः, टित्, पित्, प्रत्ययः, सार्वधातुकं, तिङ
ति
कर्तरि, वर्तमानः, प्रथमपुरुषः, एकवचनं
सार्वधातुकार्धधातुकयोः(७-३-८४)
धातुः
भो
शित्, पित्, प्रत्ययः
अ
लकारः, टित्, पित्, प्रत्ययः, सार्वधातुकं, तिङ
ति
कर्तरि, वर्तमानः, प्रथमपुरुषः, एकवचनं
एचोऽयवायावः(६-१-७८)
धातुः
भव्
शित्, पित्, प्रत्ययः
अ
लकारः, टित्, पित्, प्रत्ययः, सार्वधातुकं, तिङ
ति

Fig. 1 : प्रसङ्गः

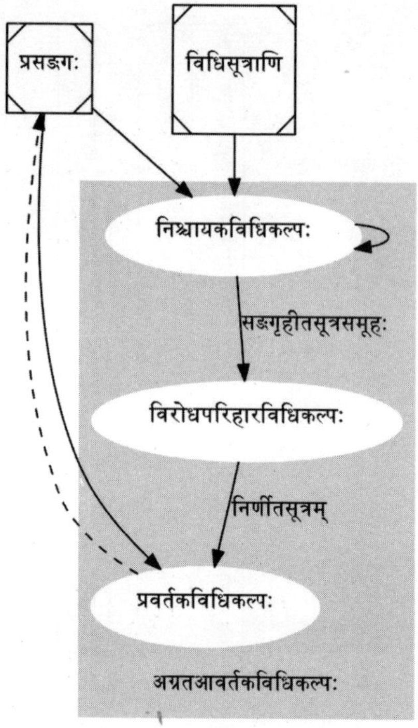

Fig. 2 : विधिप्रणयनयन्त्रम्

यन्त्रस्य मुख्यो विधिकल्पोऽयम् । अस्य द्वे निविष्टे अष्टाध्यायीगतविधिसूत्राणि, प्रसङ्गश्च । स्वगर्भितत्वेन इतरान् विधिकल्पान् उपयुङ्क्ते । अग्रतआवर्तकविधिकल्पे इमानि विधानानि क्रमशः सन्ति ।

1. निश्चायकविधिकल्पमुपयुज्य अष्टाध्यायीगतसूत्रेषु प्रत्येकमेकैकस्य सूत्रस्य प्रसङ्गे औचित्यनिश्चयः ।
2. एकस्यापि उचितसूत्रस्याभावे विधिकल्पसमाप्तिः ।
3. तादृशसूत्रस्य सत्त्वे उचितत्वेन निश्चितसूत्राणां सङ्ग्रहः ।
4. विरोधपरिहारविधिकल्पमुपयुज्य सङ्गृहीतसूत्राणां मध्ये एकस्य सूत्रस्य प्रवर्तनीयस्य निर्णयः ।
5. एकस्यापि प्रवर्तनीयस्य सूत्रस्याभावे विधिकल्पसमाप्तिः ।
6. तादृशसूत्रस्य सत्त्वे प्रवर्तकविधिकल्पमुपयुज्य प्रसङ्गे सूत्रस्य प्रवृत्तिः ।

7. नूतनसोपानेन प्रसङ्गस्योपचयः ।

8. नूतनप्रसङ्गेन प्रथमविधानमारभ्यास्य विधिकल्पस्य पुनरावर्तनम् समाप्तिपर्यन्तम् ।

अयमेव विधिकल्पः अस्मिन् चित्रे (Fig.3) सूचितोऽस्ति ।

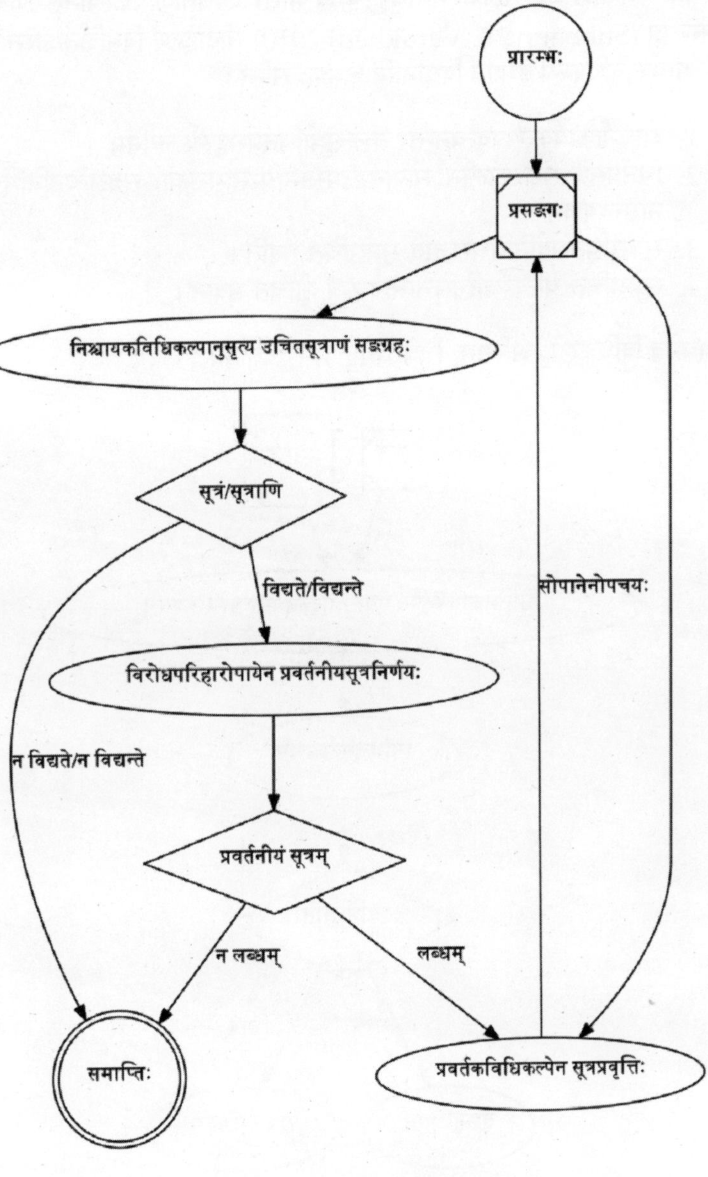

Fig. 3 : अग्रतआवर्तकविधिकल्पः

2.1.3 निश्चायकविधिकल्पः

निश्चायकविधिकल्पः सूत्राणां प्रसङ्गे औचित्यं निश्चिनोति। यद्यपि प्रसङ्गे सद्यःकालीनमेव सोपानं सूत्रौचित्यनिश्चयाय उपयुज्यते तथापि क्वचित् तत्तत्सूत्रासिद्धसूत्राणां प्रवृत्त्यनन्तरं वर्तमानं सद्यःकालीनं सोपानमौचित्यनिश्चयाय नोपयुज्यते। किन्तु असिद्धसूत्रप्रवृत्तेः पूर्ववर्ति एव। सोऽयं प्रकारः असिद्धप्रकरणमधिकृत्य विचारिते शोधनीकार्यकल्पनिरूपणावसरे अस्माभिरन्यत्र (Subbanna & Varakhedi 2010) सोदाहरणं विमर्शितोऽस्ति।

निश्चायकविधिकल्पे इमानि विधानानि क्रमशः सन्ति।

1. शोधनीकार्यकल्पप्रवृत्यनन्तरं तत्तत्सूत्रोचितप्रसङ्गस्य चयनम्।
2. चितप्रसङ्गे सद्यःकालीने सोपाने उपसामग्रि-सामग्र्योः सूत्रसूचितनिमित्तानामन्वेषणम्।
3. सूत्रसूचितसर्वनिमित्तसद्भावे सूत्रमुचितं भवति।
4. सूत्रसूचिते यत्किञ्चिन्निमित्ताभावे सूत्रं नोचितं भवति।

अयमेव विधिकल्पः अस्मिन् चित्रे (Fig.4) सूचितोऽस्ति।

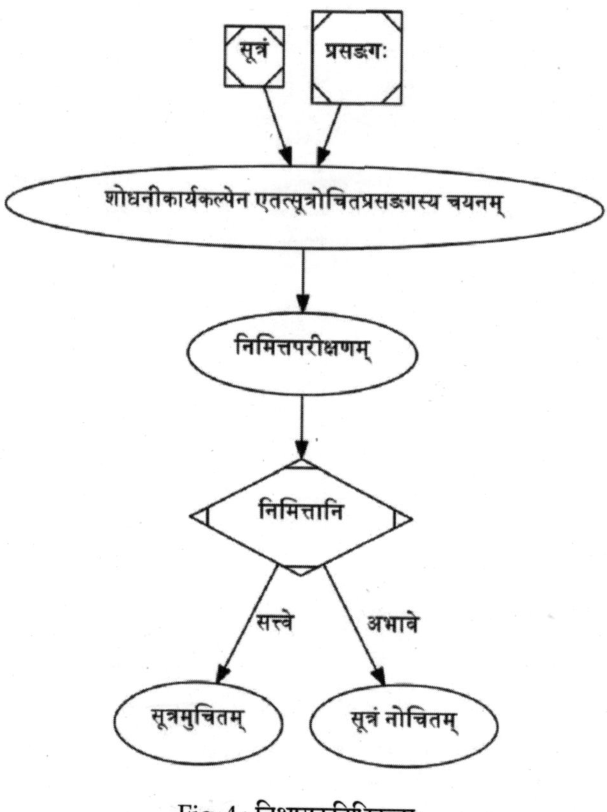

Fig. 4 : निश्चायकविधिकल्पः

2.1.4 प्रवर्तकविधिकल्पः

प्रवर्तकविधिकल्पः प्रसङ्गे सद्यःकालीनसोपाने समुचितत्वेन निर्णीतं सूत्रं प्रवर्तयति। शब्दे परिवर्तनानि (transformations) करोति। तत्रेमानि विधानानि क्रमशः सन्ति।

1. प्रसङ्गे परिवर्तनोपयोगिकर्मरूपस्य[1] स्थानिनः निश्चयः।
2. सूत्रसूचितकरणानां चयनम्।
3. परिभाषासूत्रानुसारेण एतत्सूत्रप्रवृत्तिः।

अयमेव विधिकल्पः अस्मिन् चित्रे (Fig.5) सूचितोऽस्ति।

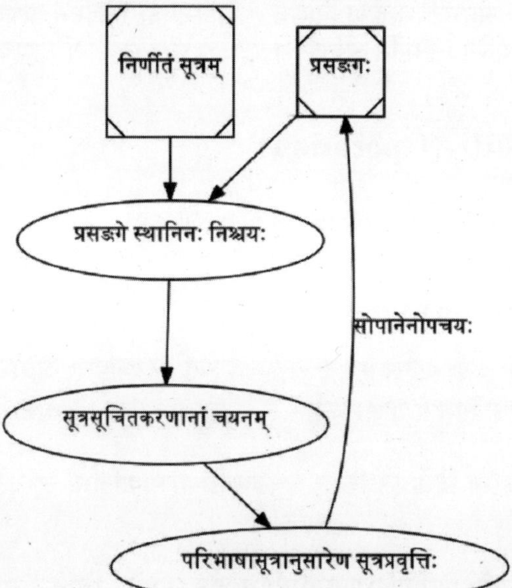

Fig. 5 : प्रवर्तकविधिकल्पः

3 विधिसूत्राणि (Prescribing Rules)

गणकतन्त्रज्ञाने निष्पादनयन्त्रमिव अष्टाध्यायी वर्तते। तस्मिन् वर्तमानानि नियमा इव अस्यामष्टाध्याय्यां विधिसूत्राणि वर्तन्ते इति पूर्वमुक्तम्।

---

[1]अत्र इदं वेदितव्यम्। यन्त्रं सूत्रेण शब्दं परिवर्तयति। शब्दे परिवृत्तिः व्यापारः। सूत्रे तत्प्रयोजकव्यापारः परिवर्तनम्। तत्प्रयोजकव्यापारः यन्त्रे। सोऽपि व्यापारः परिवर्तनशब्देनैव कथ्यते। परिवर्तनसम्बन्धि-आदेशागमादयः अवान्तरव्यापाराः। तद्व्यापारे सहकारिभूताः वर्णसमूहाः करणानि भवन्ति। तद्यथा इको यणचि इत्यत्र सूत्रं कर्तृ। इगिति स्थानी कर्म। यण् इति करणम्।

विधिसूत्राणि निमित्तानि, कर्मभूतं स्थानिनं, सहकारिणं, व्यापारांश्च निर्दिशन्ति। समुचितप्रसङ्गे सूत्रसूचितनिमित्तसद्भावे सूत्रप्रवृत्तिर्भवति। सहकारिभिः सह स्थानिनि व्यापारो भवतीत्यर्थः।

सूत्रस्य विन्यासः एवं भवति।

<निमित्तानि><स्थानिनः> <सहकारिणः> <व्यापाराः>

तद्यथा इको यणचि इति सूत्रे-

<निमित्तं-परतः स्थितः अच्> <स्थानी-इक्>
<सहकारी-यण्> <व्यापारः-आदेशः>

पञ्चमीविभक्तिः सप्तमीविभक्तिश्च निमित्ते, षष्ठीविभक्तिः स्थानिनं, प्रथमाविभक्तिः सहकारिणं व्यापारञ्च दर्शयन्ति। इमानि अङ्गानि तत्तदर्थं च पुरस्कृत्य विधिप्रणयनयन्त्रं प्रवर्तते।

4 सूत्रेषु व्यापाराः (Operations)

त्रिविधा व्यापारा भवन्ति सूत्रेषु। आगमः आदेशः लोपश्चेति।

4.1 आगमः (Insertion)

स्थानिना सह नूतनः वर्णः वर्णसमूहो वा संयुज्यते चेत् स व्यापारः आगमः इति कीर्तयन्ति। तदा व्यापारात्पूर्वं स्थानिनि ये वर्णाः वर्तन्ते ते तु नापगच्छन्ति। यथोक्तं मित्रवदागमः इति।

आगमो न कण्ठतो विधीयते किन्तु उपसामग्रिपरिभाषादिभिः सूच्यते। तत्सूचनञ्च त्रिप्रकारम् ।

1. ट्, क्, म् इत्येतैः द्वितीयविधोपसामग्रीभिः इत्-नामकैः संयुक्तेन सूत्रगतेन प्रथमाविभक्त्यन्तेन पदेन सूचनम् ।
2. परश्च इति परिभाषारूपेण अधिकाररूपेण च विद्यमानेन 'परश्च' (३.१.२) इति सूत्रेण सूचनम् । 'आद्युदात्तश्च' (३.१.३) सूत्रतः 'निष्प्रवाणिश्च' (५.४.१६०) पर्यन्तं विद्यमानेभ्यः सूत्रेभ्यः सूचितो व्यापारः आगमः इत्यर्थः।
3. साक्षान्निर्दिष्टेन द्वित्वेन सूचनम् ।

अत्र प्रथमप्रकारः देशविशेषेण त्रिविधो भवति। 'ट् '-रूपोपसामग्र्या यदा आगमः सूच्यते तदा स्थानिनः आदौ सः भवति। क्-रूपोपसामग्र्या यदा आगमः सूच्यते तदा स्थानिनः अन्ते सः भवति। म्-रूपोपसामग्र्या यदा आगमः सूच्यते तदा स्थानिनः अन्त्यात् अचः परं सः भवति। अयञ्च नियमः परिभाषासूत्रद्वयेन निर्दिष्टः - 'आद्यन्तौ टकितौ' (१.१.४६) 'मिदचोऽन्त्यात्परः' (१.१.४७) इति। तद्यथा -

1. 'आर्धधातुकस्य इड् वलादेः' (७.२.३५) इत्यत्र इ-इत्यागमः 'ट्'-इत्युप- सामग्र्या सूचितः। अतः वलादेः आर्धधातुकस्य स्थानिनः आदौ इ-इत्यागमः भवति। 'लव् ता' इति स्थिते 'ता'रूपस्थानिनः आदौ इडागमे 'लव् इता = लविता' इति भवति।
2. 'भियो हेतुभये षुक्' (७.३.४०) इत्यत्र 'ष्'-इत्यागमः 'क्'-इत्युपसामग्र्या सूचितः। अतः हेतुभयार्थकभीधातोः स्थानिनः अन्ते 'ष्'-इत्यागमः भवति। भीषयते इत्यत्र भी-धातोः परः 'ष्'-इत्यागमः भवति।
3. 'नपुंसकस्य झलचः' (नुम्) (७.१.७२) इत्यत्र न्-इत्यागमः म्-इत्युपसामग्र्या सूचितः। अतः नपुंसकस्य झलन्तस्य स्थानिनः अन्त्यात् अचः परः 'न्'-इत्यागमो भवति। 'यशांसि' इत्यत्र 'यशस्' इत्यस्य नपुंसकस्य झलन्तस्य स्थानिनः अन्त्यात् 'अ'-इति अचः परः 'न्'-इत्यागमः भवति।

द्वितीयप्रकारेऽयं विशेषः। तत्रत्यसूत्रेषु स्थानी न निर्दिष्टः। पञ्चमीविभक्त्या सूचितात् निमित्तात् परः व्यापारः भवतीत्येतन्मात्रं गम्यते। ततश्च निमित्तात् परः आगमः भवति। स्थानी तु अभावरूपः। शून्यस्योपरि आगमः इति वेदितव्यम्। तद्यथा-

'स्त्रियां क्तिन्' (३.३.९४) इत्यनेन 'क्तिन्' इति प्रत्ययस्यागमः विधीयते। पराधिकारे वर्तमानत्वेन सूचितः। विवृतमेतत् काशिकायाम् (Mishra 1979)- "भावे अकर्तरि च कारके ति वर्तते। स्त्रीलिङ्गे भावादौ धातोः क्तिन् प्रत्ययो भवति। कृतिः।" इति। 'कृञ्'[1] इत्यस्माद्धातोः परः 'ति'[2] इत्यागमः भवति। 'कृतिः' इति शब्दः निष्पद्यते।

तृतीयप्रकारे तु द्वित्वं साक्षान्निर्दिष्टमित्युक्तम्। द्वित्वं नाम वर्णानां द्विवारमुच्चारणम्। तद्यथा-

'एकाचो द्वे प्रथमस्य' (६.१.१)। विवृतम् एतत् काशिकायाम्- "अधिकारोऽयम्। एकाचः इति च, द्वे इति च, प्रथमस्य इति च त्रितयम् अधिकृतं वेदितव्यम्। इत उत्तरं यद् वक्ष्यामः प्राक् सम्प्रसारणविधानात् तत्र एकाचः प्रथमस्य द्वे भवतः इत्येवं तद् वेदितव्यम्। वक्ष्यति 'लिटि धातोरनभ्यासस्य' (६.१.८) इति। तत्र धातोरवयवस्य अनभ्यासस्य प्रथमस्य एकाचो द्वे भवतः। जजागार। पपाच। इयाय। आर।"

4.2 आदेशः (Substitution)

अयं व्यापारः उत्सर्गतः प्राप्तः। उपसामग्रि आगमस्य सूचनाभावे लोपरूपव्यापारस्य चानिर्देशे तत्सूत्रसूचितः व्यापारः आदेशरूप इत्यर्थः। त्रिविधाः आदेशाः परिभाषासूत्रचतुष्टयेन निर्दिष्टाः। स्थानिनः देशविशेषनिमित्तकः अयं विभागः।

---

[1]कृञ् इत्यत्र 'ञ्' इत्येतत् उपसामग्रि भवति।

[2]क्तिन् इत्यत्र 'क्', 'न्' इत्येते उपसामग्रि भवतः।

1. उत्सर्गतः स्थानिनः अन्त्यवर्णस्य आदेशः भवति।
   तदुक्तं 'अलोऽन्त्यस्य'(१.१.५२) इति परिभाषासूत्रे। तद्यथा -
   'इद्गोण्याः' (१.२.५०) इत्यत्र पञ्चगोणीशब्दस्य 'ई' इत्यस्य अन्त्यवर्णस्य 'इ' इत्यादेशः भवति- पञ्चगोणि। अपि च 'ङ्' इत्युपसामग्रिसूचित आदेशश्च अन्त्यवर्णस्यैव भवति।
   तदुक्तं 'ङिच्च' (१.१.५३) इति परिभाषासूत्रे। तद्यथा-
   'देवताद्वन्द्वे च' (आनङ्) (६.३.२६) इत्यत्र इन्द्रश्च वरुणश्च इत्यत्र द्वन्द्वे इन्द्रशब्दस्य अन्त्यवर्णस्य 'आ' इत्यादेशः भवति - इन्द्रावरुणौ।
2. यदा सहकारिणः अनेकवर्णत्वं 'श् '-इत्युपसामग्रियुक्तत्वं वा अस्ति तदा सर्वस्य स्थानिनः आदेशः भवति। तदुक्तं 'अनेकाल्शित्सर्वस्य' (१.१.५५) इति परिभाषासूत्रे। तद्यथा-

   'अस्तेः भूः' (२.४.५२) इत्यत्र 'अस् ' धातोः 'भू' इत्यादेशो भवति सहकारिणः 'भू' इत्यस्य अनेकवर्णत्वात् सर्वस्य तद्भवति - भविता। 'जश्शसोः शिः' (७.१.२०) इत्यत्र जश्शसोः 'इ' इत्यादेशो भवति सहकारिणः 'इ' इत्यस्य 'श् ' इत्युपसामग्रियुक्तत्वात् सर्वस्य तद्भवति -कुण्डानि।
3. यत्र पञ्चमीनिर्देशः तत्परे शिष्यमाणं कार्यं परस्य आदेः वर्णस्य भवति। तदुक्तं 'आदेः परस्य' (१.१.५४) इति परिभाषासूत्रे। तद्यथा-
   'ईदासः' (७.२.८३) इत्यत्र पञ्चमीनिर्दिष्टात् 'आस् ' इत्यस्मात् परस्य 'अन' इत्यस्य आदेः 'अ' इति वर्णस्य 'ई' इत्यादेशो भवति - आसीनः।

4.3 लोपः (Elision)

प्रसक्तस्य वर्णस्य अदर्शनं लोप इत्युच्यते। अयं व्यापारः आदेशरूपव्यापारस्य प्रकारविशेष इत्यपि विश्लेषितुं शक्यते। शून्येन आदेशः इत्यर्थः। प्रायः लोप इति कण्ठत एव लोपविधानं भवति। तद्यथा - 'लोपः शाकल्यस्य' (8.3.19) इत्यत्र 'द्वाव् अत्र' इति स्थिते वकारस्य लोपविधानात् 'द्वा अत्र' इति भवति।

क्वचित् प्रत्ययानां लोपविधाने लुक्, श्लु, लुप् इत्येतैः लोपः विधीयते। तत्र एतत्संज्ञाविशेषैः निर्देशनं प्रत्ययलोपे कृते प्रत्ययहेतुकं कार्यं भवतीति सूचनार्थम्। तदुक्तं - 'प्रत्ययस्य लुक्श्लुलुपः' (१.१.६१), 'प्रत्ययलोपे प्रत्ययलक्षणम् ' (१.१.६२) इति।

4.3.1 विरोधपरिहारोपायः (Conflict Resolution Strategy)

यन्त्रप्रणयनपद्धतौ विरोधपरिहारस्यावश्यकत्वं पूर्वमुक्तम् (sec. 2.1.1, p. 119)। तस्य पद्धतिः विधिकल्पश्च इदानीं विव्रियेते। अनेकसूत्राणाम् औचित्यसद्भावे एकस्यैव निर्णयाय अस्योपयोगः। तन्निर्णयश्च द्वेधा। सूत्रेभ्यः परिभाषाभ्यश्च। उत्सर्गापवादन्यायेन सिद्धासिद्धन्यायेन च परिहारः सूत्रेभ्य एव सूचित इति भाति। तथापि तन्निर्णयप्रकारः न साक्षादुक्तः।

साक्षात्तु 'विप्रतिषेधे परं कार्यम्' (१.४.२) इति सूत्रमात्रमुपलभ्यते। सूत्राणां विरोधे सति परं सूत्रं बलीय इति तस्यार्थः। सम्प्रदायस्तु अयं नियमः सर्वत्र विरोधपरिहारे उपयुज्यते इति मन्यते। तथापीदं सूत्रं एकसंज्ञाधिकारे एव प्रवर्तते न तु सर्वत्रानुस्यूतमित्याधुनिकाः। ततश्च कण्ठतः कश्चिदपि विरोधपरिहारोपायः सूत्रैः एवोक्त इति तु न सर्वाभिमतम्। तत्र परिभाषा (Keilhorn 1985, Abhyankar 1967) एव शरणम्। सङ्गणकीयतन्त्रदृष्ट्या अस्य विरोधपरिहारोपायस्य विचारः अस्माभिरन्यत्र (Subbanna & Varakhedi 2009) कृतः।

5 उपसंहारः

अष्टाध्यायी किञ्चित् स्वयंचलद्यन्त्रमिव सङ्गणकप्रतिमानरूपेणानुचिन्तयितुमनुरूपा भवतीति प्रतिपादितम्। तस्यां च अष्टाध्याय्यां विद्यमानाः काश्चित् कल्पनाः संज्ञा प्रक्रियेत्यादयः सङ्गणकशास्त्रस्योचितकल्पनाभिः उपसामग्रि (metadata), निष्पादनयन्त्रपरिकल्पनं (concept of production system) च विवृतम्। तेन च पाणिनेः सङ्गणकमूलतत्त्वपरिकल्पनं स्पष्टमासीदिति विज्ञायते। यच्च परिकल्पनं अत्याधुनिकं तत् त्रिसहस्रवर्षेभ्यः प्रागपि पाणिन्युपज्ञमिति साधितम्। अहो भारतीयविज्ञानवैभवम्!

References

1. Abhyankar K.V. Paribhāṣāsaṁgraha, Bhandarkar Research Institute, Poona, 1967.
2. Bullinaria, John A. `http://www.cs.bham.ac.uk/~jxb/IAI/w7.pdf`, 2005
3. Giri, S.P., Satyanarayanashastri, पाणिनीयः अष्टाध्यायी , Krishnadas Academy, Varanasi, 1984.
4. Kalpan, Randy M. Constructing Language Processors for Little Languages , John Wiley and Sons, New York, 1994.
5. Kielhorn, F. Paribhāṣenduśekhara of Nāgojibhaṭṭa, Parimal Publications, Delhi, 1985.
6. Mishra, Srinarayana. Kāśikā, Chaukhamba Samskrita Samsthan, Varanasi, 1979.
7. Subbanna, Sridhar and Shrinivasa Varakhedi. Computational Structure of the Aṣṭādhyāyī and Conflict Resolution Techniques, Springer Third International Symposium, Hyderabad, pp. 56-65, Hyderabad, 2009.
8. Subbanna, Sridhar and Shrinivasa Varakhedi. Asiddhatva Principle in Computational Model of Aṣṭādhyāyī, Springer Fourth International Symposium, New Delhi, pp. 231-38, New Delhi, 2010.

Completeness Analysis of a Sanskrit Reader

Pawan Goyal and Gérard Huet

INRIA Paris-Rocquencourt,
BP 105, 78153 Le Chesnay Cedex, France

Abstract. We analyse in this paper differences of linguistic treatment of Sanskrit in the Sanskrit Heritage platform[1] and in the Pāṇinian grammatical tradition.

1 General Methodology

The general assumption behind the design of the Heritage Sanskrit Reader is that sentences from classical Sanskrit may be generated as the image by a regular relation R of the Kleene closure W^* of a regular set W of *words* over a finite alphabet Σ. Think of W as the vocabulary of (inflected) words (*pada*s) and of R as *sandhi.*

The computerized lexer underlying the Heritage Reader essentially proceeds by inverting relation R over the candidate sentence w in order to produce a finite sequence w_1,w_2,..., w_n of word forms, together with a proof that $w \in R(w_1 \cdot w_2 \cdot ... \cdot w_n)$. The word forms w_i must be justified being valid word forms of Sanskrit (i.e. *pada*s), and some justification must be offered that the combination of such word forms makes sense. The first justification consists in exhibiting w_i as the lemmatization of some root stem, according to valid rules of morphology. The second justification consists in giving some dependency analysis of sentence w using assignments of semantic roles for the individual w_i's consistent with their morphological analysis. Both kinds of justifications must be ultimately related to the traditional methods of Sanskrit grammar (*vyākaraṇa*). That is, that each w_i corresponds to some w_i', obtainable by a valid Pāṇinian derivation sequence, and that the concatenation of the sequence

[1] `http://sanskrit.inria.fr`

$w'_1, w'_2, ..., w'_n$ yields by some valid Pāṇinian derivation a final sequence of phonemes w' equivalent in a strong sense to the original w.

Thus, to fix ideas with a concrete trivial example, the sentence (in Roman transliteration):
rāmogrāmaṃgacchati, equivalently represented as:
rāmogrāmaṅgacchati[2], may be analysed as the sequence:
[*rāmaḥ* { nom. sg. m. }[*rāma*]⟨aḥ|g →og⟩]
[*grāmam* { acc. sg. m. }[*grāma*]⟨m|g →ṅg⟩]
[*gacchati* { pr. [1]ac. sg. 3 }[*gam*]⟨⟩]

where the various forms are lemmatizations of the basic stems (*prātipadikas*) *rāma*, *grāma* and the root *gam*, respectively. The root *gam* (to go) being transitive (*sakarmaka*) and its form *gacchati* being in the active voice, we may assign the agent role (*kartṛ*) to the nominative form *rāmaḥ* and the goal role (*karman*) to the accusative form *grāmam*, yielding the interpretation "Rāma goes to the village". It should then be a routine exercise (for a *vyākaraṇa* specialist) to use the sequence of lemmas and phonetic rewrite rules as a guide to the generation of a Pāṇinian derivation of the original sentence.

The method looks hardly original, in view of modern computational linguistics, and it could be applied *mutatis mutandis* to many natural languages, with Σ representing the set of phonemes of the language, W being the vocabulary of (inflected) words and R being some phonetic smoothing (called *sandhi* in Sanskrit). Often, at least in Western languages such as English or French, the phonetic treatment is given separately as a layer of speech understanding, words are strings over an alphabet of written characters, isolated by blanks in the written sentence, and more importance is assigned to a structural notion of *syntax* where word order is important. The basic assumption is that there is a clear hierar-

[2] The normalization procedure implemented in the Heritage Reader, where the *anusvāra* before a consonant is replaced by the homogeneous nasal of the consonant, corresponds to the following rule in Pāṇini's grammar:

8.4.58 *anusvārasya yayi parasavarṇaḥ*: In *saṁhitā*, if *ṁ* is followed by a consonant in *pratyāhāra yay*, it is replaced by the homophonic nasal of the consonant.

chy of levels of linguistic description (traditionally called phonetics, phonemics, morphology, syntax, semantics, pragmatics), corresponding to more or less modular computational processes, and that the interfaces between these processes are the essential components allowing generation in one direction, and analysis in the reverse direction in a general model of universal linguistics. It could thus appear that the treatment of Sanskrit is just slightly biased, in having a significant *sandhi* component because of the faithfulness of its written representation to oral enunciation, and in having a shallow *syntactic* component because of the richness of its morphology. Indeed, the treatment of Sanskrit linguistics by Paul Kiparsky (2009) is essentially a precise elaboration of such processes, at least in the synthesis direction. One is thus hardly surprised at the general presentation of the methodology.

However, things are not that simple. For one thing, if this methodology was straightforward, one wonders why the traditional methods of linguistics analysis (*vyākaraṇa*) do not explain sentence formation in this simple, intuitive, modular fashion. Indeed, the traditional Pāṇinian presentation of Sanskrit grammar by the trinity of the three sages (*trimuni*) of ancient India is an extremely complex interweaving of formal transformations operating at all levels in parallel, and it has been copiously criticized by linguists of the nineteenth century such as Whitney. However, there exists to this date no grammatical description of Sanskrit that is as precise and as complete as the traditional one, and Sanskrit grammar experts well aware of modern linguistics theories such as George Cardona and Peter Scharf (2009) maintain that mixing of levels is unavoidable for accounting for the complexity of Sanskrit grammar. Thus it remains a challenge to provide a modular description of computational linguistics processes adequate to recognize correct Sanskrit sentences, and there is to this date no better justification of such than to relate their operations to that of the tradition. We shall attempt to meet this challenge in the present paper, and to provide a rationale for the completeness of the Heritage Reader with respect to a well-identified subset of classical Sanskrit.

2 Morphology

2.1 Limiting the Recursion

The first difficulty we are facing is in the definition of the set W of *words* (*padas*). It cannot simply be explained as the set of inflected forms of a finite set of "atomic" words. For instance, it is possible to form compounds of arbitrary length, making the set of substantive bases (*prātipadikas*) infinite. Furthermore, the process of turning a substantive base into a denominative verb is productive,[3] even for compounds, although this last possibility is infrequent. If we examine the diagram given in (Kulkarni and Shukl, 2009), which purports to explain the recursive structure of Sanskrit morphology as authorized by the traditional grammar, it seems hopeless to invert it directly in order to obtain a complete parser. By contrast, the (simplified) finite-state diagram underlying the Heritage transducer given in Fig.1 reduces drastically the allowed recursions. For one thing, it forbids denominative verbal forms, except for the conjugated forms of a finite set of lexicalized verbal stems. Also,

[3] As per Pāṇini's grammar, the main *sūtras* corresponding to the nominal verbs ordain six different suffixes:

- *kyac*: 3.1.8 *supaḥ ātmanaḥ kyac*. E.g. *ātmanaḥ putram icchati* →*putrīyati*.
- *kāmyac*: 3.1.9 *kāmyac ca*. E.g. *ātmanaḥ putram icchati* →*putrakāmyati*.
- *kyaṅ*: 3.1.11 *kartuḥ kyaṅ salopaḥ ca*. E.g. *śyena iva ācarati* →*śyenāyate*.
- *kyaṣ*: 3.1.13 *lohitādiḍājbhyaḥ kyaṣ*. E.g. *alohito lohito bhavati* →*lohitāyate*.
- *ṇiṅ*: 3.1.20 *pucchabhāṇḍacīvarāt ṇiṅ*. E.g. *puccham udasyati* →*utpucchayate*.
- *ṇic*: 3.1.21 *muṇḍamiśraślakṣṇalavaṇavratavastrahalakalakṛtatūstebhyaḥ ṇic*. E.g. *miśraṃ karoti* →*miśrayati*.

Suffix *ṇiṅ* is specific only to three nominal bases, *kyaṣ* is specific to the *lohitādigaṇa*, while the other suffixes are applicable to any nominal base. Among these suffixes, the suffix *ṇic* is the most productive and there is a *gaṇasūtra: tatkaroti tadācaṣṭe*, which specifies this suffix after any nominal base in the sense of 'he does that', 'he behaves like', 'he says that'.

it makes many assumptions on compounding which must be explained and justified.

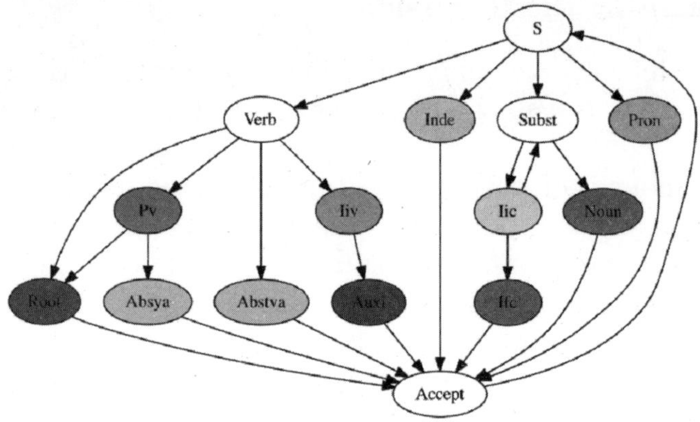

Fig. 1: A simplified lexical analyser

Let us explain briefly Fig.1, in order to relate it to the traditional terminology. Each colored oval, called a *phase* of the underlying automaton, corresponds to a finite set of forms. Going from top (node S) to bottom (node Accept) consists in following the arcs, selecting forms from the intervening phases, and glueing them with *sandhi*, in order to obtain one word (*pada*). The subdiagram below the Subst node builds substantival forms (*subantas*). The subdiagram below the Verb node builds verbal forms (*tiṅanta*s). The Inde node builds indeclinable forms, the Pron node builds pronominal forms. Phase Noun contains declined forms of autonomous atomic substantive and adjective stems, found in the lexicon with their attested gender parameters. Phase Ifc contains the non-autonomous ones, usable only as the right-hand component of a compound, such as root substantival forms, *-gam* (gone to). Phase Iic contains bare stems of nouns (*prātipadikas*) such as *deva-*. Phase Root contains conjugated forms of roots, phase Pv contains attested sequences of preverbs (*upasarga*s) such as *ā, sam, nirā*, and *samabhivyā*. Phase Auxi contains conjugated forms of the three auxiliary roots *bhū*, *as* and *kr̥*, phase Iiv contains periphrastic forms of a substantive formed with an *-ī* suffix (technically designated as *cvi* in Pāṇinian terminology). The path Iiv-Auxi allows generation of compound verbal forms such as *pavitrīkaroti* (he purifies). Phase Inde contains a mix of indeclinable forms, such as grammatical words (*ca, vā, api*, etc.) and adverbs (*yathā*). Absolutives in *-tvā* (*kr̥tvā*) are stored in Abstva, whereas absolutives in *-ya*, necessarily prefixed with a preverb, are put in phase Absya. Infinitive forms (*kartum*), which may or may not be prefixed with a preverb, appear both in Inde and in Absya.

This diagram is a simplification of the actual automaton transition graph of the Sanskrit Heritage lexical analyser, that has numerous other phase databanks to account for constructions such as periphrastic perfect, but it suffices to give a general idea and start the discussion.

2.2 Morphology Generation

Each of the coloured nodes of the diagram of Fig.1 represents a databank of forms. These data banks are filled in during a series of preliminary passes. First the lexicon is analysed to gather stems and their morphological parameters, such as permitted genders of nominal stems, allowed present classes (*gaṇa*) and attested preverbs for roots. In a second phase, more stem generation occurs for roots, accounting for the various tenses/moods (*lakāra*s), as well as absolutives and infinitives, but also participles (adjectival *kṛdanta*s) in ten varieties. Finally, inflexional morphology paradigms derive the inflected forms according to the morphological parameters, some of which being read from the lexicon, some of which being defined in specific tables.

It is not simple to relate our paradigmatic derivations and the operations of Pāṇinian grammar. Some stem operations relate to morpho-phonetic operations well identified in the central rules (*sūtra*s), such as taking the phonetic grades of *guṇa* or *vṛddhi*. Some are dispersed in various parts of the grammar such as stem substitutions. Still others, such as retroflexion, occur in the final section (*tripādī*) of the *Aṣṭādhyāyī*, which comprises a list of rewrite rules which are applied iteratively at the end of the derivation process, in some kind of "phonetic smoothing" phase. Since the forms stored in our databanks are to be matched to the surface realization of the sentence, this phonetic smoothing must be applied at the time of generation of these forms. Some careful analysis must be done in order to understand the mutual interaction of the retroflexion rules and of the external *sandhi* rules (which are used in segmentation in the Heritage Reader). This analysis will be given in Section 4.4 below.

The main discrepancy between the Pāṇinian processes and our reader operations is in the order of rewritings. Often the *sūtras* relevant to a given operation are dispersed in different sections of the *Aṣṭādhyāyī*, and thus it is hard to give the trace of the needed *sūtras*. However, in many cases, one can recognize the *sūtra* operations from the computer program. A complete analysis, in the specific case of future passive participles in *-ya* (*yat, kyap, ṇyat*), is given in Appendix A.

2.3 Variations in *Sandhi*

One related difficulty concerns the precise definition of the *sandhi* relation labeling implicitly the arcs of the diagram. For most arcs, it is what Western linguists call "external *sandhi*". However, for the arcs issued from the Pv phase, it adds retroflexion rules, necessary to explain verbal forms of verbs (or participles) prefixed by preverb sequences. Furthermore, the forms stored in the various databanks (Noun, etc.) use such retroflexion rules in the formation of their stems and of their inflexions.

The correctness and completeness of our method involves thus a careful assessment of the mutual interaction (feeding, bleeding) between the rules of the morpho-phonetic processes of stem formation and inflection, the rules of external *sandhi*, and the final *tripādī* rules.

3 Specific Problems of Compounding

3.1 Pre-Compounds vs. Compounds

Another set of difficulties concerns compounding. First of all, what our analyser recognizes by using the loop going through phase Iic in Fig. 1 is not strictly speaking a compound (*samāsa*), but what we call a *pre-compound* a mere sequence of Iic bare stems ended in an inflected substantival form. Several possible compounds may be mapped to a unique pre-compound, representing the common frontier of the corresponding binary trees. Thus the sequence *ānandamayakośaḥ* will parse as a unique pre-compound *ānanda-maya-kośaḥ*, which has two possible interpretations as compositions of binary compounding, one of which is the intended one (*ānanda*<*maya*)<*kośa* in Gillon's notation (2009). This has advantages (a unique pre-compound parse instead of C_n parses of an $n+1$-component compound, where C_n, the $_{n^th}$ Catalan number, is an exponential function of n, as explained in (Huet, 2009), and drawbacks (some ulterior computation will be needed in order to resolve the ambiguity if one wants to get a handle on its meaning). Only at this ulterior stage one will be able to relate the precise compound construction to the relevant *sūtra*s.

3.2 Forms Allowed as Left Components of Compounds

Heritage Treatment

Another problem is that the left component of a compound is not always a bare stem - it may be a gendered stem (e.g. *durgāpūjā*). It may even be a fully inflected form, like in so-called *aluk* compounds such as *gavāmayana* ("cows' travel" or year), where *gavām* is the genitive plural of *go*. We consider this last construction as non-productive and assume that the finite set of such attested frozen forms is lexicalized. Other possible left components of compounds are particles which are not bare stems of stand-alone substantives, such as *su, vi, dur*. They must be accommodated in the Iic bank.

Aṣṭādhyāyī Treatment

The left component of a compound may undergo some operations as enumerated in Pāṇini's grammar and, therefore, is not always a bare stem. First, we have the problem of *aluk* compounds, where Iic can be a fully inflected form. The rules corresponding to *aluk* compounds are discussed in Pāṇini from 6.3.1 to 6.3.24. For example:

> 6.3.4 *manasaḥ saṁjñāyām*: *aluk* applies to a *tr̥tīyā*, which occurs after *manas*, when a constituent in combination follows and the derivate denotes a *saṁjñā*. Thus, *manasādattā*. The Iic *manasā* is the inflected form of *manas* in instrumental case (*tr̥tīyā*).
>
> 6.3.7 *vaiyākaraṇākhyāyāṃ caturthyāḥ*: *aluk* applies to a dative form (*caturthī*), which occurs after *ātman*, when a constituent in combination follows and the derivate denotes a

name assigned by the grammarians. Thus, *ātmanepadam*. The Iic *ātmane* is the inflected form of *ātman* in *caturthī*.

Similar to the rules as enumerated above, the rules for *aluk* compounds are very specific and generate a finite set of compounds. Thus, this formation is non-productive and as a design decision in the Heritage system, we consider these compounds as frozen expressions and the finite set of these forms is lexicalized.

Another problem is that in some cases, the Iic stems may undergo some changes and may not be the same as the bare stem. These cases correspond to Pāṇini's rules 6.3.25 to 6.3.139. For example:

> 6.3.52 *pādasya padājyātigopahateṣu*: The word *pāda* is replaced by *pada*, when *āji*, *āti*, *ga* or *upahata* combine to follow. Thus *padopahataḥ*, *padagaḥ*.
> 6.3.70 *kāre satyāgadasya*: Augment *mum* is introduced to *satya* and *agada*, when *kāra* combines to follow. Thus *satyaṅkāraḥ*.

Similar to these rules, the rules in this section ordain various changes in the Iic of a compound. While most of the rules in this section are non-productive and the cases like 6.3.52 are being taken care of by declaring additional Iic stem *pada* for the word *pāda*, some of the rules which are productive and may require special treatment are:

> 6.3.34 *striyāḥ puṁvat bhāṣitapuṁskādanūṅ samānādhikaraṇe striyām apūraṇīpriyādiṣu*: In the place of a feminine word, the corresponding masculine form is substituted, when the feminine word has an actual corresponding masculine and does not end in the suffix *ūṅ*, if followed by another feminine word, but not when this word ends in a *pūraṇa* suffix or belongs to the list headed by *priyā*. Thus, *darśanīyabhāryā* and not *darśanīyābhāryā*.
> 6.3.61 *ikaḥ hrasvaḥ aṅyaḥ gālavasya*: The final of a nominal which ends in a vowel belonging to the *pratyāhāra ik*, with the exception of *ṅī*, is optionally replaced by its short counterpart in the opinion of Gālava. Thus, *grāmaṇiputraḥ* and *grāmaṇīputraḥ*.

A careful assessment of the rule 6.3.34 reveals that we actually take care of the words generated using this rule without any special treatment. The Iic stems which may qualify for this rule are those feminine stems, which have been derived from a masculine stem and as a result of this rule application, these stems will be substituted by their masculine stems. In the Heritage system, the corresponding masculine forms will always be stored in the Iic banks and thus, analysing these compounds will not raise a special problem.

The case with the rule 6.3.61 is different because the Iic stem is shortened and may not be present in our Iic bank. However, this is an optional rule and some statistics from the corpora is required to figure out the productive nature of this optional shortening.

3.3 Forms Allowed as Right Components of Compounds

Heritage Treatment

Still another problem concerns the forms allowed as right components of compounds. Sometimes, and this is the case of the important class of *tatpuruṣa* compounds, there is gender preservation of the right component. We are thus assured of finding the corresponding form in the Noun database, which contain forms of words consistent with their lexicalized gender. But this is not true of the exocentric (*bahuvrīhi*) compounds, where a substantive may be lifted to an adjective used in a different gender, such as *caturmukhaḥ* "who has four heads", since *mukhaḥ* is not an autonomous form of neuter stem *mukha*. This forces us to add forms such as *mukhaḥ* to the Ifc database. A similar problem arises with the so-called *avyayībhāva* compounds, where an adverb "turns to indeclinable" its right component, usually by coining a neuter-like form, like in *yathāśraddham* (according to your convictions), where the right component is similar to the accusative form of a hypothetical neuter stem *śraddha* induced from the originally lexicalized feminine stem *śraddhā*.

Aṣṭādhyāyī Treatment

Pāṇini's *sūtra* 2.2.24 (*anekam anyapadārthe*) states that many syntactically related *pada*s combine in a *bahuvrīhi* compound and the compound denotes the meaning of something other than its own constituents. Therefore, it acts as an adjective and, like other adjectives in Sanskrit, can take any gender.

In the case of *avyayībhāva* compounds, the Ifc is changed to neuter (shortened)[4] and the compound gets the *saṁjñā* '*avyaya*'[5] and, therefore, the nominal case ending is deleted.[6] Some exceptions where the nominal case ending is not deleted are stated in the following rule:

> 2.4.83 *na avyayībhāvāt ataḥ am tu apañcamyāḥ*: A case ending occurring after an *avyayībhāva* compound is not deleted when the compound ends in *a*, instead the case ending is replaced by *am* except when it is in ablative (*pañcamī*).

The generation of *avyayībhāva* compounds can be implemented by adding two phases. The first phase corresponds to the possible left-hand sides which can be listed as a finite set of words, corresponding to the *sūtras* 2.1.5 to 2.1.19, such as {*adhi, pari, anu, antar, upa, su, dur, nir, ati, iti, tat, prati, yathā, sa, yāvat, apa, bahir, prāk, ā, abhi, pāre, madhye*} and the set of numbers. The second phase corresponds to the forms of the second component, which must be constructed from ordinary *prātipadika*s by various changes, as described in the grammar. If the *prātipadika* ends in a long vowel, it is changed to the corresponding short vowel (neuter stem). Some other stem changes are described in the rules 5.4.107 to 5.4.112. For example:

> 5.4.107 *avyayībhāve śaratprabhr̥tibhyaḥ*: For the *prātipadika*s listed in the *śaradādigaṇa*, the suffix *ṭac* is added. Thus, *śarad* can be stored as *śaradam*, obtained by the following sequence:
> *śarad* + *ṭac* $\xrightarrow{5.4.107}$ *śarada* $\xrightarrow{2.4.83}$ *śaradam.*
> 5.4.111 *jhayaḥ*: For the *prātipadika*s ending in a consonant belonging to *pratyāhāra jhay* (the first four letters of the sound classes), a suffix *ṭac* (*a*) is optionally added. Thus, the right hand side corresponding to *sarit* can be stored as two forms {*sarit, saritam*}, where *saritam* is obtained by the same process as described above for *śaradam.*

---

[4] 2.4.18 *avyayībhāvaḥ ca* and 1.2.47 *hrasvaḥ napuṁsake prātipadikasya*
[5] 2.1.5 *avyayībhāvaḥ*
[6] 2.4.82 *avyayāt āpsupaḥ*

In effect, the forms of the second component correspond to the following two-stage method:

1. Stem changes from long to short and other changes as prescribed in the rules 5.4.107 to 5.4.112.
2. If the stem obtained from the first step ends in *a*, add the suffix *am* to it.

3.4 Intra-Compound *Sandhi*

Finally, we have to make sure that the components of a compound are glued together according to the *sandhi* rules that are assumed by our transition transducer. In general, external *sandhi* is used. However, it may happen that retroflexion occurs, as in *rāmāyaṇa*, which is therefore not obtainable by external *sandhi* from its components *rāma* and *ayana*. We shall assume that such frozen forms, usually occurring only in proper names, are not the result of a productive process, and can be obtained by proper lexicalization. But another class of compounds, called *prādi* compounds, take retroflexion regularly. This is specially frequent with participles prefixed with preverbs, but also with other primary substantival formations (*kr̥dantas*) from roots. In order to deal with those, we have to introduce new databanks of participial forms, accessible from yet another copy of preverb sequences, with retroflexion allowed on the corresponding transition, as shown in the more complete state diagram of Fig. 2. This extension demanded an extension of our morphological generator, which had to provide derivational morphology and not just flexional morphology. The *aṣṭādhyāyī* treatment of the retroflexion across word and compound boundaries has been dealt with exclusively in Section 4.4.

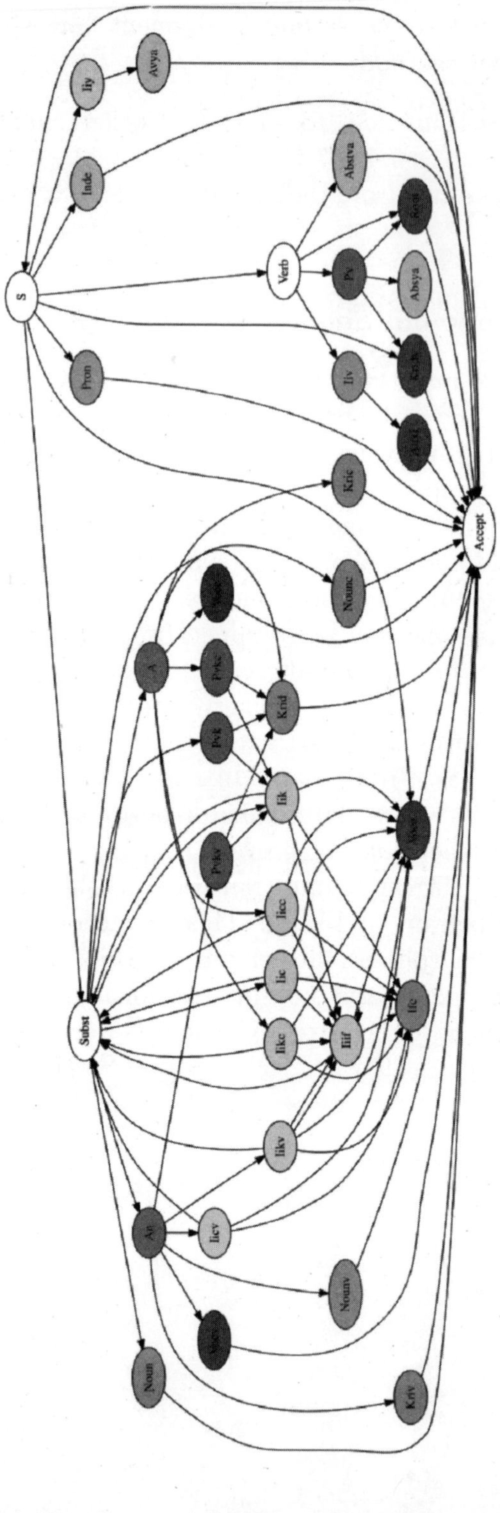

Fig. 2: A more complete lexical analyser.

Such intricate problems of compounding have already been discussed at length in other papers. We shall concentrate in the following on the justification that the morpho-phonetic devices used in our parser are indeed consistent, from both points of view of correctness and of completeness, with the rules defined in the *Aṣṭādhyāyī*, specially in view of their different order of application.

4 Completeness of the Segmenter

4.1 Basic Zen Technology

The Heritage platform is based on a functional toolkit for computational linguistics called Zen (Huet, 2002). This technology builds on a central applicative data structure of *tries* or lexical trees. Tries are a commonly used data structure for representing lexicons. One may see a trie as a deterministic finite state automaton recognizing the lexicon as a regular set of words. The maximal sharing of this data structure obtained by representing the underlying tree as a dag (directed acyclic graph) yields the corresponding minimal automaton. The Zen toolkit generalizes this observation to the case of general (i.e. possibly infinite) regular sets by representing the control graph of finite state machines such as finite automata and transducers as an annotated trie, amenable to optimum sharing as well. Furthermore, automata and transducers are seen as specific instantiations of very general relational abstract machines, called effective Eilenberg machines, admitting uniform simulators (Huet and Razet, 2006).

The first real-scale application of this Zen technology was to show how to solve efficiently the inverse problem of external *sandhi* (Huet, 2005), represented as a *juncture rewrite system*. Let us recall briefly the key notions.

We model external *sandhi* with rewrite rules of the form $u|v \rightarrow w$, where u, v and w are words (standing for strings of phonemes). Such a rule represents the rational relation that holds between all pairs of strings (from now on we use strings and words interchangeably) $\lambda u|v\rho$ and $\lambda w\rho$, for λ and ρ any strings. The symbol $|$ stands for word juncture. The *sandhi* problem may then be posed as a regular expression problem, namely the correspondance between $(L \cdot |)^*$ and Σ^* by relation $\mathcal{R}$, where Σ is the word alphabet (our extended phoneme alphabet), L is the set of inflected forms generated from the lexicon, and $\mathcal{R}$ is the rational relation that is the concatenation closure of the union of the rational relations corresponding to the *sandhi* rules. This presentation is a standard one since the classic work of Kaplan and Kay (1994).

Note that the *sandhi* problem is expressed in a symmetric way. Going from $z_1|z_2|..., z_n| \in (L \cdot |)^*$ to $s \in \Sigma^*$ is generating a correct enunciation s with word forms $z_1, z_2, ...z_n$, using the *sandhi* transformations. Whereas going the other way means analysing the sentence s as a possible phonemic stream using words from the lexicon as amalgamated by *sandhi*. It is this second problem (*sandhi viccheda*) we are interested in solving, since *sandhi*, while basically deterministic in generation, is strongly ambiguous in analysis.

Huet (2005) explains how to use the Zen toolkit to perform this analysis automatically. It then goes on to give a formal justification of the methodology, under two assumptions, called *strictness* and *non-overlapping*. In a nutshell, the algorithm is sound (all outputs are plausible solutions in the sense of yielding the input sentence by *sandhi*), complete (all such solutions are enumerated), and terminating (the set of solutions is finite and the enumeration algorithm always terminates). Let us now examine the correctness assumptions. The strictness condition is simply that in every *sandhi* rule $u|v \rightarrow w$ the right-hand side word w is not empty and this is trivially satisfied. The non-overlapping condition involves both the lexicon L component and the rewrite rule R component. It expresses that there can be overlap of juncture rules of R within one word of L. We say that there is overlapping of rules $u|v \rightarrow w$ and $u'|v' \rightarrow w'$ within word $z \in L$ whenever the right-hand side v of the first rule, initial substring of z, overlaps with the terminal substring of z identical with the left-hand side u' of the second rule: $|z| < |v| + |u'|$. In other words, the first rule potentially *bleeds* the second one (in the sense of blocking its application). Since rules of external *sandhi* are very local ($|v| = 1$, and $|u| = 1$ or $u = a\d{h}$ or $u = \bar{a}\d{h}$), such overlapping can occur only for very short words in L, of length at most 2. Furthermore, since neither *aḥ* nor *āḥ* are legal autonomous forms, this leaves us to consider only the rare words of length 1. There are basically two such words to consider in classical Sanskrit, besides the Vedic exclamation u which is not used in an autonomous manner in classical Sanskrit, but only in combination with other particles, marking a hiatus situation not amenable to *sandhi* (*pragṛhya*). These two words are the preverb/preposition *ā*, and the negation prefix *a*. We shall deal with these two monophonemic words in the following two sections.

4.2 Phantom Phonemes

We are dealing in this section with *sandhi* interference in the case of the *ā* preverb. Let us start with an example, the simple imperative sentence "come here". The sentence is built up from the word *iha* (here) and the imperative form *ihi* of root *i* (to go), prefixed by preverb *ā*. If we build the imperative form *ehi* (come), and consider the sequence *iha ehi*, we would obtain by *sandhi* the wrong **ihaihi*. The mistake comes from a too hasty glueing of the preverb to the root form, in a situation where *sandhi* is indeed not associative, precisely because of overlapping. We should first glue *iha* and *ā*, getting *ihā*. Now glueing *ihā* and *ihi* by *sandhi* leads to the correct sentence *ihehi*. This example shows that the terminology "preverb" is actually misleading. Preverbs are just particles which have shifted from the Vedic language to the Classic one from a role of postposition to a preferred position of prefix to root and primary derivatives (*kṛdanta*s). But they have kept enough autonomy as individual words to interact with their predecessor, in left-to-right phonetic interaction, before the resulting utterance interacts with the root form. This vindicates our choice not to generate precooked forms obtained by glueing preverbs to root forms, but rather to consider (sequences of) preverbs as an autonomous phase in lexical analysis. This has the added interest to keep only one root form, instead of all the verb forms with preverbs attached.

Still, some special mechanism is required, in order to circumvent the violation of the Zen segmenter non-overlapping requirement in case of preverb *ā*. This mechanism uses so-called *phantom phonemes*, and was first described in (Huet, 2003, 2006). The idea is to pre-cook special forms, encoding the *ā*-prefixed root forms. Such forms are needed only for root forms starting with a vowel, say v. We add to such a form v-w a special form $^*v$-w, with $^*v$ a new symbol, called the *phantom phoneme* of the *varṇa* of vowel v. Phantom phonemes obey new *sandhi* rules, which are coined to simulate the left-to-right application of *sandhi*, should preverb *ā* have occurred before the standard form v-w. We have four such symbols, noted respectively **a*, **e*, **o* and **r*, for the four vowel *varṇas*. Thus **a* replaces *a* or *ā*, **e* replaces *i* or *ī*, **o* replaces *u* or *ū*, **r* replaces *ṛ* or *ṝ*. The new rules of *sandhi* are all instances of $u|{*v} \rightarrow w$, for u any vowel, $*v$ the phantom of vowel v, w the result of *sandhi* of z and v, for z the result of *sandhi* of u and $\bar{a}$. For the above example, we add to the bank of root forms the special form **ehi*, and we analyse *ihehi* as the glueing of *iha* with **ehi*, using special *sandhi* rule $a| *e \rightarrow e$.

Correspondence with *Aṣṭādhyāyī* Treatment

In terms of Pāṇinian derivation, the concept of phantom phonemes can be shown to be in correspondence with the following rules:

> 6.1.85 *antādivat ca*: A replacement in the place of the preceding and following sound segments in *saṁhitā* is treated as the final of what precedes and initial of what follows.
> 6.1.95 *omāṅoḥ ca*: When a vowel *a* is followed by the *ā* of *āṅ* or *o* of *om*, the second is a replacement in place of both.

So, when we reach at the stage *iha* + *ehi* in the Pāṇinian derivation, because of the metarule 6.1.85, the second word is as if starting with *ā* of *āṅ* and therefore, 6.1.95 finds its scope and replaces the *a* of *iha* and *e* of *ehi* by the second (which is *e*), giving the desired form *ihehi*. If we try to make a correspondence between the Pāṇinian derivation and phantom phonemes, we can think of these phantom phonemes as an indication that these have been obtained because of *sandhi* between *ā* and another vowel and, therefore, will follow the *sandhi* rule 6.1.95. In general, if we have a *sandhi* rule such that:

$$[\bar{a} + \text{Vowel x} = \text{Vowel y}],$$

we can replace the Vowel y with a phantom phoneme *y which follows the following *sandhi* rule after the vowel *a*:

$$[a + {}^{*}\text{y} = \text{y}].$$

Replacing y by *y corresponds to the metarule 6.1.85, where the phonetic form is preserved but an indication is provided that it comes from the element *ā*, while the *sandhi* rule 'a + *y = y' corresponds to 6.1.95, where the two phonemes are replaced by the second.

4.3 Privative Compounds

Treatment of Privative Compounds in the Heritage Platform

In this section, we shall examine possible overlappings with the privative particle *a*. First of all, we emphasize that the morpheme *a* used for augment forms of the past tenses such as imperfect or aorist is not to be considered here, since it applies only in the generative morphology of root forms, which is assumed to be done in a previous phase (the construction of the Verb database of forms).[7]

It turns out that the privative particle does not lead to an interference situation, due to its dual nature; indeed, it is marked by the *pada a* in front of consonants, but by the *pada an* in front of vowels. Since *a* combines with a preceding phoneme either to form a syllable ended in *a* in case of a consonant, and to a vowel otherwise, it is clear that no *sandhi* overlap of the result may occur with the following *prātipadika*. Note that the alliteration nasal *n* forbids the analysis of phoneme *ā* as an arbitrary succession of negations, should *a* alone be cumulative, leading to hopelessly ambiguous statements.

Thus it is enough to give the analysis of privative compounds by splitting the Noun database into two subsets Nounc (starting with a consonant) and Nounv (starting with a vowel), and by having distinct phases A or An, corresponding to unit databases representing the two respective strings *a* or *an*. The state space of the segmenter links phases A to Nounc and An to Nounv. A similar duplication is needed for the Iic phase, as well as for the Voc phase of vocative forms. This leads to a significant increase of the number of phases, as witnessed by Fig. 2, but no essential complication.

It should be emphasized, though, that the duplication of some phase does not lead to a duplication of the corresponding database. It is straightforward to share Noun, Nounc, and Nounv by only duplicating the first layer of the corresponding dags, and profiting of the fact that vowels are listed before consonants, leading to more

[7] Indeed, if Sanskrit analysis was attempted without this initial generative phase, the inverting of augment would be a major hurdle, as well as retroflexion analysis; we do not believe such analysis, inverting Pāṇini's grammar rules fully down to root stems, to be computationally tractable.

sharing. There is thus very little increase of the space requirements of these databases, in good adequacy with the regime of economy (*lāghava*) of the Zen machinery.

Treatment of Privative Compounds in the *Aṣṭādhyāyī*

The *nañ* compounds correspond to the following rules in Panini's grammar:

> 6.3.73 *nalopaḥ nañaḥ*: In a compound, when *nañ* is followed by another word, the *n* of *nañ* is deleted.
> 6.3.74 *tasmāt nuṭ aci*: In a compound, if *nañ* is followed by a word starting with a vowel, the augment *nuṭ* is inserted after the *n* has been deleted.

Together, these two rules imply that *nañ* is replaced by *a* and *an* if the following word in the compound starts in a consonant and vowel respectively. In the Heritage system, *a* and *an* are denoted by two distinct phases A and An and the noun database is split into Nounc and Nounv for the nouns starting with a consonant and the nouns starting with a vowel, respectively. The phase A is linked to Nounc (6.3.73) and An is linked to Nounv (6.3.74).

4.4 Analysis of Retroflexion Across Word and Compound Boundaries

The retroflexion rules in Pāṇini's grammar appear in the *tripādī* section and as the other rules in this section, are applied as phonetic smoothing of the final forms. The retroflexion rules can be divided into two categories:[8]

> Retroflexion rules for *n*→*ṇ*.
> Retroflexion rules for *s*→*ṣ*.

For a system that only uses word generation mechanism for handling sentences, handling retroflexion rules is not trivial. A parser based on an underlying word-generating device works on the principle that the word forms are stored and a compound as well as a *pada*

[8] Please note that we will not discuss the *sandhi* rules such as 8.4.41 *ṣṭunā ṣṭuḥ*, which can also cause the changes from *s* →*ṣ* and *n* →*ṇ*.

with external *sandhi* is analysed by glueing together the constituent word elements using external *sandhi.* These external *sandhi* rules are assumed by the transducer *a priori* and do not include retroflexion rules. So, while the constituent words themselves would have gone through retroflexion if the conditions are present within that word, it would not be the case if the condition for retroflexion is present in another word. Let us go back to the example *rāmāyaṇa.* The two constituent words forming this compound are *rāma* and *ayaṇa* (*ayana*, the independent entry). A parser based on an underlying word generating device would have problems recognizing the term *ayaṇa* because the independent word *ayana* does not have such retroflexion and the condition for retroflexion in *ayana* is triggered by the preceding segment *rāma.* We shall look into this issue by analysing the two cases of retroflexion separately.

Retroflexion Rules for *n*→*ṇ*

The main rules for this retroflexion in Pāṇini's grammar are the following:

> 8.4.1 *raṣābhyāṃ naḥ ṇaḥ samānapade*: A replacement in *ṇ* comes in place of *n* when *n* occurs in close proximity, preceded by *r* or *ṣ* in the same word.
> 8.4.2 *aṭkupvāṅnumvyavāye api*: The above replacement takes place even if intervened by any phoneme in the set {*aṭ*[9], *ku*[10], *pu*[11], *āṅ*, *num*}.

The main rule 8.4.1 uses the term *samānapade* (in the same word), which implies that this retroflexion can be applied in a single *pada* only. It clearly overrides the possibility of retroflexion in the case of external *sandhi* across word boundaries. Thus *agnir* + *nayati* = *agnirnayati.*[12] This settles the problem of retroflexion in the case

[9] *aṭ* = Vowels ∪ {*h*, *y*, *v*, *r*}.

[10] *ku* = {*k*, *kh*, *g*, *gh*, *ṅ*}.

[11] *pu* = {*p*, *ph*, *b*, *bh*, *m*}.

[12] This example is interesting because of the fact that the generative model of *Aṣṭādhyāyī* uses the context from the complete sentence, in contrast with a generative model that first generates the separate final forms and, then, glues these together to generate the sentence. For this specific case of *agnirnayati*, the separate final forms in a word-

of external *sandhi*. However, Pāṇini lists many rules for retroflex-

generating device would be *agniḥ* and *nayati*. However, there is no rule in *tripādī* which can give the following desired form *agnirnayati*, starting with the input *agniḥ* + *nayati*, i.e.

$$agni\d{h} + nayati \not\rightarrow agnirnayati.$$

In this example, the final form stored by a word-generating device will not give the correct form in external *sandhi*. However, it is to be noted that the only instances, which can lead to this problem are the rules which have a specific condition of *avasāna*. A *pada* in context of other words does not get this condition unless it is the final *pada* of a sentence. There are two rules in *tripādī* with the condition of *avasāna*:

8.3.15 *kharavasānayoḥ visarjanīyaḥ*: The phoneme *r* is changed to *ḥ* if followed by a phoneme in *pratyāhāra khar* or in *avasāna*.
8.4.56 *vā avasāne*: A phoneme belonging to the set *jhal* is changed to a phoneme in the set *car* optionally if the right context is *avasāna*.

Thus, the rule 8.4.56 changes *vāg* to the optional forms *vāk, vāg* in *avasāna*, which would be stored as the final forms in a word-generating device. It might have caused problem if the external *sandhi* between *vāk* + *hari* gives a different form that $v\bar{a}g + hari \xrightarrow{8.4.62} v\bar{a}gghari$. Thankfully, there is another rule 8.2.39 (*jhalāṁ jaśaḥ ante*), which can convert this final *k* back to *g*. Thus,

$$v\bar{a}k + hari \xrightarrow{8.2.39} v\bar{a}g + hari \xrightarrow{8.4.62} v\bar{a}gghari$$

gives the same form as *vāg* + *hari* and the *sandhi* rules $\{k + h = ggh, g + h = ggh\}$ will give the correct *sandhi*, in correspondence with *tripādī* rules.

We will now discuss the methodology adopted by the system to handle this situation created by the condition of *avasāna* in 8.3.15. The system stores the final form as to what it would be before applying that particular rule. So, the final form is stored as ending in *r* and the following external *sandhi* rules are applied:

$r + khar \xrightarrow{8.3.15,8.3.34} s + khar.$
r + all phonemes $-khar \rightarrow$ no change.
r (end of *pada*) $\xrightarrow{8.3.15}$ *ḥ* (end of *pada*).

ion across constituent words in a compound formation, specifically rules 8.4.3 to 8.4.13. Let us consider rule 8.4.3 here:

> 8.4.3 *pūrvapadāt sañjñāyām agaḥ*: A replacement *ṇ* comes in place of *n*, when *n* occurs in a *pada*, combined after another *pada*, containing *r* or *ṣ* as the condition of replacement, but not containing *g*, provided the derivate denotes a name.

This rule clearly gives the cases for retroflexion across constituent words (*pada*) in a compound (*samāsa*). Now, questions have been raised in the tradition whether 8.4.3 is an operational rule or a restrictive rule (Sharma, 2003), that is, whether the retroflexion across *pada* was available from the rules 8.4.1 and 8.4.2. Let us describe these two views in brief below.

Operational view: A compound cannot be accepted as a single *pada*. Therefore, in *dru–nasa*, the retroflexion is not available by the previous rules and 8.4.3 prescribes this operation, making 8.4.3 to be an operational rule.

Restrictive view: Since nominal endings are introduced after a compound nominal stem to derive a single *pada*, the compound as a whole constitutes a single pada. Therefore, retroflexion in compounds was available from the previous rules. The rule 8.4.3 restricts this availability only to the compounds, denoting a name.

Whether we accept the operational view or the restrictive view, it leads to the same interpretation, i.e., in the case of compounds, retroflexion across pada occurs only in the case of *saṁjñā* (names) such as *rāmāyaṇa* and *śūrpaṇakhā*. It suggests that these compounds can actually be lexicalized as frozen expressions.

Apart from 8.4.3, other rules dealing with retroflexion across *pada* in a compound have a limited scope since the conditions for these rules are the specific lexical entries. For instance:

> 8.4.4 *vanaṃ puragāmiśrakāsidhrakāsārikākoṭarāgrebhyaḥ*: When *vana* occurs in combination after *r* or *ṣ* contained within a previous *pada* constituted by *puragā*, *sidhrakā*, *sārikā*, *koṭarā* or *agre*, the *n* of *vana* undergoes retroflexion.
>
> 8.4.8 *vāhanam āhitāt*: When *vāhana* occurs in combination after *r* or *ṣ* contained within a previous *pada* constituted by a word signifying 'that which is carried', the *n* of *vāhana* undergoes retroflexion.

Similarly, other rules in this section also have a limited scope and these cases can be lexicalized. However, there is another rule in this section, which is general enough:

> 8.4.11 *prātipadikāntanumvibhaktiṣu ca*: A replacement in *ṇ* comes optionally in place of *n*, which either occurs at the end of a nominal stem or occurs as a part of *num* or *vibhakti*, if preceded by a *pada* containing *r* or *ṣ* as the condition of replacement. For example,
> *māṣa–vāpin* + nominative dual → *māṣavāpiṇau* (*n* occurs at the end of the nominal stem *vāpin*)
> *māṣa–vāpa* + nominative plural → *māṣavāpāṇi* (*n* of *num*)
> *māṣa–vāpa* + instrumental singular → *māṣavāpeṇa* (*n* of *vibhakti*).

Rule 8.4.11 is a general rule, not specific to the proper names only and, therefore, it is not clear whether lexicalizing such occurrences would suffice. This rule, however, is an optional rule and it needs to be verified that there are sufficient corpus occurrences of this specific case of retroflexion. To access the number of compounds which may fall in this category, that is, satisfy the conditions of 8.4.11, we gathered some statistics from the attested compounds in the Monier-Williams (MW) (1999) dictionary. The compounds satisfying the conditions for 8.4.11 can fall in the following two categories:

> The compounds ending in *n*, where the left constituent of the compound may trigger the retroflexion in the right constituent: There are fifty-seven such compounds attested in MW. Example, *agra–gāmin* might decline as {*agra–gāminau*, *agra–gāmiṇau*}.
> The compounds where there is no *n* in the right constituent but the left constituent may trigger the retroflexion when the compound word declines: There are 509 such compounds, attested in MW. Example, *śāra–bhūmi* might decline as {*śāra–bhūminā*, *śāra–bhūmiṇā*}.

We are now left with the question whether the optional retroflexed forms allowed by 8.4.11 actually appear in the corpus and if they do, how many such forms are there? An analysis into corpus statistics is needed for all these forms.[13] As of now, we do not have

[13] It is not possible to get these statistics from MW because this retroflexion occurs for the inflected forms.

any statistics regarding the occurrences of such forms with/without retroflexion in a corpus.

Retroflexion rules dealing with preverbs for the cases of *prādi* compounds as well as in a single *pada* are listed from 8.4.15 to 8.4.35. The main *sūtra* 8.4.14 states:

> 8.4.14 *upasargād asamāse api ṇopadeśasya*: If a preverb (*upasarga*) contains the *r* or *ṣ* as the condition of retroflexion, it can cause retroflexion in the following verb if the verb contains *ṇ* in the initial citation (*upadeśa*). Thus *praṇāyakaḥ*.

Retroflexion Rules for *s*→*ṣ*

The main rules in Pāṇini's grammar corresponding to this retroflexion case are the following:

> 8.3.55 *apadāntasya mūrdhanyaḥ*: A replacement in *mūrdhanya* (retroflex) comes in place of that *s*, which does not occur at the end of a *pada*.
> 8.3.57 *iṇkoḥ*: A non-final *s* is replaced with *ṣ*, when the same occurs after *iṇ*[14] or *ku*.
> 8.3.58 *numvisarjanīyaśarvyavāye api*: The replacement takes place even if intervened by *num*, *visarjanīya* or *śar*.[15]

For this case of retroflexion, Pāṇini does not use the term *samānapade*. Therefore, we need to consider both the word and compound boundary cases in our analysis. However, this retroflexion has a different property. The number of intervening phonemes can at most be 1 and, therefore, it limits the cases where this retroflexion can occur across words. We will enumerate all the possibilities where the condition for this retroflexion may be obtained across the word boundaries. Before going into that, we define the following sets:

> C_s: The set of phonemes that trigger this retroflexion: (8.3.57: *iṇ* ∪ *ku*).
> I_s: The set of phonemes that can intervene between any phoneme $p \in C_s$ and 's', which is to be retroflexed: (8.3.58: *n*, *ḥ*, *ś*, *ṣ*, *s*).

[14] *iṇ* = {Vowels - {*a*, *ā*}} ∪ {*h*, *y*, *v*, *r*, *l*}.
[15] *śar* = {*ś*, *ṣ*, *s*}.

Let us denote the left and right constituents under consideration by P_1 and P_2, respectively. We are looking for the cases where a phoneme in P_1 can trigger retroflexion in P_2. We will have the following cases:

> **Case 1:** $p \in C_s$, $q \in I_s$ and P_1 ends in 'pq', P_2 starts with an s.
> 8.3.111 *sātpadādyoḥ* states that if the s occurs in the beginning of a word, it will not undergo retroflexion. In this case, s occurs in the beginning of P_2 and, therefore, this case is overruled by the grammar.
> **Case 2:** $p \in C_s$, P_1 ends in p.
> As per 8.3.111, if P_2 starts with an s, it will not undergo retroflexion. So, for this case to apply, s has to be the 2nd phoneme of the word P_2 and P_2 should start with a phoneme $q \in I_s$. Clearly, it requires that P_2 should start with a conjunct consonant from the set {*ns, ḥs, śs, ṣs, ss*}. The language does not allow such words, starting with this pattern. Internal *sandhi* rules explicitly eliminate the last four, and general sonority hierarchy rules out the first in syllable structure.
> **Case 3:** So, we are left only with the case where the first phoneme p of P_2 is not in the set C_s and by external *sandhi* with P_1, changes to the set C_s. Also, the second phoneme of P_2 should be s after external *sandhi* of P_1 and P_2, so that the first phoneme $p \in C_s$ of P_2 will provide a condition for retroflexion in the second phoneme s. Let us now look into this case in further details, taking the two exhaustive cases, where the first phoneme of P_2 did not belong to C_s and external *sandhi* changed it into a phoneme in C_s, either consonant or vowel.

Let us consider the first possibility. Due to the language constraints, the consonant $p \in C_s$ has to be k and only k, because other consonants in set C_s do not occur before s or ṣ, while starting a word. Let us consider the rules which can change a consonant $q \notin C_s$ to k.

8.2.30. *coḥ kuḥ*: A phoneme in the set cu = {*c, ch, j, jh, ñ*} will be changed to the corresponding phoneme in the set ku = {*k, kh, g, gh, ṅ*}, if a phoneme in *pratyāhāra jhal* follows. Though s belongs to the *pratyāhāra jhal*, this rule would not qualify for our analysis since this rule does not look at the phoneme preceding cu

and therefore, would have been applied on the original word itself and the original word would have the retroflexion.

The same reasoning can be applied to the following rule as well:

> 8.2.41. *ṣaḍhoḥ kaḥ si*: A phoneme in the set {*ṣ*, *ḍh*} will be changed to *k* if *s* follows.

So, we will never have a case where external *sandhi* changes a consonant $q \notin C_s$ to a consonant $p \in C_s$, such that p is the first phoneme and s is the second phoneme of P_2 after external *sandhi*.

Let us now consider the second possibility, which is common enough and the language does not constrain the vowels to be used before *s*. However, the only possible cases here are if any vowel q in the set $A = \{a, \bar{a}\}$ is changed to a vowel $p \in C_s$ by external *sandhi*. Such a case arises. Consider the following example:

ka ḥ + *asicat* → *ka u* + *asicat* (6.1.109 *ato roraplutādaplute*)
ka u + *asicat* → *ko* + *asicat* (6.1.84 *ādguṇaḥ*)
ko + *asicat* → *kosicat* (6.1.105 *eṅaḥ padāntādati*).

At this stage, the *o* could have triggered the retroflexion in *s*. However, this application is prevented because of the following rule:

> 6.1.86 (*ṣatvatukorasiddhaḥ*): A single replacement of two sound elements is suspended when a replacement in *ṣ* or insertion of *tuk* is to take place. Therefore, this case is prevented by the grammar itself.

We have now exhausted all the possibilities and from this discussion, we can safely say that the general case for *s* → *ṣ* retroflexion is that the retroflexion does not happen across *pada*, even though the term *samānapade* has not been used by Pāṇini for this case. There are certain rules, allowing retroflexion across the constituent words in a compound. These rules are treated as exceptions of the rule 8.3.111. Some of the examples are:

aṅguli – *saṅga* → *aṅguliṣaṅga* (8.3.80 *samāse aṅguleḥ saṅgaḥ*)
agni – *stoma* → *agniṣṭoma* (8.3.82 *agneḥ stutstomasomāḥ*)
mātṛ – *svasṛ* → *mātṛṣvasṛ* (8.3.84 *mātṛpitṛbhyāṃ svasā*).

These examples provide a finite list, which can easily be lexicalized. Retroflexion rules corresponding to the compounds are also discussed in 8.3.65 to 8.3.77. In tradition, these rules are also treated as exceptions of 8.3.111. In this section, there are specific rules for various verbs and preverbs, and each pair of preverb and verb is to be handled separately.

While we are discussing retroflexion, we will also like to draw the attention of the readers to a specific case of non-retroflexion in the case of *kurvanti*.

The Case of *Kurvanti*

A Sanskrit student who does not know Pāṇini's grammar by heart may find it difficult to give a quick answer as to why there is no retroflexion in *kurvanti*? As stated before, the standard rules for retroflexion *n*→*ṇ* in Pāṇini are 8.4.1 and 8.4.2. The word *kurvanti* has an *n* preceded by *r* in a single word (8.4.1) and the intervening phonemes *a* and *v* fall in the set *aṇ*, matching the criteria of 8.4.2. Therefore, it appears as if the form *kurvanti* should undergo retroflexion. But it does not, the reason being two other rules stated in Pāṇini's grammar.

> 8.3.24 *naḥ ca apadāntasya jhali*: If *n* is followed by a consonant in *pratyāhāra jhal*, it is replaced by *ṃ*.
> 8.4.58 *anusvārasya yayi parasavarṇaḥ*: If *ṃ* is followed by a consonant in *pratyāhāra yay*, it is replaced by the homogeneous nasal.

Consider the set T = consonants− {{*ṅ*, *ñ*, *ṅ*, *n*, *m*} ∪ {*y*, *v*, *r*}}, which denotes the phonemes in the *pratyāhāra* set *jhal*. If *n* is followed by a phoneme from the set T, the rule 8.3.24 gets the application, bleeding the retroflexion rules. For the set $H = T - \{h, ś, ṣ, s\}$, the rule 8.3.24 feeds the rule 8.4.58. Specifically, in the case under consideration,

$$kurva(n)ti \xrightarrow{8.3.24} kurva(\dot{m})ti \xrightarrow{8.4.58} kurva(n)ti.$$

So, effectively no change took place. On the other hand, if it has to undergo retroflexion, the process would be:

$kurvanti \xrightarrow{8.4.2} kurvaṇti$

The second process does not correspond to the desired form *kurvanti*. There is no rule in Pāṇini's grammar that allows converting the form *kurvaṇti* to *kurvanti*.

What prevents one from following this wrong process is the control structure of *tripādī*. The rules in *tripādī* are to be applied sequentially. The rule 8.3.24 appears before 8.4.2 and, therefore, should be applied before 8.4.2. Once the form is *kurvaṁti* by the application of 8.3.24, 8.4.2 does not get the application (bleeding by 8.3.24) and the process directly goes to 8.4.58 (feeding by 8.3.24), which converts *kurvaṁti* back to *kurvanti* by changing *ṃ* to the homonasal of *d*, which is *n* in this case.[16]

Now, let us have a look at how this process is implemented in the Heritage site. In addition to coding the rules 8.4.1 and 8.4.2, an additional criteria is employed for retroflexion. As per this criteria, the right-hand side of *n* is checked and only if it does not contain any consonant in *pratyāhāra jhal*, it can undergo retroflexion. Clearly, the retroflexion process is not exactly Pāṇinian and if asked to enumerate the rules leading to the form *kurvanti* in the Heritage system, it will definitely not list the rules 8.3.24 and 8.4.58, which actually cancel the effect of each other. However, it might be looked as a much more complete rule for the retroflexion condition.

5 Idiosyncracies of Phonology

5.1 Phonemic Variations

The Heritage engine computes on words and sentences represented as phonemic lists, with phonemes represented as integers, in the simplistic but efficient style of the Zen library. The user interface interprets user input in four common transliteration styles and immediately converts it to normalized words, where normalization, explained in footnote 2, replaces (non genuine) *anusvāra* by the equivalent nasal. All computed forms and morphemes are stored in this normalized form, avoiding useless non-determinism at segmenting time.

One important remark is that these stored forms are generally in terminal *sandhi* form, *except* that final *r* is preserved, and *not* turned into *visarga*. This is necessary to parse phrases such as *punarapi*, analysable as the *sandhi* of *punar* and *api*. Storing *punaḥ* instead would prevent this analysis and allow the wrong **punopi*.

[16] We thank Malhar Kulkarni for his explanation of this intricate Pāṇinian process.

Gemination, allowing e.g. *karmma* for *karma*, is not allowed, although allowed (optionally) by 8.4.46.[17] In that we follow the opinion of Śākalya.[18] Degemination, for instance of *vārtā* for *vārttā*, is allowed for a few lexical items.[19]

The data structure of *pratyāhāra* is not used in the Heritage machinery. The corresponding sets of phonemes are represented by unions of integer intervals.

5.2 Finer Phonemic Distinctions

The Heritage machinery makes finer phonemic distinctions than the tradition, in order to simplify some morpho-phonemic treatment. Specifically, we consider three versions of phoneme *h* and two versions of phoneme *j*.

Variants of Phoneme *h*

The standard (cerebral) version of phoneme *h* combines with *t* in *sandhi* to yield *ḍh*. Thus, for example, root *gāh* admits as past participle *gāḍha*. But sometimes *gdh* is obtained, like in *dugdha* for root *duh*, whose final *h* has kept a guttural character. And rarely

---

[17] 8.4.46 *acaḥ rahābhyāṃ dve*: A phoneme in the *pratyāhāra yar*, when occurring in close proximity after a vowel followed by *r* or *h*, is optionally doubled.

[18] 8.4.51 *sarvatra śākalyasya*: In the opinion of Śākalya, there is no doubling.

[19] In *tripādī*, there are two optional rules regarding degemination:

> 8.4.64 *halaḥ yamāṃ yami lopaḥ*: A phoneme in the *pratyāhāra yam* is deleted optionally if it is preceded by any consonant (*hal*) and is followed by another phoneme in the *pratyāhāra yam*.
> 8.4.65 *jharaḥ jhari savarṇe*: A phoneme in the *pratyāhāra jhar* is deleted optionally if it is preceded by any consonant and is followed by a homogeneous phoneme in the *pratyāhāra jhar*.

As an interesting observation, the two *pratyāhāra* sets, *yam* and *jhar* are exclusive and exhaustive to cover all the consonants. Thus, after any consonant, if two homogeneous consonants follow in the close proximity, the first of the two can optionally be deleted by these two rules.

ddh is obtained, like in *naddha* for root *nah*, whose final *h* has kept a dental character.

These *sandhi* rules are handled in the Heritage site by a finer phoneme distinction than in the traditional view, with extra phonemes *h'* and *h"*, subject to the following *sandhi* rules:

> *h'* + *t* → *gdh* and *h"* + *t* → *ddh* (and other similar rules for consonants other than '*t*').

As per Pāṇini's grammar, the general rule for *sandhi* between *h* and any phoneme in *jhal* is

> 8.2.31 *haḥ ḍhaḥ*: *h* is replaced by *ḍh* if any phoneme in *jhal* follows. For the specific case of *h* followed by *t*, this rule feeds some other rules, yielding the following derivation sequence:
>
> $h + t \xrightarrow{8.2.31} ḍh + t \xrightarrow{8.2.40}$[20] $ḍh + dh \xrightarrow{8.4.41} ḍh + ḍh \xrightarrow{8.3.13}$[21] $ḍh$.

However, there are rules, exception to 8.2.31, which in addition to looking at the phonemes, also look for the lexical criteria such as the actual root word and the *sandhi* rule for the *h* appearing in such roots is different. For example:

> 8.2.32 *dādeḥ dhātoḥ ghaḥ*: For the roots starting with *d*, *h* is replaced by *gh* if any phoneme in *jhal* follows. Roots such as {*dah, dih, duh*} fall in this category.
> 8.2.33 *vā druhamuhaṣṇuhaṣṇihām*: For the roots {*druh, muh, ṣṇih, ṣṇuh*}, *h* is optionally replaced by *gh* if any phoneme in *jhal* follows.

For the specific case of *h* followed by *t* in these roots, these rules can yield the following derivation sequence:

---

[20] 8.2.40 *jhaṣaḥ tathoḥ dhaḥ adhaḥ*: The phonemes *t* and *th* are replaced by *dh*, if they follow after a phoneme in the set *jhaṣ*, with the exception of the root *dhā*.

[21] 8.3.13 *ḍhaḥ ḍhe lopaḥ*: The phoneme *ḍh* is deleted, when followed by *ḍh*.

It is to be noted that the rule 8.3.13 has been applied here after 8.4.41 and, therefore, is an exception of the *asiddha* principle. These cases of *āśrayāt siddham* have been discussed in detail by Cardona in (2011).

$h + t \xrightarrow{8.2.32|8.2.33} gh + t \xrightarrow{8.2.40} gh + dh \xrightarrow{8.4.53}$[22] $g + dh$.
8.2.34 *nahaḥ dhaḥ*: '*h*' of the root *nah* is replaced by '*dh*' if any phoneme in *jhal* follows. For the specific case of *h* followed by *t* in *nah*, this rule can yield the following derivation sequence:
$h + t \xrightarrow{8.2.34} dh + t \xrightarrow{8.2.40} dh + dh \xrightarrow{8.4.53} d + dh$.

In the Heritage system, the phoneme *h* corresponding to the rules 8.2.32 and 8.2.33 is denoted by *h'*, while that corresponding to 8.2.34 is denoted by *h"*.

Variants of phoneme *j*

Similarly, phoneme *j* in its usual guttural version combines with *t* in *sandhi* to yield *kt*. Thus *yukta* for past participle of root *yuj*. But sometimes it acts similarly to the sibilant *ś* and yields rather *ṣṭ*. Thus *mṛṣṭa* for past participle of root *mṛj*. The Heritage site recognizes this distinction with a variant *j'* such that *j'* + *t* → *ṣṭ* in order to accommodate forms of roots such as *mṛj*. The roots concerned are *bhrāj*, *mṛj*, *yaj*, *rāj*, *vraj*, and *sṛj*.

As per Pāṇini's grammar, the general rule for *sandhi* between *j* and any phoneme in *jhal* is:

> 8.2.30 *coḥ kuḥ*: A phoneme belonging to the set *cu* (palatals) is replaced by the corresponding phoneme in the set *ku* if any phoneme in *jhal* follows or at the end of a word.

Under specific conditions, this rule can feed another rule in the grammar:

> 8.4.55 *khari ca*: A phoneme belonging to the set *jhal* is replaced by the corresponding phoneme in set *car*, if followed by a phoneme in set *khar*.
> *khar* = {*kh*, *ph*, *ch*, *ṭh*, *th*, *c*, *ṭ*, *t*, *k*, *p*, *ś*, *ṣ*, *s*}
> *car* = {*c*, *ṭ*, *t*, *k*, *p*, *ś*, *ṣ*, *s*}.

---

[22] 8.4.53 *jhalāṃ jaś jhaśi*: A phoneme in the set *jhal* is replaced by a phoneme in the set *jaś*, if followed by a phoneme in the set *jhaś*. In effect, this rule replaces a phoneme in the set *jhal* by the third letters, if followed by fourth letters of a group.

In effect, the rule 8.4.55 changes the second, third and fourth phonemes of the sound set to its first phoneme, if followed by a phoneme in set *khar*. So, in general, when *j* combines with *t*, both the rules 8.2.30 and 8.4.55 apply, yielding the following:

$$j + t \xrightarrow{8.2.30} g + t \xrightarrow{8.4.55} k + t.$$

However, there is an exception to rule 8.2.30:

> 8.2.36 *vraścabhrasjasr̥jamr̥jayajarājabhrājachaśāṃ ṣaḥ*: The last phoneme of the roots *vraśc*, *bhrasj*, *sr̥j*, *mr̥j*, *yaj*, *rāj*, *bhrāj* and roots ending in *ch* or *ś* are substituted by *ṣ* if any phoneme in *jhal* follows or at the end of a word.

Focusing on the combination of *j* and *t*, this rule gives an exception for the roots {*bhrasj*, *sr̥j*, *mr̥j*, *yaj*, *rāj*, *bhrāj*} and changes the *j* to *ṣ* instead of *g*, as specified by the general rule 8.2.30. The phoneme *ṣ* before *t* then feeds the following rule:

> 8.4.41 *ṣṭunā ṣṭuḥ*: A phoneme in the set *stu* ({*s*, *t*, *th*, *d*, *dh*, *n*}) is substituted by the corresponding phoneme in the set *ṣṭu* ({*ṣ*, *ṭ*, *ṭh*, *ḍ*, *ḍh*, *ṇ*}), if it occurs before or after a phoneme in the set *ṣṭu*.

Together, these rules yield the following *sandhi* rule for these specific roots:

$$j + t \xrightarrow{8.2.36} ṣ + t \xrightarrow{8.4.41} ṣ + ṭ.$$

In the Heritage system, the phoneme *j* corresponding to the rule 8.2.36 is denoted by *j'*.

The variant phonemes which are dealt with in the Heritage engine may be justified by comparative linguistics, as remnants from earlier language substratum. They yield a more unified *sandhi* processing. The Pāṇinian tradition recognizes them indirectly, by giving specific rules for specific roots, but the end result is equivalent.

6 Soundness and Completeness

Evaluation of a computational linguistics platform is usually discussed in terms of the parameters of precision and recall, measuring the quality of response to a query. For a query admitting *rv* relevant answers, let *rt* be the number of retrieved answers returned by the platform and *right* be the number of retrieved relevant answers. The precision is defined as *right*/*rt*, the recall as *right*/*rv*. The recall measures the completeness of the system. A low recall means that the system performs badly, in not recognizing correct sentences. Increasing the recall usually decreases the precision; we say that the system overgenerates, its correct answers being drowned in irrelevant ones.

We shall not give here precise figures of precision and recall for the Heritage platform, for lack of a statistically significant tagged corpus consistent with our system of tags and our assignment of homonymy indexes. Furthermore, many evaluation criteria may be envisioned, for the generational aspect as well as for the recognition aspect.

We shall however discuss the known incompletenesses of the system with respect to the Pāṇinian framework, and try to assess their statistical relevance. Before discussing recall, i.e. completeness, we discuss the mechanisms which limit overgeneration.

6.1 Curbing Overgeneration

Direct inversion of *sandhi* on a non-trivial sentence would result in literally millions of potential segmentations, most of them being sterile, with segments un-recognizable as *pada*s. We curb this overgeneration by having our segmenter lexicon-directed non-compound *pada*s are stored in pre-generated databases of forms arranged in lexical categories, compounds are analysed recursively as sequences of lexicalized forms, and the lexical analyser search is constrained by the phase transitions, which reflect the morphological geometry. Still, certain situations lead to important branching factors of the non-deterministic search. For instance, the form *parā* leads to a potential 164 legal choices, as explained in Huet (2005).

In order to curb overgeneration, a semantic filter is applied to the potential segmentations, using a simplified semantic roles (*kāraka*) analysis. This mechanism has been described in Huet (2007). Every segmentation candidate is expanded into the set of all its tagged interpretations. Each tagged interpretation is given a penalty, reflecting the lack of match between the semantic roles of the substantive items and the regime of the verbal items (*sakarmaka/akarmaka*), determining its expectations (*ākāṅkṣā*). In this simplified analysis, only the roles of agent (*kartṛ*) and goal/patient (*karma*) are taken into account. Every segmentation is then assigned as penalty the minimum penalty of its interpretations, and the system truncates all solutions below a given threshold. This semantic filtering reduces drastically the number of returned solutions, with a clear increase in precision, without too much loss in recall.

Two remarks are in order. The first one is that the inner structure of compounds is not relevant to this simplified semantic analysis, since no inner component of a compound may feed direct roles in Sanskrit. Note that the examples of *asamartha* compounds exhibited by Gillon (1993, 2002) concern only cases where the inner component of a compound has an exocentric argument as Bhartṛhari puts it, this component expresses a relation. This vindicates our flat analysis of pre-compounds, since a pre-compound with $n+1$ components may correspond to C_n possible binary compounds, where the Catalan number C_n is exponential in n, as noted earlier.

The second remark is that, none the less, certain good segmentations may be discarded because of ellipses (typically, the agent may be implicit from the context as the current topic). This means that the *kāraka* analysis ought to be done at the level of discourse, rather than individual sentences.

Another device that curbs overgeneration in the Heritage platform is the regular nature of the segmenting automaton, the phases of the lexical analyser being constrained by a regular expression limiting the recursion. Thus small lexical items such as root substantives (*-pa*, *-ga*, *-nī*, etc.) can generally occur only in Ifc position (right component of a compound), limiting drastically their combinatorics.

Still another important device is that vocatives are allowed only as terminal strings of the various segments. This avoids frequent ambiguities of stems in *-a* as bare stems usable as left components of compounds and as vocative interjections. While Pāṇini does not exclude the vocatives from undergoing *sandhi*, it is a rare phenomena to obtain the vocatives as a non-final segment and it can be justified by the prosody constraints. It still adds to the incompletenesses of the system, as the systems cannot recognize the vocatives which appear as a non-final segment.[23]

Finally, two distinct modes of the Sanskrit Reader are offered to the user. The so-called Simplified mode uses the simple state diagram shown in Fig. 1. It forbids vocatives and does not use the productive devices of participle generation and privative compounds such stems must be lexicalized in order to be recognized. The simplified mode is adequate for simple sentences and has very good precision (often, a unique segmentation is proposed). For more complex sentences, the Complete mode, using the full databank of participles and the complete analysis of privative compounds, is necessary. Let us now indicate in which ways this "Complete" mode is still incomplete.

6.2 Known Incompletenesses

One basic limitation of the Sanskrit Heritage engine is that it relies on lexicalization of atomic items. At the time of writing, its lexicon lists 588 roots and 9,200 non-compound stems. 1,560 combinations of preverbs and roots provide as many verbs, each allowed in all finite conjugation paradigms available in Classical Sanskrit (present, imperfect, optative, imperative, future, perfect, aorist/injunctive), plus infinitive and absolutive (with transitions allowing absolutives in *-tvā* only from roots, and those in *-ya* only when a preverb is present). Ten forms of participles are generated. Secondary conjugation stems (causative, desiderative and intensive) are lexicalized on demand. Other primary derivatives (*kr̥dantas*) are available only when lexicalized. The same is true of secondary derivatives, which is certainly a strong limitation, that will have to be lifted at some future point, since many *taddhita* suffixes are very productive (*-tā*, *-tva*, *-tr̥*, etc.)

[23] In the *Bhagavadgītā* (Bh.G.), for instance, there are at least three verses where the vocatives appear as a non-final segment:

- Bh.G. 3.22: *na me* ***pārthāsti*** *kartavyaṁ triṣu lokeṣu kiñcana*
- Bh.G. 3.28: *tattvavit tu* ***mahābāho*** *guṇakarmavibhāgayoḥ*
- Bh.G. 5.3: *nirdvandvo hi* ***mahābāho*** *sukhaṃ bandhāt pramucyate.*

The segments containing the non-final vocatives are shown in bold. The first verse also gives an example *pārthāsti*, where the vocatives can undergo *sandhi*.

A few lexical items have been omitted from the lexicon because they caused too much overgeneration. For instance, the substantive *vi* (bird), for obvious clash with the homophonic particle or the rare substantive *atra* (food) for similar confusion with the adverb. Also the substantive *āya* for its conflict with dative forms as well as the form *nā* (nominative of *nṛ*). It is hoped that such difficulties will be overcome at some stage, when the system will be tuned by statistical training.

The analysis given in Section 3 ought to convince the reader that most productive schemes are correctly dealt with. Non-productive schemes (*aluk*, retroflexion) assume lexicalization of the corresponding compound stem.

The strongest limitation concerns substantival verbs, such as *yantrayati*. At present, such verbal stems must be lexicalized. Dealing with substantival verbs in all generality, including for past forms with augment, seems out of reach with the present technology.

Sanskrit is a complex language, whose literature covers many styles over three millenia. It has an extremely productive morphology, allowing the generation of extravagant items such as *cicandrīyīṣakāyamāṇena* (Dīkṣita et. al., 1905). Current technology does not permit the automatic analysis of such complex forms. However, compounds with any number of components, such as *pravaranṛpamukuṭamaṇimarīcimañjarīcayacarcitacaraṇayugalaḥ* (attested in Pañcatantra), do not pose particular problems.

7 Conclusion

The Sanskrit Heritage reader recognizes simple sentences from Classical Sanskrit. In Simplified mode (Fig. 1), it is precise but incomplete. In Complete mode (Fig.2), it exhibits a good recall of sentences whose vocabulary is covered by the lexicon. The system is fast and robust. This paper made an attempt at relating its operations to those of the Pāṇinian tradition. Although the details of derivation vary, there seems to be no major discrepancy. The most difficult problems left to solve are the analysis of denominative verbs, and the proper treatment of ellipsed agents and double accusative verbs (*dvikarmaka*).

References

1. von Böhtlingk, O. *Pāṇini's Grammatik.* Language and Linguistics Series. Motilal Banarsidass, Delhi, 1998.
2. Cardona, G. *Pāṇini: His Work and Its Traditions.* Motilal Barnasidass, Delhi, 1988.
3. Cardona, G. *Pūrvatrāsiddham and Āśrayāt Siddham.* D.K. Printworld, Delhi, 2011.
4. Dīkṣita, B., S. Vasu, and B. Das Basu. *The Siddhānta Kaumudi of Bhattoji Dikshita.* Number v. 3 in *The Siddhanta Kaumudi of Bhattoji Dikshita.* The Panini Office, 1905.
5. Gillon, B.S. 'Bartṛhari's solution to the problem of asamartha compounds. *Études Asiatiques/Asiatiche Studien*, 47,(1): 117–133, 1993.
6. Gillon, B.S. *Indian linguistic studies: Festschrift in Honour of George Cardona*; eds. Madhav M. Deshpande et Peter E. Hook, chapter 'Bartṛhari's Rule for Unexpressed Kārakas: The Problem of Control in Classical Sanskrit. Motilal Banarsidass, Delhi, 2002.
7. Gillon, B.S. 'Exocentric (Bahuvrīhi) Compounds in Classical Sanskrit. In G. Huet and A. Kulkarni, eds., *Proceedings, First International Symposium on Sanskrit Computational Linguistics*, pp. 1–12, 2007.
8. Gillon, B.S. 'Tagging Classical Sanskrit Compounds. In A. Kulkarni and G. Huet, eds., *Sanskrit Computational Linguistics 3*, pp 98–105. Springer-Verlag LNAI 5406, 2009.
9. Huet, G. *The Zen Computational Linguistics Toolkit.* Technical report, ESSLLI Course Notes, 2002.
10. Huet, G. 'Towards Computational Processing of Sanskrit. In *International Conference on Natural Language Processing (ICON)*, 2003.
11. Huet, G. 'A Functional Toolkit for Morphological and Phonological Processing, Application to a Sanskrit Tagger. *J. Functional Programming*, 15,(4): 573–614, 2005.
12. Huet, G. *Themes and Tasks in Old and Middle Indo-Aryan Linguistics*, eds. Bertil Tikkanen and Heinrich Hettrich, chapter 'Lexicon-directed Segmentation and Tagging of Sanskrit, pp. 307–25. Motilal Banarsidass, Delhi, 2006.
13. Huet, G. and B. Razet. 'The Reactive Engine for Modular Transducers. In K. Futatsugi, J.-P. Jouannaud, and . Meseguer, eds., *Algebra, Meaning and Computation, Essays Dedicated to Joseph A. Goguen on the Occasion of His 65th Birthday*, pp. 355–74. Springer-Verlag LNCS, vol. 4060, 2006.
14. Huet, G. 'Shallow Syntax Analysis in Sanskrit Guided by Semantic Nets Constraints. In *Proceedings of the 2006 International Workshop on Research Issues in Digital Libraries*, New York, NY, USA, 2007. ACM.

15. Huet, G. 'Sanskrit Segmentation. XXVIIIth South Asian Languages Analysis Roundatable, University of Denton, Texas, 2009.
16. Joshi, S. and J. Roodbergen. *Patañjali's Vyākaraṇa-Mahābhāṣya Sthānivadbhāvāhnika: Introduction, Text, Translation and Notes.* Number v. 1 in Research Unit Series. Bhandarkar Oriental Research Institute, 1990.
17. Joshi, S. and J. Roodbergen. *The Aṣṭādhyāyī of Pāṇini with Translation and Explanatory Notes.* Number v. 11 in The Aṣṭādhyāyī of Pāṇini. Sāhitya Akādemī, 2004.
18. Kaplan, R.M. and M. Kay. 'Regular Models of Phonological Rule Systems. *Computational Linguistics*, 20,(3): 331–78, 1994.
19. Kielhorn, F. *The Paribhashendusekhara of Nagojibhatta.* Parimal Publications, Delhi (reprint), 1871.
20. Kiparsky, P. 'On the architecture of Pāṇini's grammar. In G. Huet, A. Kulkarni, and P. Scharf, eds., *Sanskrit Computational Linguistics 1 & 2.* Springer-Verlag LNAI 5402, 2009.
21. Kulkarni, A. and D. Shukl. 'Sanskrit Morphological Analyser: Some Issues. *Indian Linguistics*, 70(1-4): 169–77, 2009.
22. Monier-Williams, M., E. Leumann, and C. Cappeller. *A Sanskrit-English Dictionary: Etymological and Philologically Arranged with Special Reference to Cognate Indo-European Languages.* Asian Educational Services, 1999.
23. Munśī, O., E. Unithiri, and N. Unithiri. *Dhāturūpaprapañca (A Dictionary of All the Forms of All the Roots in Sanskrit).* Number pt. 2 in Calicut University Sanskrit Series. Publication Division, University of Calicut, 2004.
24. Scharf, P. 'Levels in *Pāṇini*'s *Aṣṭādyāyī.* In A. Kulkarni and G. Huet, eds., *Proceedings, Third International Symposium on Sanskrit Computational Linguistics*, volume LNAI 5406, pp. 66–77. Springer, 2009.
25. Sharma, A., K. Deshpande, and D. Padhye. *Kāśikā: A Commentary on Pāṇini's Grammar.* Sanskrit Academy series. Sanskrit Academy, Osmania Universtiy, 2008.
26. Sharma, R. *The Aṣṭādhyāyī of Pāṇini: English translation of adhyāyas seven and eight with Sanskrit text, transliteration, word-boundary, anuvṛtti, vṛtti, explanatory notes, derivational history of examples, and indices.* The Aṣṭādhyāyī of Pāṇini. Munshiram Manoharlal Publishers,Delhi, 2003.
27. Vasu, S. *The Aṣṭādhyāyī of Pāṇini.* Motilal Banarsidass, Delhi, 1980.

Appendix A

Let us consider the derivation of future passive participles (pfp) ending in *ya* and we will draw parallel between the Heritage system and the rules in *Aṣṭādhyāyī*.

Aṣṭādhyāyī Treatment

In *Aṣṭādhyāyī*, there are three different *kṛtya* suffixes, which are used for the pfp ending in *ya*: {*yat, kyap, ṇyat*}. The treatment of this pfp formation can be considered a two-stage process of first identifying the proper suffix out of the three, and second stem changes according to the suffix.

Identifying the Proper Suffix

Main rules in Pāṇini's grammar corresponding to identifying the pfp suffixes are:

> 3.1.97 *acaḥ yat*: The suffix *yat* is added to the roots ending in a vowel.
> 3.1.98 *poḥ adupadhāt*: The suffix *yat* is added to the roots ending in a vowel and having *a* as the penultimate phoneme.
> 3.1.109 *etistuśāsvṛdṛjuṣaḥ kyap*: The suffix *kyap* is applied to the roots {*i, stu, śās, vṛ, dṛ, juṣ*}.
> 3.1.110 *ṛdupadhāt ca akḷpicṛteḥ*: The suffix *kyap* is applied to the roots having short *ṛ* in the penultimate, with the exception of *kḷp* and *cṛt*.
> 3.1.124 *ṛhalor ṇyat*: The suffix *ṇyat* is applied to the roots ending in *ṛ* or a consonant.

Together, these rules along with some specific rules in 3.1.97 to 3.1.132 determine which of the three suffixes should be applied to a root.

Stem Changes

Once the suffix is decided, the rules in the grammar corresponding to the stem changes are applied. For example, **for suffix *yat***:

> 6.1.45 *āt ecaḥ upadeśe aśiti*: For a root ending with one of the {*e, ai, o, au*} in the *upadeśa*, the last phoneme is substitued by *ā*, if a suffix not having an indicatory *ś* follows.
> 6.4.65 *īt yati*: If suffix *yat* follows an *aṅga* ending in *ā*, the last *ā* is replaced by *ī*.

Because *yat* is an *ārdhadhātuka* suffix, the *aṅga* gets the *guṇa* by 7.3.84 (*sārvadhātukārdhadhātukayoḥ*).

For suffix *kyap*, the main stem changes occur because of the following rule:

> 6.1.71 *hrasvasya piti kṛti tuk*: When a short vowel is followed by a *kṛt* suffix having an indicatory *p*, it gets an insertion of *tuk* (*t*).

Because *kyap* has an indicatory *k*, it does not cause *guṇa* because of 1.1.5 *kkṅiti ca*.

For suffix *ṇyat*, the main stem changes occur because of the following rules:

> 7.2.115 *acaḥ ñṇiti*: An *aṅga* ending in a vowel gets *vṛddhi* before a suffix having an indicatory *ṇ* or an indicatory *ñ*.
> 7.2.116 *ataḥ upadhāyāḥ*: The penultimate *a* of an *aṅga* gets *vṛddhi* before a suffix having an indicatory *ṇ* or an indicatory *ñ*.

Because *ṇyat* is an *ārdhadhātuka* suffix, when the *aṅga* does not satisfy the above two rules, it gets the *guṇa* by 7.3.86 (*pugantalaghūpadhasya ca*).

After the stem gets *vṛddhi*, there are some phonetic changes because of the following rule:

> 7.3.52 *cajoḥ ku ghiṇyatoḥ*: The final *c* or *j* of an *aṅga* are replaced by *k* and *g*, respectively, if a suffix having an indicatory *gh* or the suffix *ṇyat* follows.

There are some exceptions to 7.3.52, such as:

> 7.3.59 *na kvādeḥ*: The change from *c* or *j* to *k* and *g* does not take place if the root starts with a velar.
> 7.3.66 *yajayācarucapravacarcaḥ ca*: The change from *c* or *j* to *k* and *g* does not take place for the roots {*yaj, yāc, ruc, pravac, ṛc, tyaj*}. The inclusion of the root *tyaj* is because of a *vārtikā* on this rule.

Heritage Treatment

The Heritage system does not implement pfp as a two-stage process as described above but the rules for identifying suffix and stem changes are implemented together. Given a root, the function **pfp-ya** builds the stem pfp-stem. Once the pfp-stem is built, the condition of phonemic change due to 7.3.52 is checked by a function **fix-pfp-ya** and the specific exceptions of 7.3.52 are encoded in the function **palatal-exceptions**. We will give a brief pseudocode of these three functions along with the reference to Pāṇini's rules on pages 170 and 171. The function pfp-ya takes care of all the roots, which take *yat* and *ṇyat* suffixes and the roots ending in a consonant, which take *kyap* suffix. The roots which take *kyap* suffix and end in a vowel, are dealt with specifically in a separate function, which also generates the supplementary pfp forms.

It is clear from the pseudocode that every operation in the Heritage system emulates the corresponding operations in Pāṇini's grammar. A single line of code (phonetic rewrite rule) corresponds to one or many rules (*sūtra*) in *Aṣṭādhyāyī*; as discussed in section 1, these rewrite rules could be used as a guide to the generation of the Pāṇinian derivation.

pfp-ya (root)

pfp-stem =
*(** if root ends in a vowel **)*
match last phoneme of root with
a →root *(3.1.97)*
ā | *ai* | *o* | *au* →replace last with *e* *(3.1.97, 6.1.45, 6.4.65, 7.3.84)*
i | *ī* | *u* | *ū* →*guṇa* of root *(3.1.97, 7.3.84)*
r̥ →*vr̥ddhi* of root *(3.1.124, 7.2.115)*
*(** if root ends in a consonant **)*
match last and penultimate phoneme with
{x,*a*} →if x ∈ {*p,ph,b,bh,m*} then root *(3.1.98)*
else replace *a* by *ā* *(3.1.124, 7.2.116)*
{x,r̥} →root *(3.1.110)*
else →*guṇa* of root *(3.1.124, 7.3.86)*

fix-pfp-ya (root, pfp-stem)

pfp-stem-new =
if palatal-exception (root) →pfp-stem
else if pfp-stem starts with a velar →pfp-stem *(7.3.59)*
else match the last phoneme of pfp-stem with
    c →replace *c* with *k* *(7.3.52)*
    j →replace *j* with *g* *(7.3.52)*
    else →pfp-stem

palatal-exception (root)

match root with
aj | *vraj* →True *(7.3.60)*
yaj | *yāc* | *ruc* | *r̥c* | *tyaj* →True *(7.3.66)*
sr̥j | *vr̥j* | *pr̥c* →True *(** because these roots take kyap (3.1.110) **)*
else →False

Googling the Ṛṣi

Graph Based Analysis of Parallel Passages in Sanskrit Literature

Oliver Hellwig

South-Asia Institute, University of Heidelberg,
hellwig7@gmx.de

Abstract. Citations and parallel passages are important clues for analyzing the internal transmission structure of the Sanskrit literary tradition. The paper describes quantitative approaches for automatically constructing citation networks from lexically and Part-of-Speech (POS) tagged Sanskrit texts, and proposes numeric measures for filtering out "interesting" citations. In addition, it discusses how the resulting data can be evaluated in philological research.

1 Motivation and Structure

Sanskrit literature, one of the most voluminous literary corpora of mankind, is characterized by a strong awareness of its own tradition and a high degree of self-referentiality.[1] As a consequence, citations and plagiarism are found in most Sanskrit works. While, however, intensive, unreferenced citations are not highly estimated in modern Western society,[2] Indian tradition accepts them as one kind of hommage to important works and thinkers of the past.[3]

[1] Thanks to W. Petersen for helping me with graph terminology. The title of the paper itself is a citation it refers to the line "Googling the bard", which is the subtitle of a stage review, published by J. Rodrigues on 29 February 2012 in *The Providence Phoenix.*

[2] Consider the case of the German Secretary of Defense v. Guttenberg, who resigned from office because he had copied parts of his doctoral thesis without giving the sources.

[3] Refer to Buelow (1990) for an overview of post-Renaissance European discussions about plagiarism and originality.

Although Indological research is well aware of the importance of citations for in-depth research in the intellectual history of ancient India, it is not able to explore these connecting lines to their full extent. This situation is due to the enormous amount of Sanskrit literature and to the intensity of cross-references between texts. In this situation, quantitative approaches may support and promote traditional text-oriented research by formalizing the problem of citations in Sanskrit literature and by developing computational models for an approximate solution.

The paper has three aims: all of which belong rather to Computational Philology than to pure Computational Linguistics. First, it aims at defining criteria and quantitative methods by which citations or parallel passages can be detected in Sanskrit literature. Second, the paper describes methods with which networks of strongly citing texts can be explored. The third aim of the paper is formalizing the notion of "importance" that is assigned both by tradition and modern research to certain Sanskrit texts. Most scholars would probably agree that the *Manusmṛti* and the *Mahabhārata* are important texts, without being able to give a formal or even quantitative criterion for defining "importance". Formalizing this philological notion has numerous areas of application. It may, for instance, be used to determine the authoritative texts in complex, weakly explored text traditions, thereby facilitating the philological examination of Sanskrit literature. In addition, a formalized notion of "importance" is useful for assigning weights to query results from Sanskrit corpora.

The paper is divided into six parts. After a short overview of previous research in Section 2, Section 3 defines basic terms used in this paper, and Section 4 describes the data used for citation detection. The actual implementation of citation search is discussed in Sections 5 and 6. While Section 5 describes how citations are detected in morphologically and lexically annotated texts and how they are transformed into a graph structure, Section 6 sketches the philological evaluation of this structure. Section 7 summarizes the main findings.

2 Previous Work

Detection of citations and of intentional parallels is a well investigated topic in Computational Linguistics and in neighbouring disciplines. Many authors make use of similar, quite stable technologies, which frequently rely on (partial) sequence alignment. Baker (1992), one of the early approaches to duplication detection on the text level, applies suffix trees to search efficiently for exact matches in text pairs. Irving (2004) makes use of the Smith–Waterman algorithm (Smith and Waterman, 1981) for detecting plagiarism by local alignments. Similar methods are proposed in Gipp and Meuschke (2011) or Su et al. (2008).

The present paper interprets parallel passages as links between texts. To formalize this model, texts are represented by vertices in a citation graph and the links between them are represented by edges. Citations constitute, in general, unidirectional connections between text vertices, because the later text cites the earlier one. The temporal directionality produces acyclic graphs, although this condition is violated in several cases when constructing the network of citations in Sanskrit literature (refer to page 182). These ideas, which are heavily used in research on citation networks, make it possible to apply methods of graph and network analysis to the citation structure of Sanskrit literature.[4] In this field, several methods have been developed for assessing the importance of single vertices in graphs. This paper applies the well-known Page rank algorithm (Brin and Page, 1998) to this problem and tries to formalize the philological idea of "importance" of a text in this way. In addition, it uses clique detection algorithms for finding strongly citing, closed subcorpora in an automatic way. The paper uses the `igraph` library of `R` (R Development Core Team, 2007) for creating and analyzing the citation network.

3 Definition and Preliminaries

In this paper, the term "citation" is defined as a pair of sentences from two texts that are as long as possible and that share as much "interesting" lexical units as possible. Several points in this definition need further clarification.

[4] Refer to Price (1965) and Leicht et al. (2007), for instance.

Citations are generally defined as intentional references of an author to another text, which include the name of the cited text and the cited passage. Leaving apart the problem that text and author are modern Western concepts and that these concepts are difficult to apply to major parts of the Sanskrit literature, this definition must be relaxed in several points when dealing with algorithms for finding parallel passages in Sanskrit literature. First, many texts, especially those from the Purāṇic tradition do not give the sources of citations. *Garuḍa Purāṇa* 146ff., for example, cites literally from several chapters of the *Aṣṭāṅgahṛdaya Saṁhitā.*[5] The text does not mention its source explicitly. Instead, it opens Chapter 146 by mentioning the physician Suśruta, from whose work the *Aṣṭāṅgahṛdaya Saṁhitā* is probably derived (cf. Meulenbeld, 2000). Although scholarly Sanskrit treatises and the commentary literature frequently mention the sources of citations, we are facing the problem that many (possible) citations consist only of the cited text and leave out the bibliographical reference. As a consequence, the intentionality of citations and, therefore, the direction of edges in the citation graph are difficult to establish.

Closely connected is the problem of the historical dimension, whose preliminary solution is addressed on page 182. Obviously, the citing text is composed later than the cited one. The algorithm for citation detection that is proposed in Section 5 only detects similar passages, without giving the temporal relation between them. Therefore, the temporal relation between the texts linked by parallel passages, which is crucial for establishing edge directionality in the graph structure of the citation network, must be deduced from external, philological sources. At the current stage of research in the history of Sanskrit literature, this historical dimension introduces a large amount of uncertainty in the citation network. Any conclusion drawn from it must, therefore, be checked carefully against the results of philological research.

Contrary to string-based approaches to citation detection as described, for instance, in Irving (2004) or Prasad and Rao (2010) we compare sequences of lexical units, thereby abstracting to a higher level of linguistic annotation. This choice has been made due to the linguistic complexity of Sanskrit. The rich morphology, *sandhi* rules, a comparatively free word order, and the weakly regularized

[5] See also Kirfel (1954) for Āyurvedic content in the *Garuḍa Purāṇa*.

orthography of many Devanāgarī prints frequently create suboptimal alignments on a phonetic level even if the linguistic structure of two passages is nearly identical. Consider the following trivial example, where the *Garuḍa Purāṇa* most probably refers to a verse found in the *Manusmr̥ti*:

Manusmr̥ti, 1.35	*maricim atryaṅgirasau pulastyaṃ pulahaṃ kratum* /
Garuḍapurāṇa, 1.87.2	*mariciratryaṅgirasau pulastyaḥ pulahaḥ kratuḥ* /

While an alignment on the character level would involve several insert and delete operations, we observe a perfect match if both verses are interpreted as sequences of lexemes (*marici* → *atri* → *aṅgiras* → *pulastya* → *pulaha* → *kratu*). In the same way, high measures of correspondence can still be achieved even if the positions of few lexical units have been exchanged in a sentence.

In most cases of sentencewise similarity, bibliographical data are not recorded in the citing text or they are not captured by the algorithm described in this paper. Therefore, it is a challenge to distinguish "true" citations from those passages that use similar phraseology, but are not necessarily intentional citations. This problem is difficult to solve by performing alignment on the lexical level alone, and without inspecting the context of each similar passage. As the algorithm yields several 10,000 parallels, a manual inspection cannot be performed in acceptable time. Therefore, the intentionality of sentencewise parallelisms is estimated by two additional measures: the "interestingness" of the lexical composition and the length of the two parallels. The interestingness, which is dealt with in Section 5.2, reflects the notion that two passages sharing extraordinary, rare vocabulary are more likely to be intentional citations than two passages with common vocabulary. The length of a common sequence is another important clue when evaluating the intentionality of parallel passages. Very short passages need "impressive" lexical, semantic or (text-)historical contexts to be identifiable as citations. *Tat tu* would hardly be acceptable as a valid citation in any context, while the Upaniṣadic *tat tvam asi* is mostly accepted as a citation, due to its famous literary origin. As a consequence, the length of a parallel passage is an important piece of information in a quantitative approach.

4 Data

The Digital Corpus of Sanskrit (DCS) (Hellwig, 2010-12) is used as the database for finding citations. While preparing this paper (February 2012), the DCS contains about 3,200,000 lexically and morphologically annotated words in 430,628 sentences or verses. In addition to the Sanskrit source text, the corpus disposes of several layers of linguistic annotations that store, among others, the lexical and morphological analyses of all words (Hellwig, 2009b). This linguistic information forms the foundation of the citation search described in this paper, and its availability is the reason of why this comparatively small corpus has been chosen for citation detection.[6]

To limit the execution time of citation search and to prevent overinclusion of short high-frequency expressions such as "[XY] *uvāca*", the evaluation has been restricted to sentences that contain between $n_1 = 5$ and $n_2 = 12$ lexemes. Setting the two thresholds to these specific values includes about 90 percent of the 430,628 sentences that are contained in the DCS, as can be seen in Fig. 1.

5 Building the Citation Graph

This section describes how parallel passages are found (Section 5.1), how their lexical "interestingness" is evaluated (Section 5.2), and how they are transformed into a graph structure (Section 5.3).

5.1 Extracting Parallel Sequences

Due to the comparatively small size of the text database (refer to Sectinn 4), we evaluate every pair of sentences (s_i, s_j) that contain

[6] We are currently preparing an unsupervised analysis of the complete Gretil corpus for which an average accuracy of over 95 peercent can be expected for combined *sandhi* splitting and lexical analysis (tokenization and lemmatization). This data will give access to a much more representative view of the Sanskrit tradition, including, for instance, the Buddhist canon and numerous texts from the *ṣaḍdarśanas*, which are only scarcely represented in the DCS at the moment. It is to be expected that this enlarged corpus will also generate a different citation network of Sanskrit literature.

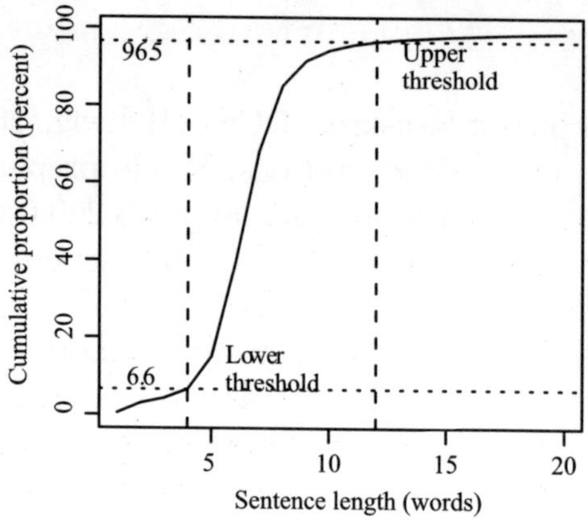

Fig. 1: Cumulative proportions of sentence lengths in the DCS; data in Table 1

Table 1: Absolute counts and cumulative percentual proportions of sentence lengths in the DCS

Length	Total Number	Cummulitive Proportion
1	2,178	0.51
2	10,891	3.03
3	5,498	4.31
4	9,956	6.62
5	36,172	15.02
6	10,4552	39.30
...		
12	3,574	96.52
13	2,301	97.06
...		
20	0,562	98.77

between 5 and 12 lexemes. Evaluation and alignment are performed in two steps.

If l_i and l_j denote the ordered sets of unique lexemes contained in sentences s_i and s_j,[7] high-frequency and closed-class lexemes

[7] In database terminology, these sets are created using the `DISTINCT` and `ORDER BY` operators.

such as *tad*, *etad*, *ca* or *api* are removed from l_i and l_j. Now, the size of the intersection between l_i and l_j is divided by the size of their union. This results in a measure $e^1 = \frac{|l_i \cap l_j|}{|l_i \cup l_j|}$, which can be calculated efficiently for preordered sets. Pairs of sentences (s_i, s_j) with e^1_{ij} being larger than a given threshold are passed to a more detailed examination in the next step, because results found using this approach are frequently not related in content and, therefore, not relevant from a philological point of view. Consider an artificial example with s_i as *ṛṣayoḥ paśyatāṃ rāmaś ca sītā ca vanānnirgacchataḥ* and s_j as *rāmaḥ sītāṃ paśyati.* Although the two sentences share a triple of lexemes (*rāma*, *sītā*, *paś*), they express completely different ideas. As long as Sanskrit sentences cannot be annotated with discourse semantic information, correspondence in content is approximated by taking into account word order, which is done in the next step.

After the first step has detected intersections in the vocabulary without taking into account the order of lexemes, an alignment algorithm is now applied to (s_i, s_j). We use the Smith–Waterman algorithm (Smith and Waterman) to obtain the optimal (local) alignment score of the two sentences. The following update rule is used for filling the $|s_i| \times |s_j|$ matrix m:

$$m[a,b] = \max \begin{cases} m[a-1,b-1]+2 & \text{if } s_{ia} = s_{jb} \\ \max(m[a-1,b]-1, & \text{else} \\ m[a,b-1]-1) & \end{cases}$$

Because long parallel sequences should be given a greater weight (Section 3), the highest (local) score in m is divided by twice[8] the possible maximal length of compared sentences, resulting in $e^A = \frac{\max m}{2 \cdot 12}$.

The extraction step generates 54,206 pairs of parallel sequences from the DCS.

5.2 Evaluating the "Interestingness" of Citations

As mentioned in the Section 3, the "interestingness" or semantic relevance of a parallel passage can be measured by the semantic

[8] Twice because the weight for an identical pair of lexical symbols is set to +2.

weight of the lexemes it contains. While, for instance, the mention of *tad* or *rājan* does not yield a strong indication for the common origin of two passages, high frequency of vocabulary from restricted subdomains supports the conclusion that two parallel passages constitute a pair of citations.[9] This philological idea is demonstrated nicely when comparing the following two pairs of parallel passages. The verse *tato devāḥ sagandharvāḥ siddhāś ca paramarṣayaḥ* is repeated literally in several texts from epic and Purāṇic tradition (among others, in *Rāmāyaṇa, Bā.*, 14.4 and *Matsya-Purāṇa*, 111.10); the verse *pinākaṁ darduraṁ nāgaṁ vajraṁ ceti caturvidham*, which enumerates four types of the mineral *abhra*, is found in *Ānandakanda*, 1, 7.154 and *Bhāvaprakāśa*, 6, 8.118. From a philological point of view, the second parallel is definitely a stronger indication of a citation (or at least a common textual source) than the first one, because it is composed of unusual, domain-specific vocabulary.

In a more formal approach, high semantic weight is assigned to those lexical units that occur only in few texts. Such distributional properties can be expressed by the entropy of lexical units over texts. In this paper, however, an easier, "binary" method is used. If δ_{ij} is the Kronecker delta with

$$\delta_{ij} = \begin{cases} 1 \text{ if lexeme } i \text{ is } \textit{not} \text{ contained in text } j \\ 0 \text{ else} \end{cases}$$

and N is the total number of text in the DCS, we define the lexical "interestingness" of lexeme i as $d_i = \frac{\sum_{j=1}^{N} \delta_{ij}}{N}$. This measure yields low values for common, well distributed lexemes, but high values for specialized domain vocabulary. The lexical weight e^L_{ij} of the pair of sentences (s_i, s_j) is defined as the average of d_k for all lexemes k in $s_i \cap s_j$: $e^L_{ij} = \frac{\sum_{l_k \in (s_i \cap s_j)} d_k}{|s_i \cap s_j|}$.

5.3 Transforming the Data into a Graph

After each pair of sentences (s_i, s_j) has been associated with the normalized alignment score e^A_{ij} from the Smith–Waterman algorithm and the average lexical weight e^L_{ij}, the parallel passages are

[9] Refer to Hellwig (2009a) for a case study from the Sanskrit alchemical corpus.

filtered based on these two measures and transformed into a graph structure. It should be emphasized at this point that the structure and the complexity of the final citation graph are strongly influenced by parameter selection described in the following paragraphs. Comparatively strict thresholds were chosen for this paper to generate a well visualizable citation network.

Removing Self-citations: Parallel passages for which source and destination texts are identical are removed from the database of citations. Although this information is important when examining, for example, traces of oral composition or the stratification of a text,[10] self-citations distort the weighting scheme applied in this paper, because highly self-referential texts obtain high weights in Page rank. In this step, the initial number of 54,206 pairs of parallel sentences is reduced to 32,127 pairs.

Filtering Using Alignment Scores and Lexical Weights: The 50 percent and 75 percent quantiles of the Smith–Waterman alignment scores e^A and of the average lexical weights e^L are calculated. Only those pairs (s_i, s_j) are retained for which both measures are in the upper 50 percent of the respective distributions or for which at least one measure is in the upper 25 percent of the respective distributions, which results in a further reduction to 18,722 pairs of parallel passages. Quantiles are used instead of mean and standard deviation because the distribution of e^A has a positive skew.

Grouping by Texts: The remaining pairs of parallel passages are grouped by containing texts, which results in 981 quadruples $(t_i, t_j, n_{ij}, a_{ij})$, with t_i and t_j denoting a pair of different texts, n_{ij} denoting the number of parallel passages shared by t_i and t_j, and a_{ij} being a normalized measure of association between t_i and t_j. If l_i denotes the number of sentences in text t_i, a_{ij} is defined as $a_{ij} = \frac{n_{ij}}{l_i \cdot l_j}$, i.e. by dividing the observed number of linking passages by the highest possible number of sentence-wise links between t_i

[10] See, for instance, Brockington (1970) or Hellwig (2008) for studies on the *Rāmāyaṇa*.

and t_j.[11] a_{ij} is used as edge weight in the resulting citation network. Quadruples with $n_{ij} < 3$ are removed. This step reduces the number of quadruples from 981 to 477.

In graph terminology, the texts constitute the vertices of the citation graph. The fact that two texts t_i and t_j share parallel passages is expressed by inserting an edge between the corresponding vertices. The weight of this edge is given by parameter a_{ij}, calculated as described above.

Removing Single Linkage Texts: To keep the final structure intelligible, all texts that are linked to only one other text are removed from the citation network, even if linkage strength a_{ij} is high. This step, which further reduces the number of vertices to 459, removes philologically interesting microstructures such as the *Spandakārikā*, which is only linked to the *Śivasūtravārttika* from the same Kashmirian tradition, the *Nāḍīparīkṣā*, which is closely connected to parts of the *Śārṅgadhara Saṁhitā*, or the component consisting of *Toḍalatantra* and *Mātṛkābhedatantra*.

Directionality of Edges: The direction of the linking edges is established using the historical stratification of the DCS described in Hellwig (2010). A directed edge pointing from t_i to t_j replaces the undirected edge between these vertices if t_i and t_j share enough parallel passages and if t_i is later than t_j according to the historical stratification. Because the stratification is only a coarse approximation of the true historical structure of the corpus, about 100 temporal relations are added manually, most of which describe the temporal relation of texts that are assigned to the same historical layer in Hellwig (2010). If, as in the case of *Mahābhārata* and *Manusmṛti*, the temporal relation between two texts cannot be determined with reasonable certainty, two directed edges $t_i \rightarrow t_j$ and $t_j \rightarrow t_i$ are inserted in the graph. Inserting such double edges, of course, violates the acyclicity, which is a central feature of citation networks Leicht et al. (2007).

[11] The maximal number of $l_i \cdot l_j$ linking passages is obtained, if every sentence in t_i is linked to every sentence in t_j. This scenario only occurs when both texts consist completely of the repetition of the same sentence, which is a slightly unrealistic assumption.

The resulting list of vertices and edges is processed using the `R` (R Development Core Team, 2007) package `igraph`, which offers high-level functions for the exploration of the citation graph. Figure 2 shows the resulting network. The graph is produced using the Fruchterman–Reingold layout algorithm as a starting point and manually refining the layout in the `tkplot` interface such that overlapping labels are avoided, but without rearranging the basic layout produced by `igraph`. The weights of edges a_{ij} are indicated by their hues.

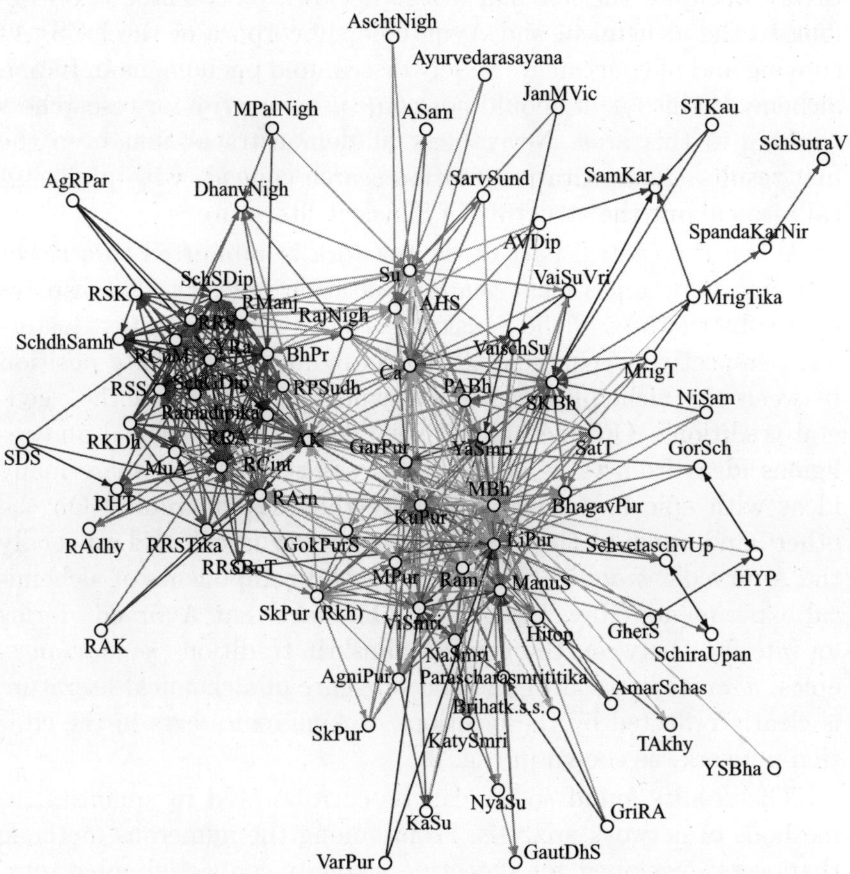

Fig. 2: Full network of citations in the DCS

6 Philological Evaluation of the Citation Network

6.1 Detecting Strongly Linked Subcorpora

Even a short look at the citation network in Fig. 2 reveals a clearly observable substructure in the graph, because the texts in the DCS can be divided into two groups. A cluster of strongly linked texts, which is indicated by the dark edges connecting its vertices (= texts), occupies the left half of the network plot. These texts belong to the alchemical and Āyurvedic subcorpora of the DCS. As copying and plagiarism are widely distributed phenomena in Indian alchemy,[12] this result should not come as a surprise for researchers working in this area. Neverthless, it demonstrates that even the first results of quantitative citation search coincide with philological ideas about the structure of Sanskrit literature.

When the central part of the network is submitted to a closer scrutiny, it becomes clear that the citation network also displays finer substructures of the Sanskrit corpus. Seen from a text historical perspective, Āyurvedic texts occupy an intermediate position between the alchemical subcorpus and the texts from the "general tradition". On one hand, they take up philosophical and religious ideas from texts of the *ṣaḍdarśana*s, and they share many ideas with epic literature, especially the *Mahābhārata*.[13] On the other hand, medical theories found in the Āyurveda and especially the Āyurvedic *materia medica* are central components of alchemical experiments (Ray, 1907, 1909). The fact that Āyurveda forms an interface between the general Sanskrit tradition (*ṣaḍdarśana*s, epics, *dharma* literature) and the subgenre of alchemical literature is clearly reflected by the positions of Āyurvedic texts in the citation network, as shown in Fig. 2.

The results found so far can be corroborated by quantitative methods of network analysis. From among the numerous methods that were developed for detecting strongly-connected subgraphs,

---

[12] Refer, for instance, to Hellwig (2009a)and Bendixen (1990) for a detailed study of the *Rasaratnasamuccaya* and the *Rasendracūḍāmaṇi*.

[13] Refer to Comba (1987) and Hellwig (2009c) for contact points between Āyurveda, Vaiśeṣika and Sāṁkhya.

the largest clique algorithm is applied to the citation network.[14] The algorithm yields ten cliques, nine of which are slightly differing subgraphs from the alchemical subcorpus,[15] while the tenth clique contains central texts from the general Sanskrit tradition such as the *Mahābhārata* and the *Manusmṛti*. Results of largest cliques detection thus prove the value of this approach for research in complex, highly interlinked text traditions as, for example, medieval religious schools or subdomains of scientific literature.

6.2 Determining the Importance of Texts

The results presented in the previous section have shown that a visual inspection as well as a quantitative evaluation of citation networks support philological ideas about the history and the composition of a large Sanskrit corpus. The second part of the evaluation addresses the question of how citation networks can be used for formalizing the notion of importance that traditional scholarship has assigned to different texts in the Sanskrit tradition, and of whether numeric measures of importance corroborate those traditional ideas.

As mentioned in the beginning of this paper, Sanskrit scholarship assigns high importance to texts such as the *Mahābhārata* or the *Manusmṛti*, while, for instance, alchemical texts are not assumed to be integral components of the textual tradition. Taking a slightly simplified approach, the importance of a text can be measured by the frequency with which other authors refer to this text: If the text is mentioned and cited frequently, over a long period of time, and by a well diversified group of important authors, it is certainly more important for the general intellectual picture of the Sanskrit tradition than texts from an almost closed, though strongly linked subcorpus as constituted by alchemical literature.

The Page rank algorithm (Brin and Page, 1998) is the quantitative method of choice for automatically detecting texts that are important according to this definition. Generally speaking, the algorithm assigns a weight to each vertex in a directed graph. The

[14] The implementation `largest.cliques` from the `igraph` library is used in this paper.

[15] The core of this subcorpus is constituted by the *Rasārṇava*, the *Rasaratnasamuccaya* and the *Rasendracūḍāmaṇi*.

weight is calculated by recursively inspecting the weights of those vertices that link to the given vertex. The solution of the problem can be given by calculating the eigenvector of a matrix representing the linking structure.

Table 2 displays the texts with the highest and the lowest Page ranks. A threshold of 0.02, by which the high-ranking texts are delimited, has been selected by inspecting Fig. 3, which plots the Page ranks of all texts in decreasing order. The threshold corresponds to the "turning point" of the curve. Even the snapshot displayed in Table 2 shows that the Page rank algorithm, when applied to the citation data, is able to filter out texts such as the *Mahābhārata* or the *Manusmṛti*, which traditional scholarship deems to be important, while the algorithm assigns lowest weights to peripheral texts such as the *Janmamaraṇavicāra* or the *Gṛhastharatnākara.*

The efficiency of the weighting algorithm is further demonstrated by the plot of the citation network with weighted vertices (Fig. 4), where the radius of each vertex is scaled linearly with its weight. Most interestingly, the texts from the alchemical tradition, though interlinked strongly in the citation graph (cp. Fig. 2), obtain only low weights, while the *Mahābhārata* and the *Manusmṛti* occupy the central positions that are assigned to them by scholarly tradition. Results of the Page rank algorithm also make sense when the Āyurvedic "interface texts" are inspected, where the *Caraka Saṁhitā* is the dominant text. This weight clearly coincides with the text historical position of the *Caraka Saṁ mhitā*, because it is an important source for the *Aṣṭāṅgahṛdaya Saṁhitā*, which, again, influenced the medieval medical tradition (cf. Meulenbeld), and because it is linked strongly to the early philosophical literature and to the philosophical strata of the *Mahābhārata.*

7 Conclusions and Outlook

The paper has discussed quantitative approaches to citation detection in Sanskrit literature. It has presented numeric measures whose combination enables the researcher to extract interesting and relevant parallel passages in an unsupervised way. In the second part, the paper has described applications of citation search in "practical" philology and especially in the discussion of textual traditions. It is to be hoped that methods such as the Page rank

Text	Page Rank
Mahābhārata	0.0986
Manusmṛti	0.0578
Rāmāyaṇa	0.0547
Viṣṇusmṛti	0.0544
Garuḍapurāṇa	0.0531
Carakasaṃhitā	0.0519
Yājñavalkyasmṛti	0.0409
Nāradasmṛti	0.0385
Kātyāyanasmṛti	0.0294
Liṅgapurāṇa	0.0252
Kūrmapurāṇa	0.0217
Rasaratnākara	0.0215
Bṛhatkathāślokasaṃgraha	0.0205
...	
Amaraughaśāsana	0.0019
Āyurvedadīpikā	0.0019
Āyurvedarasāyana	0.0019
Gṛhastharatnākara	0.0019
Janmamaraṇavicāra	0.0019

Table 2: Texts with highest and lowest Page rank scores; threshold determined using Fig. 3

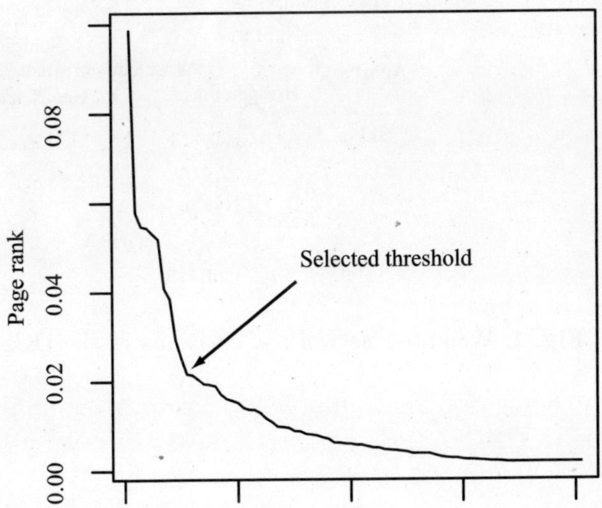

Fig. 3: Determining the threshold for "important" texts

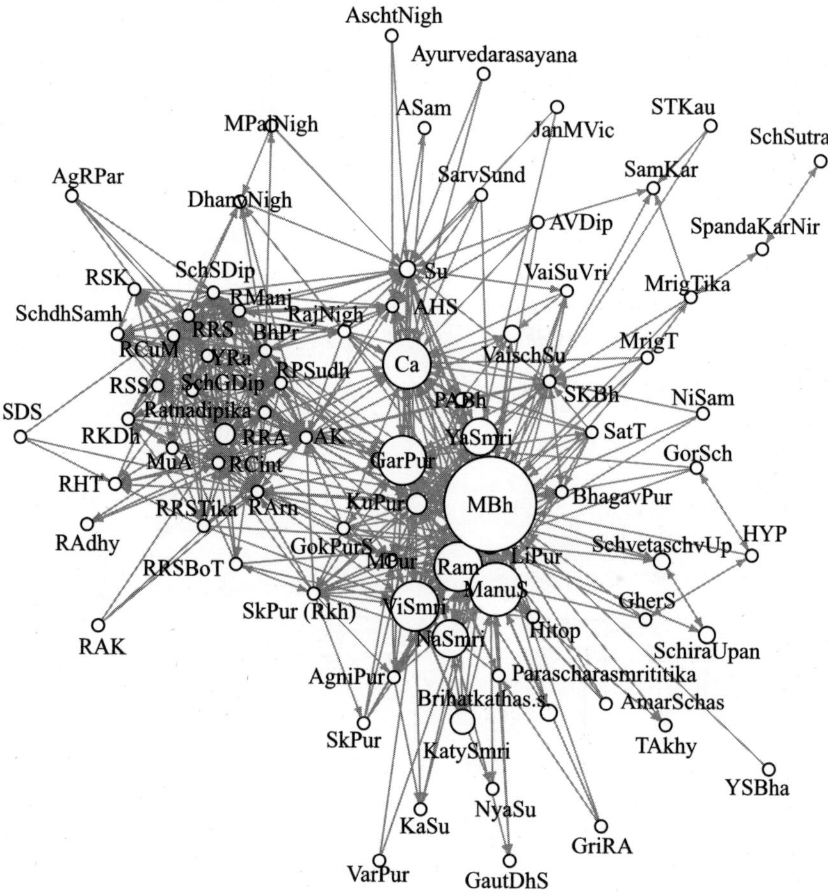

Fig. 4: Weighted network of citations in the DCS

algorithm are applied more frequently to philological questions to supplement traditional scholarship with the findings from quantitative approaches.

References

1. Baker, B. S. A program for Identifying Duplicated Code, *Computing Science and Statistics* 24: 4957, 1992.
2. Bendixen, A. Überlegungen zu *Rasaratnasamuccaya* (Kapitel 1-11) und zu *Rasendracūḍāmaṇi*, *Journal of the European Āyurvedic Society* 1: 165–66, 1990.
3. Brin, S. and Page, L. The anatomy of a large-scale hypertextual web search engine, *Computer Networks and ISDN Systems*, Elsevier Science Publishers, pp. 107–17, 1998.
4. Brockington, J. Stereotyped expressions in the Rāmāyaṇa, *Journal of the American Oriental Society* 90.2: 210–27, 1970.
5. Buelow, G. J. Originality, Genius, Plagiarism in English Criticism of the Eighteenth Century, *International Review of the Aesthetics and Sociology of Music* 21(2): 117–28, 1990.
6. Comba, A. Carakasaṃhitā, Śārīrasthāna I and Vaiśeṣika philosophy, *in* G. J. Meulenbeld and D. Wujastyk (eds), *Studies on Indian medical history*, Egbert Forsten, Groningen, pp. 43–61, 1987.
7. de Solla Price, D.J. Networks of scientific papers, *Science* 149(3683): 510–15, 1965.
8. Gipp, B. and Meuschke, N. Citation pattern matching algorithms for citation-based plagiarism detection: Greedy citation tiling, citation chunking and longest common citation sequence, *Proceedings of the 11th ACM Symposium on Document Engineering (DocEng2011)*, 2011.
9. Hellwig, O. Frequent Phrases and Their Application to Text Segmentation, *Studien zur Indologie und Iranistik* 25: 55–72, 2008.
10. Hellwig, O. *Quecksilber und Chronometrie. Eine computerphilologische Analyse der mittelalterlichen indischen Alchemie*, Shaker Verlag, Aachen, 2009a.
11. Hellwig, O. `SanskritTagger`, A Stochastic Lexical and POS Tagger for Sanskrit, *in* G. Huet, A. Kulkarni and P. Scharf (eds), *Sanskrit Computational Linguistics. First and Second International Symposia*, Lecture Notes in Artificial Intelligence, 5402, Springer Verlag, Berlin, pp. 266–77, 2009b.
12. Hellwig, O. The theory of the puruṣa in Carakasaṃhitā, Śārīrasthāna 1.1 and its connection with the early history of Indian philosophy, *Studien zur Indologie und Iranistik* 26: 27–69, 2009c.

13. Hellwig, O. Etymological trends in the Sanskrit vocabulary, *Literary and Linguistic Computing* 25(1): 105–118, 2010.
14. Hellwig, O. *DCS - The Digital Corpus of Sanskrit*, Heidelberg., 2010-2012.
15. Irving, R. Plagiarism and collusion detection using the Smith-Waterman algorithm, *Technical Report TR-2004-164*, University of Glasgow Computing Science Department, 2004.
16. Kirfel, W. Ein medizinisches Kapitel des Garuḍapurāṇas, *in* J. Schubert and U. Schneider (eds), *Asiatica. Festschrift Friedrich Weller zum 65. Geburtstag gewidmet von seinen Freunden, Kollegen und Schülern*, Otto Harrassowitz, Leipzig, pp. 333–356, 1954.
17. Leicht, E. A., Clarkson, G., Shedden, K. and Newman, M. E. J. Large-scale structure of time evolving citation networks, *European Physical Journal B – Condensed Matter* 59(1): 75 – 83, 2007.
18. Meulenbeld, G. J. *A History of Indian Medical Literature*, Egbert Forsten, Groningen, 2000.
19. Prasad, A. S. and Rao, S. Citation matching in Sanskrit corpora using local alignment, *in* G. N. Jha (ed.), *Sanskrit Computational Linguistics - 4th International Symposium*, Lecture Notes in Computer Science 6465, Springer, pp. 124–36, 2010.
20. R Development Core Team *R: A Language and Environment for Statistical Computing*, R Foundation for Statistical Computing, Wien, 2007.
21. Ray, P. C. *A History of Hindu Chemistry from the Earliest Times to the Middle of the Sixteenth Century A.D.*, Williams and Norgate, London, 1907, 1909.
22. Smith, T. and Waterman, M. Identification of common molecular subsequences, *Journal of Molecular Biology* 147: 195–197, 1981.
23. Su, Z., Ahn, B.-R., Eom, K.-Y., Kang, M.-K., Kim, J.-P. and Kim, M.-K. Plagiarism detection using the Levenshtein distance and Smith-Waterman algorithm, *Proceedings of the 2008 3rd International Conference on Innovative Computing Information and Control*, IEEE Computer Society, Washington, 2008.

Parsing Sanskrit Texts

Some Relation-specific Issues

Amba Kulkarni[1] and K.V. Ramakrishnamacharyulu[2]

[1] Department of Sanskrit Studies,
University of Hyderabad,
Hyderabad
apksh@uohyd.ernet.in
[2] Department of Vyakarana,
Rashtriya Sanskrit Vidyapeetha,
Tirupati
kvrkus@gmail.com

Abstract. Building a sentential parser following a dependency framework needs a well-defined set of relations. In Sanskrit, various texts on *Śābdabodha* theories discuss such relations. These relations are critically examined from the point of view of feasibility of building a rule-based parser. We propose an intermediate parse with nice computational properties of a tree structure and then propose another layer to make this tree structure more useful for information retrieval and user understanding.

Keywords: Sanskrit, parser, *kāraka* relations

1 Introduction

Parsing unfolds a linear string of words into a structure which shows explicitly the relations between words. The parse of positional languages such as English are well expressed by constituency structure while languages like Sanskrit, which are morphologically rich and to a large extent free word order, are better represented by a dependency tree. A possible parse of

(1) *rājā viprāya gāṁ dadāti.*
gloss: King brahmin{dat.} cow{acc.} gives.
Eng: A king gives a cow to a brahmin.

is shown in Fig. 1 as a dependency tree.

Texts dealing with the *Śābdabodha* theories describe an

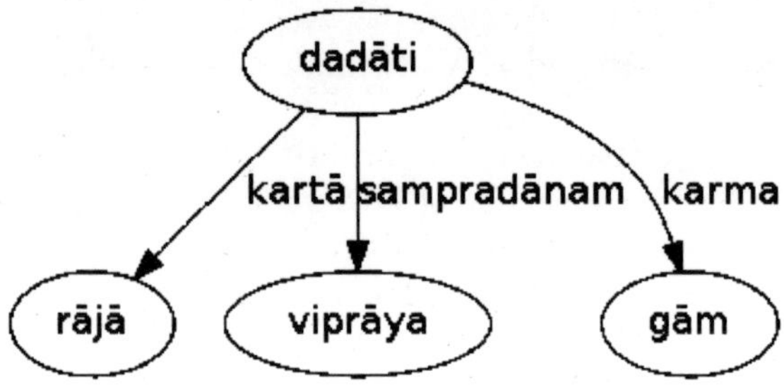

Fig. 1

understanding arising from the sentences in terms of the relations between various constituents. For example the Vaiyākaraṇa's *śābdabodha* of (1) is

rājakartr̥ka-gokarmaka-viprasampradānaka-dānānukūla-vyāpāraḥ.

Thus, according to Vaiyākaraṇas when a person hears sentence (1), the understanding that he gets is of an activity of *dāna* whose *kartā* (agent) is a king, whose *karma* (goal) is a cow and whose *sampradāna* (recipient) is a brahmin.

For a Naiyāyika, however, the structure of the verbal cognition resulting from this utterance is different. The Naiyāyika's *śābdabodha* is

gokarmaka-viprasampradānaka-dānānukūla-kr̥timān rājā.

So, according to a Naiyāyika, sentence (1) results in the cognition of a king who is the agent of an activity of giving, whose goal is a cow and whose recipient is a Brahmin.

Thus the chief qualificand is different in both the cases, however the relations between the *padārtha*s 'referent of words' are the same. Various relations described in the traditional grammar books have been compiled and classified by Krishnamacharyulu (2009) under the two broad headings inter-sentential and intra-sentential relations. This work provided a starting point for developing guidelines for annotation of Sanskrit texts at *kāraka* level and also for the development of an automatic parser for Sanskrit.

Unlike English where special efforts were put in as described in PARC (King et al., 2003) and Stanford dependency manual (Marneffe and Manning, 2008) for defining the set of relations, we are fortunate to have a well-defined, time-tested tagset for Sanskrit. This tagset can be put to use for two tasks: (a) to develop an annotated corpus and (b) to develop a parser that produces a parse tree of a given sentence. One question we would like to ask before putting it to actual use is whether the granularity of this tagset is suitable for the above two tasks?

The suitability of a tagset for manual annotation can be judged on the basis of the following parameters:

- (a) The inter annotator agreement for various tags, and
- (b) The grey/fussy tags which lead to errors in annotation.

A statistical parser that uses manually annotated data will also have these as the main concerns. A rule-based parser, on the other hand, will have different considerations. A rule-based parser performs better the less it depends on extra-linguistic information. For example, consider a manually annotated text where *kartā* is subclassified further into *anubhavī kartā* (experiencer), *karaṇa kartā*, *karma kartā*, etc. If the tagged data is sufficiently large, it is possible that machine learns the distinction between a *kartā* and an *anubhavī kartā* from the tagged examples. On the other hand, to decide whether something is an *anubhavī kartā* or not, one needs to appeal to the semantics of the verb involved. Deciding whether the *padārtha* 'the referent of a word' is a *kartā* or not is relatively easier as it involves only the syntactic and morphological information. So with a goal to build a rule-based parser, we critically examined all the tags in Krishnamacharyulu (2009). The basic principles we followed during this critical examination were:

- (a) The relations should be binary, and
- (b) information / clue for extracting any relation should be coded in the language string.

In the next section, we describe the notation for representing the relations and, in Section 3, we discuss various clues for extracting the relations. Section 4 discusses various criteria used for the choice of a relation and Section 5 deals with the issues of granularity. In Section 6, we describe the post-processing for making the parse more useful.

2 Convention for Marking the Relations

Let the *padārtha*s associated with the two words[3] 'a' and 'b' be related by relation 'R'. To be precise, 'b' has the property of 'R_ness' conditioned/determined by 'a'. We represent this graphically as in Fig. 2.

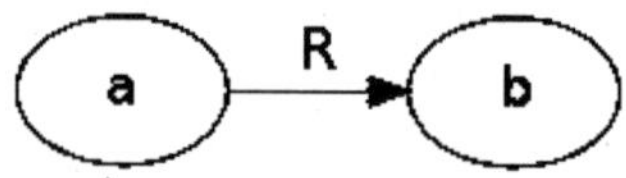

Fig. 2

Note the arrowhead at 'b'. This is a directed labelled graph where 'a' and 'b' represent the nodes, joined by a labelled arrow 'R'. For example, in a sentence *rāmaḥ gacchati*, *rāma* is the *kartā* of the going activity. Figure 3 shows the corresponding graph.

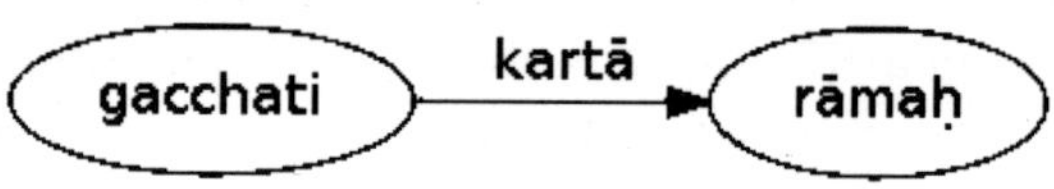

Fig. 3

For the ease of annotation, instead of annotating the sentences in graphical mode, we represent them as a text with three fields separated by a tab. The first field contains the word number, the second field the word and the third field the relation. The first

[3] Henceforth we shorten the phrase 'the *padārtha*s associated with the word' by simply 'the word'.

line of a sample annotation below then means: The word *rāmaḥ* at position 1 is the *kartā* of the word at the third position, viz. *gacchati*.

```
1.  rAmaH  kartA,3
2.  vanam  karma,3
3.  gacchati
```

3 Clues for Extracting the Relations[4]

Sanskrit being inflectionally rich, the inflectional suffixes mark the relation between words. Similarly, certain indeclinables mark some grammatical relations. Agreement between the words also indicate certain grammatical relations. We discuss below these clues for extracting relations.

1. *Abhihitatva* (property of being expressed)
   The Pāṇinian *sūtra anabhihite* (2.3.1) (if not already expressed) is an important *sūtra* that governs the *vibhakti* assignment to the nominals. The *vārttika*[5] on this *sūtra* explains *abhihita* as the one which is expressed either by *tiṅ* (a finite verbal suffix), *kṛt* (a non-finite verbal suffix), *taddhita* (derivational nominal suffix) or *samāsa* (compound). for example, in the sentence

   (2) *rāmaḥ vanaṁ gacchati*

   the verb being in the active voice (*kartari prayogaḥ*), the verbal suffix *ti* expresses the *kartā*, while in the following sentence in passive voice (*karmaṇi prayogaḥ*).

   (3) *rāmeṇa vanaṁ gamyate*

   the *karma* is expressed by the verbal suffix. As such, in both cases, the one which is expressed (*kartā* and *karma*, respectively) is in the nominative case and shows number and

[4] These have been discussed in Kulkarni et al. (2010). For the sake of completeness, we repeat the relevant portion here.

[5] *tiṅkṛttaddhitasamāsaiḥ parisaṁkhyānam* (Ma. Bhā. 2.3.1 vā.).

person agreement with the verb form.

Unlike the *tiṅ* suffix which is inflectional, *kr̥t*, *taddhita* and *samāsa* mark the derivation process, and in the process the derivation generates a new lexical head from the old one. For example, in

(4) *dhāvan aśvaḥ*

the *kr̥t* suffix in *dhāvan* expresses the relation of *kartā* (*kartari kr̥t* (3.4.68)) and indicates the one which performs the action of *dhāv* 'running'.

2. *Vibhakti*
   The verbal as well as nominal suffixes in Sanskrit are termed *vibhaktis*. We have already seen that verbal suffixes (*tiṅ*), through *abhihitatva*, mark the relations between words. Now we consider the nominal suffixes. They fall under three broad categories.

   a. *Vibhakti* indicating a *kāraka* relation
      This marks a relation between a noun and a verb known as a *kāraka* relation. Sanskrit uses seven case suffixes to mark six *kāraka* relations *kartā, karma, karaṇa, sampradāna, apādāna* and *adhikaraṇa.* The genitive suffix, in addition to marking a *kāraka* relation,[6] is predominantly used to mark a noun–noun relation.

   b. *Upapada vibhakti*
      In addition to the noun–noun relations expressed by the sixth case, there are certain words, most of them indeclinables called *upapadas*, which also mark a special kind of noun-noun relation. These indeclinable, mark a relation of a noun with another noun, and in turn demand a special case suffix for the preceding noun. For example, the *upapada saha* demands a third case suffix for the preceding noun as in:

[6] *kartr̥karmaṇoḥ kr̥ti* (2.3.65).

(5) *rāmeṇa saha sītā vanaṁ gacchati.*

c. Special *vibhakti*

*Vibhakti*s are also used to indicate various other relations such as

atyantasaṁyoga 'intimate and total contact' (as in *māsamadhitaḥ* 'he studied for a month without any break'),
kriyaviśeṣaṇa 'adverbial usage' as in *vegena dhāvati* 'runs fast',
aṅgavikāra 'defect in a body-organ' as in *akṣṇā kāṇaḥ* 'blind with an eye',
nirdhāraṇa 'specifying one out of many' as in *nareṣu śreṣṭaḥ* 'best among the men' ,
vibhakta 'distinct/different' as in *gopālāta śyāmaḥ avaraḥ* 'Śyāma is better than Gopāla'.

3. Indeclinables (*avyaya*)

The indeclinables mark various kinds of relations such as negation, adverbial (manner adverbs only) and co-ordination. Sometimes they also provide information about interrogation, emphasis, etc. We distinguish the *upapada*s from the *avyaya*s, mainly because, though most of the *upapada*s (which are termed *karmapravacanīya* by Pāṇini) are also indeclinables, they demand a special case suffix on the preceding word, whereas it is not so with indeclinables.

For example, the relation of *na* with *gacchati* in the sentence

(6) *rāmaḥ gṛhaṁ na gacchati*

is that of 'negation (*niṣedha*)'. Similarly, the relation of *mandam* with *calati* in the sentence

(7) *rāmaḥ mandaṁ calati*

is that of 'adverbial (*kriyāviśeṣaṇa*)'. The relation of *eva* with *rāma* in the sentence

(8) *rāmaḥ eva tatra upaviṣati*

is that of 'emphasis (*avadhāraṇa*)'.

4. *Samānādhikaraṇa*
   Agreement in gender, number and case suffix marks *samānādhikaraṇa* (having the same locus), or the modifier-modified relation between two nouns as in

   (9) *śvetaḥ aśvaḥ dhāvati.*
   (10) *aśvaḥ śvetaḥ asti.*

   In (9) and (10), the words *aśvaḥ* and *śvetaḥ* have the same gender, number and *vibhakti* indicating *samānādhikaraṇa.* However, there is a subtle difference between the information being conveyed. In (10), the word *śvetaḥ* is a predicative adjective (*vidheya viśeṣaṇa*), while in (9) it is an attributive adjective.

4 Choice of Relations and Their Representation

These clues now lead us to the following questions.

- Should the inflectional suffixes and derivational suffixes be treated at par?
- How to treat the function words? Should they be treated as a node in a tree or an edge?
- How to represent the inter-sentential relations?
- Should anaphoric resolution be part of this annotation?

The basic principles we follow in arriving at the decision and the rationale behind them are:

1. Preserve one–one mapping between the nodes of a tree and the words in a sentence.[This is more of a topological requirement than a linguistic one. If this condition is relaxed, the parse ceases to be a tree, loosing its nice computational properties.[7]]

---

[7] Amba Kulkarni acknowledges fruitful discussions with Gérard Huet.

2. In case of derived nouns, consider only the inflectional suffix for establishing the relations.[This also is a topological requirement with the same reasoning as above.]
3. In case of derived indeclinables, use the derived suffix to mark the relations.[Since there is a deletion (*lopa*) of the inflectional suffix in case of derived indeclinables, the information encoded by the derived suffix is considered for the marking of relations.]
4. In case of indeclinables (other than the derived *kr̥dantas*), the words themselves mark the relations.
5. A suffix or a word can represent one and only one relation.[Any meaningful unit in an interpretation under consideration expresses only one meaning.]

We present below various cases and explain the rationale behind these principles. These principles themselves provide answers to the questions raised above.

1. *Abhihita*

   The verbal inflection in addition to marking various features associated with the verbal form also shows an agreement with the noun – a *kartā* in *kartari prayogaḥ* (active voice) and a *karma* in *karmaṇi prayogaḥ* (passive voice). So the question is, in case of an active voice, what is the head of the *kartā* relation – a verb or a noun? If we refer back to our convention for naming the relations, if 'b' has R_ness conditioned by 'a', then we mark the relation 'R' as a relation of 'a' in 'b'. In a sentence *rāmaḥ gacchati*, the nominal case suffix in *rāma* does not indicate any *kāraka* relation.[8] And hence on the basis of agreement, we mark the relation of *kartā* in *rāma*. If *kartr̥ pada* is missing in the sentence as in *gacchāmi*, we do not mark it.

   Now consider another example:

   (11) *dhāvantam aśvaṁ paśya.*

   In this sentence, there are two verbs *dhāv* 'run' and *paśya (dr̥ś)* 'see'. *Dhāv* has a *kr̥t* suffix (*śatr̥*) which is in the sense of *kartā*. *Aśva* is the *karma* of *paśya*, and is also the *kartā* of *dhāv*. Further *dhāvantaṁ* and *aśvaṁ* have same *vibhakti* and hence

[8] *prātipadikārthaliṅparimāṇavacanamātre prathamā* (2.3.46).

there is a *viśeṣya–viśeṣaṇa bhāva* (modifier–modified relation) between them. Now the question is which relation to mark for the word *aśva-* a *karma* of *paśya*, a *kartā* of *dhāv* or a *viśeṣya* of *dhāvat* or all of them? Marking all these three relations may generate a loop or multiple inheritance for the word *aśvaṁ* as shown in Fig. 4.
A loop destroys the nice tree structure of a parse, and hence we decide to mark only relations indicated through the inflectional suffixes and not through the derivational suffixes. Hence we propose to represent the relations as in Fig. 5.

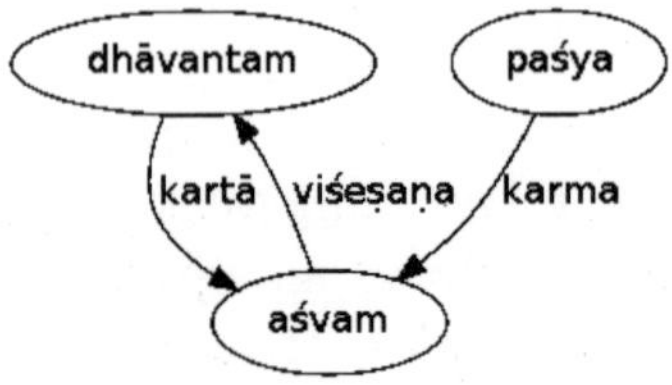

Fig. 4

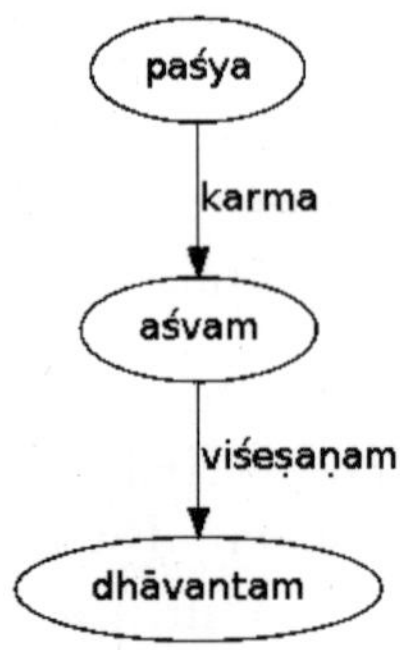

Fig. 5

Now one may raise an objection that this representation is not faithful to the information content in the given string. The answer to this objection is: there is no loss of information in this representation. The information that *dhāvantam* marks the *kartā* of the verb *dhāv* is still available in the derivational suffix *śatṛ*, which we can still use during the post-processing to add the missing information. The advantage of postponing the marking of this information is that the resulting parse is a tree and we can use the existing computational tools for extracting a tree from the graph.

2. Treating indeclinables
   Should an indeclinable be treated as a function word or a content word? The indeclinables fall into three categories viz. *kṛdanta*, *upapada* and the rest. The treatment of each of them is discussed below with an example.

– *kr̥danta avyayas*
Consider the following example:

(12) *rāmaḥ dugdham pītvā śālāṁ gacchati.*

Here the word *pītvā* is a *kr̥danta-avyaya* derived from the verbal root *pib* by adding a *kr̥t* suffix *ktvā*. This *ktvā* which is a derived suffix marks the relation of precedence (*pūrvakālaḥ*) with reference to the main verb.[9]
Here we mark the relation of precedence, though it is denoted by the derivational suffix. Since this is an indeclinable, there is an elision of inflectional suffix, and hence we mark the information encoded by the derivational suffix as a relation.
The *sūtra samānakartr̥kayoḥ pūrvakāle* (3.4.21) states that the action, denoted by the verb with *ktvā* suffix preceding another action, shares the *kartā* with it. Thus in the above example, *pib* precedes the action of going, denoted by *gam* in *gacchati. Rāmaḥ* is the *kartā* of *gacchati* and is also *kartā* of the drinking action denoted by *pib*. Graph indicating the relations is shown in Fig. 6.

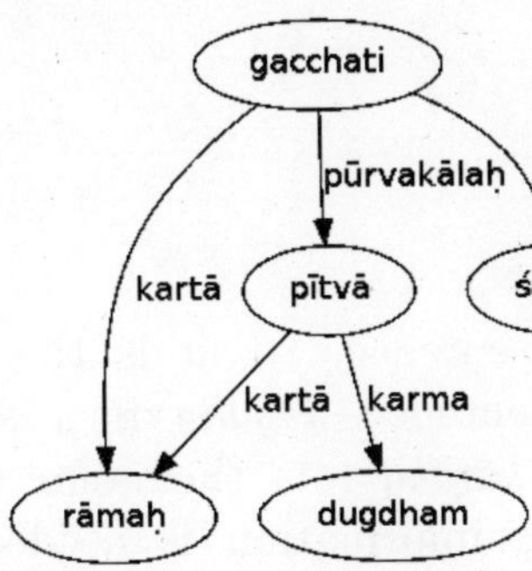

Fig. 6

Rāmaḥ is the *kartā* of both an action of going as well as drinking. However, the nominal suffix in *rāmaḥ* can express only one relation. Further, because of two incoming arrows into a single node, the graph results in nodes having multiple inheritances which prohibits this parse from being a tree. Hence we do not mark the relation of *kartā* between

9 *samānakartr̥kayoḥ pūrvakāle* (3.4.21).

rāmaḥ and *pītvā*, since it is not expressed by any suffix. This relation will be restored at the post-processing stage.

- *upapada avyayas*
  The *upapada avyayas* such as *saha* demand a specific *vibhakti* for the noun with which it is connected. For example, Pāṇini's *sūtra sahayukte apradhāne* (2.3.19) assigns a third case to the noun to which *saha* is attached as in *rāmeṇa saha*. Consider the sentences:

  (13) *sītā rāmeṇa saha vanaṁ gacchati.*
  (14) *sītā dugdhena saha roṭikāṁ khādati.*

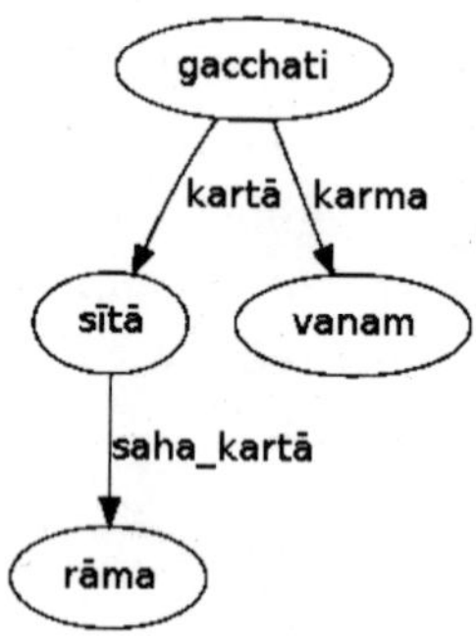

Fig. 7

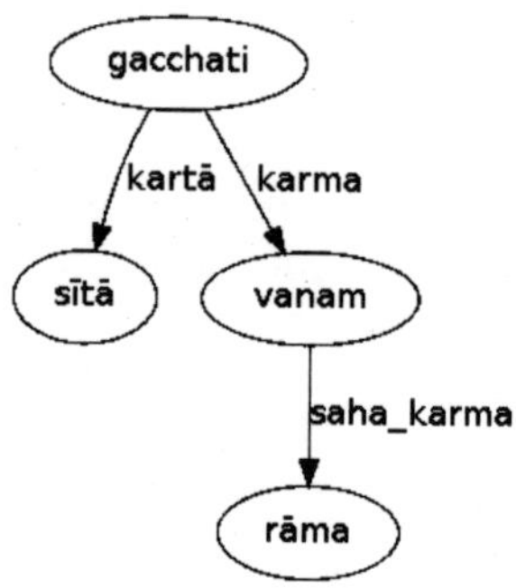

Fig. 8

In the first sentence, *rāma* is the *saha-kartā* while in the second sentence *dugdha* is a *saha-karma*. Thus to decide what *kāraka* role the noun with *saha* will have, extralinguistic information is needed in the absence of which machine will end up producing two possible parses (one correct and the other wrong) for sentence (13) as in Figs. 7 and 8.
To arrive at the correct parse one needs to check the meaning- compatibility (*yogyatā*) of associated words. Further, in order to reduce the number of relations, we mark this relation as *saha-sambandha*, following the tradition, ensuring that there is no loss of information in doing so.

Now the next question is whether to treat this *upapada* as a content word or as a function word? In other words which parse to prefer – the one represented in Fig. 9 or Fig. 10?

The *upapada* acts more like a function word (*dyotaka*) than a content word (*vācaka*). So it is desirable to group the *upapada* together with the preceding content word and mark the relation with the content word as in Fig. 9.

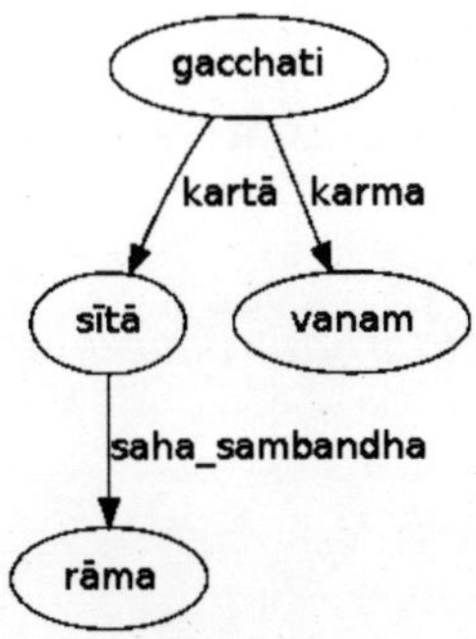

Fig. 9

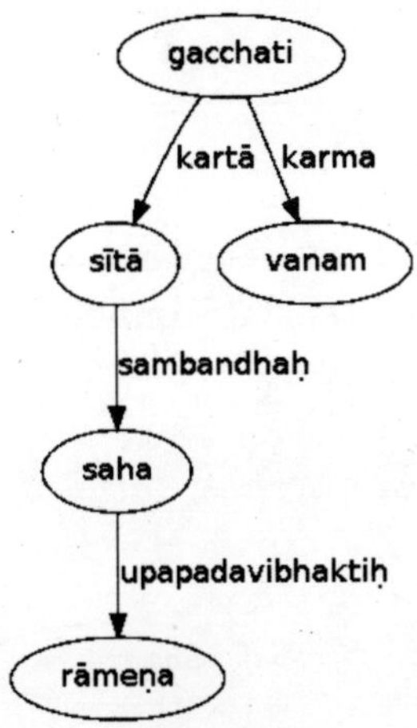

Fig. 10

Though this solution is desirable, it creates a mismatch between the number of words and the nodes in the graph. To avoid this mismatch, we propose to generate a graph as in Fig. 10 and then we collapse the intermediate node to generate the graph in Fig. 9 mechanically later.

rest of the indeclinables

Certain indeclinables such as *eva*, *iva* and *na* also mark relations like *avadhāraṇā* 'emphasis', *sādharmya* 'similarity' and *niṣedhya* 'negation'. These are all more like function words than content words. However, in order to preserve the one–one relation between the number of words in a sentence and the nodes in a graph, we treat these words as content words and mark the relations as in Figs. 11 and 12.

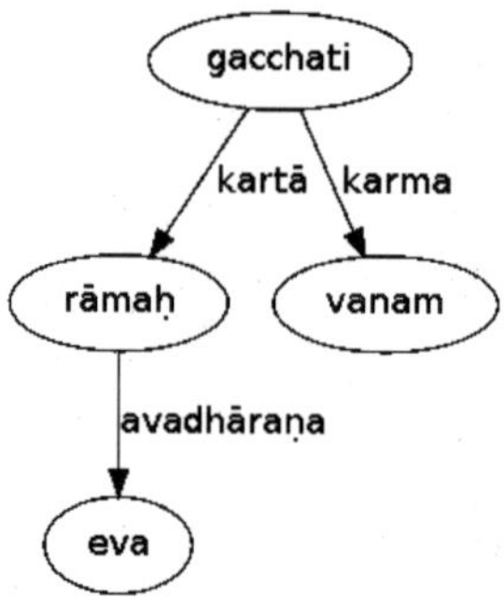

Fig. 11

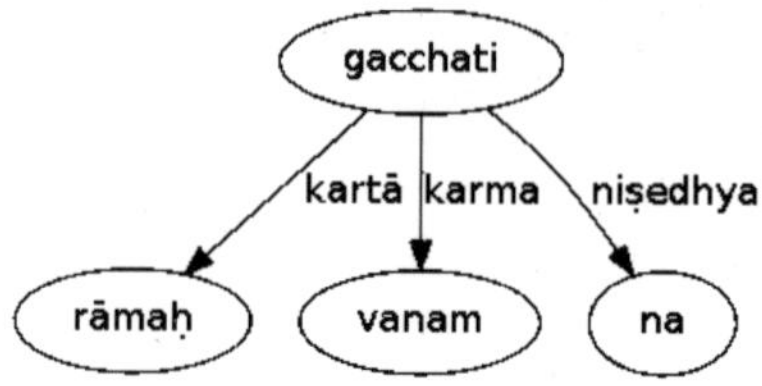

Fig. 12

3. Treatment of inter-sentential connectives
   The inter-sentential connectives connect two sentences. For example, consider:

   (15) *yadi tvam icchasi tarhi ahaṁ bhavataḥ gṛhaṁ āgacchāmi.*

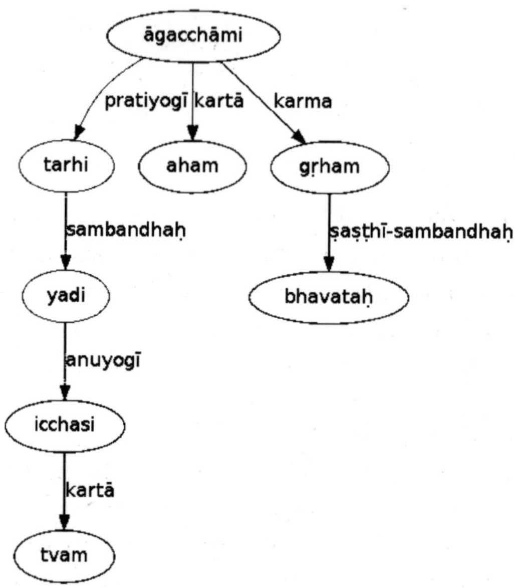

Fig. 13

Here *tvam icchasi* and *ahaṁ bhavataḥ gr̥haṁ āgacchāmi* are two independent sentences and the words *yadi-tarhi* connect them. Now this connection is through the main verbs *icchasi* and *āgacchāmi.* Figure 13 shows one proposed parse.

Following the Navya-Nyāya convention, the relations are named *anuyogī* and *pratiyogī* (roughly relata 1 and relata 2). The words *yadi–tarhi* might be grouped together to form a node, but since this will create a mismatch between the number of words and the nodes, we name the relation between *yadi* and *tarhi* as *sambandhaḥ.* This scheme then can be extended to handle cases of ellipsis where either *yadi* or *tarhi* is dropped as below.

(16) *tvam icchasi tarhi ahaṁ bhavataḥ gr̥haṁ āgacchāmi.*
(17) *yadi tvam icchasi ahaṁ bhavataḥ gr̥haṁ āgacchāmi.*

The corresponding graphs are shown in Figs. 14 and 15, respectively.

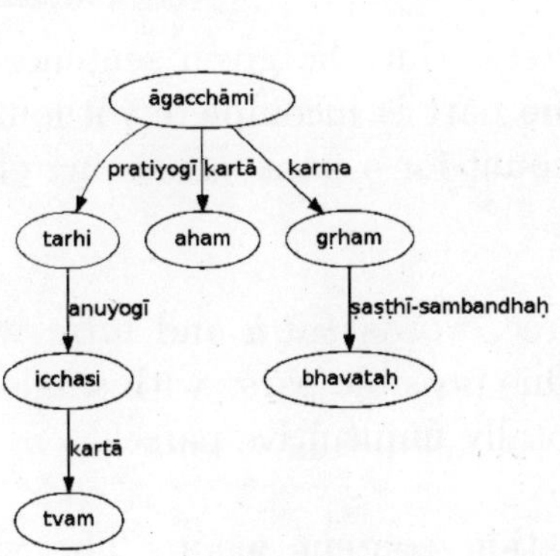

Fig. 14

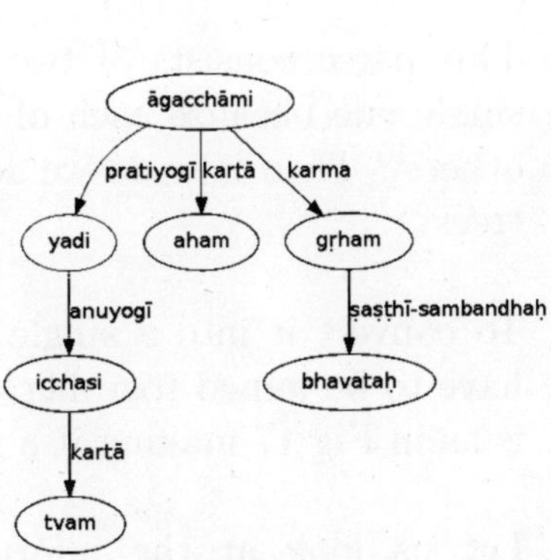

Fig. 15

During the post-processing stage, we provide the missing words *yadi*/*tarhi* for proper interpretation of the graph.

4. Treatment of anaphoras
The convention for showing the anaphoric references is by co-indexing. Consider the sentence:

(18) *yatra nāryaḥ pūjyante ramante tatra devatāḥ.*

The parse for this may be represented as in Fig. 16a,b.

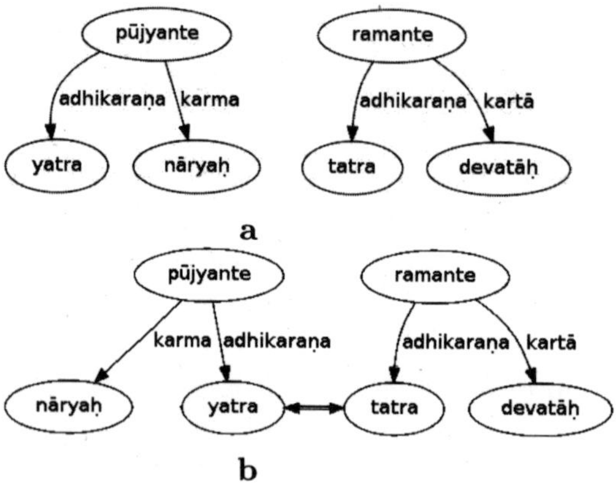

Fig. 16a,b

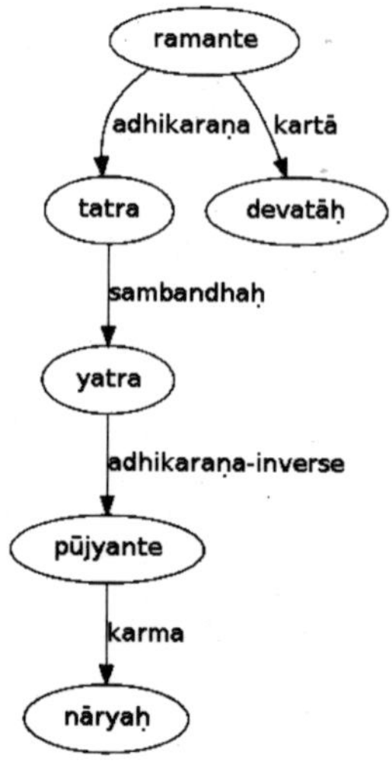

Fig. 17

This parse consists of two trees. But the given sentence is a single one because each of the part is incomplete without the other.[10] Then how do we account for a parse consisting of two trees?

To convert it into a single tree, words *yatra* and *tatra* would have to be joined together. One possible parse with single tree is as in Fig 17 making it a totally unintuitive parse!

Let us look at the information content again. The words *yatra* and *tatra* are in the seventh case with *yat* and *tat* as the nominal stems. The inflectional suffixes mark the relation of *adhikaraṇa* with the verbs. Now the anaphoric relation between them is due to the *nitya sambandhaḥ* between the pronominal stems and not because of any suffixes. The relations we are marking are due to the suffixes and, therefore, we do not mark the relation between the *prātipadikas yat* and *tat* leaving the parse structure as a forest. The co-indexing

[10] *arthaikatvāt ekaṃ vākyaṁ sākāṅkṣaṁ ced vibhāge syāt.*

(denoted by double arrow) as in Fig. 16a will turn the forest into a tree.

5. Treatment of conjunctions and disjunctions
The problem in the representation of conjunction and disjunction is deciding the head. Following a Naiyāyika we mark the conjunctive or disjunctive particle as a head. Figure 18 shows the analysis of sentence (19).

(19) *rāmaḥ sītā lakṣmaṇaḥ ca vanaṁ gacchanti.*

This is represented in Fig 18. Thus the *kartr̥tva* is in *rāma, sītā and lakṣmaṇa* together, and not in individuals separately. This is represented by the box which in turn contains all the individuals, joined by the conjunctive particle *ca.* In case of two sentences joined by the conjunctive particle, the later sentence is marked as a head (see Fig. 19) as in

(20) *rāmaḥ śālāṁ gacchati pāṭhaṁ ca paṭhati.*

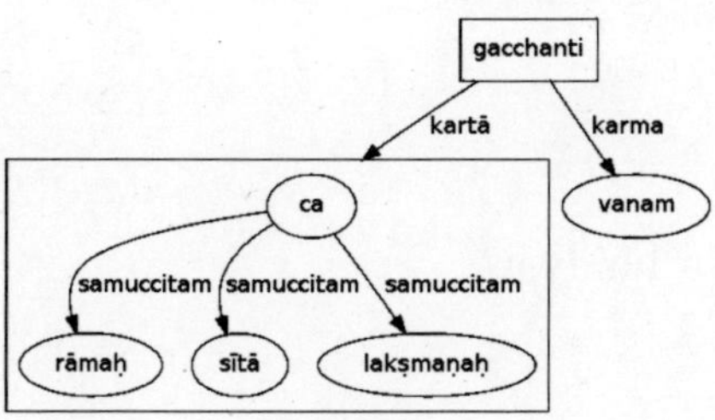

Fig. 18

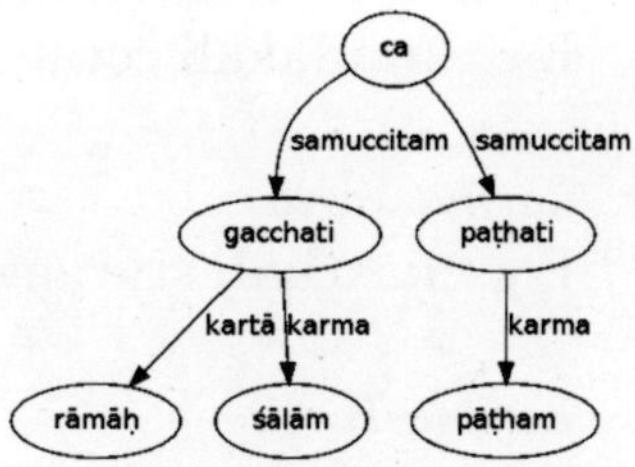

Fig. 19

Note here that *rāmaḥ* which is the *kartā* for the verb *paṭhati* as well is not explicitly marked in this parse. The reason being, this information is not explicitly coded by any morpheme but is inferred through the property of the conjunctive particle. Such an information resulting due to inference will be shown in the post-processed parse structure.

5 Granularity

The criterion for deciding the granularity is simple. If one can tell one relation from the other purely on the basis of syntax or morphology, then the two relations may be treated as distinct. We illustrate this with an example. Krishnamacharyulu (2009) subclassifies the relation of *kartā* into the following subcategories.

anubhavī kartā
E.g.: **ghaṭo** naśyati

amūrtaḥ kartā
E.g.: **krodhaḥ** āgacchati

prayojaka kartā
E.g.: **devadattaḥ** viṣṇumitreṇa pācayati

prayojya kartā
E.g.: devadattaḥ **viṣṇumitreṇa** pācayati

madhyastha kartā
E.g.: devadattaḥ **yajñadattena** viṣṇumitreṇa pācayati

abhipreraka/utpreraka kartā
E.g.: **modakaḥ** rocate

karma-kartā
E.g.: **kāṣṭhaḥ** svayameva bhidyate

karaṇa-kartā
E.g.: **asiḥ** chinatti

ṣaṣṭhī kartā
E.g.: **ācāryasya** anuśāsanaṁ

In case of *prayojaka* and *prayojya kartā*, the verbal form (causative suffix *ṇic*) along with the *vibhakti* marker of the noun provide the necessary clue. In case of *ṣaṣṭhī kartā*, the *kṛt* and the genitive suffix provide the clue. It is also possible to decide whether the *kartā* is *utpreraka* or not. The list of special verbs (which is a closed list) such as *ruc*[11] provide the necessary hint. In all other cases, merely

[11] *rucyarthānām prīyamāṇaḥ* (1.4.33).

on the basis of syntax and morphology it is not possible to decide the subcategory of the relation.

Morphology and syntax are necessary to mark the *prayojaka kartā*, *prayojya kartā* and *ṣaṣṭhī kartā* mechanically. But these are not sufficient. The sufficiency comes in the form of *yogyatā* 'compatibility'. For example, in *devadattena annam pācayati. devadatta* is a *prayojya kartā*, and in *devadattaḥ agninā annam pācayati, agni* is *karaṇa.* The third case suffix in *devadatta* and *agni* are only the eligibility criterion for *devadatta* and *agni* to be either *prayojya kartā* or *karaṇa.* The sufficiency comes from their referents. Similarly the genitive case marks the necessity for a relation to be either *kartā* or *karma* as in *ācāryasya anuśāsanam* and *kāṣṭhasya jalanam.* The *yogyatā* between the referents decide the precise relation. Thus in case of these relations, morphology and syntax provide the necessary conditions. But this is not so with other relations. For example, only on the basis of morphology and syntax one cannot claim that *asiḥ* is a *karaṇakartā* for *chinatti.* It is *karaṇakartā* because the referent of *asiḥ* also happens to be the *karaṇa* of the verb *chid.* Thus in the case of *karaṇakartā* and *karmakartā*, only if the referent is a *kartā* as well as *kara dna* or *karma* of the action indicated by the verb concerned, one can assign such relations. After examining all the 103 tags proposed by Krishnamacharyulu (2009), we arrived at a set of only thirty one relations (see Appendix A) for which only morphology and syntax play as a necessary criterion.

6 Towards a More Useful Parse

Though the principles described above are good from the computational point of view, from a user's perspective some of these constraints are not good. Even from the point of view of information extraction, these constraints pose limitations. An information retrieval system or even an ordinary user interested in understanding the Sanskrit texts would like to

- mark the relations involving *upapada*s treating them as function words rather than content words.
- mark the relation between two sentences by semantic labels such as cause-effect (*kāryakāraṇa*) or

reason(*hetu-hetumadbhāva*) etc. rather than just marking them by too general terms such as *anuyogi*, *pratiyogi* or *sambandhaḥ*.

- indicate the sharing of *kāraka*s in case of conjunctive and disjunctive particles.
- mark the relations indicated by the derivational suffix in case of *kr̥danta* nouns.
- show the co-indexing for anaphora resolution.

The post-processing module caters to this need. We show the relations added after this post-processing step by 'dotted arrows' so as to distinguish them from the ones which are marked before. Figures 20 and 21 show the graphs of sentences (21) and (22) after post-processing, respectively.

(21) *rāmaḥ dugdham pītvā mohanena saha śālāṁ gacchati.*
(22) *rāmaḥ śālāṁ gacchati pāṭhaṁ ca paṭhati.*

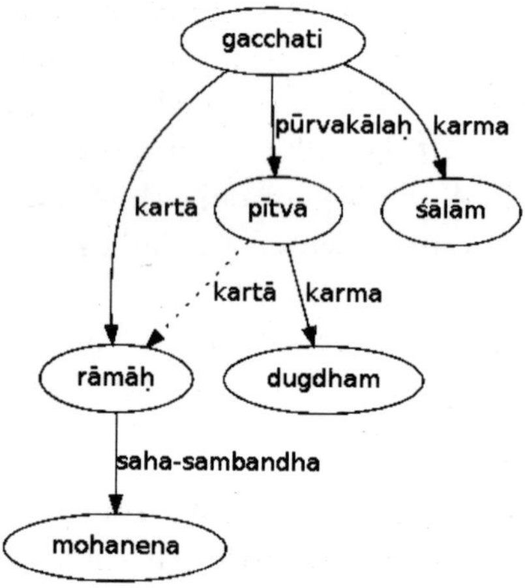

Fig. 20

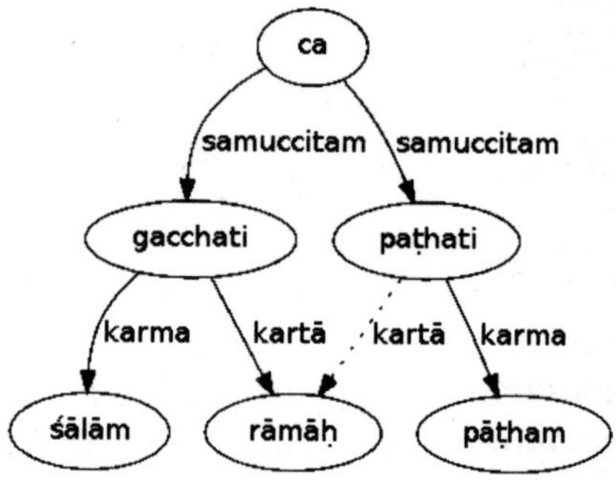

Fig. 21

7 Conclusion

In this paper we discussed various issues in deciding the tagset of relations for parsing Sanskrit sentences. We followed a two-stage procedure to account for the topological requirement of one–one mapping between the words and the nodes, no multiple inheritance, and no loops. In order to be faithful to the coded information and also from the point of view of information retrieval, we process the parsed tree further: (a) collapse nodes corresponding to function words, (b) make the information related to sharing explicit, and (c) show the co-indexing.

This two-stage parser has been implemented and is available as a part of Sanskrit-Hindi Machine Translation system at `http://sanskrit.uohyd.ernet.in/scl/SHMT/shmt.html`.

8 Acknowledgement

Authors thank the anonymous reviewers for useful suggestions. This work is a part of the Sanskrit Consortium project entitled 'Development of Sanskrit Computational Toolkit and Sanskrit–Hindi Machine Translation System' sponsored by TDIL Programme, DIT, Government of India.

Appendix: The Recommended Relations

kartā	*prayojya kartā*	*prayojaka kartā*	*karma*
karaṇam	*sampradānam*	*apādānam*	*ṣaṣṭhī-sambandhaḥ*
adhikaraṇam	*sambodhana-sūcakam*	*sambodhyaḥ*	
hetuḥ	*prayojanam*	*tādarthya*	*niṣedhyaḥ*
kriyāviśeṣaṇam	*viśeṣaṇam*	*śeṣasambandhaḥ*	*nirdhāraṇam*
upapada-sambandhaḥ	*sambandhaḥ*	*pratiyogī*	*anuyogī*
samuccitam	*anyataraḥ*	*kartṛsamānādhi-karaṇam*	*karma-samānādhi-karaṇam*
samānakālaḥ	*anantarakālaḥ*	*pūrvakālaḥ*	*vīpsā*

References

1. Bharati, Akshar and Rajeev Sangal. *Parsing Free Word Order Languages in the Paninian Framework* In Proceedings of ACL: 93.

2. Bharati, Akshar, Vineet Chaitanya and Rajeev Sangal. *Natural Language Processing: A Paninian Perspective* Prentice-Hall, New Delhi, 1995.
3. Bhaṭṭāchārya, Gadādhara. *Vyutpattivādaḥ*, Chaukhamba Sanskrit Sansthanam, Varanasi, 1988.
4. Carroll, John , Guido Minnen and Ted Briscoe. *Corpus Annotation for Parser evaluation.* In Proceedings of the EACL, 1999
5. Charniak, Euguen and Mark Johnson. *Coarse-to-fine n-best Parsing and MaxEnt Discriminative Re-ranking* In Proceedings of the 43rd Annual Meeting of the ACL, pp.173-80, 2005.
6. Copestake, Ann and Dan Flickinger. *An Open-source Grammar Development Environment and Broad-coverage English Grammar Using HPSG.* In Proceedings of the Second Conference on Language Resources and Evaluation (LREC-2000), Athens, Greece, 2000.
7. de Marneffe, Marie-Catherine and Christopher D. Manning. *The Stanford Typed Dependencies Representation.* In COLING Workshop on Cross-framework and Cross-domain Parser Evaluation, 2008. URL`http://nlp.stanford.edu/pubs/dependencies-coling08.pdf`.
8. King, Tracy H., et. al. *The PARC 700 Dependency Bank.* In 4th International Workshop on Linguistically Interpreted Corpora (LINC-03).
9. Kulkarni, Amba, Sheetal Pokar and Devanad Shukl. *Designing a Constraint-based Parser for Sanskrit* In 4th International Sanskrit Computational Symposium, ed. G N Jha, LNAI Springer Verlag, 2010.
10. Kulkarni, Amba, Devanad Shukl and Sheetal Pokar. *Mathematical Modelling of Akāṅkshā and Sannidhi for Parsing Sanskrit* In 15th World Sanskrit Conference, 2012, Delhi (forthcoming).
11. Krishnamacharyulu, K.V.R. *Annotating the Sanskrit Texts Based on the Śābdabodha systems* In 3rd International Sanskrit Computational Symposium, eds. Amba Kulkarni and Gérard Huet, LNAI Springer Verlag, 2009.
12. Schröder, I. *Natural Language Parsing with Graded Constraints.* PhD thesis, Hamburg University, 2002.
13. Tatachārya, N.S.R. *Śābdabodhamīmāṃsā: The Sentence and Its Significance Part-I, Institute of Pondicherry and Rashtriya Sanskrit Sansthan, New Delhi, 2005*

Text Normalizer for Sanskrit

Diwakar Mishra[1], Kalika Bali[2] and Girish Nath Jha[1]

[1]Jawaharlal Nehru University, New Delhi, [2]Microsoft Research India

diwakarmishra@gmail.com, kalikab@microsoft.com, girishjha@gmail.com

Abstract. Though Sanskrit writing system is very close to phonetic, there are, like other languages, many other words in running text which are not pronounced as they are written, or they are not in word form but are pronounced. Converting such words and other utterable tokens into standard word form is known as text normalization. Normalization, with many other uses, plays an important role in speech synthesis or Text-to-Speech (TTS) systems. The normalization process mainly can be divided into two main stages – recognition of Non-Standard Words (NSWs) and converting them to standard words. The ambiguity resolution also can be an intermediate stage or a part of the recognition stage. Normalizer does some other secondary, but not less important, tasks like cleaning of text, appropriate placing of punctuation marks (in current case, isolating attached symbols from words). The present paper describes an effort of a system which recognizes a few types of NSWs and converts them into standard Sanskrit word sequence. The program is developed in Java and recognizes and converts into words a few formats of numbers and short forms of words, primarily text names in Unicode Sanskrit text. The system applies lexical approach for short forms of words and rule-base approach for different formats of numbers.

Keywords: Text normalization, speech synthesis, Sanskrit, NSWs, TTS.

1 Introduction

Any language processing system is supposed to deal with real text. Real text includes many types of elements which are in different format from the general text. So the systems which can process general text need a module that can transform the real text with non-standard elements into the general standard text. Speech synthesis is also such type of a system which needs such module to normalize the text to standard format. Text normalization is the process of transforming a text in some way to make it consistent. In the sense the word is used here is to identify NSWs and convert them to the standard word form. As a part of speech synthesis (and its other applications) this module identifies the NSWs and converts them to words formed with alphabetical letter-sequence, called standard words in this specific context. NSWs are those which are either not written as alphabetical sequences (like numbers, formulae) or written with alphabetical or alphanumeric sequence but pronounced differently from which sound sequence they generally represent in that language. Developing such a system for any language (here the case is Sanskrit) requires keeping in mind the traditional conventions of writing and pronunciation as well as those formats which can be or have been adopted as the result of interaction with other languages. Translation of news into Sanskrit is one of the most effecting elements and teaching Sanskrit through other media is another one. The coming sections will describe the Sanskrit text normalizer developed by the authors. Before that there will be a literature survey and, in the end, it will describe the development methodology with a sample of the system's output.

2 Text Normalization Survey

The development of speech synthesis systems has started long back in the history of language processing, and the speech synthesis necessarily involves text normalization. Considerable work has been done in text normalization for European–American languages, Chinese, Japanese and many Indian languages. Most of them follow some common basic process- tokenization, identification, disambiguation and word expansion. Panchapagesan et al. (2004) have developed Hindi text normalizer. They have dealt with representation of NSWs – cardinal, ordinal words, roman numerals, fractions, ratio, decimal numbers, time, date, year, telephone number, url, range, percentage and alphanumeric strings. Soman et al. (2011) have developed Malayalam text normalizer as a part of Malayalam TTS synthesis. Filip et al. (2006) have developed text normalizer for Polish language and described it in the context of machine translation. Raj et al. (2007) described text normalization for Indian languages in general. They dealt with several Indian languages

Gujrati, Hindi, Kannada, Malayalam, Marathi, Tamil and Telugu. In fact every full-fledged TTS system has inbuilt text normalization. In Indian languages also the TTS systems are built. Alam et al. (2009) have developed text normalization system for Bangla. Some more works on text normalization can be cited (Yarowasky, 1999; Olinsky, 2000; Taylor, 2007; Khair Md. et al., 2006). For Sanskrit, a few speech synthesis systems have been developed (Mahananda, 2010; Acharya Project; Jain, 2004) but they do not report incorporated text normalizer module. Among these only (Mahananda, 2010) is specific to Sanskrit.

3 Sanskrit Text Normalizer

Sanskrit text normalizer described here, developed by the authors, recognizes and converts several types of NSWs into standard word form that is into the spelling or the representative sequence of Sanskrit alphabet characters. This section will describe the development of the normalizer system and its coverage and performance. The program takes input Sanskrit text in Devanāagarī Unicode UTF-8 format. Numbers in both Devanāagarī and Roman scripts are accepted. The program runs on input text and recognizes the suspected tokens for their NSW category, and then expands them accordingly.

3.1 Data Structure

The Sanskrit text normalizer system recognizes some of the categories by their structure and for others it uses the information from three data-files. One data-file is for recognition purpose only one for expansion only, and one is both for recognition and expansion. The three data-files are as follows.

Abbreviation File. This file contains abbreviations or short forms of the words which are frequently found in the running Sanskrit texts. Each line contains an abbreviation and its expansion separated by tab. Most of the short forms are text names which occur mostly in citing reference. Some others are short forms of modern words like rupee and doctor (title). This file is used both for identification of abbreviations and their expansion. Though mostly these are not shortened multi-word expressions like conventional meaning of abbreviation, but some words like ka.u. (for *Kaṭhopaniṣad*) ma.bha. (for *Mahābhāṣya* or

Mahābhārata) fall in same category. Therefore, these short forms are here taken under general word abbreviation.

Context File. This file contains the list of words which can fall in the context of that particular NSW category. The category name is separated from the context words list by tab and the words in the list are tokens, separated by space. This file is used only for identification of NSW category.

Number Pronunciation File. This file has data in three columns separated by space in each line. The first column is numbers in digits of both Devanāagarī and Roman. The second column has the pronunciation of that digit(s) as final word. The third column is the pronunciation of digit(s) in non-final form, i.e. when some more string is going to be concatenated after that in case of higher place value. The digits expression in third column is suffixed with *uttara* to be later added expression of higher place value. The file contains only the expressions of one and two digit numbers. Higher place-value expressions are generated by the system with these basic data. The number pronunciation is able to process till twenty-one place values of numbers.

3.2 Process of Identification and Expression

The system reads the input file line by line and writes the output in output file after each line processing. It reads the words in line, tokenized by space, and creates list. Then it looks for presence of suspicious character in each token. Suspicious characters are Devanāagarī and Roman digits, symbols and punctuation marks. If a suspicious character is found, the token is taken as suspicious, and then processed for various kinds of NSWs. They are checked for abbreviations. If the token is found in abbreviations, then it is replaced with its expansion value. If not found in abbreviations, then it is checked for different kinds of NSWs. Some of them are identified by their structure, sometimes by both the structure and context words and sometimes only by contexts. The words not identified in any of the category and having all digits are, as default action, expanded as numbers.

The suspected token is checked for following the categories and in the following order:

Abbreviations
Time
Money
Phone number
Date or reference (text)
Normal number.

To avoid unnecessary processing, first restriction is, as said earlier, it checks only suspected tokens for NSW categories. Among these categories, to avoid checking further categories after correct recognition, a condition is added, to check for next category only if the current token is same as the original token (means, not changed by previous categories). The identification functions are included in the conversion function to avoid duplication of process. In the complex structured tokens, first the structure needs to be processed and then it can be identified as a specific NSW category. If the expression of token is done differently, the same process of breaking down structure is required to be repeated. The present Sanskrit text normalizer does not have ambiguity resolution component, it depends on the ordering of checking categories. For example, date is processed first. If it is not processed there, then only it is passed further to recognize as reference.

The lack of ambiguity resolution causes problem sometimes. For example, date and reference have similar structure as considered here, only with difference of context words. Two categories of NSWs with same structure cannot be recognized without ambiguity resolution. One of them can be assigned default category and placed later in order but it may be wrong, as done for date and reference here. For the same problem the range (20-25) and proportion (12:45) could not be included in current system because these resemble the structure with time and former with reference also. Sometimes context word also cannot decide whether *9-10 vādane* is 'nine hours ten minutes' or 'nine to ten' hours. Context here is decided by only one word back and forth. Therefore in the sample input below, one phone number 05212-236516 could not be recognized as its correct NSW category and expanded as unconfirmed reference. The reason is, the context word after the digits is interrupted by another word *iti*.

3.3 Recognized Formats

The present system recognizes above mentioned categories in different formats as follows:

Abbreviations
Having abbreviation mark, zero or dot and present in abbreviation file
Time
12:45 (without context)
7:05 (without context)
1020 (with context)
10.40, 22-30 (with context)
Money
With or without comma and decimal followed by /-
With or without comma and decimal (with context)
Phone numbers
Beginning with (+, (0, (० ; including up to next four tokens till they are digit only (without context)
Beginning with (+, (0, (० ; including next token whether containing hyphen (without context)
All-digit token with or without hyphen (with context)
Examples (+91) 9899 78 01 61; (0091) 11 2674 1308; (011) 2674 1308; (+91) 11-26741308; 2232100; 0522-2232100
Date
Dd/mm/yyyy (with context)
Yyyy/mm/dd (with context)
Separator may be slash, hyphen or dot
Date and month can be one digit but year must be four digits
Reference
Format like date but any number of tokens of any length (with context)
Converted as default ordinals (without context)
Default number
With or without decimals

There are many other formats under the covered categories, especially in the dates which are not covered by the current system. There are also a few more categories like range, proportion, percentage and Roman scripts characters which are not covered.

3.4 Development Methodology

The text normalizer program is developed as a stand-alone program in Java. There is a main class and two processing classes. One of those reads input file and identifies the NSW category. The other class generates different kinds of numbers' expressions- ordinal, cardinal, decimal and individual digits. The latter class is used by the previous one to generate different kinds of number expressions. The input text must be in Devanāagarī Unicode UTF-8 encoding. It may contain numerals in Roman digits also. Following is a NSW-mixed input text and output of it generated by the present Sanskrit text normalizer. The NSWs are randomly inserted in the text to have representation of maximum formats in minimum text.

Input text

text with abbreviations

डॉ. रमेशः अद्य माम् अमिलत् । आवां बहु वार्तालापम् अकुर्वा ।

text with time and dates and phone numbers

डॉ. रमेशः अद्य ९-५-२०१२ 12:45 वादने माम् अमिलत् । आवां बहु वार्तालापम् अकुर्वा । सः माम् अवदत् यत् मया सह दूरभाषेण वार्ता करणीया । मम अनेके दूरभाषक्रमाङ्काः सन्ति । प्रथमः अस्ति (+९१) ५२२-२२३२१०० । अन्यः मम व्यक्तिगतं चलभाषमस्ति- (०) ९८९९ ७८ ०१ ६१ । मया सह 05212-236516 इति संपर्कसूत्रे अपि संपर्कः साधयितुं शक्यते ।

text with reference

अहं पूर्वमपि अकथयम् यथा ऋ. १०/१२५/४ कथितम् यत् अस्माभिः सहयोगेन समत्वेन च वस्तव्यम् ।

mixed-text

दत्त्वा 5 सुलभः 12 ॐ सत्योऽयं (+91) 522-2232100 स्वप्नः १ २ ३ स्वप्नः
12:45 वादने त्वं ऋ. 10/20 हरिः । (+91) 522-2232100 वादने (+91) 24 90
44 777 4557 गच्छ 20,020 रु. मिथ्याऽनेन रु. 47918 भाव्यं ऋ. (+91) 522-
2232100 234 वित्तमेव 10001 - ओ३म् दिनांकम् 27/03/2007 (+91) 522-

2232100 गच्छ abhinav 10444.09 रु. 45 877665532 9888767655 54544667987 (+91) 24 90 44 777

Output text

text with abbreviations

डॉक्टर-रमेशः अद्य माम् अमिलत् । आवां बहु वार्तालापम् अकुर्वा ।

text with time and dates and phone numbers

डॉ रमेशः अद्य नवमम् दिनांकम् पञ्चमे मासे द्वादशोत्तर-द्विसहस्रतमे वर्षे द्वादश पञ्चचत्वारिंशत् वादने माम् अमिलत् । आवां बहु वार्तालापम् अकुर्वा । सः माम् अवदत् यत् मया सह दूरभाषेण वार्ता करणीया । मम अनेके दूरभाषक्रमाङ्काः सन्ति । प्रथमः अस्ति धनम् नव एकम् पञ्च द्वे द्वे द्वे द्वे त्रीणि द्वे एकम् शून्यम् शून्यम् । अन्यत् मम व्यक्तिगतं चलभाषमस्ति शून्यम् नव अष्ट नव नव सप्त अष्ट शून्यम् एकम् षट् एकम् । मया सह द्वादशोत्तर-द्विशतोत्तर-पञ्चसहस्रतमम् षोडशोत्तर-पञ्चशतोत्तर-षट्त्रिंशत्सहस्रोत्तर-द्विलक्षतमम् इति संपर्कसूत्रे अपि संपर्कः साधयितुं शक्यते ।

text with reference

अहं पूर्वमपि अकथयम् यथा ऋग्वेदे दशमे पञ्चविंशत्युत्तर-एकशततमे चतुर्थम् कथितम् यत् अस्माभिः सहयोगेन समत्वेन च वस्तव्यम् ।

mixed text

दत्त्वा पञ्च सुलभः द्वादश ओ३म् सत्योऽयं धनम् नव एकम् पञ्च द्वे द्वे द्वे द्वे त्रीणि द्वे एकम् शून्यम् शून्यम् स्वप्नः एक द्विः त्रिः स्वप्नः

द्वादश पञ्चचत्वारिंशत् वादने त्वं ऋग्वेदे दशमे विंशतम् हरिः । धनम् नव एकम् पञ्च द्वे द्वे द्वे द्वे त्रीणि द्वे एकम् शून्यम् शून्यम् वादने धनम् नव एकम् द्वे चत्वारि नव शून्यम् चत्वारि चत्वारि सप्त सप्त सप्त सप्तपञ्चाशदुत्तर-पञ्चशतोत्तर-चतुःसहस्रम् गच्छ विंशत्युत्तर-विंशतिसहस्रम् रुप्यकाणि मिथ्याऽनेन रुप्यकाणि अष्टादशोत्तर-नवशतोत्तर-सप्तचत्वारिंशत्सहस्रम् भाव्यं ऋग्वेदे धनम् नव एकम् पञ्च द्वे द्वे द्वे द्वे त्रीणि द्वे एकम् शून्यम् शून्यम् चतुस्त्रिंशदुत्तर-द्विशतम् वित्तमेव एकोत्तर-दशसहस्रम् - ओ३म् दिनांकम् सप्तविंशतम् दिनांकम् तृतीये मासे सप्तोत्तर-द्विसहस्रतमे वर्षे धनम् नव एकम् पञ्च द्वे द्वे द्वे द्वे त्रीणि द्वे एकम् शून्यम् शून्यम् गच्छ abhinav चतुश्चत्वारिंशदुत्तर-चतुःशतोत्तर-दशसहस्रम् दशांशाः शून्यम् नव रुप्यकाणि पञ्चचत्वारिंशत्द्वात्रिंशदुत्तर-पञ्चशतोत्तर-पञ्चषष्टि-सहस्रोत्तर-षट्सप्ततिलक्षोत्तर-सप्ताशीतिकोटिः ' सप्ताशीत्युत्तर-नवशतोत्तर-सप्त-षष्टिसहस्रोत्तर-षट्चत्वारिंशत्लक्षोत्तर-चतुष्पञ्चाशत्कोटि-चतुष्पञ्चाशत्-अर्बुदोत्तर-पञ्चपञ्चाशत्खर्वोत्तर-षट्सप्ततिनीलोत्तर-षट्सप्ततिपद्मोत्तर-अष्टाशीति-शङ्खोत्तर-अष्टानवतिमहाशङ्खम् धनम् नव एकम् द्वे चत्वारि नव शून्यम् चत्वारि चत्वारि सप्त सप्त सप्त

4 Future Work

The normalizer system still misses some of the NSW categories and many formats under the covered categories. It needs to be extended to those categories and formats. Also, for some types of NSWs, a generalized expression is used. It can be made more customized according to specific format. The normalizer has been developed as a part of speech synthesis to be developed. The normalizer program is not yet evaluated and hence performance statistics could not be given. The normalizer in this phase only checks one token back and forth for context. It can be extended to more words- based on the evaluation. A very important thing to be added is ambiguity resolution module. Without which, many types of tokens are likely to be identified incorrectly.

5 Conclusion

The text normalizer is an important module for many language processing systems which work on a standard format of the text. The presented text normalizer is aimed as a part of Sanskrit speech synthesizer system to be developed. The system needs to be fine-tuned to generate correct speech. But it's use is not limited to speech synthesis only, but is useful for other systems like machine translation also as described in Filip et al. (2006). Its evaluation will help to improve its results.

References

1. Acharya project by IIT Madras, Sanskrit TTS Demo <http://acharya.iitm.ac.in/disabilities/tts.php>
2. Alam, Firoz, S.M. Murtoza Habib, Mumit Khan: 'Text Normalization System for Bangla'. In *Proc. Conference on Language and Technology* (CLT09), Pakistan, 2009.
3. Filip, Gralinski, et al.: 'Text Normalization as a Special Case of Machine Translation'. In *Proc. International Multiconference on Computer Science and Information Technology*, pp. 51-56, 2006.
4. Jain, Harsh, Varun Kande, Kartik Desikan: *Vani: An India Language Text to speech Synthesizer,* Final tage Report. Dept. of Computer Science and Engineering, IIT Mumbai, (April 2004).

5. Khair Md., et al.: 'Analysis of and Observations from a Bangla News Corpus'. In *Proc. 9th International Conference on Computer and Information Technology*, Dhaka, Bangladesh, 2006.
6. Mahananda, Baiju, et al..: 'Building a Prototype Text-to-Speech for Sanskrit'. In *Proc. 4i-SCLS*, LNCS-6465, 2010.
7. Olinsky, C., Black, A.: 'Non-Standard Word and Homograph Resolution for Asian Language Text Analysis'. In *Proc. ICSLP2000*, Beijing, China 2000.
8. Panchapagesan, K., et al.: 'Hindi Text Normalization'. In *Proc. Fifth International Conference on Knowledge Based Computer Systems (KBCS)*, Hyderabad, India, 2004.
9. Raj, A., Sarkar, et al.: 'Text Processing for Text-to-Speech Systems in Indian Languages'. In *Proc. ISCA SSW6*, Bonn, Germany, pp. 188-93, 2007.
10. Soman, A., S.,et al.: 'Corpus Driven Malayalam Text-to-Speech Synthesis for Interactive Voice Response System'. In *J. Computer Application*, 29(4), September 2011.
11. Taylor, Paul: *Text to Speech Synthesis*. University of Cambridge, pp. 71-111, 2007.
12. Yarowsky, D.: 'Homograph Disambiguation in Text-to-Speech Synthesis'. In *Proc. 2nd ESCA/IEEE Workshop on Speech Synthesis*, New Paltz, NY, pp. 244-47, 1999.

Extended Nyāya-Vaiśeṣika Ontology as Applied to Amarakośa KnowledgeNet

Sivaja S. Nair[1], Shrinivasa Varakhedi[2] and V. Sheeba[3]

[1] Post-doctoral Research Associate
IIT, Bombay
sivaja.s.nair@gmail.com
[2] Dean and Director
State Samskrit Education
Karnataka Samskrit University, Bangalore
shrivara@gmail.com
[3] Deputy Director
Chinmaya International Foundation Shodha Sansthan, Ernakulam
v.sheeba@gmail.com

Abstract. *Amarakośa* is a thesaurus which provides list of words to the concepts categorized based on different domain and context. Knowledge in this *kośa* concerns with many non-observational and culture-specific facts that connect many concepts within and outside the domain. In this paper, we present a few representative examples of the concept clusters from Amarakośa KnowledgeNet (A-KN) where the extended Nyāya-Vaiśeṣika (NV) ontology is applied. We will also show how the knowledge base of *Amarakośa* requires an extension for NV ontology when we tried to apply the same.

Keywords: Ontology, *Amarakośa, jāti, upādhi, jātibādhaka*s

1 Introduction

Indian tradition of transmitting knowledge orally is on the verge of vanishing. As the oral transmission demands, Indian traditional educational culture was organized to be 'formal and intensive' as opposed to the modern culture which is more 'informal and extensive' (Wood, 1985). The close inspection of the structure of the *Amarakośa* gives much more insight into the way the words are organized. When a student memorizes it, though in the beginning it appears as a linear list of words, as he starts understanding the meaning of the words, reads the commentaries on this text and starts using these words, the linear structure unfolds into a knowledge web with various links.

In this paper, we present a few examples from the Amarakośa KnowledgeNet (A-KN) Ver. 0.1 (Nair, 2010), which necessitated the extension of Nyāya-Vaiśeṣika (NV) ontology when it was applied. Any knowledge structure involved with many concepts and the relations needs an ontological system in its base. Without a sound ontological grounding, building a knowledge structure on top of it may create problems. In order to provide a strong base, we chose NV ontological system for building A-KN. When the ontological systems applied, we find many incompletions and inconsistencies. To get rid of them, an extended ontology on the basis of NV system is developed. In this process many ideas from other disciplines are also taken care.

2 Amarakośa

Amarakośa primarily named as *Nāmaliṅgānuśāsana* (a work that deals with instructions related to the gender of nouns) is authored by Amarasiṁha - fourth century C.E (Oka, 1981) - and is the most celebrated and authoritative ancient thesaurus of Sanskrit with around sixty commentaries and translations into modern Indian as well as foreign languages such as Chinese, Tibetan and French (Patkar, 1981). It consists of 1,608 verses composed in *anuṣṭup* meter and are divided into three chapters called *kāṇḍa*s.

3 Ontology for A-KN

The word 'ontology' with Greek origin means "the study of being or existence or reality". The study of existence of entities, their classification based on similarities or differences, and the hierarchy involved in it is very close to the philosophical studies. Historically, ontologies arise out of the branch of philosophy known as metaphysics, which deals with the nature of reality of what exists. Ontology also plays an important role in Knowledge Representation which is a way of specification or representation of a concept. J.F. Sowa (2000, p.492) explains: "The subject of ontology is the study of the categories of things that exist or may exist in some domain." The traditional goal of ontological inquiry in particular is to divide the world 'at its joints', to discover those fundamental categories or kinds, into which the worlds objects naturally fall.

History of ontology records various traditional ontological schools. In the East, especially in India, each school of thought has developed its own ontology. Among the major ones, NV ontology is considered as prominent one as it is grounded on sound logic and widely applicable to any domain. Because of that nature, this ontology is admitted as the best candidate to govern the semantics of *Amarakośa.*

Many upper-level ontologies to capture the relation between the concepts used in common human understanding are based on Western ontology. It cannot be directly adopted to develop KnowledgeNet for Indian languages, especially for Sanskrit. The concepts like *svarga, viṣṇu, asura,* equipments of deities and animals of deities. cannot be accommodated in these upper-level ontologies. So we thought of the necessity to make an upper-level ontology using Indian traditional Śāstras to accommodate the concepts that are specific to Indian languages and culture.

4 NV Ontology

The choice of NV ontology for this purpose was on the basis of simple reason that NV ontology has a clear tree structure of categories that are based on experience of common people and it has also given scope for reasoning. Nyāya School of thought started by Gautama in 300 BCE, deals with the epistemology, i.e. means of knowledge fallacies, art of debates, justifications, etc. On the other hand Vaiśeṣika school, established by Kaṇāda, is a realistic school, which focuses on ontology of the whole world and the characteristic relations of the entities. Both these schools have merged into one stream with some additions and omissions by complementing each other. The new NV school reduced the total cosmic entities into seven *padārthas* or the ontological categories.

They are *dravya* (substance), *guṇa* (quality), *karma* (motion), *sāmānya* (universal), *viśeṣa* (particularity), *samavāya* (inherence) and *abhāva* (absence).[4] These are further subdivided. The details of each classification is given in Fig.1.

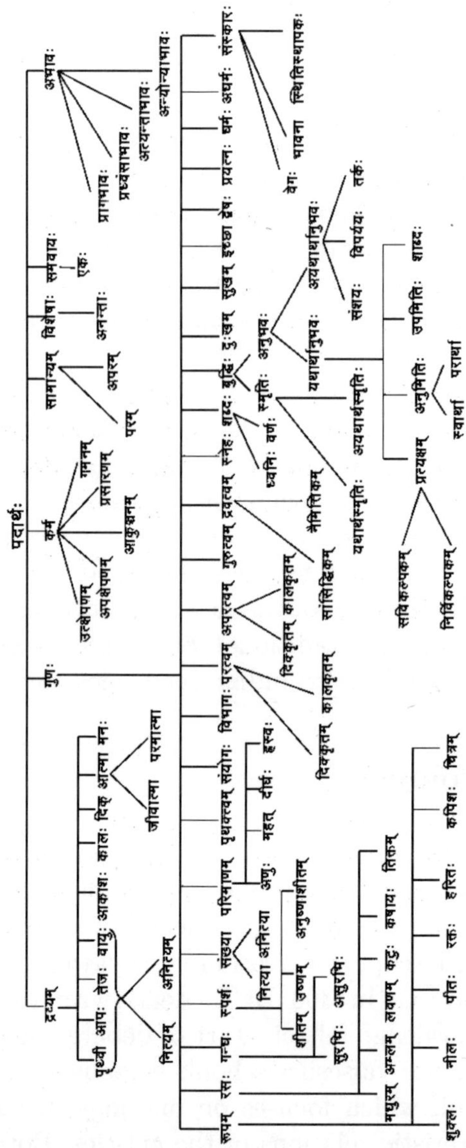

Fig. 1: Vaiśeṣika classification of objects

[4] *Tarkasaṁgraha*, p. 2.

5 NV Categories

Among the seven categories, first three belong to the phenomenon world. Any common man through his senses can perceive substances, their qualities and action. Substance is the abode of the qualities and actions. Qualities are twenty-four in number enumerated by the NV system and actions or motions of different kinds are inherent in the substance which does not have independent existence. The substances both eternal and non-eternal are classified into nine.[5] The other four categories are called Śāstrik categories, their existence is established by the reasons provided by Śāstra. Common man without proper understanding of Śāstra cannot comprehend the notion of these categories. The notion of universals, inherence relation and particularities is inevitable for constructing NV system of ontology and making it whole and complete. The unique relation *samavāya* (inherence) gets the first three categories connected. The universals, common properties of special kind put the entities in a common basket that show up in a tree structure. The particularities on the other hand keep the entities belonging to common categories, unique and protect their individuality. Therefore, without these metaphysical notions, the whole and complete ontological system is impossible. The last category *abhāva* (absence) also finds an independent existence in the NV ontological system on par with the other being categories.

The core feature of this ontology is its wider applicability. The ontology is not just a prototype of the reality, rather it is a complete description of the real phenomenon world. Hence the definitions and categories of any ontological system must find a consistent and clear application in the real objects of the world.

6 NV Theory of Universal

The NV theory of universal (*jāti*) does not recognize all general characteristics as universal. According to them the universal is a natural and eternal class-essence like *gotvam* (cowness) and

[5] *Pr̥thvī* (earth), *āpaḥ* (water), *tejas* (fire), *vāyu* (air), *ākāśa* (ether), *kāla* (time), *dik* (direction), *ātman* (soul) and *manas* (mind) (*Tarkasaṁgraha*, p. 5).

ghaṭatvam (potness) which is a permanent feature of a particular thing. Other general characteristics such as *unnatatvam* (tallness) and *nīlatvam* (blueness), which are adventitious features, are not universal but termed as *upādhi*s. The properties that are not considered as universals for some reasons become *upādhi*s.

6.1 The Impediments or *Jātibādhaka*s

The logical basis for the distinction of *jāti* and *upādhi* is explained by Udayana by enumerating six 'impediments' called *jātibādhakāḥ*. Presence of anyone of these six is sufficient to disqualify a characteristic as an universal. The six impediments are described in *Nyāyasiddhāntamuktāvalī* as *vyakteḥ abhedaḥ, tulyatvam, saṅkaraḥ, anavasthitiḥ, rūpahāniḥ* and *asambandhaḥ.*[6]

Vyakteḥ abhedaḥ: Any property that resides in a single object is not universal. e.g. *ākāśa* being single, *ākāśatva*, a property of being *ākāśa* is not universal.

Tulyatvam: Two general names which are the synonyms and thus describe exactly same *padārtha* do not stand for different universals. e.g. *ghaṭatva* and *kalaśatva.* Here either *ghaṭatva* is a universal or *kalaśatva* is a universal but not both, since both reside in the same set of individuals are indicating the same thing itself.

Saṅkara: The cross-dividing properties which co-exist in some instances and also exclude one another in others are not to be recognized as universals. Consider the five elements *pṛthvī, jala, tejas, vāyu* and *ākāśa. Bhūtatva* (being an element) is a property that exists in all these five elements. Of these the first four have *mūrtatva* (mobility). Now the question is, should *mūrtatva* be considered as universal? We know that other than the first four elements, even the *manas* is also *mūrta* and hence it has *mūrtatva.* So *mūrtatva* is located in *manas* and not in *ākāśa.* Similarly, *bhūtatva* exists in *ākāśa* excluding *manas.* Both *mūrtatva* and *bhūtatva* reside in four elements. Therefore, both these mutually

6 *vyakterabhedatulyatvaṁ saṅkaro'thānavasthitiḥ, rūpa-hānirasambandhaḥ jātibādhakasaṅgrahaḥ.* (*Pratyakṣakhaṇḍa, Nyāyasiddhāntamuktāvalī,*) p. 25.

exclusive properties have a shared location. This situation leads to *saṅkara*. Hence both the properties are not considered as universals.

Anavasthitiḥ: The character recognition of which as a universal, leads to infinite regress, means universality (*jātitva*) is not to be considered as *jāti*, it can be *upādhi*. If universality was regarded as a universal, then another universality will be required to synthesis the former with the latter and this process becomes infinite. Therefore, the concept of universal is not to be regarded as corresponding to one more universal, namely, universality.

Rūpahāniḥ: Ultimate difference cannot have any principle of unity, as it would contradict their essential nature (*viśeṣāstu anantāḥ eva*). If *viśeṣatva* was regarded as an identity or universal, inhering in the *viśeṣa*s, then mutual difference would not be there. *Viśeṣa*s being principles of ultimate differences, they cannot be differentiated from one another on the basis of any other characteristics. So *viśeṣatva* is also considered as *upādhi*.

Asambandhaḥ: The universal by definition is, 'inherent' in its subject. This implies that the thing in which nothing can inhere cannot be the substrate of a universal. The categories of inherence (*samavāya*) and non-existence (*abhāva*) cannot have anything inhering in them. If *samavāyatva* is regarded as a universal, inhering in inherence, then it would have to inhere in both its substrate and its relation with it, which is absurd. Such a position would also lead to infinite regress. Hence, nothing can be conceived as inhering in inherence. Similarly, no universal can be conceived to inhere in negation, because, it is not a positive entity. Therefore, *samavāyatva* and *abhāvatva* are not to be regarded as universals.

7 Application of NV Ontology on A-KN

The words of *Amarakośa* are categorized according to this scheme. Each *Amarakośa* entry is classified into a class which helped us to evolve the ontological classification just as an upper-level ontology does. We followed both the top-down as well as bottom-up approach simultaneously in order to arrive at the ontological classification. For the top-down approach, though our starting point was Vaiśeṣika ontology, we deviated from it a bit. Further, we have also introduced *upādhis* wherever the need arouse. While adopting Vaiśeṣika ontology to classify words in *Amarakośa*, it is noticed that some of the classes (since there are no instances of those in the *Amarakośa*) are not needed, while we also required further subclassification of some of them. Out of these *Amarakośa* has instances only corresponding to *dravya, guṇa, karma, sāmānya* and *abhāva.* By this enterprise of applying NV ontology on *Amarakośa* has improved the A-KN in many aspects. Some of them are given below:

1. *Amarakośa* categories are brought into the classification of an ontological system.
2. The tree structure has given the scope for reasoning about the properties and relations of the categories.
3. With this application new types of *upādhis* have been emerged in the A-KN. This has enhanced the understanding of *Amarakośa* categories.
4. On the other hand, the limitation of the NV ontology is shown while its application on a world of real-time categories.

Thus, these *jātibādhakas* impose constraints in the selection of *jātis*, and leads to multiple ways of classification. Choice of one way of classification forces other universal properties to be *upādhis*. This choice is typically guided by the application in hand where we build the NV ontology further and provide detailed classification, so that we can classify the *padārthas* in *Amarakośa.* The detailed description of this scheme is given below. The graphical representation is also given in Figs. 2 and 3.

The result in classification of *padārthas* in *Amarakośa* that emerged after the adaptation of NV ontology is shown in Fig. 2, where the additions or deletions of some of the nodes are justified. According to Vaiśeṣika, *padārtha* (reality) is the entity encompassing all things, *dravya, guṇa, karma, sāmānya, viśeṣa, samavāya* and *abhāva* as classified into seven. Out of these, *Amarakośa* has instances only corresponding to *dravya, guṇa, karma, sāmānya* and *abhāva.* All those words which could not be classified are put under *śeṣaḥ.*

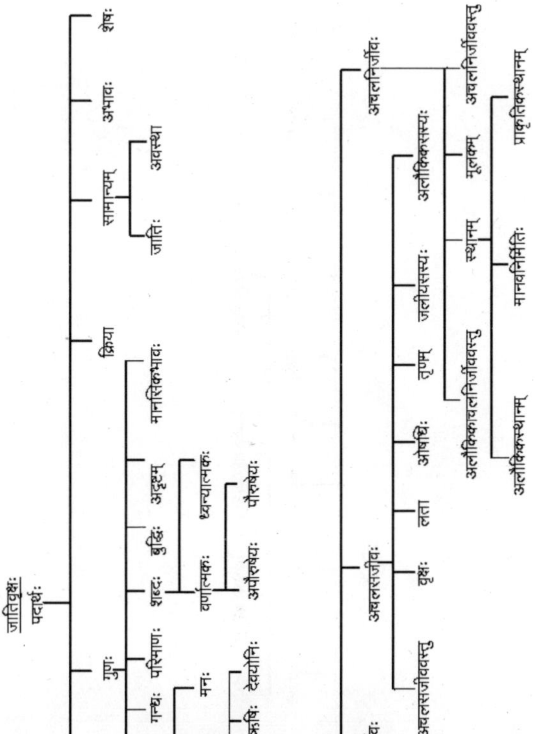

Fig. 2: *Jāti* chart

8 *Dravya* Classification

According to Vaiśeṣika, *dravya* is classified into nine *pṛthvī*, *jala*, *tejas*, *vāyu*, *ākāśa*, *kāla*, *dik*, *manas* and *ātman*, which are taken as

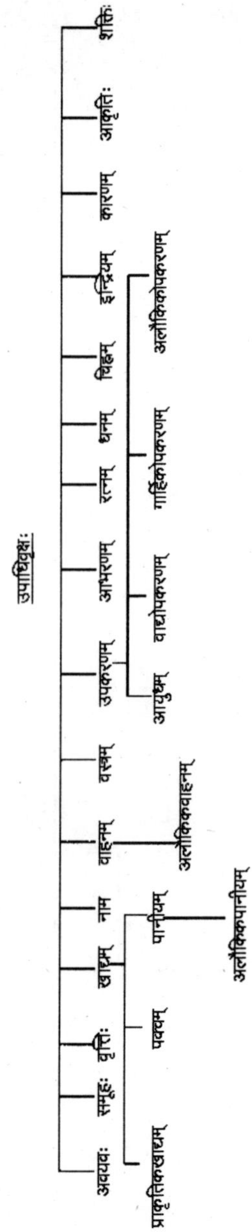

Fig. 3: *Upādhi* chart

it is in NV ontology. The first eight elements are classified into *nitya* and *anitya* as well as *ātman* into *jīvātman* and *paramātman.* Since we are looking at *Amarakośa* from Natural Language Procesing (NLP) point of view, this classification does not give us much mileage. Hence we deviated a bit from Vaiśeṣika ontology and further subclassified three of them *pṛthvī, tejas* and *ātman* as described below.

8.1 The Subclasses of *Pṛthvī*

There are different kinds of elements which come under *pṛthvī* in *Amarakośa.* All the elements under *pṛthvī* are classified on the basis of two properties *cala/acala* and *sajīva/nirjīva.*[7] In addition to these, we have created one more node viz. *alaukika* and its subnodes to account celestial objects. The classification describing each node with definition and examples is given below. The number of subnodes is shown in parenthesis against each node.

Pṛthvī (5)

1. *calasajīvaḥ* (3)
   – the thing which is alive and mobile [e.g. *manuṣyaḥ* and *jantuḥ*]
2. *calanirjīvaḥ* (0)
   – the thing which is not alive but is mobile [e.g. *rathaḥ, ḍolā* and *pālakī*]
3. *alaukikacalanirjīvaḥ* (0)
   – the thing which is not alive, mobile and celestial [e.g. *puṣpakam*]
4. *acalasajīvaḥ* (7)
   – the thing which is alive and is not mobile [e.g. *vṛkṣaḥ* and *bhrūṇam*]
5. *acalanirjīvaḥ* (4)
   – the thing which is not alive and is not mobile [e.g. *chatram* and *mārgaḥ*].

The Subclasses of Calasajīvaḥ

The category *calasajīvaḥ* is classified into three as *manuṣyaḥ, manuṣyetaraḥ* and *alaukikacetanaḥ.* All these nodes contain qualities of the body, not of the soul.[8] The classification is given here:

---

[7] These properties are not found in NV ontology. But these are added to accommodate the concepts found in *Amarakośa* for the chosen ontology.

[8] The human body comes under *pṛthvī* according to Vaiśeṣika

1. *alaukikacetanaḥ* (0)
   – all the celestial beings [e.g. *śacī* and *aruṇaḥ*]
2. *manuṣyaḥ* (0)
   – human beings [e.g. *dhīvaraḥ* and *rājā*]
3. *manuṣyetaraḥ* (2)
   – non-human beings [e.g. *siṁhaḥ* and *matsyaḥ*].

The Subclasses of Manuṣyetaraḥ

Manuṣyetaraḥ node is classified into two *jantuḥ* and *alaukikaprāṇī*. The second node represents the celestial non-human beings. The *jantuḥ* node represents all non-human beings. The classification is given below:

1. jantuḥ (6)
   – non-human living being [e.g. *sarpaḥ* and*kūrmaḥ*]
2. *alaukikaprāṇī* (0)
   – non-human celestial being [e.g. *airāvatam* and *garuḍaḥ*].

The Subclasses of Jantuḥ

1. *jalīyaḥ* (0)
   – water body [e.g. *matsyaḥ* and *śaṅkhaḥ*]
2. *ubhayacaraḥ* (0)
   – the animals which can live in both water and earth [e.g. *maṇḍūkaḥ* and *kūrmaḥ*]
3. *sarīsṛpaḥ* (0)
   – reptiles [e.g. *sarpaḥ* and *saraṭaḥ*]
4. *stanapāyī* (0)
   – mammals [e.g. *vānaraḥ* and *hiraṇaḥ*]
5. *pakṣī* (0)
   – birds [e.g. *śukaḥ* and *kākaḥ*]
6. *kīṭaḥ* (0)
   – insects [e.g. *jalaukaḥ* and *vṛścikaḥ*].

The Subclasses of Acalasajīvaḥ

The node *acalasajīvaḥ* classifies the plant world and non-moving living things. It is divided into seven categories as given below. The node *alaukikasasyaḥ* marks celestial plants.

1. *acalasajīvavastu* (0)
   – the living things which are not mobile. [e.g. *aṇḍam, kalalam*]

2. *vṛkṣaḥ* (0)
   – trees [e.g. *āmraḥ, kharjuraḥ*]
3. *latā* (0)
   – creepers [e.g. *mallikā, yūthikā*]
4. *oṣadhiḥ* (0)
   – shrubs [e.g. *nīlī, bākucī*]
5. *tṛṇam* (0)
   – grasses [e.g. *elā, jaṭāmāṁsī*]
6. *jalīyasasyaḥ* (0)
   – water plants [e.g. *padmam, kumudam*]
7. *alaukikasasyaḥ* (0)
   – celestial plants [e.g. *devavṛkṣaḥ*].

The Subclasses of Acalanirjīvaḥ

Acalanirjīvaḥ node is classified into four according to the necessities as follows:

1. *alaukikācalanirjīvavastu* (0)
   – celestial non-living things which are not mobile [e.g. *viṣṇoḥ* and *maṇiḥ*]
2. *sthānam* (3)
   – places [e.g. *mārgaḥ* and *nadī*]
3. *mūlakam* (0)
   – minerals [e.g. *abhrakam* and *pāradaḥ*]
4. *acalanirjīvavastu* (0)
   – non-living thing which are not mobile [e.g. *chatram* and*cāmaram*].

8.2 The Subclasses of *Sthānam*

1. *alaukikasthānam* (0)
   – celestial places [e.g. *indravanam* and *kuberapurī*]
2. *mānavanirmitiḥ* (0)
   – places or things which are created by men [e.g. *kūpaḥ* and *mārgaḥ*]
3. *prākṛtikasthānam* (0)
   – natural places (not created by men) [e.g. *nadī* and *parvataḥ*].

The extended classification of *pṛthvī* shown above is to accommodate the concepts enumerated in the *Amarakośa.* One may note that this extension not only uses *jāti* but also the various *upādhis*. Without this extension with the mixture of *jāti* and *upādhi*, the A-KN cannot be described on the basis of an ontological scheme. NV ontology gives scope for both *jāti* and *upādhi.* Though it does not provide with an entry to *upādhis* in the tree constructed on the basis of *jāti*, this merging of two notions in one tree will not be contradictory.

8.3 The Subclasses of *Tejas*

According to the Vaiśeṣika ontology *tejas* is divided into four *bhauma, divya, udarya* and *ākaraja*, however, in this scheme *udarya* and *ākaraja* are considered under *bhauma. Tejas* is divided into *bhauma* and *divya* in the present scheme. *Bhauma* is again subdivided into *dhātu* and *dahana.* The node *dahana* is divided into two *śarīra* and *indhanaja.* The node *divya* has three divisions as *nakṣatra, graha* and *vidyut.* The classification is given below:

bhauma (2)

1. *dhātu* (0)
   - all kinds of metals [e.g. *suvarṇam* and *rajatam*]
2. *dahana* (2)
   - fire [e.g. *agniḥ* and *yāgāgniḥ*]
     - *śarīraja* (0)
       * the fire produced in body [e.g. *gharmaḥ*]
     - *indhanaja* (0)
       * the fire produced from fuel [e.g. *āhavanīyāgniḥ* and *saṁskṛtāgniḥ*].

divya (3)

- *nakṣatra* (0)
  - all kinds of stars [e.g. *dhruvaḥ* and *kārtikā*]
- *graha* (0)
  - all planets [e.g. *sūryaḥ* and *candraḥ*]
- *vidyut* (0)
  - lightning [e.g. *vajrāgniḥ* and *taḍit*]

8.4 The Subclasses of *Ātman*

Ātman in Vaiśeṣika ontology is divided into two as *jīvātman* and *paramātman*. *Ātman* can be classified as *siddhaḥ, sādhakaḥ* and *sāmānyaḥ*. *Sāmānyaḥ* can be classified into *devayoniḥ* and *manuṣyayoniḥ*. But in the present scheme *ātman* is divided into four *īśvaraḥ, devatā, ṛṣiḥ* and *devayoniḥ*. The category *siddhaḥ* is named as *devatā, sādhakaḥ* as *ṛṣiḥ* and *devayoniḥ* is taken as it is. In *Amarakośa* there is not a single entry which is related to *manuṣyayoni*. There are entries like *puruṣaḥ and, strī* and are considered under the category named *manuṣyaḥ*, which comes under *pṛthvī*, because the gender and the like are *śārīrikaguṇas* (qualities of the body) of *manuṣya*, not *ātmaguṇas*. The classification is given below.

ātman

1. *īśvaraḥ* (0)
   – *trimūrtis* [e.g. *brahmā, viṣṇuḥ and maheśvaraḥ*]
2. *devatā* (0)
   – all deities [e.g. *indraḥ, lakṣmī, yamaḥ*]
3. *ṛṣiḥ* (0)
   – sages [e.g. *buddhaḥ* and *agastyaḥ*]
4. *devayoniḥ* (0)
   – demi-gods or demons [e.g. *rākṣasaḥ, yakṣaḥ* and *kinnaraḥ*].

9 *Guṇa* Classification

In the Vaiśeṣika ontology *guṇa* is classified into twenty-four subdivisions. The *Amarakośa* classification does not require all these divisions. The classes that are necessary to classify *Amarakośa* words are taken into consideration in this scheme. Some of the classes from Vaiśeṣika ontology are merged into a single category. According to this scheme *guṇa* is classified into eight classes *rūpam, rasaḥ, gandhaḥ, parimāṇam, śabdaḥ, buddhiḥ, adṛṣṭam* and *mānasikabhāvaḥ*. *Adṛṣṭam* marks both *dharma* and *adharma*. The last class in this classification named as *mānasikabhāvaḥ* contains all kinds of mental feelings like *sukham, duḥkham, dveṣa* etc.

The classification is given here.
guṇaḥ (7)

1. *rūpam* (0)
   – colour [e.g. *śuklaḥ* and *nīlaḥ*]
2. *rasaḥ* (0)
   – taste [e.g. *madhuram* and *amlaḥ*]
3. *gandhaḥ* (0)
   – smell [e.g. *sugandhaḥ* and *durgandhaḥ*]
4. *parimāṇam* (0)
   – measurements [e.g. *alpam* and *anekam*]
5. *śabdaḥ* (2)
   – sound [e.g. *akṣaram* and *hastigarjanam*]
6. *buddhiḥ* (0)
   – intelligence [e.g. *buddhiḥ* and *jñānam*]
7. *adr̥ṣṭam* (0)
   – unforeseen merit or demerit [e.g. *dharmaḥ* and *adharmaḥ*]
8. *mānasikabhāvaḥ* (0)
   – mental condition [e.g. *icchā* and *spr̥hā*].

9.1 The Subclasses of *Śabdaḥ*

The node *śabda* is divided into two *varṇātmakaḥ* and *dhvanyātmakaḥ*. *Varṇātmakaḥ* marks articulate sounds like letters and *dhvanyātmakaḥ* marks all the instrumental sounds. *Varṇātmakaḥ* is divided into two *apauruṣeyam* and *pauruṣeyam*. The node *apauruṣeyam* marks the divine knowledge which is available between the Vedic time and the Purāṇic time. The *pauruṣeyam* node represents the origin of other knowledge. The classification is given below.

1. *varṇātmakaḥ* (2)
   – articulate sounds [e.g. *akṣaram*]
   - *apauruṣeyaḥ* (0)
     * divine knowledge [e.g. *vedāḥ* and *mantraḥ*]
   - *pauruṣeyaḥ* (0)
     * the knowledge which are created by man [e.g. *vyākaraṇam* and *nyāyaḥ*]
2. *dhvanyātmakaḥ* (0)
   – instrumental sounds [e.g. *vīṇānādaḥ* and *tālaḥ*].

10 *Kriyā, Sāmānya* and *Abhāva* Classification

In Vaiśeṣika ontology, *kriyā* is classified into five. Since *Amarakośa* does not have any instance of verbs, this class is not required. *Sāmānya* has two divisions as *param* and *aparam*. This scheme also adopted two subclasses named *jātiḥ* and *avasthā*. *Jātiḥ* is the permanent property in all things but *avasthā* is the concurrent property. The words indicating absence are classified as *abhāva*s, e.g. *vr̥ṣṭyabhāvaḥ* and *vidyābhāvaḥ*.

11 *Upādhi* and Its Classification

Any property i.e. qualified to be the universal as per the conditions is considered as *upādhi*. The category of *upādhi* is an open list. Here in this scheme, the *upādhi* nodes are taken on the basis of necessity. *Upādhi* is divided into sixteen subclasses according to the A-KN. Some nodes have subdivisions also. *Upādhi* nodes are: *avayavaḥ, samūhaḥ, vr̥ttiḥ, khādyam, nāma, vāhanam, vastram, upakaraṇam, ābharaṇam, ratnam, dhanam, cihnam, indriyam, kāraṇam, ākr̥tiḥ* and *śaktiḥ*. The classification is given in the Fig. 3. The classification describing each node with example is given below. The number of sub-nodes also shown in bracket against each node.

11.1 *Upādhi* Classification

1. *avayavaḥ* (0)
   – part of a living body [e.g. *phaṇaḥ, śākhā* and *pādaḥ*]
2. *samūhaḥ* (0)
   – groups [e.g. *tr̥ṇasamūhaḥ, jantusamūhaḥ* and *paśusaṁghaḥ*]
3. *vr̥ttiḥ* (0)
   – profession [e.g. *ābhīrī, vaidyaḥ* and *adhyāpakaḥ*]
4. *khādyam* (3)
   – eatable things [e.g. *grāsaḥ* and *bhuktocchiṣṭam*]
5. *nāma* (0)
   – names of the individuals [e.g. *br̥haspatiḥ, śukrācāryaḥ* and *gaṅgā*]
6. *vāhanam* (1)
   – vehicles [e.g. *krīḍārathaḥ, śakaṭikā* and *naukā*]

7. *vastram* (0)
   – cloths [e.g. *dhautakauśeyam, paṭṭavastram* and *uparivastram*]
8. *upakaraṇam* (4)
   – instruments [e.g. *kamaṇḍaluḥ, śarādhāraḥ* and *mūṣā*]
9. *ābharaṇam* (0)
   – ornaments [e.g. *śiromaṇiḥ, kirīṭam* and *karṇābharaṇam*]
10. *ratnam* (0)
    – gems [e.g. *maratakamaṇiḥ, pravālamaṇiḥ* and *hāramadhyamaṇiḥ*]
11. *dhanam* (0)
    – different types of prizes [e.g. *baliḥ, mūladhanam* and *rajatarūpyakam*]
12. *cihnam* (0)
    – signs [e.g. *rājacihnam, puṇḍram* and *viṣṇulāñchanam*]
13. *indriyam* (0)
    – organs [e.g. *śabdādīndriyam, cakṣurādīndriyam* and *pāyvādīndriyam*]
14. *kāraṇam* (0)
    – cause [e.g. *mukhyakāraṇam* and *sādhakatamam*]
15. *ākr̥tiḥ* (0)
    – shape [e.g. *vr̥ttam* and *golaḥ*]
16. *śaktiḥ* (0)
    – power [e.g. *rājaśaktiḥ* and *siddhiḥ*].

12 Conclusion

This extended NV ontology is emerged as a result of the application of NV ontology for building A-KN. This model is based on the classification of *jāti* and *upādhi* which gives scope for extension of ontology.

13 Acknowledgement

Authors thank Prof. K.V. Ramakrishnamacharyulu and Dr Amba Kulkarni for extending their help for the completion of the work.

References

1. Chandra, Vidyabhusana Satis (1978): *History of Indian Logic.* Motilal Banarsidass, Delhi.
2. Dravid, Raja Ram (1972): *The Problem of Universals in Indian Philosophy.* Motilal and Banarsidass, Delhi.
3. Gruber, Tom (2009): *'Ontology'*, In The Encyclopedia of Database Systems, ed. Ling Liu and M. Tamer zsu (Eds.), Springer-Verlag.
4. Guha, D.C. (1979): *Navya Nyāya System of Logic.* Motilal Banarsidass, Delhi.
5. Halbfass, Wilhelm. (1992): *On Being and What There Is: Classical Vaisesika and the History of Indian Ontology.* State University of New York Press, Albany.
6. Jha, Ramachandra (1997): *Tarkasaṁgrahaḥ.* Chaukhamba Sanskrit Serise Office, Varanasi.
7. Jha, V.N. (2001): *Dictionary of Nyāya Terms (Sanskrit-English).* CASS, University of Pune, Pune.
8. Jha, V.N. (2010): *Tarkasangraha of Annambhatta (English Translation with Notes).* Chinmaya International Foundation Shodha Sansthan, Kerala.
9. Kiryakov, Atanas, Kiril Iv. Simov and Marin Dimitrov (2001): *OntoMap: Portal for Upper-Level Ontologies* FOIS 01, October 17-19, Ogunquit, Maine, USA.
10. Liu, H. and Singh P. (2004): 'ConceptNet: A Practical Commonsense Reasoning Tool-kit'. *BT Technology Journal*, vol. 22(4), October.
11. Nair, Sivaja S. and Kulkarni Amba (2010): 'The Knowledge Structure in Amarakośa'. *4th International Symposium on Sanskrit Computational Linguistics*, Springer (LNAI 6465), Germany.
12. Nair, Sivaja S. (2011): *The Knowledge Structure in Amarakośa.* Doctoral dissertation submitted to the University of Hyderabad, Hyderabad.
13. Oka, Krishnaji Govind (1981): *The Namalinganushasana: Amarakośa of Amarasiṁha with the Commentary (Amarakośodghāṭana) of Ksheraswamin.* Upasana Prakashan, Delhi.
14. Patkar, M.M. (1981): *History of Sanskrit Lexicography*, Munshiram Manoharlal, Delhi.
15. Sasibalagauda (1987): *Darśanaśāstrasyetihāsaḥ*, Chaukhamba Surabharati Prakashan, Varanasi.
16. Sastri, Dharmendra Nath (1976): *The Philosophy of Nyāya-Vaiśeṣika and Its Conflict with the Buddhist Dignāga School (Critique of Indian Realism).* Bharatiya Vidhya Prakashan, Delhi.

17. Sastri, Dharmendra Nath (1985): *Nyāyasiddhāntamuktāvalī.* Motilal Banarsidass, Delhi.
18. Sastri, Haragovind (2006): *Nāmaliṅgānuśāsana or Amarakośa of Amarasiṁha with the Rāmāśramī Commentary*, Chaukhambha Sanskrit Sansthan, Varanasi.
19. Sivadatta, Pandit (1915): *Nāmaliṅgānuśāsana (Amarakośa) with the Commentary of (Vyākhyāsudhā or Rāmāśramī) of Bhanuji Dikshit.* Nirnaya Sagar Press, Bombay.
20. Sowa, John F. (2000): *Knowledge Representation: Logical, Philosophical, and Computational Foundations.* Pacific Grove, Brooks/Cole, USA,.
21. Wood, Ananda (1985): *Knowledge Before Printing and After: The Indian Tradition in Changing Kerala.* Oxford University Press, Delhi.

Gaveṣikā

A Search Engine for Sanskrit

Srigowri and Karunakar

Department of Sanskrit Studies,
University of Hyderabad,Hyderabad
{amrutham.gowri,kannaiah.chinni}@gmail.com

Abstract. The paper discusses the complexity in Sanskrit language when it comes to searching and retrieving data from Sanskrit corpus. Gaveṣikā, a Sanskrit search engine that extends the functionality of Lucene search engine by plugging in a morphological generator and a spelling variation module is described here.

Keywords: Sanskrit, search engine, search and retrieval of Sanskrit text.

1 Introduction

The corpus of Sanskrit literature ranges from literary, religious, scientific, technical to philosophical texts. A vast amount of Sanskrit text is now available on the web. With the increasing interest in Sanskrit from different parts of the world there is a demand for the retrieval of adequate and relevant information. Further, Sanskrit being a classical language, there is a demand to provide authentic information whenever one quotes from Sanskrit text even in vernacular languages.

Searching and retrieving of Sanskrit data has three major issues. The first one relates to various encodings used in digitizing Sanskrit texts. Even though standards such as Indian Script Code for Information Interchange (ISCII) (BIS, 1992) and Indian Script Font Code (ISFOC) (CDAC, 1991) existed, most of the Sanskrit texts prior to the Unicode standard were in proprietary fonts. After the emergence of Unicode standard, and integration of keyboard and display drivers into editors and display tools, Sanskrit texts are becoming available in Unicode. Typically the texts originating from India are in Unicode Devanāgarī and those originating from outside India have a tendency to be in Unicode Roman Diacritic. Thus even if one restricts the search to only Unicode texts, one still needs to handle multiple encodings for Sanskrit.

Second issue is related to the rich *sandhi* formation in Sanskrit. Most of the text available on the Web is in sandhi form. During the *sandhi* formation of words w_1 and w_2, a terminal phonemic sequence, say u, of w_1 and the initial phonemic sequence, say v, of w_2 undergo some changes resulting in possibly a totally new set of phonemes, say w. So the resultant string may not have either u or v as a part of it. Therefore, a search for w_1 or w_2 will fail on such *sandhi*ed texts.

The third issue is related to the Sanskrit morphology. Sanskrit has a rich morphology and especially its derivational morphology is very productive. Sanskrit being an inflectional language, use of regular expressions for search has a disadvantage. There is a danger of missing out some forms. For example, the third case singular form of *ramā* is *ramayā*. The use of regular expression *ram**[1] will lead to over generation whereas *ramā** will miss out the form *ramayā*, in spite of possible over generation.

Apart from these language-specific issues, there are various user perspectives, especially with regard to Sanskrit search. The search requirements vary from a layman to a scholar. A layman is typically interested and satisfied with simple 'string matches', where most of the times, the input is a *sandhi*ed text. For example, one may like to know in which text of Kālidāsa, one finds *astyuttarasyām diśi devatātmā*. In such cases even a simple web search will produce the result.

Then there are students of Sanskrit or research scholars, who are interested in knowing the text, preferably the oldest one, where a word, say, *draviḍa* occurs. Now, here, the student is not interested in a particular form, but is searching for *any* inflected form of the word *draviḍa*. As pointed out earlier, Sanskrit being an inflectional language, a regular expression search with a possible stem may either overgenerate or miss out some of the forms. Further since the text available on the web is typically in *sandhi* form, there are chances of missing some of the instances. So the existing search engines may not provide the desired results.

---

[1] Here the '*' stands for any number of characters.

Finally, there is a third class of users, who is interested in finding linguistic evidence, such as the use of a particular verb in a particular tense, number and person in collocation with a noun with some morphological features or use of a verb in particular meaning, etc.

With the availability of various computational tools for Sanskrit it is now possible to build a better search engine for Sanskrit, which fulfils some of these demands. In what follows we describe an effort to provide a significant search for Sanskrit by plugging in a morphological analyzer to the core search engine.

2 Sanskrit Search Engine

2.1 Core Engine

Our main focus is on providing language-specific features rather than building a core search engine from scratch. Between several search engines available on the web we chose Apache Lucene. It has an architecture that employs best practice relevancy ranking and querying, as well as state of the art text compression and a partitioned index strategy to optimize both query performance and indexing flexibility. It is suitable for any application which requires full text indexing and searching capability. Lucene's logical architecture allows only a corpus containing fields of text. This constraint allows Lucene's API to be independent of the file format. Therefore, texts in PDFs, HTML, Microsoft Word, and Open Document format can all be indexed provided their textual information can be extracted. Lucene is portable, scalable, fast and allows incremental indexing. It has full support for complex search patterns and finally has a capability to sort results of search queries according to various parameters such as relevance and date.

2.2 Search Corpus

The next decision was to go for a crawler-based search engine or build directories and provide search from the local corpus. As mentioned earlier, Sanskrit texts are available in more than one encodings. Further languages other than Sanskrit- Marathi, Hindi and Nepali also use Devanāgarī script. So to use a crawler-based search engine, one needs to detect the language and then convert it to a common encoding before building an index. However, if we go for a directory-based search engine, one can choose the corpus and it's encoding in advance and we can do away with the language detection and the encoding-specific issues. Moreover, the directory structure allows a domain-specific search providing better search options for the user. Finally, the availability of Sanskrit corpus at various websites which are edited and checked by humans, prompted us to go for directory-based search engine.

2.3 Storage and Index Encoding

The third issue is regarding the encoding for storage of the corpus. The available corpus was in different encodings such as Unicode Devanāgarī and Unicode Roman diacritic (most of the corpus in GRETIL and DCS sites). Sanskrit Library has it optionally in SLP1 notation, the corpus with University of Hyderabad is in WX notation and so on. The encoding schemes used for Sanskrit - WX, Velthuis, Kyoto-Harward, SLP1, Itrans map the Devanāgarī phonemes to the Roman letters, and thus effectively use ASCII. Between these SLP1 and WX, use one Roman letter for each Devanāgarī *varṇa*, and thus consume less space as compared to other coding schemes. Unicode for Devanāgarī, which is based on ISCII, is not purely *varṇa* based, but uses a mixture of *varṇa* and *akṣara* in its encoding. This leads to two different representations for vowels - इ and ि. And eventually, if a search is performed on a Unicode-encoded Devanāgarī Sanskrit text, there is a chance to miss out some of the occurrences. For example, the string पद्मपि is stored in Unicode as प द् म प ि, whereas its constituent *varṇa*s are प् अ द् अ म् अ प इ. While the WX encoding which encodes it as 'padamapi', finds अपि in पद्मपि, the Unicode encoding does not have an instance of अपि in पद्मपि. Because of this mixing one needs special routines in Lucene to handle different representation of the same letter in different contexts while creating index and during search.

Another important problem with Unicode is the size. Since the default standard for storage is UTF-8, a Devanāgarī unicode string occupies almost three times the space of corresponding text in WX notation. Hence we decided to go for WX notation for the storage, index and search.

3 Architecture and Functionality

Sanskrit search engine uses various Sanskrit corpora available on the web. All these corpora are downloaded from the respective websites to the Department of Sanskrit Studies server.

- Sanskrit corpus at GRETIL
- *Mahābhārata* from BORI
- Digital corpus for Sanskrit from DCS website
- Sanskrit texts from Sanskrit library
- Sanskrit texts developed by the Department of Sanskrit Studies, University of Hyderabad
- Sanskrit corpus developed by the Sanskrit Consortium.

The Sanskrit corpus developed by the Sanskrit Consortium is annotated at various levels such as *sandhi* and compounds. However, we have not used the information of annotation effectively in searching yet. These corpora were all in various encodings. They were first converted to Devanāgarī Unicode and also to WX notation. The corpus in WX notation is used for building the index, while the text in Unicode was used for display. Table 1 gives the size of the various corpora.

Corpus	**Size in bytes (MB)**	
	WX	**UTF**
GRETIL	225	514.4
Mahābhārata	12.5	27.1
DCS	20.8	54.8
Sanskrit Library	48.2	114.3
University of Hyderabad	14.6	37
Sanskrit Consortium	34.4	82.6

The search engine works as a web service. The user sends his query, which is parsed and sent to the analyzer. The analyzer then consults the index and the indexed pages and sends the links to the indexed pages back to the user (Fig. 1).

For Sanskrit, we do a little more processing on the search string before passing it to the query parser.

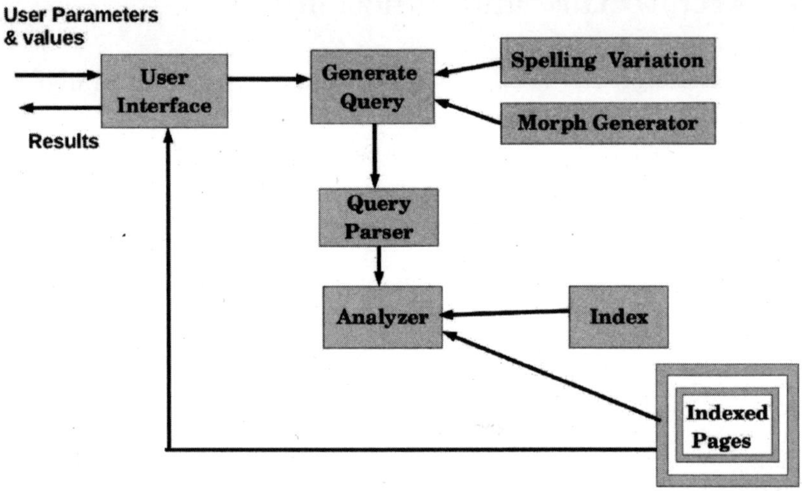

Fig. 1: Working of Sanskrit Search Engine

- Spelling variation: A given query string may use a different spelling than the one in the corpus. For example, look at the words अङ्कम् and अंकम्. Both these spellings are accepted. We would like the engine to search both these alternative spellings irrespective of the input spelling and irrespective of the spelling in the corpus. The variations in Sanskrit are well defined. For example, an *anusvāra* and a homorganic nasal of the following consonants are variants.
- Morphological generator: In a query string we allow a query with a *prātipadikam* or a *dhātu*. With this query, then engine uses the morphological generator to generate all possible inflected word forms corresponding to a given string and searches for all these generated forms along with their variant spellings in the corpus.

  The verb conjugation module requires various attributes of the verbal root such as the class it belongs to. Instead of asking the user to type in the information, we provide a drop-down menu of all verbs. Currently it handles only the finite verb forms. This needs to be expanded to handle the non-finite verb forms as well as the verb roots with prefixes.

4 User Interface

Following options are provided to the users.

- **Source:** This field allows one to choose the corpus for search.
- **Encoding:** Input string may be given in any of the following encodings: Unicode Devanāgarī, Unicode Roman diacritic, Itrans, Velthuis, Kyoto-Harward, SLP1 and WX.
- **Type of query to search:** User can search either any of the inflected forms of a *prātipadikam* or a verb conjugation corresponding to a verbal root. Alternately, he may choose any one of the following options related to *padam*.

Sr. No.	Pattern	Description
1	*pada*	a *pada* as specified
2	?	Preceding character may or may not be present
3	*	Any number of characters
4	str1 AND str2	Both str1 and str2
5	str1 OR str2	Either str1 or str2
6	"a b"	Literal string "a b"
7	str1+str2	May contain str1 and must contain str2

The results are displayed in Unicode Devanāgarī. Along with search results a link is provided where a user can navigate to a border look of the content. Gaveṣikā, a Sanskrit search engine is available at `http://sanskrit.uohyd.ernet.in:8080/searchengine/`.

5 Conclusion

Sanskrit is rich in morphology. It is also the practice of scholars to retain in their editions the expressions in their original *sandhi* form. This makes the normal search engine less effective for Sanskrit. In this paper, we described our efforts to plug-in the morphological generator and a spelling variation module to enhance the performance of a search engine. Enhancing this further by incorporating a *sandhi* module is a real challenge, since *sandhi* involves morphophonemic changes.

6 Acknowledgement

We acknowledge the morph engine provided by Sanskrit Consortium project, 'Development of Sanskrit Computational Tools and Sanskrit-Hindi Machine Translation System' sponsored by TDIL Programme, DIT, Government of India. We thank Oliver Hellwig and Peter Scharf who have shared their corpora, and Amba Kulkarni for guiding us in developing the search engine for Sanskrit.

References

1. Kulkarni, Amba and Devanand Shukl (2009):'Sanskrit Morphological Analyzer: Some Issues', In the Festscrift volume of Bh. Krishnamoorty, *Indian Linguistics*, 70(1-4), 15 Dec.
2. Bureau of Indian Standards (1992): *Indian Script Code for Information Interchange: ISCII Standard*, New Delhi.
3. Doug Cutting (2005): *Open Source Search*, Information Retrieval Seminar, 5, December, Israel.
4. Huet, G. (2009), 'Formal Structure of Sanskrit Text: Requirements of a Mechanical Sanskrit Processor', in Huet, Kulkarni & Scharf (2009), pp. 162-99.
5. Perner, Petra (2007): *Machine Learning and Data Mining in Pattern Recognition*: 5th International Conference. Springer. pp. 387-89.
6. Scharf, Peter M. and Malcolm D. (2012): Hyman, *Linguistic Issues in Encoding Sanskrit*, Motilal Banarsidass,First Edition, Delhi.
7. Unicode Consortium (2006): *The Unicode Standard, Version 5.0*, Addison-Wesley, Boston.

Websites

8. `http://bori.ac.in/` Critical edition of Mahābhārata available at Bhandarkar Oriental Research Institute.
9. `http://sanskritlibrary.org/` Corpus developed by Peter Scharf available at Sanskrit Library.
10. `http://kjc-fs-cluster.kjc.uni-heidelberg.de/dcs/` Corpus developed by Oliver Hellwig available at DCS.
11. `http://sanskrit.uohyd.ernet.in/` Corpus developed by the Department of Sanskrit Studies, University of Hyderabad.
12. `http://fiindolo.sub.uni-goettingen.de/gretil.html` Gretil Corpus.

13. Official Web page of Department of Sanskrit Studies `http://sanskrit.uohyd.ernet.in/`, गवेषिका (Sanskrit Search Engine) `http://sanskrit.uohyd.ernet.in:8080/searchengine/` and Apache Lucene `http://lucene.apache.org/core/`.
14. `http://pune.cdac.in/html/gist/standard.aspx`, 1991 (accessed on 1st May 2012). Standards for Indian Languages in IT.

A Screen-Shots

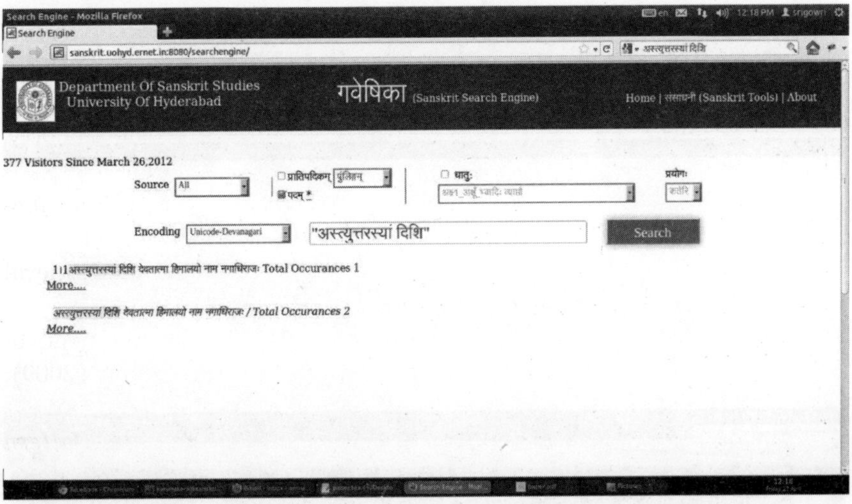

Fig. 2: Search results for phrase "अस्त्युत्तरस्यां दिशि"

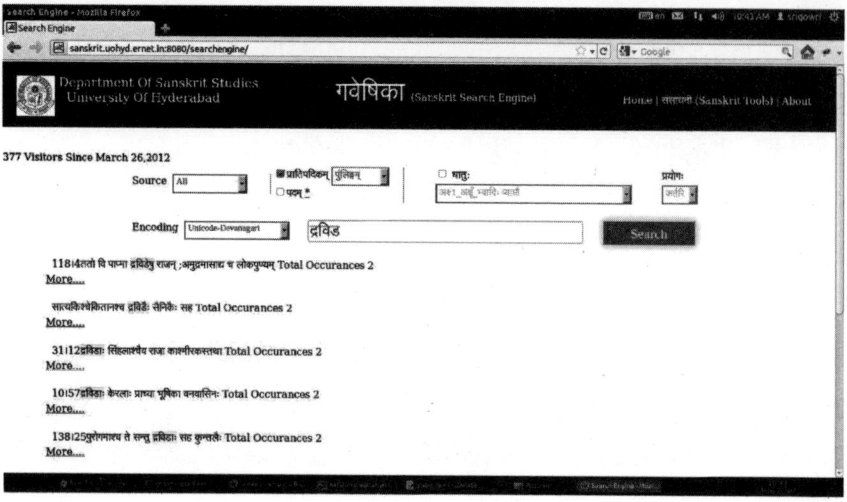

Fig. 3: Search results for द्रविड using प्रातिपदिकम्

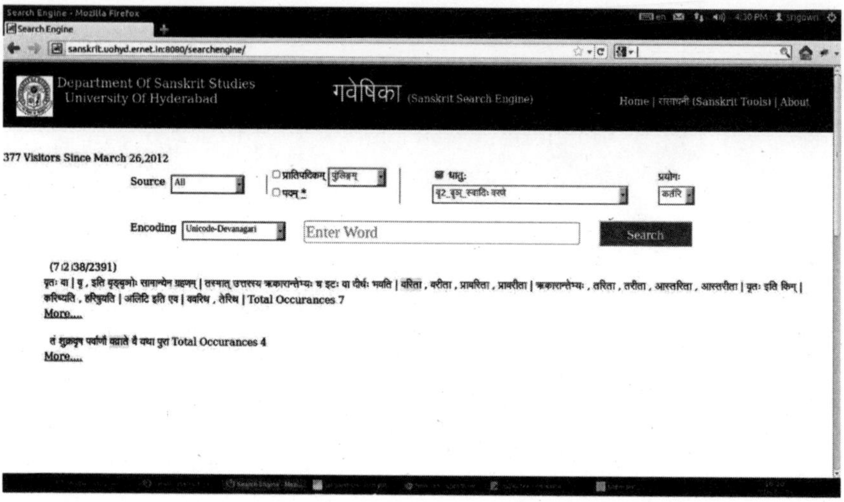

Fig. 4: Search results for धातु: "वृ2 वरणे"

वेदान्तसंस्कृतम्

सङ्गणकीयोपकरणानाम् उपयोगेन आरम्भिकवेदान्ताध्ययनोपयोगिनः संस्कृतपठ्यस्य प्रस्तावना

डॉ. तिरुमल पि कुलकर्णी

पूर्णप्रज्ञविद्यापीठस्नातक-स्नातकोत्तराध्ययनकेन्द्रम्, बेङ्गळूरु-२८

1 प्रस्तावना

संस्कृतज्ञा वयं तदा तदा अनुभवामः यत् जनाः संस्कृतविषये अभिरुचिं प्रेम च दधते। बहून् 'अहमपि संस्कृतं ज्ञातुमिच्छामि' 'शालासमये मया संस्कृतमधीतम्। इदानीं सर्वं विस्मृतप्रायम्।' इत्यादि वदतः श्रुणुमश्च।

इतोऽप्यग्रे केषाञ्चित् इमां स्थितिमहं बहुवारं दृष्टवान्। नैके युवानः उपपञ्चत्रिंशत्तमे वयसि वेदान्तविषयेषु आसक्तिं दधतः तत्र तत्र गुरुभ्यः पठितुमारभन्ते। अनुवादग्रन्थानां पठतां तेषां कतिभ्यश्चित् मासेभ्यः अनन्तरं 'मया मूलग्रन्थाः अध्येतव्याः' इति भावना आविर्भवति। गुरून् सम्प्रार्थ्य वेदान्तपाठैः सह संस्कृतपाठमपि श्रोतुमारभन्ते। चतुःपञ्चमासेषु अपेक्षितां प्रगतिम् अनवलोकयन्तः क्रमेण मूलग्रन्थपठनाशां परित्यजन्ति।

अपरे केचन एतादृशजनाः सन्ति ये स्वीये मध्यवयसि संस्कृतं पठितुमपारयन्तः वार्धकेऽपि वा यदि शक्यं तर्हि चिकीर्षवः षष्टि-सप्ततिवर्षीयाः उत्साहिनः ज्ञानपिपासवः।

तदेतादृशानां परस्सहस्रजिज्ञासूनाम् उपकाराय, नानापरियोजनान्तर्गततया सज्जीक्रियमाणानां सङ्गणकीयोपकरणानां समाजोपयोगितासम्पादनाय च अस्मिन् प्रबन्धे काचित् प्रस्तावना विदुषां पुरतः संस्थाप्यते।

2 प्रस्तुतस्थितिः

संस्कृताध्ययने द्वयी रीतिः सम्प्रति दृश्यते। एका गुरुकुलेषु दृश्यमाना साम्प्रदायिकी पद्धतिः। द्वितीया आधुनिककाले शाला-प्रौढशाला-कलाशाला-विश्वविद्यालयेषु अनुस्त्रियमाणा रीतिः। उभयोः रीत्योः

आरम्भे पठ्यपुस्तकानि[1] उपयुज्यन्ते इत्येतत् समानम्। गुरुकुलपद्धतौ कोष-काव्यादीनां मूलग्रन्थाः विशेषतः अभ्यस्यन्ते, कण्ठस्थीकरणाय अधिकमवधानं दीयते इति विशेषः। पठ्यपुस्तकेषु छात्राणां लिङ्ग-वचन-विभक्ति-पुरुषादिभेदेन अकारान्तेकारान्तादि-सुबन्त-तिङन्तशब्दानां परिचयः यथा स्यात् तथा पाठाः संयोजिताः भवन्ति। महता श्रमेण बहुकालीनपाठानुभवाधारेण च इमानि पुस्तकानि रचितानि इत्यत्र नास्ति संशयलेशोऽपि। एतेषां पठ्यपुस्तकानां लक्ष्यं भवति सर्वशास्त्रसाधारण-सामान्यसंस्कृतपरिचायनम्। एतदनुसारेण रचयितारः आदौ सरलशब्दान् प्रस्तूय क्रमेण सर्वेषां लिङ्ग-वचन-पुरुष-लकारादीनां तत्रापि त्रिष्वपि लिङ्गेषु अकारान्त-इकारान्ताद्यजन्तशब्दानां नानाहलन्तशब्दानां च परिचयं कारयन्ति। इदं सर्वं सम्यगेव कृतमित्यपि पठितॄणां अवलोकयितॄणां च स्पष्टम्।

परन्तु, आधुनिक-मध्यवयस्क-बुद्धिमत्-जिज्ञासूनां कृते एतैः पठ्यपुस्तकैः अतीव उपयोगः न जातः इत्यपि अनुभवसिद्धम्। तत्कुतः इति चेत्, ते यत् शास्त्रं, प्रकृते वेदान्तं, पठितुमिच्छन्ति केवलं तस्य परिचायनं न तेषां पठ्यपुस्तकानां लक्ष्यम्। एकमुदाहरणं पश्यामः - वेदान्तग्रन्थेषु कानिचित् द्विशतक्रियापदानि उपयुज्यन्ते।[2] तत्रापि न सर्वलकाराः उपयुज्यन्ते, उपयुक्तलकारेष्वपि न सर्वपुरुषाणां

---

[1] मया दृष्टानि पठ्यपुस्तकानि १. आदर्शपुस्तकानि (बालादर्श-प्रथमादर्श-द्वितीयादर्श-तृतीयादर्शनामकानि) २. M. R. काळे महोदयरचितं Higher Sanskrit Grammer, Motilal Banarasidas, 1961

[2] भवति स्वीक्रियते स्यात् व्याकरवाणि विद्धि वर्तते वदन्ति युज्यते परिषस्वजाते निश्चीयते करोति उपपद्यते आह आसीत् आनय अस्तु अस्ति असि अभिचाकशीति हरति स्वीक्रियन्ते स्वीकरोति स्युः स्याम् संगच्छते सिञ्चति सम्भवन्ति सम्भवति सम्बोधयेत् सम्बध्यते सम्पादयति सम्पत्स्ये समवलीयन्ते सन्ति सङ्गच्छते श्रृणोमि श्रूयते श्रुणु शृणोति शक्यते व्यावर्तयति व्याप्रियते व्याप्नुतः व्यवह्रियते व्यपदिश्यते व्यनक्ति व्यथन्ति विविच्येत विविच्यताम् विरम्यते विमुच्यते विभाति विभज्यताम् विध्ये विधीयते विदधाति विजानीयात् विचचार वाति वर्तन्ते वर्णयन्ति वदतः वदति वक्ष्यामः वक्ष्यते वक्ष्यति लभते लक्षयति रक्षिष्यति योजयति यान्ति मन्यन्ते मन्यते मनुते भ्रियते भिद्यते भासते भाति भविष्यामः भवन्ति ब्रूयात् ब्रुवते बोधयति बृंहयति बृंहति बाधते बभूवुः बध्यते बधान प्रोक्षति प्रीयताम् प्राकृतम् प्रसज्येते प्रविशति प्रवर्त्तते प्रयुंक्ते प्रयुञ्ज्यात् प्रयन्ति प्रपद्यते प्रदर्श्यन्ते प्रतीयन्ते प्रतीयते प्रतिषेधयति प्रतिषेधति प्रतिवसति प्रतिपादयामः प्रतिपादयन्ति प्रतिपद्यते प्रजायेय पृच्छयते पृच्छामि पूर्यते पायात् पान्ति पश्येत् पश्यामि पश्यन्ति पश्यति पवते निर्दिश्यते निर्दिशति निरूप्यन्ते निरूप्यते निराचष्टे निन्द्यते निगद्यते नश्येत् नम ध्यायेत्

सर्वाणि वचनानि। पठ्यपुस्तकेषु तु सर्वेषामेषां परिचयः भवति। अतः इमानि पुस्तकानि प्रकृतोद्देशाय नातीवोपयुक्तानि भवन्ति।

3 परिहारोपायः - लेखसङ्ग्रहाधारितभाषाध्ययनम् (Corpus Linguistics)

1990तमवर्षानन्तरं सङ्गणकस्य उपयोगः भाषाक्षेत्रे आरब्धः। ततः नूतनसम्भावनाः भाषाविज्ञानिनां दृष्टिपथमागताः। तत्रैका सम्भावना लेखसङ्ग्रहाधारितभाषाध्ययनम्[3] सङ्गणके टङ्कितानां लेखानां/ग्रन्थानां सङ्ग्रहस्य उपयोगः बहुभिः प्रकारैः कर्तुं शक्यते। भाषाविश्लेषकः सङ्ग्रहे अपेक्षानुसारेण विभिन्नान् ग्रन्थान् चेतुं शक्नोति। उदाहरणाय प्रकृते केवलं वेदान्तग्रन्थान्, तत्रापि आरम्भिकग्रन्थान् चित्वा तदुपरि उपलभ्यमानसङ्गणकीयोपकरणानि उपयुज्य विश्लेषणं कर्तुं शक्यम्।

धावति द्वेष्मि दृश्यते दिशति ददाह ददाति तेज तिष्ठन्ति तरति जीवन्ति जिघ्राणि जायन्ते जायते जानामि जानाति जाग्रति जहाति जनयति जज्ञिरे छिद्यन्ते चेतयते चेतयति चिन्तयामि चालयेत् चलन्ति ग्राहयन्ति ग्रसते गोचरयति गृह्यते गृह्णीयात् गृह्णन्ति गच्छन्ति गच्छति क्षीयन्ते क्षरति क्रियेते क्रियते क्रियताम् कुर्मः कुरु कल्प्यते कल्पते करोमि करिष्ये कथ्यन्ते ऐक्षत एति उपासीत उपासते उपयुज्यते उपपादयामः उपपादयन्ति उपदेक्ष्यन्ति उपदिशेत् उपजायन्ते उपगच्छन्ति उद्भावयति उदेति उदाहरिष्यामः उत्पद्यन्ते उत्पद्यते उत्क्रामन्ति उच्यन्ते उच्यते ईशते ईडे ईक्षामहे ईक्षते इष्यते इच्छामि इच्छन्ति इङ्गते आहुः आस्ते आसम् आवहेत् आराधयति आरभ्यन्ते आरभ्यते आरभते आम्नायते आमनन्ति आपि आपादयति आतिष्ठन्ते आच्छादयति आचष्टे आचक्षते आख्यानि आक्षिपति अस्वाप्सम् अस्मि असृजत अवेहि अवेदिषम् अवाप्नोति अवभासते अवतिष्ठते अभ्युपगच्छन्ति अभ्यवहरति अभूत् अभिसंविशन्ति अभिव्यज्यते अभात् अब्रवीत् अपेक्षते अपनुदति अनुसरति अनुशेते अनुवर्तन्ते अनुमीयते अनुमापयति अनुप्राविशत् अध्यस्यन्ति अदर्शि अत्ति अतितराम अतप्यत अजानन् अङ्गीक्रियते अकामयत शार्ङ्गायते

3 Corpus Linguistics: What It Is and How It Can Be Applied to Teaching, Daniel Krieger, The Internet TESL Journal at http://iteslj.org/Articles/Krieger-Corpus.html

3.1 *सङ्गणकीयोपकरणानि*

अधुना नानाविध-सङ्गणकीय-उपकरणानां सिद्धत्वात् एतादृशजिज्ञासूनाम् उपकाराय नूतनः उपायः शक्यः। तस्य विवरणम् इदानीं दीयते।

Development of Sanskrit Computational Toolkit and Sanskrit-Hindi Machine Translation System, funded by Department of Information Technology, Ministry of Communication and Information Technology, Govt. of India, इत्येका परियोजना 2008तः प्रवर्तते।[4] एतदन्तर्गततया बहूनि उपकरणानि सज्जीकृतानि सन्ति। एतानि उपकरणानि <http://sanskrit.uohyd.ernet.in/scl> इत्यत्र अन्तर्जाले उपलभ्यन्ते। पाणिनीय-व्याकरणानुसारेण पदविश्लेषकं वाक्यविश्लेषकं सन्धिविच्छेदकं सन्धिसंयोजकम् एवमादीनि बहूनि उपकरणानि साधितानि। अस्मिन् प्रबन्धे प्रस्तूयमानः सर्वोऽपि विषयः इमानि उपकरणानि उपयुज्य प्रस्तुतः।

3.2 *स्वीकृतग्रन्थाः*

द्वैत-अद्वैत-विशिष्टाद्वैत-निम्बार्कसम्प्रदायस्य आरम्भिकग्रन्थाः अत्र विश्लेषणाय स्वीकृताः। ते च -

---

4 This is a consortium mode project.
Consortium Leader - University of Hyderabad
Consortium Members
Poorna Prajna Vidya Peetha, Bangalore
Jawaharlal Nehru University, New Delhi
International Institute of Information Technology, Hyderabad
Rashtriya Sanskrit Vidya Peetha, Tirupati
Jagadguru Ramanandacharya Rajasthan Sanskrit Uinversity, Jaipur Sanskrit Academy, Hyderabad

1. श्रीजयतीर्थभिक्षुविरचितं श्रीमदानन्दतीर्थभगवत्पादाचार्यविरचिततत्वसङ्ख्यानविवरणम्
2. श्रीमत्परमहंसपरिव्राजकाचार्यसदानन्दविरचितो वेदान्तसारः
3. श्रीनिवासदासेन विरचिता यतीन्द्रमतदीपिका
4. श्रीअनन्तरामेण विरचितो वेदान्ततत्वबोधः
5. छलारीशेषाचार्यविरचिता प्रमाणचन्द्रिका

3.3 *सन्धिविच्छेद-समस्तपदविच्छेदौ*

ग्रन्थानां टङ्कनानन्तरं अक्षरशोधः (proof reading) क्रियते। तदनु सन्धिविच्छेदः क्रियते। उदाहरणाय अत्र एकं शोधितदोषं वाक्यं दर्श्यते -

ननु पर्वते वर्तमानो धूमो गृहान्तवर्तिनः पुरुषस्य किमित्यग्निप्रमां न जनयति ? उच्यते। न प्रत्यक्षवदनुमानमज्ञातकरणम्। किन्तु ज्ञातमेव।

तत्र सन्धिविच्छेदे कृते एवं भवति -

ननु पर्वते वर्तमानः+ धूमः+ गृहान्तवर्तिनः पुरुषस्य किम्+इति+अग्निप्रमाम्+ न जनयति ? उच्यते। न प्रत्यक्षवत्+अनुमानम्+अज्ञातकरणम्। किन्तु ज्ञातम्+एव।

तत्र पुनः समस्तपदविच्छेदे विहिते एवं जायते -

ननु पर्वते वर्तमानः+धूमः गृह-अन्तर्-वर्तिनः पुरुषस्य किम्+इति+अग्नि-प्रमाम्+ न जनयति ? उच्यते। न प्रत्यक्ष^वत्+अनुमानम्+ नञ्-ज्ञात-करणम्+। किन्तु ज्ञातम्+एव।[5]

एवं सर्वेषां ग्रन्थानां परिष्कारः कृतः।

---

[5] अत्र क्रमः परियोजनायां निर्धारितरीत्या विहितः । तदीयविवरणाय पश्यत – Sanskrit Compound Processor, Anil Kumar, Vipul Mittal and Amba Kulkarni In Proceedings of the International Sanskrit Computational Linguistics Symposium, Springer, 2010.

3.4 *पदावृत्तिः* (Frequency of words)

इतः सङ्गणकीयविधीनामुपयोगस्य समयः। प्रथमतः समग्रपदपट्टिका निर्मिता।[6] आहत्य 40,000 पदानि लब्धानि। sort filename | uniq -c > newfile इत्यादेशस्य साहाय्येन पदानामावृत्तिसङ्ख्या लब्धा। sort -u filename > newfile इत्यादेशेन असाधारणपदपट्टिः सम्पादिता।

आहत्य पञ्चग्रन्थस्थपदानि (Total words of five texts) – 40,000.			
असाधारणपदानि (Unique words) – 70,00[7]			
विविधाः आवृत्तयः (Different frequencies)			
सुबन्तानि (नामपदानि) 6,020		**वचनावृत्तिः *(Vachana freq.)***	
6,020 सुबन्तानां प्रातिपदिकानि[8]	2,800	एकवचनम्	4,170
नञ्समासभिन्नप्रातिपदिकानि[9]	2,300	बहुवचनम्	598
अव्ययानि	338	द्विवचनम्	228
तिङन्तानि (क्रियापदानि)	273		
उभयात्मकानि (उदा. नाम, यत्, नमः - इमानि सुबन्तान्यपि अव्ययान्यपि भवन्ति)	29		

6 यत्र रिक्तस्थलं +चिह्नं -चिह्नं वा वर्तते तत्र new line स्थापने पदपट्टिः सिद्ध्यति ।

7 अत्र आनुकूल्याय पूर्णसङ्ख्याः दर्शिताः । यथावत्सङ्ख्यास्तु क्रमेण 40,605 तथा 6,649 ।

8 सुबन्तेषु अनेकेषां पदानां प्रातिपदिकं एकं भवति । यथा `यस्य येन येषां यस्मिन्' इत्यादीनां यद् इत्येव प्रातिपदिकम् । एवं 6020सुबन्तानां प्रातिपदिकानि 2800 भवन्ति ।

9 अनभिहितम्, अश्रुतम्, अचेतनम् - इत्यादौ प्रातिपदिकं यद्यपि भिन्नम् । तथापि अभिहित-श्रुत-चेतनेत्यादिप्रातिपदिकज्ञानेन सह नञ्समासप्रकारज्ञानं भवति चेत् एतादृशशब्दाः ज्ञातुं शक्यन्ते । नञ्समासोदहारणानि ४००तः अधिकानि सन्ति । अतः ज्ञातव्यप्रातिपदिकानि २३००+ भवन्ति ।

सुबन्तेषु अन्त्यवर्णावृत्तिः.		**हलन्तपदानि 450**	
अकारान्तम्	3,618	नकारान्तानि	161
आ	344	त	146
इ	361	स	46
ई	52	द्	10
उ	99	च	7
ऊ	1 (भू)	श	6
ऋ	52	ज	5
ओ	4	र	4
विभक्त्यावृत्तिः *(Vibhakti freq.)*		प	1 (अप् शब्दः)
प्रथमा	2,028	**लिङ्गावृत्तिः *(Linga freq.)***	
समासपूर्वपदम् (उदा. पूर्वज्ञनम् इत्यत्र पूर्वशब्दः)	976	पुं.	2,152
द्वितीया	464	नपुं.	1,007
षष्ठी	436	पुं-नपुं.	921
तृतीया	372	स्त्री	650
सप्तमी	369	पुं-स्त्री	129
पञ्चमी	297	पुं-स्त्री-नपुं.	120
चतुर्थी	49	नपुं-स्त्री.	16

3.5 *फलितांशोपयोगः*

उपरि दर्शितानां फलितांशानामाधारेण वैज्ञानिकरीत्या नूतनपठ्यपुस्तकानां निर्माणं कर्तुं शक्यते। अस्मिन् पुस्तके न क्रमेण सर्व-लिङ्ग-अन्त-विभक्ति-वचन-पुरुषाणां परिचयः भवति। साम्प्रदायिकपठ्येषु अजन्तशब्दानां परिचायनानन्तरं हलन्तानां परिचयः भवति। परन्तु आश्चर्यजनकः अयं विषयः यत् अकारान्तानामावृत्तेः (3,618) अनन्तरं हलन्तानामावृत्तिः (405) अधिका ! तदनु आकारान्तानामावृत्तिः (344)!!

अयमप्यंशः परिशील्यताम् – 2,300 प्रातिपदिकानां 338 अव्ययानां 273 क्रियापदानां च परिचयेन वेदान्ताध्ययनं परिनिष्ठिततया कर्तुं शक्यते! तत्रापि बहवः संस्कृतसुबन्तशब्दाः भारतीयभाषासु उपयुज्यमानाः भवन्ति। ततश्च अपरिचितानां शब्दानां, परिचितानामपि भिन्नवचनविभक्तिषु कीदृशानि रूपाणि भवन्तीति परिचेयम्।

एवं सर्वस्तरेष्वपि भाषासम्बन्धिनामंशानां परिचायने नूतना रीतिः आविष्करणीया भवति। एतादृशपठ्यानामध्ययनं कृतवतां वेदान्ताध्ययनं सुलभं भवतीति नवीनेयं सम्भावना नूनं पाठक-पाठयितॄणां प्रमोदावहा भवति।

3.6 *एकः प्रयत्नः*

अस्मिन् सन्दर्भे एतन्मार्गे गच्छतः ममैकं प्रयत्नमधिकृत्य वक्तुमिच्छामि। षट् छात्राः उपचत्वारिंशद्वर्षीयाः अध्ययनाय आगताः। तेभ्यः आदौ सर्वभाषासम्बन्धिनः इमे केचन विषयाः कन्नडभाषोदाहरणपुरस्सरं पाठिताः। ते च विषयाः -

वाक्यस्वरूपम्	विशेषणविशेष्यभावः
पदस्वरूपम्	क्रियापदेषु तिङन्त-कृदन्ते
पदविभागः-क्रियापद-नामपद-अव्ययानि	कारकाणि (अस्य विषये अधिकमवधानं दत्तम्)
लिङ्गम्	पदानाम् अकाराद्यन्तत्वम्
वचनम्	नामपदानाम् अकाराद्यन्तभेदेन रूपभेदः
विभक्तिः	माहेश्वरसूत्रपरिचयः

प्रत्याहारपरिचयः (अग्रे अच्-हल् इत्यादिशब्द-प्रयोग-सौलभ्याय)

एतेन संस्कृतव्याकरणसम्बन्धिनः बहवः विषयाः विना अतिक्लेशम् अवगामिताः। एतेषां परिचायनाय आवर्तनाय च आहत्य ४.५ घण्टाः व्ययीकृताः। तदनु उपरिदर्शितावृत्त्यनुसारं प्रथमतः अकारान्तस्य तदनु हलन्तस्य नामपदस्य क्रमेण इतरपदानां च विभक्तिरूपाणि परिचायितानि। २५ अव्ययानां क्रियापदानां च परिचयः कारितः। एतदर्थं पञ्च घण्टाः अपेक्षिताः। एवमेव सन्धीनामावृत्तिमनुसृत्य प्रथमतः विसर्गसन्धेः तदनु इतरसन्धीनां परिचयः कारितः। एतदर्थं पुनः तिस्रः घण्टाः यापिताः। मम अनुभवानुसारेण विंशतिघण्टात्मककाले छात्राणां यथा वेदान्ताभ्यासे आत्मविश्वासः सोत्साहा अभिरुचिश्च उत्पद्येत तथा पाठनं शक्यम्।

4 अग्रिमसोपानानि

उपरिदर्शितान् विषयान् आधृत्य नूतनपठ्यपुस्तकानां रचनं करणीयम्। प्रतिपाठं विस्तरेण अभ्यासाः रचनीयाः येन पाठितांशाः दृढाः स्युः।

यथेदं वेदान्तक्षेत्रे कृतं तथा 'आयुर्वेदाय संस्कृतम्' 'योगाय संस्कृतम्' इत्यादिरूपेण प्रयत्नान् विधाय तत्तच्छास्त्रजिज्ञासूनामुपकारः कर्तुं शक्यः। ये अल्पकालं संस्कृतमभ्यस्य संस्कृतविश्वविद्यालयेषु पठितुमिच्छन्ति तेषां कृते लघुकक्ष्याः (crash course) निर्माय तेषामध्ययनस्य मौलिकता अभिवर्धयितुं शक्या। यदि अल्पकाले सफलसंस्कृताध्ययनं शक्यमिति वार्ता प्रसृता स्यात् तर्हि नवीनाः अपि जनाः संस्कृताध्ययनाय आगच्छेयुः। संस्कृतसीमा विस्तृता स्यात्।

श्लेषालङ्कारः

संस्कृतविश्लेषणसाधनानां परीक्षणाय एकः समाह्वयः

Śleṣa Alaṁkāra

A Challenge for Testing Sanskrit Analytical Tools

वरलक्ष्मीः

संस्कृत अकादमी, हैदराबाद्

Abstract. प्रबन्धसारः – संस्कृतसाहित्यस्य अध्ययनाध्यापनन्तु पदच्छेदः, पदविश्लेषणं, समस्तपदविच्छेदः, समस्तपदविश्लेषणम् अन्वयश्चेति सम्प्रदायमनुसृत्य गुरुशिष्यपरम्परया वैदिककालात् प्रचलति। तमेव सम्प्रदायमनुसृत्य प्राचीनशास्त्राणाम् आधुनिकशास्त्राणाञ्च ज्ञानं समालोड्य, अहरहरः परिश्रम्य विद्वांसः संस्कृतसङ्गणकीयसंसाधनानि निरमान् इतोऽधिकानि निर्मान्ति च। एभिः विद्वद्भिः निर्मितः संसाधनसमुच्चयः नैकेषु अन्तर्जालपुटेषु हस्तलभ्यः वर्तते। संस्कृतविश्लेषकसंसाधनानि पठनपाठने कथमुपकुर्वन्तीति श्लेषालङ्कारस्य विश्लेषणं सोदाहरणं प्रदर्श्य सङ्गणकसाधनानां सामर्थ्यं वैशिष्ट्यञ्च पत्रेऽस्मिन् निरूप्यते। अष्टौ श्लेषप्रकाराः सभङ्गाभङ्गोभयात्मकश्लेषश्च सयान्त्रिकविश्लेषणाः प्रस्तूयन्ते।

1 परिचयः

अधुनातनाध्ययनक्षेत्रे अध्ययनाध्यापनविधौ नूतनपरम्परा समारब्धा। वैद्युतकग्रन्थाः, वैद्युतकग्रन्थालयाः, वैद्युतकाध्ययनकक्ष्याः, वैद्युतकाध्ययनं, संङ्गणकोपकरणानीति विद्याक्षेत्रे अध्ययनसौलभ्याय उपकल्पिताः। आ बहोः कालात् गुरुशिष्यपरम्परया अविरतं प्रचाल्यमाने संस्कृताध्ययनक्षेत्रेऽपि ईदृशानि उपकरणानि उपकल्पनीयानीति सत्सङ्कल्पेन कर्मकुशलाः, विद्वत्तल्लजाः संस्कृतसङ्गणकसाधनोपकल्पने कार्यरतास्सन्ति। साम्प्रतम् उपलभ्यमानानां साधनानां परिचयः, तेषाम् उपयोगिता, कार्याचरणे उत्पद्यमाना भ्रान्तिः तस्याः निवारणञ्च शोधपत्रेणानेन क्रियते।

2 संस्कृतसङ्गणकीयसंसाधनानि

फ्रान्सदेशस्थायाः इन्रियासंस्थायाः प्राचार्यः जेरार्ड ह्युयेट्, ब्रौन् विश्वविद्यालयीयः आचार्यः पीटर् षार्फ्, प्राचार्यः ओलिवर् हेल्विग्, जवाहरलालनेहरूविश्वविद्यालयीयः

प्राचार्यः गिरीशनाथझावर्यः, हैदराबादनगरस्थकेन्द्रीयविश्वविद्यालयीया प्राचार्या अम्बाकुलकर्णिवर्या अन्ये च गण्याः संस्कृतसाहित्याध्ययनाय विश्लेषणाय नैकानि संस्कृतसङ्गणकीयसंसाधनानि निरमान्। तानि च संसाधनानि विभिन्नेषु अन्तर्जालपुटेषूपलभ्यन्ते। सन्धिसंश्लेषिका, सन्धिविच्छेदिका, पदविश्लेषिका, सुब–न्ततिङ्न्तकृदन्ततद्धितरूपाणाम् उत्पादिकाः, संस्कृत–हिन्दी अनुवादकम् अनुसारकं लिप्यन्तरीकरणञ्चेति नैकानि संसाधनानि दैनन्दिनोपयोगे समानयन्।

2.1 संसाधनोपयोगे जायमानाः क्लेशाः

संस्कृतवाङ्मयस्य विश्लेषणावसरे मानवः स्वीयं पुस्तकज्ञानं प्रापञ्चिकपरिज्ञानञ्च उपयुङ्क्ते। विषयान् इदमित्थतया स्पष्टयति। सङ्गणकयन्त्रं केवलदत्तनिधिसङ्ग्रहा–धारेण वाङ्मयं विश्लेषयति। तानि विश्लेषणानि भ्रान्तिजनकानीव प्रतिभान्ति। तं विषयमत्र प्रस्तुमः।

यान्त्रिकसन्धिविच्छेदनम् जेरार्ड ह्यूयेट् महोदयेन **सेग्मेण्टर्**, गिरीशनाथवर्येण **सन्धि एनलैजर्**, अम्बाकुलकर्णिमहाभागया **सन्धिविच्छेदिका**, चेति सन्धिविच्छेदनसाधनानि निर्मितानि। इमानि यान्त्रिकसाधनानि 'तवातिमहानलाभः' 'महेशः' इत्युदाहरणानि कतिधा छिन्दन्तीति तालिकायां प्रस्तूयन्ते।

Table 1 : तालिका–1 सन्धिविच्छेदनानां संख्यात्मकविश्लेषणम्

क्र.सं	उदाहरणम्	सेग्मेण्टर्	सन्धि एनलैजर्	सन्धिविच्छेदिका
1	तवातिमहानलाभः	41	0	62
2	महेशः	1	2	8

यान्त्रिकपदविश्लेषणम् जेरार्ड ह्यूयेट् महोदयेन **स्टेम्मर्**, गिरीशनाथवर्येण **सुबन्त एनलैजर्**, **तिङ्न्त एनलैजर्** च अम्बाकुलकर्णिमहाभागया **पदविश्लेषिका**, पीटर् षार्फवर्येण **मार्फलाजिकल् एनलैजर्** चेति पदविश्लेषणसाधनानि निर्मितानि। यान्त्रिकसाधनानि सुबन्तानि तिङ्न्तानि च बहुलतया विश्लेषयन्ति। सोदाहरणमत्र प्रस्तूयते।

Table 2 : तालिका–2 सुबन्ततिङन्तयोः यान्त्रिकविश्लेषणम्

क्र. सं	संसाधनानि	उदाहरणम्	यान्त्रिकविश्लेषणानि
1	स्टेम्मर्–पदविश्लेषिका–सुबन्त एनलैजर्–मार्फलाजिकल् एनलैजर्	वलयः–सुबन्तम्	**वलि**-स्त्री.प्र.वि.ब.व. **वलय**–पुं.प्र.वि.ए.व.
2	स्टेम्मर्–पदविश्लेषिका–तिङन्त एनलैजर्	वक्ष्यति–तिङन्तम्	**वह्** कर्तरि, लृट्, प्र, ए.पर.वहँ अदादिः– **वच्** कर्तरि लृट् प्र ए पर वचँ भ्वादिः– **ब्रू** कर्तरि लृट् प्र ए पर ब्रूञ् अदादिः–

यान्त्रिकसमस्तपदविच्छेदनम् सालकाननशोभिनीति समस्तपदं विभिन्नतया विविधसंसाधनानि भञ्जन्ति। साहित्ये तु समस्तपदमिदं स–अलक–आनन–शोभिनी, साल–कानन–शोभिनीति च द्वेधैव विभज्यते।

Table 3 : तालिका – 3 : समस्तपदविच्छेदनस्य संख्यात्मकविश्लेषणम्

1	सेग्मेण्टर्	18
2	समासविच्छेदिका	52

समस्तपदविश्लेषणम् 'विपल्लवाः' इति समस्तपदविश्लेषणं यन्त्रेण बहुधा क्रियते। विपद्–लवाः – षष्ठी– तत्पुरुषसमासः, वि–पल्लवाः – प्रादितत्पुरुषसमासश्चेति द्विविधसमासौ प्रयुक्तौ। यान्त्रिक– पदविश्लेषणानि 31 प्राप्यन्ते।

समेषां संस्कृतसङ्गणकसंसाधनानां संख्याबाहुल्योपेतविश्लेषणानि संलक्ष्य उपयोक्ता अवश्यं भ्रान्तिमनुभवति। कथं बहूनि विश्लेषणानि यन्त्रं जनयति? कतमं विश्लेषणमर्थवदस्ति? निरर्थकानि विश्लेषणानि कुतो यन्त्रं जनयति?

3 दत्तनिधिसङ्ग्रहः

प्रातिपदिककोशः, अव्ययकोशः, संख्यासंख्येयपूरणकोशः सर्वनामकोशः, क्रियापद–कोशः, कृदन्तपदकोशश्च दत्तनिधिसङ्ग्रहरूपेण यन्त्रे निवेशिताः। तस्याधारेणैव सन्धिविच्छेदनं पदविश्लेषणं यान्त्रिकानुवादश्चेति संक्लिष्टकार्याणि सङ्गणकयन्त्रेण सिद्ध्यन्ति। नैकमपि विच्छेदनं, विश्लेषणञ्च निरर्थकमस्तीति निश्चप्रचं वक्तुं शक्यते। संस्कृतभाषा सहजतयैव वैशिष्ट्यपूर्णास्ति। एकमेव पदं बहुधा छेत्तुं शक्यते। अथवा

एकमेव पदं बहून् अर्थान् व्यनक्ति। अत एव एकस्यैव ग्रन्थस्य वा काव्यस्य वा शास्त्रस्य वा नैकानि व्याख्यानानि अथवा भाष्याणि क्रियन्ते। ईदृशं संस्कृतभाषागतवैशिष्ट्यं मनसि निधाय कविपण्डिताः श्लेषालङ्कारकाव्यानि रचयित्वा चमत्कारं जनयन्ति।

4 अलङ्कारः

श्लेषालङ्कारस्य विश्लेषणात्पूर्वं काव्यं नाम किम्? काव्ये अलङ्कारस्य स्थानं कीदृशम् अस्ति? को वा अलङ्कारः? स च कतिधा वर्तत? इति सङ्क्षिप्ततया ज्ञातव्यम्।

अ. **शब्दार्थौ सहितौ काव्यमिति** काव्यालङ्कारकर्ता भामहः काव्यस्य लक्षणं वक्ति।

आ. काव्यालङ्कारसूत्रवृत्तिकारः वामनः **काव्यं ग्राह्यमलङ्कारादिति** काव्ये अलङ्कारप्राधान्यं, **सौन्दर्यमलङ्कारः** इति अलङ्कारस्वरूपञ्च विवृणोति।

इ. **काव्यशोभाकरान् धर्मानलङ्कारान् प्रचक्षते** इति काव्यादर्शकारः दण्डी अलङ्कारप्राशस्त्यं स्तौति। स च अलङ्कारः शब्दालङ्कारः अर्थालङ्कारश्चेति द्वेधा वर्तते। अलङ्कारेषु अन्यतमः श्लेषः।

4.1 श्लेषालङ्कारः

श्लेषालङ्कारविषये त्रयः आलङ्कारिकाः तुल्याभिप्रायं वहन्ति। श्लेषः अष्टधेति साहित्यदर्पणकारः विश्वनाथः[1], काव्यप्रकाशकर्ता मम्मटश्च अभिप्रेतः[2] शृङ्गारप्रकाशकर्ता भोजराजस्तु षोढा इति अभिप्रैति।[3]

Table 4 : तालिका – 4 : श्लेषालङ्कारप्रकाराः

क्र.सं	साहित्यदर्पणम्	काव्यप्रकाशः	शृङ्गारप्रकाशः
1	वर्णश्लेषः	वर्णश्लेषः	–
2	प्रत्ययश्लेषः	प्रत्ययश्लेषः	प्रत्ययश्लेषः
3	लिङ्गश्लेषः	लिङ्गश्लेषः	–
4	प्रकृतिश्लेषः	प्रकृतिश्लेषः	प्रकृतिश्लेषः

[1]श्लिष्टैः पदैरनेकार्थाभिधाने श्लेष इष्यते। वर्णप्रत्ययलिङ्गानां प्रकृत्योः पदयोरपि। श्लेषाद् विभक्तिवचनभाषाणामष्टधा च सः।। साहित्यदर्पणः 10.13

[2]वाच्यभेदेन भिन्ना यद् युगपद्भाषणस्पृशः। श्लिष्यन्ति शब्दाः श्लेषोसावक्षरादिभिरष्टधा।। अर्थभेदेन शब्दभेदः इति दर्शने काव्यमार्गे स्वरो न गण्यते इति च नये वाच्यभेदेन भिन्ना अपि शब्दा यत् युगपदुच्चारणेन श्लिष्यन्ति भिन्नं स्वरूपमपह्नुवते स श्लेषः। स च वर्ण–पद–लिङ्ग–भाषा–प्रकृति–प्रत्यय–विभक्ति–वचनानां भेदादष्टधा। काव्यप्रकाशः 9.84

[3]द्वयोस्तन्त्रेणाभिधानं श्लेषः। स षोढा– प्रकृतिश्लेषः, प्रत्ययश्लेषः, विभक्तिश्लेषः, वचनश्लेषः, पदश्लेषः, भाषाश्लेषः इति। शृङ्गारप्रकाशः 10

5	पदश्लेषः	पदश्लेषः	पदश्लेषः
6	विभक्तिश्लेषः	विभक्तिश्लेषः	विभक्तिश्लेषः
7	वचनश्लेषः	वचनश्लेषः	वचनश्लेषः
8	भाषाश्लेषः	भाषाश्लेषः	भाषाश्लेषः

श्लेषालङ्कारः पुनः शब्दश्लेषः अर्थश्लेषश्चेति द्वेधा विभक्तोऽस्ति। शब्दश्लेषः सभङ्गाभङ्गोभयात्मकश्चेति त्रेधा विभक्तः। उपरितनाष्टौ प्रकाराः शब्दश्लेषस्य त्रिषु विभागेषु अन्तर्भवन्तीति मम्मटः विश्वनाथश्च अभिप्रेतः।

श्लेषालङ्कारः

शब्दश्लेषः — अर्थश्लेषः

त्रिविधः

1. सभङ्गः–वर्ण–प्रत्यय–लिङ्ग–प्रकृति–पद–विभक्ति–वचन–भाषा–प्रभेदाः
2. अभङ्गः–वर्ण–प्रत्यय–लिङ्ग–प्रकृति–पद–विभक्ति–वचन–भाषा–प्रभेदाः
3. उभयात्मकमः–वर्ण–प्रत्यय–लिङ्ग–प्रकृति–पद–विभक्ति–वचन–भाषाप्रभेदाः

5 श्लेषालङ्कारोदाहरणानि-यान्त्रिकविश्लेषणम्

व्युत्पन्नमतयः कविवरेण्याः सभङ्गाभङ्गोभयात्मकश्लेषस्य अष्टौ प्रकारान् सन्धेः अथवा समासस्य विभिन्नविच्छेदनानाम्, पदानां नैकविश्लेषणानाञ्चाधारेणैव काव्येषु प्रयुञ्जते। श्लेषालङ्कारवैचित्रिं यान्त्रिकसंसाधनानाम् अनुपममद्भुतञ्च सामर्थ्यं सोदाहरणं विवृणुमः। साहित्यदर्पणं, काव्यप्रकाशः, शृङ्गारप्रकाशः चेति त्रिभ्यः साहित्यशास्त्रग्रन्थेभ्यः, नैषधीयचरितं नलचम्पूश्चेति द्वाभ्यां काव्याभ्याञ्च उदाहरणश्लोकाः उद्धृताः।

5.1 वर्णश्लेषः

प्रतिकूलतामुपगते हि **विधौ** विफलत्वमेति बहुसाधनता।
अवलम्बनाय दिनभर्तुरभून्न पतिष्यतः **करसहस्रमपि**।।[1]

[1]साहित्यदर्पणम् 10

बहुषु साधनेषु सत्सु अपि (अ)विधौ प्रतिकूले सति (आ)विधौ अथवा चन्द्रे उदिते सति (अ)सहस्रं हस्ता अपि (आ)सहस्रं किरणा अपि (अ)कार्त्यवीर्यार्जुनं (आ)सूर्यं रक्षितुं न प्रभवन्ति। विधौ चन्द्रे विधातरि वा, कराः किरणाः हस्ताश्च। श्लोके वर्णश्लेषं प्रयुज्य विधौ इति पदेन चन्द्रं विधातारञ्च, करसहस्रमिति पदेन हस्ताः किरणाश्चेति द्वन्द्वार्थं साधयित्वा कार्त्यवीर्यार्जुनं सूर्यञ्चावर्णयत् कविः।

Table 5 : तालिका – 5 : वर्णश्लेषस्य यान्त्रिकपदविश्लेषणम्

श्लेषप्रकारः – वर्णश्लेषः
उदाहरणम् – विधौ
१. उकारान्तः पुं.लि. विधु शब्दः स.वि.ए.व
२. इकारान्तः पुं.लि. विधि शब्दः स.वि.ए.व.
'विधि' शब्दस्य 'विधु' शब्दस्य च सप्तमीविभक्तेः उभे रूपे तुल्ये स्तः।

अलङ्कारः शङ्काकरनरकपालं परिजनो
विशीर्णाङ्गो भृङ्गी वसु च वृष एको बहुवयाः।
अवस्थेयं स्थाणोरपि भवति सर्वामरगुरो
विधौ वक्रे मूर्ध्नि स्थितवति वयं के पुनरमी॥[1]

शिवस्य अलङ्कारः मानवकपालं, तस्य सेवकः शिथिलाङ्गः भृङ्गी, तस्य सम्पत्तिः वृद्धवृषभः, तस्य शिरसि (अ)चन्द्रकला (आ) प्रतिकूलविधिः। विधातरि प्रतिकूले सति देवगुरोः एव ईदृशी स्थितिः अस्ति चेत् मनुष्याणाम् अस्माकं का वा स्थितिः भवेत्? श्लोकेऽस्मिन्नपि विधौ इति विधुशब्दस्य विधिशब्दस्य च तुल्यं सप्तम्यन्तरूपं द्वन्द्वार्थे प्रयुज्य चमत्करोति कविः।

5.2 प्रत्ययश्लेषः

रजनिरमणमौलेः पादपद्मावलोक
क्षणसमयपराप्तापूर्वसंपत्सहस्रम्।
प्रमथनिवहमध्ये जातुचित्त्वत्प्रसादाद्
अहमुचितरुचिः **स्यान्नन्दिता** सा तथा मे॥[2]

[1]काव्यप्रकाशः 9.369
[2]काव्यप्रकाशः 9.374

शिवस्य पादपद्मावलोकनात् सहस्रधा सम्पत्तिं प्राप्य, तत्प्रसादेन भक्तिञ्च सम्प्राप्य अहं (अ)प्रथमगणमध्ये नन्दकः स्याम् (आ) नन्दिता नाम गणभावः स्यात्। 'नन्दिता' इत्येकमेव पदं, 'तृच्', 'तल्' इति द्वौ प्रत्ययौ प्रयुक्तौ, द्वावर्थौ च साधितौ। स्यान्नन्दितेति स्यां स्यादित्युत्तमप्रथमयोः नन्दितेति तृच्तलोस्तुल्यं रूपम्। पदविश्लेषिकेति सङ्गणकसाधनेन प्रस्तुतं यान्त्रिकविश्लेषणं परिशील्यते।

Table 6 : तालिका – 6 : प्रत्ययश्लेषस्य यान्त्रिकविश्लेषणम्

नन्दिता तृच् प्रत्ययः
नन्दिता क्त प्रत्ययः
नन्दिता नन्दि (तल्)
नन्द (लिङ्गम् स्त्री कृत् प्रत्ययः क्त टुनदिँ भ्वादिः)
नन्दिता (स्त्री प्र वि एक)
नन्दितृ (पुं) (प्र.एक)
नन्द् (कर्तरि लुट् प्र एक परस्मैपदी टुनदिँ भ्वादिः)
नन्द् (भावे लुट् प्र एक आत्मनेपदी टुनदिँ भ्वादिः)

किरणा हरिणाङ्कस्य दक्षिणश्च **समीरणः**।
कान्तोत्सङ्गजुषां नूनं **सर्वं** एव **सुधाकिरः**।।[1]

(अ) सर्वे चन्द्रकिरणाः (आ) सर्वः दक्षिणदिशायाः वायुः प्रियान् उपगच्छन्तीभ्यः योषिद्भ्यः (अ)अमृतस्यन्दिनः (आ) अमृतस्यन्दी एव (भवन्ति भवति वा)।

- बहुवचनार्थे – सर्वे किरणाः–
- एकवचनार्थे – सर्वः वायुः
- सर्वे एव – सर्व एव 'एचोऽयवायावः'[2] लोपः शाकल्यस्य'[3] इति सूत्रद्वयाधारेण 'ए' कारलोपः अभवत्।
- सर्वः एव – सर्व एव 'भोभगोअघोअपूर्वस्य योऽशि'[4] 'लोपः शाकल्यस्य' सूत्रद्वयाधारेण विसर्गलोपः अभवत्।
- अनेन वचनश्लेषः प्रयुक्तः।

[1]साहित्यदर्पणम् 10
[2]पा.सूत्रम् 6.1.78
[3]पा.सूत्रम् 8.3.19
[4]पा.सूत्रम् 8.3.17

– समीरणः – सुधाकिरः – एकवचनान्तस्य तु 'क' प्रत्ययः
– किरणाः – सुधाकिरः – बहुवचनान्तस्य विशेषणत्वे विक्षेपार्थात् कृधातोः 'क्विप्' प्रत्ययः। उदाहरणेऽस्मिन् प्रत्ययश्लेषः प्रयुक्तः।

तस्या विनापि हारेण निसर्गादिव हारिणौ।
जनयामासतुः कस्य विस्मयं न पयोधरौ ।।[1]

– हार शब्देन मतुबर्थे 'इन्' प्रत्ययः प्रयुक्तः। हारः अनयोः अस्तीति हारिणौ। हारयुक्तौ पयोधरौ इत्यर्थः।
– हृ **'णिनि'** प्रत्ययः ताच्छील्यार्थे प्रयुक्तः। मनोहारिणौ पयोधरौ इत्यर्थे प्रयुक्तः। हारेण विनापि सहजतयैव (अ)मनोहारिणौ तस्याः पयोधरौ विस्मयं जनयतः। हारेण विनापि सहजतयैव (अ)हारयुक्तौ तस्याः पयोधरौ विस्मयं जनयतः।

Table 8 : तालिका – 8 : प्रत्ययश्लेषस्य यान्त्रिकविश्लेषणम्

हारिणौ
हारिन् पुं 1 द्वि
हारिन् पुं 2 द्वि
हारिन् पुं सं प्र 8 द्वि
हारिण पुं 1 द्वि
हारिण पुं 2 द्वि
हारिण पुं सं प्र8 द्वि

5.3 लिङ्गवचनश्लेषः

भक्तिप्रह्वविलोकनप्रणयिनी नीलोत्पलस्पर्धिनी
ध्यानालम्बनतां समाधिनिरतैर्नीतेहितप्राप्तये
लावण्यस्य **महानिधी** रसिकतां लक्ष्मीदृशोस्**तन्वती**
युष्माकं **कुरुतां** भवार्तिशमनं **नेत्रे तनुर्वा** हरेः ।।[2]

– विष्णोः नेत्रे तनुश्च संसारदुःखं शमयतः इति कविः माङ्गलिकं श्लोकं ग्रथयति।

[1]शृङ्गारप्रकाशः 10.140
[2]काव्यप्रकाशः 9 37.114

- नेत्रस्य तनोश्च समानविशेषणानि प्रयुक्तानि।
- लिङ्गवचनश्लेषेण कविः चमत्कारं जनयति।
- सङ्गणकीयसाधनं श्लेषमेनं सुस्पष्टं विशदयति। विस्तरभिया नात्र प्रस्तूयते।

Table 9 : तालिका – 9 : लिङ्गवचनश्लेषस्य यान्त्रिकविश्लेषणम्

स्त्रियाम् एकवचनार्थे	नपुंसके द्विवचनार्थे
भक्तिप्रह्वविलोकनप्रणयिनी	भक्तिप्रह्वविलोकनप्रणयिनी
नीलोत्पलस्पर्धिनी	नीलोत्पलस्पर्धिनी
महानिधी	महानिधी
तन्वती	तन्वती
तनुः	नेत्रे
कुरुताम्	कुरुताम्
कृ–३ कर्तरि लोट् प्र.एक. आत्मनेपदी डुकृञ् तनादि	कृ–३ कर्तरि लोट् प्र.द्वि. परस्मैपदी डुकृञ् तनादि

विकसन्नेत्रनीलाब्जे तथा तन्व्याः स्तनद्वयी।
तव **दत्तां** सदामोदं **लसत्तरलहारिणी**॥[1]

सुन्दर्याः नेत्रे स्तने च आमोदं ददत इति वचनलिङ्गश्लेषेण एकेनैव विशेषणेन तिङन्तेन च विशेष्यद्वयं वर्ण्यते।

Table 10 : तालिका – 10 : लिङ्गवचनश्लेषस्य यान्त्रिकविश्लेषणम्

विशेषणम्	विशेष्यम्	कर्म	क्रियापदम्
लसत्तरलहारिणी इन् प्रत्ययः मतुप् स्त्री.प्र.वि.ए.व	लसन् तरलः यस्य तादृशहारवती **स्तनद्वयी**	आमोदं	दत्ताम्। दा कर्तरि लोट् प्र वि एक आत्मनेपदी डुदाञ् जुहोत्यादिः
लसत्तरलहारिणी णिनि प्रत्ययः ताच्छील्यार्थे न.पुं.प्र.वि.द्वि.व णिनि प्रत्ययः ताच्छील्यार्थे न.पुं.प्र.वि.द्वि.व	लसन्ती ते तरले तादृशी च ते हारिणी मनोहारिणी नेत्रे विकसन्नेत्रनीलाब्जे	आमोदं	दत्ताम्। दा कर्तरि लोट् प्र वि द्वि आत्मनेपदी डुदाञ् जुहोत्यादिः

[1]साहित्यदर्पणम् 10

तनुत्वरमणीयस्य मध्यस्य च भुजस्य च।
अभवन्नितरां तस्या वलयः कान्तिवृद्धये ।।[1]

सुन्दर्याः कटेः (अ) वलित्रयं, भुजस्य (आ) कङ्कणं च कान्तिवृद्धये(अ) अभवन्+नितराम् (आ)अभवत्+नितराम् इति वचनलिङ्गश्लेषः प्रयुक्तः। यान्त्रिकपदविश्लेषिका पदविच्छेदिका च समर्थतया श्लेषमिमं वर्णयति।

Table 11 : तालिका – 11 : लिङ्गवचनश्लेषस्य यान्त्रिकविश्लेषणम्

मध्यस्य	वलयः वलि स्त्री.प्र.ब.व	अभवन्+ नितराम् भू कर्तरि लङ् प्र.पु. ब.व परस्मैपदी भ्वादिः
भुजस्य	वलयः वलय पुं.प्र.ए.व	अभवत्+नितराम् भू कर्तरि लङ् प्र.पु. ए.व परस्मैपदी भ्वादिः

5.4 प्रकृतिश्लेषः

अयं सर्वाणि शास्त्राणि हृदि ज्ञेषु च **वक्ष्यति**।
सामर्थ्यकृदमित्राणां मित्राणां च नृपात्मजः ।।[2]

राजपुत्रः शास्त्राणि हृदये (अ) वहति ज्ञेषु (आ) ब्रवीति च। मित्रेभ्यः (अ) सामर्थ्यप्रदः शत्रुभ्यः (आ) सामर्थ्यहर्ता च अस्ति। वह् वच् प्रकृतिद्वयमस्ति। वक्ष्यति इति लृट्लकार–रूपमेकमेवास्ति। तद्वत् सामर्थ्यकृत्।

Table 12 : तालिका – 12 : प्रकृतिश्लेषस्य यान्त्रिकपदविश्लेषणम्

राजपुत्रः	शास्त्राणि	हृदि	वक्ष्यति वह् कर्तरि, लृट्, प्र, ए.पर.वहँ अदादिः
		ज्ञेषु	वक्ष्यति वच् कर्तरि लृट् प्र ए पर वचँ भ्वादिः ब्रू कर्तरि लृट् प्र ए पर ब्रूञ् अदादिः हृदोऽधिकरणत्वे वहिधातुर्ज्ञानार्थवाची।

[1] शृङ्गारप्रकाशः
[2] साहित्यदर्पणम्–10

Table 13 : तालिका – 13 : प्रकृतिश्लेषस्य यान्त्रिकपदविश्लेषणम्

राजपुत्रः	मित्राणां	सामर्थ्यकृत् – मित्रसम्बन्धित्वे करणार्थः। डुकृञ् तनादिः करणे
	अमित्राणां	सामर्थ्यकृत् - अमित्रसम्बन्धित्वे छेदनार्थः कृन्तति इति धातोः। कृ कृञ् स्वादिः हिंसायाम्

5.5 पदश्लेषः

पृथुकार्तस्वरपात्रं भूषितनिःशेषपरिजनं देव।
विलसत्करेणुगहनं सम्प्रति सममावयोः सदनम् ।।[1]

- देव! आवयोः गृहे तुल्ये स्तः।
- पृथुकार्तस्वरपात्रं (अ) त्वद्गेहं बृहत्स्वर्णपात्रपूर्णं (आ) मद्गेहं बालार्तनादप्रपूर्णम्
- भूषितनिःशेषपरिजनं (अ) तव परिजनः भूषितालङ्कारः (आ) मदीयाः पृथ्व्यां शयानाः
- विलसत्करेणुगहनं (अ) मत्तगजविलसितं (आ) मूषिकधूलिसंसिक्तम्
- पदश्लेषप्रयोगेण अकिञ्चनस्य राज्ञश्च सम्पत्तिः वर्णिता।

5.6 विभक्तिश्लेषः

सर्वस्वं **हर** सर्वस्य त्वं **भव**च्छेदतत्परः।
नयोपकारसांमुख्य**मायासि** तनुवर्तनम्।।[2]

विभक्तिश्लेषेण एकेनैव श्लोकेन पुत्राय चोरस्य उपदेशः शिवाय भक्तस्य निवेदनञ्चोप–वर्णितम्।
भक्तः – हर! त्वं सर्वस्य सर्वस्वम्।
चोरः – (पुत्र) त्वं सर्वस्य सर्वस्वं हर।
भक्तः – त्वं भवच्छेदतत्परः।
चोरः – त्वं च्छेदतत्परः भव।
भक्तः – नयोपकारसांमुख्यम् तनुवर्तनम् आयासि।
चोरः – उपकारसांमुख्यं नय। तनुवर्तनम् आयासि।

---

[1]काव्यप्रकाशः 9.370
[2]साहित्यदर्पणम् 10

Table 14 : तालिका – 14 : विभक्तिश्लेषस्य यान्त्रिकविश्लेषणम्

हर– पुं संबोधन एक
हर– हृ–कर्तरि लोट् मध्यम एक परस्मैपदी हृञ् भ्वादिः
भव पुं संबोधन एक ; संसार इति अर्थोऽपि अस्ति।
भव भू कर्तरि लोट् मध्यम एक परस्मैपदी भू भ्वादिः
आयासि – आयासिन् नपुं प्रथमा एक
आयासि – आङ् या कर्तरि लट् मध्यम एक परस्मैपदी या अदादिः

5.7 वचनश्लेषः

लिङ्गश्लेषस्योदाहरणेष्वेव वचनश्लेषः प्रस्तुतः।

5.8 भाषाश्लेषः

महदे सुरसंधम्मे तमव समासंगमागमाहरणे।
हर वहुसरणं तं चित्तमोहमवसर उमे सहसा।।[1]

संस्कृतप्राकृतभाषाभ्यां पार्वतीं स्तौति कविः। संसाधनैः संस्कृतभाषागतपदविश्लेषणं कर्तुं शक्यते। प्राकृतभाषायाः विश्लेषणाय साधनानि अस्मत्समीपे नोपलभ्यन्ते।

6 सभङ्गाभङ्गोभयात्मकश्लेषः

पुनस्त्रिधा सभङ्गोथाभङ्गस्तदुभयात्मकः।

- यदि पदभङ्गं कृत्वा पूर्वोल्लिखिताः अष्टविधश्लेषाः प्रयुज्यन्ते तर्हि ते सभङ्गश्लेषप्रकारा इति उच्यन्ते।
- पदभङ्गं विनैव ते प्रयुज्यन्ते चेत् अभङ्गश्लेषप्रकारा इति व्यवह्रियन्ते।
- एकस्मिन्नेव श्लोके उभयमपि प्रयुज्य अष्टौ श्लेषाः प्रयुज्यन्ते चेत् उभयात्मकश्लेषा इति कथ्यन्ते।

6.1 सभङ्गश्लेषः

बालेवोद्यानमालेयं सालकाननशोभिनी[2]

[1] साहित्यदर्पणम् 10
[2] शृङ्गारप्रकाशः 10

– इयम् उद्यानमाला (अ) स–अलक–आनन–शोभिनी बाला इव अस्ति।
– इयम् (आ) साल–कानन–शोभिनी उद्यानमाला बाला इव अस्ति।
– सभङ्गश्लेष प्रयुज्य एकेनैव विशेषणेन विशेष्यद्वयं वर्णयति।
– यान्त्रिकसमस्तपदच्छेदनेन अस्य समस्तपदस्य चत्वारिंशत्यधिकविच्छेदानि प्राप्यन्ते।
– सर्वाण्यपि विच्छेदनानि अर्थयुक्तानीति अवधातव्यम्।
– सन्दर्भमनुसृत्य कानिचन विच्छेदनानि ग्राह्याणि भवन्ति। अन्यानि च तत्सन्दर्भे अग्राह्याणि भवन्ति।

6.2 अभङ्गश्लेषः

योसकृत्परगोत्राणां पक्षच्छेदक्षणक्षमः।
शतकोटिदतां बिभ्रद्विबुधेन्द्रः स राजते।।[1]

– विबुधेन्द्रः इत्यनेन देवानां राजा इन्द्रः विदुषां श्रेष्ठः राजा च ग्राह्यौ।
– विशेषणानि सर्वाण्यपि इन्द्रे राज्ञि च पदभङ्गं विनैव अनुयन्ति।

6.3 उभयात्मकश्लेषः

येन ध्वस्तमनोभवेन बलिजित्कायः पुरास्त्रीकृतो
यश्चोद्वृत्तभुजङ्गहारवलयो गङ्गां च योऽधारयत्।
यस्याहुः शशिमच्छिरोहर इति स्तुत्यं च नामामरः
पायात्स स्वयमन्धकक्षयकरस्त्वां सर्वदोमाधवः।।[2]

– माधवः उमाधवः विष्णुः शिवश्च स्तुतः।
– सभङ्गश्लेषेण विष्णुः अभङ्गश्लेषेण शिवश्च वर्ण्येते।

विष्णुपक्षे सभङ्गश्लेषः

– **ध्वस्तमनोभवेन** - ध्वस्तं अनः शकटं वा अभवेन अजेन वा
– **बलिजित्** - बलिनो दानवान् यो जयति तादृग्येन कायः वपुः
– **पुरा स्त्रीकृतः**
– **उद्वृत्तभुजङ्गहा** - यश्चोद्वृत्तं समदं कालिकाख्यं भुजङ्गं हतवान्
– **रवलयो** - रवे शब्दे लयो यस्य
– **गङ्गां च योऽधारयत्** - गां गोवर्धनपर्वतं
– **शशिमच्छिरोहर** - शशिमथ् – राहुः –तस्य शिरोहरः
स्वयमन्धकक्षयकरस्त्वां – स्वयम् अन्धक–क्षय–करः – त्वाम् अन्धकनाम्नां जनानां येन क्षयो निवासो द्वारकायां कृतः
– सर्वदः माधवः पायात्।

[1]काव्यप्रकाशः 10.376
[2]साहित्यदर्पणम् 10

शिवपक्षे अभङ्गश्लेषः ध्वस्तमनोभवेन – ध्वस्तः मनोभवः मदनः येन सः
बलिजित्कायः पुरास्त्रीकृतः – बलेः जित् –विष्णुः पुरा – अस्त्रीकृतः
उद्धृत्तभुजङ्गहारवलयो – सर्पाभरणधरः
यो गङ्गाम् अधारयत्
यस्याहुः शशिमच्छिरोहर इति स्तुत्यं च नामामरः – चन्द्रशेखरः
स्वयमन्धकक्षयकर– अन्धकनामकराक्षसस्य हर्ता
सर्वदा उमा-धवः – पार्वत्याः पतिः शिवः पायात्।

6.4 श्रीहर्षस्य नैषधीयचरिते उभयात्मकश्लेषः

देवःपतिर्विदुषि **नैषधराजगत्या**
न निर्णीयते किमु न व्रियते किमु भवत्या।
नायं नलः खलु **तवातिमहानलाभो**
यद्येनमुज्झसि वरः कतरः पुनस्ते ।।[1]

दमयन्त्याः स्वयंवरार्थम् इन्द्राग्निवरुणयमाः नैषधराजः नलः अन्ये राजानः विदर्भदेशं सम्प्राप्नुवन्। दमयन्ती नले अनुरक्तेति ज्ञात्वा चत्वारः देवाः नलरूपधारिणः सन्तः स्वयंवरमण्डपे समासीनाः अभवन्। सरस्वती दमयन्त्याः सखी भूत्वा पञ्चनलान् संलक्ष्य सभङ्गश्लेषं प्रयुज्य तान् वर्णयति। नलपक्षे अभङ्गश्लेषं अन्येषां पक्षे सभङ्गश्लेषं प्रयुज्य श्रीहर्षः स्वपाण्डितीप्रकर्षं प्रदर्शयति।

नैषधराजगत्या

1. नलपक्षे =नैषध–राज–गत्या (निषधायां भवः –नैषधीयः–नैषधीयश्च असौ राजा च नैषधराजः–नैषधराजः एव गतिः यस्याः सा–तया)
2. इन्द्रपक्षे= न+ एषः+ धराजगत्याः (पतिः देवः)
3. अग्निपक्षे =न+ एषः +धर+ अज +गत्याः(पतिः देवः)
4. यमपक्षे = न+ एषः +धरा+ अज +गत्याः(पतिः देवः)
5. वरुणपक्षे= न+ एषः +धराज +गत्याः(पतिः देवः)

सभङ्गश्लेषमनुसृत्य नैके अर्थाः निष्पद्यन्ते।

1. नलपक्षे= नैषधराजगत्या– निषधराज्यस्य राजा नलः
2. इन्द्रपक्षे= न+ एषः+ धराजगत्याः (पृथिव्याः) पतिः किन्तु देवः अथवा एषः+ धराजगत्याः (वज्रायुधस्य अथवा शचीदेव्याः) पतिः देवः
3. अग्निपक्षे =न+ एषः +धर+ अज +गत्याः अजवाहनगतिमान् अग्निः
4. यमपक्षे = न+ एषः +धरा+ अज +गत्याः महिषवाहनगतिमान् यमः अथवा न+ एषः +धराजगत्याः+ पतिः दक्षिणदिशायाः पतिः यमः
5. वरुणपक्षे= न+ एषः +धराज +गत्याः+पतिः पृथिव्याः पतिः न अपितु वरुणः अथवा प्राणिनां नाथः

[1]नैषधीयचरितम् काव्यम् १३ सर्गः, ३३ श्लोकः

तवातिमहानलाभः

1. तव+ अति+ महाः+ नल+आभः – नलकान्तिसदृशा कान्तिः यस्य सः
2. तव +अति +महान् +अलाभः
3. तव +अति +महान् +अ+लाभः – विष्णुसदृशस्य नलस्य लाभः
4. तव +अति +महा +अनल+आभः – अग्निसदृशतेजोवान्
5. तव +अति +महा+ आन+ लाभः – सर्वप्राणिनियन्ता यमः
6. तव+ अति +महान+ लाभः – दीर्घायुप्राप्तिलाभः
7. अयं तव +अतिमहा +अनल +अभः – अग्नितेजोहर्ता वरुणः
8. अयं अति+ महाः+ नलः+ न +तदाभः – नलकान्तिसदृशः कान्तिः यस्य सः अग्निः
9. तव+ अतिम+ हान+ लाभः – ऐश्वर्ययुक्तानां देवानां त्यागेन सुखप्राप्तिः लाभः

एनम्

1. एनम् – सर्वनामविशेषणम्
2. अ +इनं –विष्णोः अग्रजः श्रेष्ठः इन्द्रः
3. अ+ इनं – विष्णुः नाथः यस्य सः वरुणः

कतरः

1. कतरः – सर्वनामविशेषणम्
2. क+ तरः – सम्पत्सु मग्नः

6.5 अन्वयाः

सभङ्गाभङ्गोभयात्मकश्लेषेण नैकानि पदविच्छेदनानि सम्प्राप्तानि। तेषामाधारेण नैके अन्वया अपि प्राप्यन्ते। तद्यथा –

1. (नलपक्षे) हे विदुषि! नैषध–राज–गत्या(नैषधराजः एव गतिः यस्याः सा तया) भवत्या अयं ना नलः देवः पतिः अस्ति इति न निर्णीयते किमु? न व्रियते किमु? तव अति–महान् अ–लाभः(न लाभः) भवति। यदि एनम् उज्झसि तर्हि पुनः ते वरः कतरः भवति?
2. (देवपक्षे) हे विदुषि! एषः धराज–गत्याः(पृथिव्याः) पतिः न अस्ति। देवः अस्ति इति भवत्या न निर्णीयते किमु? न व्रियते किमु?अयं नलः न अस्ति खलु। तव अति–महान् अ–लाभः भवति। यदि एनम् उज्झसि तर्हि पुनः ते वरः कतरः भवति?

3. (इन्द्रपक्षे) हे विदुषि! एषः धराजगत्याः (वज्रायुधस्य) पतिः देवः अस्ति इति भवत्या न निर्णीयते किमु? न व्रियते किमु? अयं नलः न अस्ति खलु। नलाभः अस्ति। (नलस्य आभा इव आभा यस्य सः) यदि एनम् (अ+इनं विष्णो अग्रजं) उज्झसि तर्हि पुनः ते वरः कतरः भवति?
4. (अग्निपक्षे) हे विदुषि! एषः धराजगत्याः पतिः देवः अस्ति इति भवत्या न निर्णीयते किमु? (धर–अज–गत्याः(धराजः (अग्निः)एव गतिः यस्याः सा – आग्नेयदिशा–आग्नेयदिशायाः पतिः) न व्रियते किमु? अयं नलः न अस्ति। अति महाः(तेजोवान्) अनलः अस्ति। यदि एनम् उज्झसि तर्हि पुनः ते वरः कतरः भवति।
5. (यमपक्षे) हे विदुषि! एषः धराजगत्याः पतिः देवः अस्ति इति भवत्या न निर्णीयते किमु? (धरा–अज–गत्या–धरां अजति–महिषः तेन गतिः यस्य सः) न व्रियते किमु? अयं नलः न अस्ति। तव अति महा–आन–लाभः भवति। अथवा अति महा अनल–आभः अस्ति। यदि एनम् उज्झसि तर्हि पुनः ते वरः कतरः भवति?
6. (वरुणपक्षे) हे विदुषि! एषः धराजगत्याः पतिः देवः अस्ति इति भवत्या न निर्णीयते किमु? (धराजस्य गतिः–जलम्–तस्य पतिः–वरुणः)न व्रियते किमु। अयं नलः न अस्ति। अति–महा–अनल–अभः अस्ति। यदि एनम् उज्झसि तर्हि पुनः ते वरः कतरः भवति?

6.6 नलचम्पूकाव्ये सभङ्गश्लेषः

भवन्ति फाल्गुने मासि वृक्षशाखा विपल्लवाः।
जायन्ते न तु लोकस्य कदापि च विपल्लवाः ।।[1]

वि–पल्लवाः विगताः पल्लवाः येषां ते वृक्षाः – प्रादितत्पुरुषसमासः
विपद्–लवाः (लोकस्य विषये) षष्ठीतत्पुरुषसमासः
द्विः प्रयुज्य एकस्मिन्नेव पदे सभङ्गश्लेषेण द्वौ समासौ प्रयुक्तौ। द्वौ अर्थौ च निष्पन्नौ।

नास्ति सा नगरी यत्र न वापी न पयोधरा।
दृश्यते न च यत्र स्त्री नवापीनपयोधरा ।।[2]

न वापी न पयोधरा – सभङ्गश्लेषेण तटाकस्य जलप्रवाहस्य च उल्लेखः
नवापीनपयोधरा – अभङ्गश्लेषेण यौवनवती पीनस्तनवती स्त्री वर्णिता।
यत्र चलतासम्बन्धः कलिकोपक्रमश्च पादपेषु दृश्यते न पुरुषेषु।[3]
लतापक्षे – यत्र च–लतासम्बन्धः कलिक–उपक्रमश्च पादपेषु दृश्यते न पुरुषेषु।
पुरुषपक्षे – यत्र चलता–सम्बन्धः कलि–कोप–क्रमश्च पादपेषु दृश्यते न पुरुषेषु।

[1]नलचम्पूः 1.27
[2]नलचम्पूः 1.26
[3]नलचम्पूः 1

भूमयो बहिरन्तश्च नानारामोपशोभिताः।
कुर्वन्ति सर्वदा यत्र विचित्रवयसां मुदम्।।[1]

नानारामोपशोभिताः

– नाना–रामा–उपशोभिताः इत्यस्मिन् पदच्छेदे सुन्दरीणामुल्लेखः।
– नाना–आराम–उपशोभिताः इति विभज्य उद्यानानामुल्लेखः च कृतः।

विचित्रवयसां

– विचित्रवयसां इत्यस्य युवानः इत्यर्थः नाना–रामा–उपशोभिताः इति पदच्छेदे अन्वेति।
– पक्षिणः इत्यर्थः नाना–आराम–उपशोभिताः इति पदच्छेदे अन्वेति।

7 संस्कृतसङ्गणकसाधनानां सामर्थ्यं वैशिष्ट्यञ्च

– अम्बाकुलकर्णीवर्यया निर्मिता सन्धिविच्छेदिका 'सालकाननशोभिनीं' नवत्यधिक–शतधा, 'नैषधराजगत्या' इति पदं चतुषष्ठ्यधिकत्रिशतधा, 'सर्वदोमाधवः' इति पदं सप्त–विंशत्यधिकद्विशतधा छिनत्ति। कस्यचित् पदस्य विश्लेषणं दशधापि भवितुमर्हति।
– जेराई ह्युयेट् वर्येण निर्मितं सङ्गणकसाधनन्तु सीमिततया विच्छेदयति विश्लेषयति तदनु कोशगतार्थान् च प्रदर्शयति।
– गिरीशनाथझावर्यस्य सङ्गणकसाधनसमुच्चयन्तु सरलतया उपयोक्तुं भ्रान्तिरहित–तया विश्लेषयितुं शक्यते।
– पीटर् षार्फ् महाभागेन निर्मितानि साधनानि कल्पितः नानाकोशसंग्रहश्च बहुलार्थ–साधकानि सन्ति।
– पत्रे प्रस्तुतानि उदाहरणानि तेषां यन्त्रीयविश्लेषणानि परिशील्य अवगन्तुं शक्यते यत् संस्कृतसङ्गणकसाधनानां सामर्थ्यं वैशिष्ट्यञ्च महद्वर्तते।
– यावन्ति यान्त्रिकपदविच्छेदनानि तावन्ति यान्त्रिकपदविश्लेषणानि प्राप्यन्ते। यावन्ति विश्लेषणानि तावन्ति व्याख्यानान्यपि भवितुमर्हन्ति। **श्रीहर्षस्य नैषधीयचरित-काव्यमेवात्र प्रमाणम्।**

[1] नलचम्पूः 1.31

7.1 नैषधीयचरितकाव्यस्थश्लोकस्य संस्कृतहेरिटेज् यन्त्रीयसभङ्गश्लेषविश्लेषणं वैशिष्ट्यञ्च

सभङ्गश्लेषविश्लेषणे जेराई ह्युयेट् वर्येण निर्मितं सङ्गणकसाधनं अतीव सामर्थ्यपूर्णं विद्यते। सेग्मेण्टर् नामकं पार्सर् नामकञ्च संसाधने महत्त्वपूर्णे वर्तेते। तद्वैशिष्ट्यमत्र सोदाहरणं प्रस्तूयते–

देवःपतिर्विदुषि नैषधराजगत्या
न निर्णीयते किमु न व्रियते किमु भवत्या।
नायं नलः खलु तवातिमहानलाभो
यद्येनमुज्झसि वरः कतरः पुनस्ते।।

सेग्मेण्टर् सङ्गणकसाधनस्य विश्लेषणप्रक्रिया –
Naiṣadhīyacharitam of Śrīharṣa

दत्तांशनिवेशः (input)
|
दत्तांशस्य पदविच्छेदनम्
|
विच्छेदितपदानां विश्लेषणम्
|
विश्लेषणानुगुणं पदानां कोशस्थनानार्थानां प्रस्तुतिः
|
तात्पर्यार्थः
(यन्त्रेण नक्रियते अपितु उपयोक्तारः निष्पादयितुं शक्नुवन्ति।)

उदाहरणम् –

– नैषधराजगत्या
– पदविच्छेदनानि – ५७
– सान्दर्भिक–अर्थपरिपूर्णानि पदविच्छेदनानि – २७
– स्थालीपुलाकन्यायेन प्रस्तुतानि – ४ – तानि च – १,३३,४२,४९

यद्यपि दैर्घ्यमस्ति तथापि संसाधनमहत्त्वनिरूपणाय यान्त्रिकपदविच्छेदनानि, विश्लेषणानि तदनुरूपं व्याख्यानानि चात्र प्रस्तूयन्ते –

क्र.सं	पद–विच्छेदनम्	पदविश्लेषणं - Lexicon	कोशगतनानार्थाः
1	नैषध राज गत्या सा	{iic} {नैषध} 1.1 {समस्तपदम्} {iic} {राजन्} 2.1 {समस्तपदम्} {तृ.ए.स्त्री} {गति} 3.1 {करण} [{स्त्री}] {प्र.ए.स्त्री} {तद्} 4.1 {कर्ता} [{स्त्री}]	{नैषध}- relating to Niṣadha, a species of grain, a prince of the Niṣadhas, n. of a people, N. of a dynasty, N. of an artificial epic poem by Śrīharṣa राजन् - a king, sovereign, prince, chief, often applied to gods, e.g. to Varuṇa and the other Ādityas, to Indra, Yama, but esp. to Soma, (also the plant and juice and the moon), a man of the royal tribe or the military caste, a kṣatriya, a Yakṣa, N. of the 18 attendants of Sūrya, of Yudhiṣṭhira गत्या - going, gait, moving, deportment, motion in general, power of going, going away, procession, march, passage, procedure, progress, movement, the going or flying of missile weapons, to die, the course of fate, the progress or course of a poem, arriving at, obtaining, acting accordingly, obeisance towards path, way, course, to recourse, a certain division of the moon's path, a means of success, refuge, resource, way or art, method of acting, stratagem, issue, running wound or sore, place of issue, origin, reason, possibility, expedient, means, a means of success, the position (of a child at birth) state, condition, situation, proportion, mode of existence, a happy issue, happiness, the course of the soul through numerous forms of life, metempsychosis, condition of a person undergoing the migration, manner, the being understood, or meant, N. of a son of Anala – a kind of rhetorical figure, a particular high number.

प्रथमविच्छेदनस्य पदविश्लेषणाधारेण प्रस्तुतानाम् अर्थानाम् आधारेण द्वेधा व्याख्यातुं शक्यते ।

१. अ. नलपक्षे–हे विदुषि नैषध–राज–गत्या (नैषधराजः एव गतिः यस्याः सा तया) भवत्या अयं ना नलः देवः पतिः अस्ति इति न निर्णीयते किमु, न व्रियते किमु.

आ. नलपक्षे–हे विदुषि भवत्या नैषध–राज–गत्या (नैषधराजः इति गत्या (अवगत्या, परिज्ञाय) अयं ना नलः देवः पतिः अस्ति इति न निर्णीयते किमु, न व्रियते किमु.

8 समुचितसान्दर्भिकश्लेषार्थाः –

1. नैषध–राज–गत्या–सा
a. related to Niṣadha (a king) refuge=(Damayantī), whose refuge is the king of Niṣadha country, i.e. Nala.
b. related to Niṣadha (a king) the being understood=having understood/ having recognized him to be the king of Niṣadha country i.e., Nala.

9 त्रयोविंशतितमम् अग्निपक्षीयं यान्त्रिकपदविश्लेषणम्–

न–एषः–धर–अज–गत्याः(पतिः देवः) अजवाहनगतिमान् अग्निः हे विदुषि एषः धर–अज–गत्याः अजवाहनगतिमान् अस्ति अथवा धराजः (अग्निः) एव गतिः यस्याः सा – आग्नेयदिशा–आग्नेयदिशायाः पतिः अग्निः अस्ति इति भवत्या न व्रियते किमु?

द्वाचतुर्विंशत्तमं यमपक्षीयं यान्त्रिकपदविश्लेषणम्– न–एष–धरा–अज– गत्या= धराम् अजति इति धराजः महिषः–महिषगतिमान् यमः हे विदुषि एषः धरा–अज–गत्याः (धरां अजति–महिषः, तेन गतिः यस्य सः) पतिः देवः (यमः) अस्ति इति भवत्या न निर्णीयते किमु ? ? न व्रियते किमु?

<table>
<tr>
<td>42</td>
<td>न<अ|इ–ऐ> एष
धरा<आ|अ–आ>
अज गत्या सा</td>
<td>{अव्य.}[न] १.१ {न}
{प्र.ए.पुं.}[एष] २.१
{कर्ता}
{iic.}[धरा] ३.१
{समास}
{iic} [अज_1] ४.१
{समास}
{iic}[अज_2] ४.२
{समास}
{तृ.ए.स्त्री.}[गति] ५.१
{करण}
{प्र.ए.स्त्री.}[तद्] ६.१
{कर्ता}</td>
<td>न–पूर्ववत्
एष – पूर्ववत्
धरा- bearer, supporter, the earth, the uterus or womb, a vein, tubular vessel of the body, marrow, a mass of gold or heap of valuables, one of the eight forms of Saraswati. N. of one of the wives of Kaśyapa (mother of the land and water-birds prob.– the earth) n. poison अज–पूर्ववत्
गत्या – पूर्ववत्</td>
</tr>
</table>

<table>
<tr>
<td>33</td>
<td>न<अ|इ–ऐ>
एष
धर<अ|अ–आ>
अज गत्या
सा</td>
<td>{अव्य.}[न] १.१ {न}
{प्र.ए.पुं.}[एष] २.१
{कर्ता}
{iic.} [धर] ३.१
{समास}
{iic} [अज_1] ४.१
{समास}
{iic} [अज_2] ४.२
{समास}
{तृ.ए.स्त्री.}[गति] ५.१
{करण}
{प्र.ए.स्त्री.}[तद्] ६.१
{कर्ता}</td>
<td>न- Not, no, nor, neither
एष
धर- bearing, supporting, holding, carrying, possessing, wearing, having, keeping, sustaining, preserving, observing, a mountain, a flock of cotton, a frivolous or dissolute man, a sword, n. of a Vasu, of a follower of the Pāṇḍavas, of the father of padma-prabha
अज_1a drove, troop, a driver, mover, instigator, leader N. of Indra, of Rudra, of one of the Maruts, of Agni, of the Sun, of Brahmā, of Viṣṇu, of Śiva, of Kāma, the leader of a flock, a he-goat, ram, the sign of Aries, the vehicle of Agni, beam of the sun, N. of a descendant of Viśvāmitra and of Daśaratha's or Dīrghabāhu's father, N. of a mineral substance, of a kind of rice, of the moon, N. of a people, of a class of Ṛiṣis, अज_2 not born, existing from all eternity, N. of the first uncreated being, Brahmā, Viṣṇu, Śiva, Kāma गत्या – पूर्ववत्</td>
</tr>
</table>

नवचतुर्विंशतितमम् इन्द्रवरुणपक्षीयं यान्त्रिकविश्लेषणम्– न–एष–धरा–जगत्या–(पतिः)= एषः पृथिव्याः पतिः न अपितु इन्द्रः अथवा वरुणः अस्ति इति भवत्या न निर्णीयते किमु ? न व्रियते किमु?

<table>
<tr>
<td>49</td>
<td>न<अ|इ–ऐ>
एष
धरा
जगत्या
सा</td>
<td>{अव्य.}[न] १.१ {न}
{प्र.ए.पुं.}[एष] २.१ {कर्ता}
{iic.} [धरा] ३.१ {समास}
{तृ.ए.स्त्री.} [जगत्] ४.१ {करण}
{प्र. ए. स्त्री.} [तद्] ५.१ {कर्ता}</td>
<td>न–पूर्ववत्
एष–पूर्ववत्
धरा–पूर्ववत्
जगत्या- moving, movable, locomotive, living, composed in the Jagati metre, air, wind, people, mankind, that which moves or is alive, men and animals, animals as opposed to men, men, within everybody's sight, the world, earth, N. of a saman, heaven and lower world</td>
</tr>
</table>

सर्वमिदं यान्त्रिकविश्लेषणं यान्त्रिकविच्छेदनञ्च अर्थयुक्तमिति प्रायोगिकपरिज्ञानेन अवगम्यते। मुद्रितग्रन्थेभ्यः नूतनव्याख्यानानि कल्पयितुं, अमुद्रितमातृकाणाञ्च सम्पादनं निर्वोढुम् अतीव उपयोगीनि भवन्ति संस्कृतसङ्गणकोपकरणानि। संस्कृतवाङ्मयस्य अध्य–यनाध्यापने अल्पव्याकरणज्ञं संस्कृतज्ञं बहुधा उपकुर्वन्ति संस्कृतसङ्गणकसाधनानी–त्युक्तौ नास्त्यतिशयोक्तिः।

10 उपसंहारः

वर्ण–पद–प्रत्यय–प्रकृति–लिङ्ग–वचन–विभक्ति–भाषेति अष्टसु श्लेषेषु नैकानि पद–विश्लेषणानि संलक्षितानि। सभङ्गाभङ्गोभयात्मकश्लेषे विभिन्नानि सन्धिविच्छेदनानि अथवा समस्तपदविच्छेदनानि संलक्ष्यन्ते। नानार्थोपेतपदानि प्रयुक्तानि। तस्मात् एकस्यैव श्लोकस्य नैके अन्वयाः व्याख्यानानि वा दृश्यन्ते।

सर्वमिदं संस्कृतभाषागतनैसर्गिकसौष्ठवात् वैशिष्ट्याच्च सिद्ध्यति। तस्मात् हेतोः त्रिविक्रमभट्टः सभङ्गश्लेषात्मकं गद्यपद्यात्मकं नलचम्पूकाव्यं, श्रीहर्षः नैषधीयचरिते श्लेष–चमत्कारोपेतपद्यानि, चिदम्बरकविः पञ्चश्लेषात्मकं गद्यपद्यमयं पञ्चकल्याणचम्पूकाव्यं, तत्सदृशाः नैके कवयः नैकानि श्लेषकाव्यानि च व्यरचयन्। पाण्डित्यप्रपूर्णव्याख्यानानि काव्यानामेतेषां श्लेषार्थम् अथवा व्यङ्ग्यार्थं विवृण्वन्ति। सहृदयहृदयेषु ब्रह्मानन्दसहोदरा–नन्दं जनयन्ति।

तादृशवैशिष्ट्योपेतसंस्कृतवाङ्मयस्य विश्लेषणाय यानि सङ्ग- णकसंसाधनानि आधुनिकयुगेऽस्मिन् निर्मितानि तेषु विशिष्य पदविश्लेषिका, सन्धिविच्छेदिका, अनुवादकम् अनुसारकञ्च नैकानि विश्लेषणानि, नैकान् विच्छेदान्, बहूनर्थान् च प्रदर्शयन्ति। अनेन क्लिष्टसंस्कृतरचनाः सरलतया अवगन्तुं शक्यन्ते। यदा सर्वे संस्कृतज्ञाः संस्कृतसङ्गणकसाधनैः परिचिताः भूत्वा तानि उपयोगे आनयन्ति तदैव संसाधननिर्मातृणां समेषां विदुषां परिश्रमः साफल्यं भजते।

कार्तज्ञ्यसमर्पणम्

कार्यमिदं भारतसर्वकारस्य संस्कृतसंङ्गणकसाधनानि एवं संस्कृतहिन्दी यान्त्रिकानुवादयन्त्रस्य निर्माणम् (Development of Sanskrit Computational Tools-kit and Sanskrit-Hindi Machine Translation System) इति नाम्न्याः परियोजनायाः भागो वर्तते। या सदा मार्गोपदेशेन मां समुद्धरति तस्यै वात्सल्यप्रपूर्णहृदयायै प्रेरणाप्रदात्र्यै प्रो. अम्बाकुलकर्णिमहाभागायै सादरं कार्तज्ञ्यं विनिवेद्यते। संस्कृतसङ्गणकभाषातत्त्वशास्त्रं परिचाययित्वा सूक्ष्मातिसूक्ष्मांशान् बोधयित्वा मम ज्ञानवर्धनाय मनोविकासाय च ये कारणीभूताः अभूवन् तान् गुरुकल्पान् श्रीमतः श्रीनिवासवरखेडिवर्यान् नतशिरसा प्रणमामि। तेषाम् अधमर्णा अस्मि। गुरुऋणात् मुक्तिं प्राप्तुम् अवसरः कल्प्यतामिति जगत्कर्तारं परमात्मानं प्रार्थये।

References

1. अनिलकुमारः, विपुलमित्तलः, अम्बाकुलकर्णी, यान्त्रिकी संस्कृतसमासप्रक्रिया, चतुर्थान्ताराष्ट्रियसंस्कृतसंङ्गणकाधिवेशने प्रस्तुतं शोधपत्रम्, गणकपाणिनीयम्, द्वितीयो भागः, पृ. सं. ६६ २०१०
2. *Anuvadacandrikā* of Chakradhar Noutiyal Hamsa Sastri, Motilal Banarsidass, Delhi.
3. *Kāvyādarśa* of Daṇḍin, edited by S.K. Belvalkar, The Oriental Book Supplying Agency, Poona.
4. *Kāvyālaṁkāra* of Bhāmaha, Pullela Sriramachandrudu, 1979, Surabharati Samiti, OU Campus, Hyderabad.
5. *Kāvyālaṁkārasūtrāṇi* of Vāmana, Pullela Sriramachandrudu, 1981, OU Campus, Hyderabad.
6. *Kāvyaprakāśa*, MM Ganganatha Jha, Bharatiya Vidya Prakashan, Varanasi.
7. *Naiṣadhīyacaritam* of Śrīharṣa, Sri Udali Subbaramasastri, Andhra Pradesh Sahitya Academy, Kalabhavan, Saifabad, Hyderabad.
8. *Naiṣadhīyacaritam* of Śriharṣa, 1952,ed. Narayana Rama Acharya, Nirnayasagar Press, Mumbai.
9. *Nalacampu* of Trivikrama Bhaṭṭa, ed. Rajendraprasad Kotyari, Chowkamba Surabharati Prakasan, Varanasi.

10. *Sāhitya Darpaṇa* of Viśwanātha, Bharatiya Vidya Prakashan, Delhi.
11. *Śṛṅgaraprakāśa* of Bhoja, ed. Reva Prasad Dwivedi, Kalidasa Sanskrit Academy, Varanasi.
12. वी. षीबा सुधीरः, संस्कृतपदविश्लेषकम् – अन्तर्जालतले एकः विनूतनः आविष्कारः, धीमहि पत्रिकायाः प्रथमसञ्चिकायां २३ तमे पृष्ठे मुद्रितः, २०१० चिन्मया इन्टर् नेषनल फौन्डेशन् शोधसंस्थान्, केरलः
13. www.sanskrit.jnu.ac.in
14. www.sanskrit.infria.fr
15. www.uohyd.ernet

Variations in Manuscripts With Reference to the Indic Collections at Brown University and the University of Pennsylvania

Anupama Ryali[1] and Peter M. Scharf[2]

[1] Department of Sanskrit Studies,
University of Hyderabad, Hyderabad
anupamaskt@gmail.com
[2] Université Paris Diderot, Paris
peter.scharf@univ-paris-diderot.fr

Abstract. Manuscripts vary in composition, script, neatness of hand, layout, design, color, numbering and material, among other factors. Such variations reveal literary material not included in editions and also provide fundamental evidence for cultural and intellectual history. Variations and remarkable features of manuscripts in the Indic collections of Brown University and the University of Pennsylvania were discovered and annotated using the Sanskrit Image-Text Alignment (SITA) software, developed in the NEH-funded project, "Enhancing Access to Primary Cultural Heritage Materials of India". The annotations allow systematic access to numerous types of remarkable features for the purpose of research and education.

Keywords: Manuscripts, variations, scribe, text-image alignment, annotation

1 Introduction

Manuscripts in India play a major role in embodying the country's knowledge, tradition, culture, and heritage. Hence preserving them plays a vital role in transmitting the knowledge they contain to future generations. Though various manual measures have been taken to copy and preserve them for centuries, these measures have become outdated since recent improvements in imaging technology. In the present era, undoubtedly digital technology is the predominant means to copy and preserve any data for posterity. The project, "Enhancing Access to Primary Cultural Heritage Materials of India: Integrating images of literary sources with machine-readable texts, lexical resources, linguistic software, and the web", funded by the U.S. National Endowment for the Humanities, aimed to preserve, and improve access to, manuscripts of the *Mahābhārata* and the *Bhāgavata Purāṇa*, housed at Brown University and the University of Pennsylvania. The manuscript pages were digitized, correlated with critical editions of the text and annotated to allow systematic access to remarkable features they contain. In the present paper, observations regarding these remarkable features, as well as the variations in various manuscripts will be discussed.

2 Sanskrit Image-Text Alignment (SITA) Software

As part of the project to catalog, digitally image, and integrate images with corresponding digital texts, Ralph Bunker, a computer scientist at Maharishi University of Management in Iowa, developed Sanskrit Image-Text Alignment (SITA) software. SITA facilitates human alignment of passages and remarkable features in digital images of manuscript pages with corresponding digital text and annotations.

SITA software is not a transcript-correlation software such as Collate2; it does not discover relationships between manuscripts automatically. Nor is it a critical edition editing software such as the Classical Text Editor; it does not transform text of various classes—base text, variants, sigla, editorial notes, etc.—into print-ready copy. It allows one to mark regions in manuscript images and to align them with passages in corresponding digital text. The corresponding digital text may be an exact transcription of the manuscript in the images, a transcription of a different manuscript, or an edition of the text. In the project undertaken at Brown University and the University of Pennsylvania, various manuscript images were correlated with an existing edition. There is no limit to the number of manuscripts that can be so correlated.

SITA does not perform automated correlation of transcripts; it assists in correlating various images with a single transcript. The alignment of images with the transcript allows searchable access to the images via the transcript. SITA provides access to all the images that have been aligned with any particular passage of interest by assembling links to the particular pages on which the passage occurs in an HTML page. Clicking a link opens the linked image with the passage marked on it. The software thereby allows an editor quick access to the original documents in order to examine and compare them.

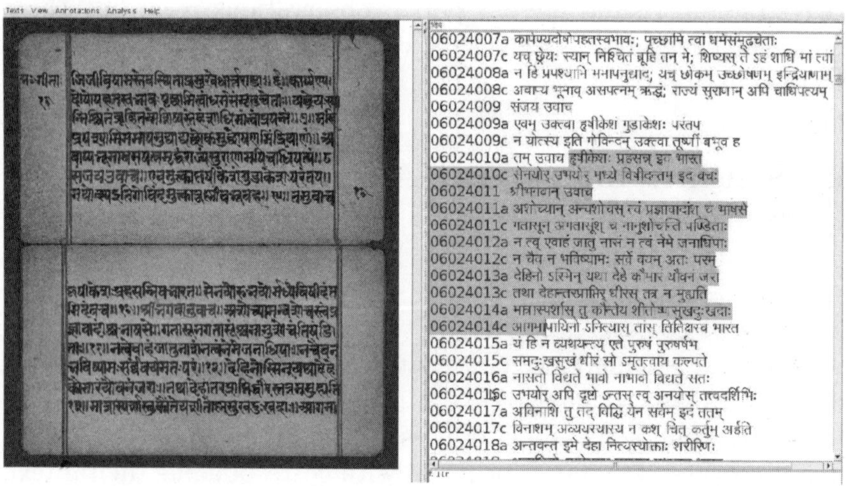

Fig. 1

SITA also allows one to mark regions on manuscript images and provide a comment. Figure 1 shows a region on f. 11r (image 11) of UPenn 559 of the *Bhagavad Gītā* marked with red corners correlated with a text selection and a comment labeling the folio and folio-side. One can mark regions that contain variants, rubrics, colophons, insertions, gaps, marginal notes, deletions or any other feature of the manuscript image of interest. Figure 2 shows the final rubric of chapter 2 of the *Bhagavad Gītā* marked on f. 18r (image 18). Annotations are saved in XML files. One can later

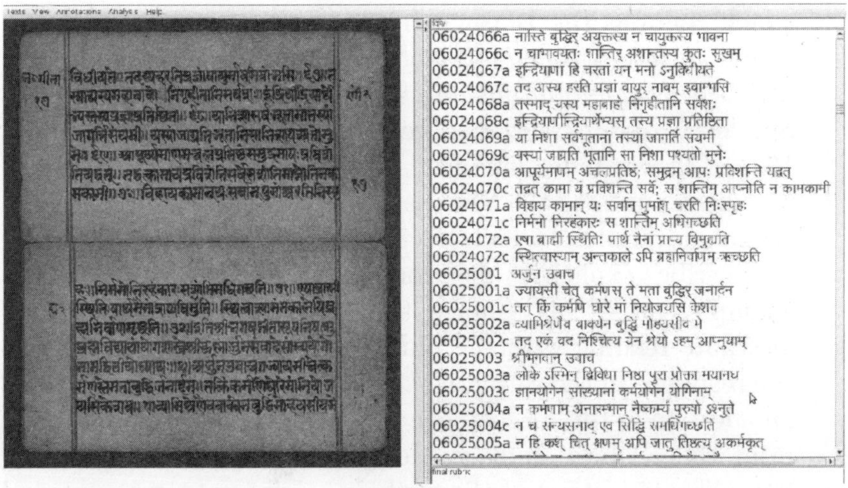

Fig. 2

then search the XML files for comments of the same type in order to locate related classes of material. For instance, one can collect all the passages in the aligned manuscripts that are not included in the existing edition with which the manuscripts were aligned to discover new literary material. Or one can collect examples of techniques of deletion and addition for pedagogical purposes for a seminar on manuscriptology.

3 Variations in Manuscripts

Variation is expected in the content of manuscripts. Variations are of different forms including composition, format and script.

3.1 Variations in Composition

- Variations in composition are found within a line or verse. For example, in Brown Indic 38, which contains the Vanaparvan, the end of the last line on f. 5v (image 107) and the beginning of the first line on f. 6v (image 108) mostly correspond with verse 3.6.10 of the Pune critical edition. However, instead of *taiḥ satkṛtaḥ sa ca tān ājamīḍho* in *pāda* c, the manuscript contains *ssatais sametyais satkṛtaḥ pāṇḍavaiḥ*. Similarly, the end of the bottom line of f. 31r (image 60) of Brown Indic 35, which contains the Bhīṣmaparvan, reads *anyonyaṁ garjatāṁ teṣāṁ sa śabdas tumulo bhavat* instead of the critical edition's 6.42.5cd *vayaṁ pratinadantaś ca tad āsīt tumulaṁ mahat.* Similar variations within a verse are found on f. 82r (image 162) of Brown Indic 35, and f. 44v (image 117) of Brown Indic 37, which contains the Śāntiparvan.

- Although variation usually occurs without remark, occasionally the scribe explicitly mentions an alternate reading. For example, on f. 93v (image 938), the scribe designates an alternate reading with the phrase *ity api pāṭhaḥ* 'such is also the reading'. In the eleventh *skandha* of the *Bhāgavata Purāṇa*, an addition in the space above the base text in a different hand from the scribe's similarly designates the alternate reading *upasādhayet* instead of the scribe's *upadhārayet* in the second line of the text on f. 94v (image 939) of UPenn 2669. Similarly, in the twelfth *skandha*, an addition in the right margin in a different hand on f. 6r (image 960) suggests the alternate reading *dharmaṁ* instead of the scribe's *sarvaṁ* at the end of the fourth line of text. On f. 12r of the same manuscript (image 966), an addition in the right margin abbreviates the designation of the alternate reading *sūkṣmajñā* instead of *sūtrajñā* with the brief phrase *ity api* followed by an elipsis mark.
- Rarely, a verse found in the manuscript that is absent in the digital text (*pāṭhāntara*) is set in parenthesis, either by the scribe or a reader. (E.g. f. 26v (image 323), f. 30v and f. 31r (image 327) of UPenn 2259 of BhP. 10).
- Particularly in the Telugu manuscripts of the *Mahābhārata*, the text diverges in large sections covering many chapters. For example, in Brown Indic 33 containing the Ādiparvan, f. 127r (image 260) proceeds from a verse corresponding with 1.128.18 to a verse corresponding with 1.155.7, excluding the entirety of chapters 129–154. Conversely, after corresponding with verses 1.155.7–15 of the critical edition, the manuscript inserts different text filling three folios before continuing with text corresponding with the critical edition on f. 130r (image 266). After aligning with the critical edition until f. 131r (image 268), again different material is found until the text again coincides with the critical edition on f. 133r (image 273).

- Variation in the content sometimes consists of a rearrangement of some of the same words. For example, on f. 37v (image 170) of Brown Indic 38 containing the Vanaparvan, the manuscript reads *pārthaṁ śrutvā mahārāja* where the critical edition reads *śakralokagataṁ pārthaṁ śrutvā.* Well known are cases where text in the model is eclipsed or repeated because a line begins with the same several syllables. It is possible that similar repetitions and mislocations of passages cause these minor rearrangements.
- Brown Indic 37, containing the Śāntiparvan, appears to include lengthy passages concerning the *varṇa*s that are absent in the critical edition. Passages containing the words brāhmaṇa, kṣatriya, or *cāturvarṇyam* in the manuscript—for example the passage on f. 55v to f. 57r (images 139–142)are entirely absent in digital text.
- Variation is commonly seen in the names used to designate a person. For instance, UPenn 2669, containing the tenth *skandha* of the *Bhāgavata Purāṇa* usually writes *śrībhagavān uvāca* where the edition writes *śrīvāsudeva uvāca*, *śrīrājovāca* where the edition writes *śrīparīkṣid uvāca*, and *bhadrovāca* where the edition writes *mitravindovāca.* Similarly, UPenn 2302 containing the sixth *skandha*, UPenn 2252 containing the tenth *skandha*, and UPenn 2259 containing the fifth, eighth and ninth *skandha*s write *śrīśuka* where the digital text writes *bādarāyaṇa.*
- Composition varies in the choice of *nipāta*s, *pādapūraṇa*s, *avyaya*s, etc. For example, where 9.21.14 of the digital edition begins *iti prabhāṣya pānīyaṁ*, UPenn 2259, containing the ninth *skandha* of the *Bhāgavata Purāṇa*, uses the word *evaṁ* instead of *iti.* The digital edition uses the pronominal adverb *yataḥ* in 9.22.44 instead of the word *nṛpaḥ* at the end of verse 43 on f. 45v (image 46) of UPenn 2304.
- Variation is seen in chapter division even where the text is otherwise the same. For example, Brown Indic 38, f. 59r (image 213) and f. 141r (image 377) contain chapter-final rubrics where the digital edition makes no chapter break between 3.8.21 and 22, nor between 3.200.28 and 29. Conversely, Brown Indic 37, containing the Śāntiparvan, makes no chapter division on f. 104v (image 237) between verses that correspond to critical edition chapters 12.142 and 12.143.

- The content of peripheral sections of the text may be entirely different in different versions of the text. For example, the *phalaśruti* on f. 113r (image 504) in Brown Indic 36, which contains the Svargārohaṇaparvan, is completely different from that contained in critical edition 18.5.40–54.

3.2 Missing Text

- Versions of texts often differ by the inclusion or omission of particular verses. For example, in the Vanaparvan, Brown Indic 38, f. 29r (image 153) and f. 29v (image 154) contain a passage consisting of several verses beginning *siddhacāraṇasaṅghāś ca* missing in the critical edition between 3.38.18d and 3.38.18e, and between 3.38.18f and 3.38.19a. Similarly, Brown Indic 37, f. 71r–71v contains several verses missing from the critical edition between 12.99.11 and 12, and ff. 87v–88r (images 203 and 204), contain a verse missing from the critical edition between 12.122.30 and 31. Conversely, the first verse of chapter 46 in the critical edition of the Vanaparvan (3.46.1), beginning *janamejaya uvāca atyadbhutam idaṁ karma*, is absent from the text on f. 37v (image 170) of Brown Indic 38. Likewise, the end of chapter 99 and beginning of chapter 100 in the critical edition of the Bhīṣmaparvan (6.99.45–47 and 6.100.1–7) are missing from the text on f. 89r (image 176) in Brown Indic 35. Similarly, Brown Indic 37, containing the Śāntiparvan omits critical edition 12.99.
- The manuscripts of the *Mahābhārata* in Telugu script at Brown University frequently include lengthy passages not included in the Pune critical edition. For example, ff. 36v–37v (images 168–170) of the manuscript Brown Indic 38, which contains the Vanaparvan, contain an entire chapter absent in the critical edition.
- Benedictions and meditations (*dhyāna*) often accompany texts transmitted in manuscript. These are usually omitted from scholarly editions. For example, almost all the manuscripts of *Viṣṇusahasranāman*, contain a *dhyāna* excluded from the established text of the critical edition. Similarly, benedictions like *sarvapraharaṇāyudha oṁ nama iti* 'oṁ obeisance to the bearer of all weapons', often present in manuscripts, are excluded from the established critical text.

3.3 Variations in Format

Manuscripts vary in form, condition of leaves, readability, legibility, size, the inclusion of borders, designs, and illustrations, neatness of hand, etc.

- Some manuscripts contain beautiful designs. For example, on the first and last pages of UPenn 2617, containing the third *skandha* of the *Bhāgavata Purāṇa*, a grapevine border in black and red frames the page, and double red lines frame the base text. Special designs, and borders with designs are found in the first and last pages of several other manuscripts as well among which are UPenn 773, 2260, and 2390 of the *Bagavad Gītā*, UPenn 2377 of the fourth *skandha* of the *Bhāgavata Purāṇa*, and UPenn 2242, 2327, and 2343 of the *Viṣṇusahasranāman*. In UPenn 2639, containing the *Saptaślokīgītā*, appear thirteen full-color illustrations, ten of which depict the ten incarnations (*daśāvatāra*) of Viṣṇu.
- In UPenn 2669 of the *Bhāgavatapurāṇa*, an empty picture frame is seen in the last folio, in which it was probably intended to put an illustration or a design never completed.

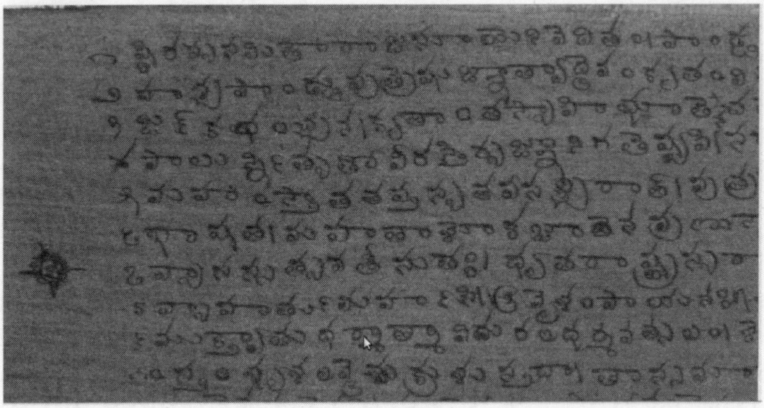

Fig. 3

- In the Telugu script manuscripts in the Brown Indic collection, a star or flower is frequently found drawn in the left margin, for example, in Brown Indic 36 containing the Anuśāsana and

Āśvamedhikaparvāns (see Fig. 3). The star or flower indicates the line on which a final rubric of a chapter is written and is clearly placed to facilitate navigation of the text by locating the final rubrics. As many final rubrics are found on a page, so many flowers appear adjacent to them in the margin. Where no indication or highlighting of the final rubric is provided and it blends in with the text, such as in UPenn 2299 of the second *skandha* of the *Bhāgavata Purāṇa*, it is very difficult to identify the end of a chapter.

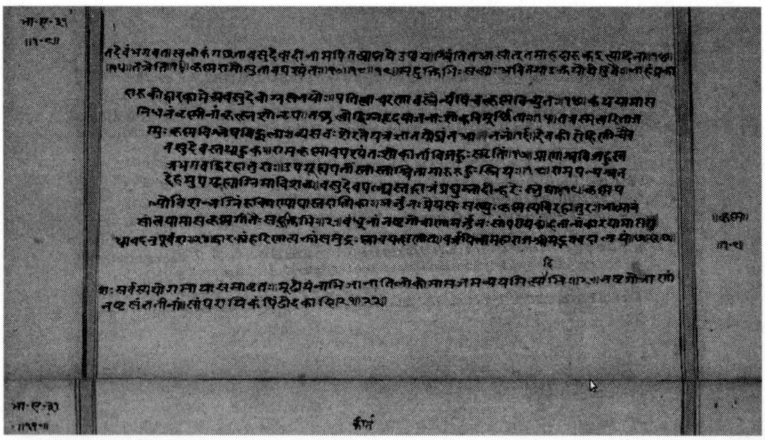

Fig. 4

- A passage is arranged in an hourglass shape on f. 109v (image 954) of UPenn 2669, containing the eleventh *skandha* of the *Bhāgavata Purāṇa* (see Fig. 4).
- In some manuscripts, final rubrics and benedictions are written in red ink (UPenn 2622 of BhP. 1, UPenn 2259 of BhP. 2, UPenn 2377 of BhP. 4, UPenn 2669 of BhP. 10) or alternating red and black ink (UPenn 2618 of BhP. 2 and 2617 of BhP. 3, UPenn 2376 of BhP. 3, and UPenn 2378 of BhP. 8). It is evident that the scribe leaves gaps for the colored ink to be filled in later where syllables alternate between color and black because the colored ink is sometimes written in a different hand or the space left for it remains blank.

- In some manuscripts, speaker introduction lines, i.e. lines in which usually a name is followed by *uvāca*, are written in red color (e.g. UPenn 2622 of BhP. 1, UPenn 2379 of BhP. 9, UPenn 2627 of BhP. 12, UPenn 2259 of BhP. 7, and UPenn 2669 of BhP. 10).
- In some manuscripts, the *daṇḍa*s surrounding verse numbers (*ślokasaṁkhyā*) are in red color (e.g. UPenn 2376 of BhP. 3).
- Generally, a final rubric, mentioning that it is the end of a chapter, is written with black ink and is highlighted by red lines. The highlighting helps to locate the end of a chapter (e.g. UPenn 2376 of BhP. 3, UPenn 2377, and UPenn 2383 of BhP. 4).
- Some manuscripts contain commentary along with the base text. In some manuscripts the base text is written in red ink while the commentary is written in black (e.g. UPenn 2249 of the *Rāsapañcādhyāyī* in BhP. 10) (see Fig. 5).

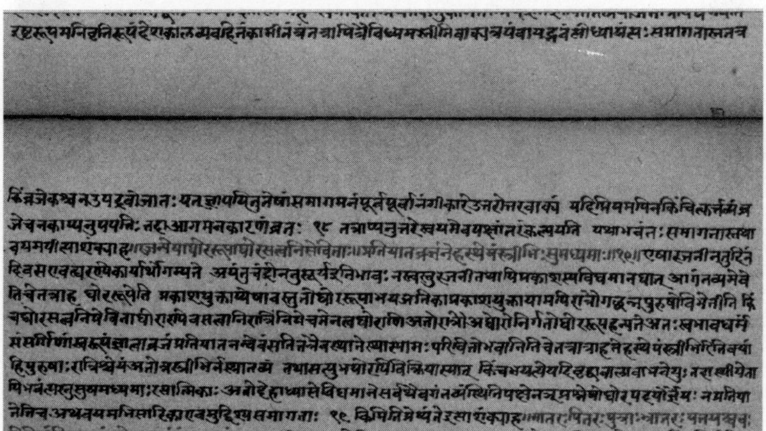

Fig. 5

- Some manuscripts are consistently characterized by scribal traits such as marginal signatures or bending partial lines up the right margin. Hence signatures appear throughout UPenn 2259 of BhP. 5. Similarly, writing final partial lines up the right margin is practiced throughout UPenn 2627 of BhP. 12, and UPenn 2669 of BhP. 1, BhP. 2.

- In UPenn 2239 of *Viṣṇusahasranāman*, a vertical mark is seen on the top of each name of Viṣṇu. The mark indicates the end of each of the thousand names of Viṣṇu. Occasionally a marginal addition is also seen which notes the end of a set of a hundred names (e.g. in f. 4r can be seen an indication of the end of the first hundred names and in f. 5r, an indication of the end of the second hundred) (see Fig.6).

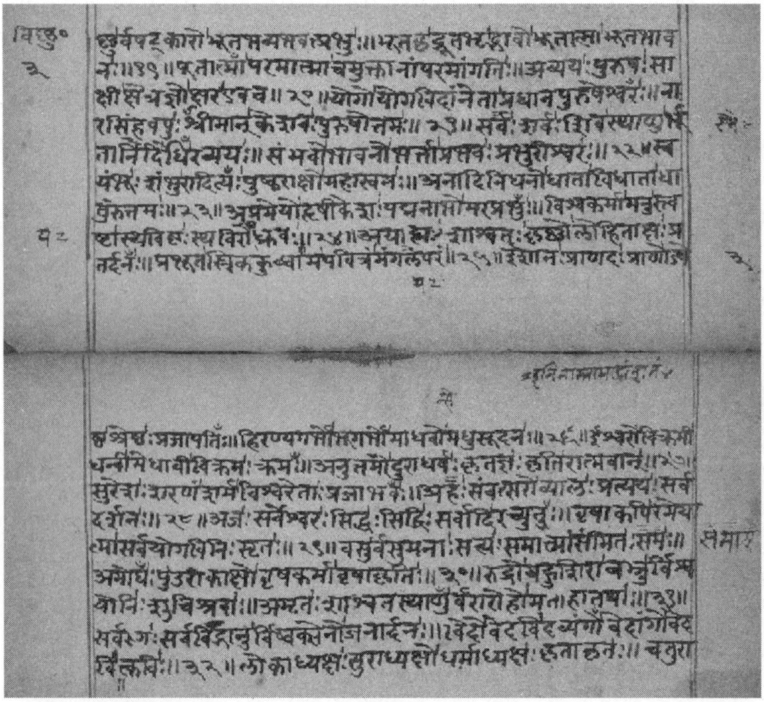

Fig. 6

3.4 Variation in Script

- Variation or inconsistency in hand writing, style of writing, and level of legibility can be seen in some manuscripts (e.g. UPenn 2609 of BhP. 7 and UPenn 2252 of BhP. 10). In UPenn 2373 of BhP. 11, highly legible scripting and aesthetically appealing character shaping can be seen from f. 1v to f. 45v, while a totally different pattern is apparent from f. 46r to f. 63v.

- Some scribes maintain a clear and systematic handwriting which appears as neat as print (e.g. f. 1v to f. 45v (image 1–45) of UPenn 2373 of BhP. 11).
- In some manuscripts, the writing of the scribe is not legible and clear. No proper stream is followed and it is not systematic (e.g. UPenn 2609 of BhP. 7).
- Some scribes simply scribbled so that the writing is difficult to read. It appears as though the scribe wrote hastily (e.g. f. 46r to f. 63v (image 46–64) of UPenn 2373 of BhP. 11).
- In some manuscripts a change of hand is apparent. In most such cases a team of scribes has undertaken the copying of the manuscript (e.g. UPenn 2303 of BhP. 7, UPenn 2623 of BhP. 10, and UPenn 2628 of BhP. 11).
- A marginal addition is written in Telugu language in a different hand on f. 61v (image 127) in Brown Indic 34 of the Droṇaparvan (see Fig. 7).

Fig. 7

- In most of the Telugu manuscripts, the letter *u* is written as *a* (e.g. f. 41r and f. 58v (image 177 and 212) of Brown Indic 38 of the Vanaparvan).

3.5 Variations in Other Concepts

- The word *uvāca* in speaker introduction lines is usually spelled out in editions whereas it is usually indicated by a zero following an *u* in the manuscripts (e.g. UPenn 2259 of BhP.).
- The word *śrī* is generally used before names in the manuscripts (e.g. UPenn 2302 and 2385 of BhP. 6), whereas it is not found in editions, though the reverse is found in some cases (e.g. UPenn 2250 of BhP. 8, UPenn 2304 of BhP. 9, UPenn 2252 of BhP. 10, and UPenn 2259 of BhP. 5, BhP. 7 and BhP. 8).
- Marginal additions

  - Many marginal additions appear in UPenn 2380 of BhP. 1, UPenn 2381 of BhP. 2, and UPenn 2259 of BhP. 9 and 10. In some manuscripts, marginal additions can hardly be seen. The absence of marginal additions may indicate that the manuscript was neatly copied and is free of errors. On the other hand, it may indicate that the manuscript has not had a careful reader. In UPenn 2381 of BhP. 2, UPenn 2250 of BhP. 8, the line number in which a marginal addition is to be inserted is invariantly indicated immediately following the marginal note. In other manuscripts it is so indicated if the marginal addition is written far away from the corrected content (e.g. UPenn 2259 of BhP. 10, f. 56v (image 911) of UPenn 2669 of BhP. 11, f. 5v (image 6), and f. 7v (image 8) of UPenn 2397 of BhP. 8).
- Reduplication (*āmreḍitam*)

  - In some manuscripts of the *Bhāgavata Purāṇa*, marginal additions are seen in many instances where the desired repetition of a word is missing. The second occurrence of the word is added as a marginal addition. For example, on f. 13r (image 123), of UPenn 2669 of BhP. 3, *yūthapa* is added in the left margin to be inserted at the insertion point just before *yūthapeṣu* in the text. Similar examples abound.
- Variations between manuscripts of UPenn and Brown
  - Regional difference can be found in the manuscripts of Brown compared with those of the University of Pennsylvania. While the manuscripts of Brown University

are all on palm leaf in Telugu script, the manuscripts of University of Pennsylvania are all on paper in Devanāgarī script.

- Generally, the paper manuscripts of University of Pennsylvania are numbered on the verso of each folio, while the palm-leaf manuscripts of Brown University are numbered on the recto.

4 Conclusion

The variations and remarkable features of manuscripts discussed in this paper were discovered and marked in the process of annotating manuscripts using the SITA, developed in the project, "Enhancing Access to Primary Cultural Heritage Materials of India". SITA allows direct access to these remarkable features by means of its analysis commands and also stores the data in XML format accessible to other search software. This focused access will allow manuscript cataloguers, critical editors, and historians who work with primary materials to utilize this information to discover relationships between manuscripts that may enhance their work. This focused access will also provide materials for training scholars to work with manuscripts. The SITA software is available from The Sanskrit Library. It is hoped that others will find it helpful in their work.

References

1. Hagel, Stefan "Zur druckfertigen Edition mit dem eigenen PC - Der 'Classical Text Editor'." In *Umgang mit Quellen heute: Zur Problematik neuzeitlicher Quelleneditionen vom 16. Jahrhundert bis zur Gegenwart*, ed. Grete Klingenstein, Fritz Fellner, Hans Peter Hye, pp. 198–201. Acta 92. Wien: Verlag der Österreichischen Akademie der Wissenschaften, 2003.
2. Hagel, Stefan "The Classical Text Editor: An Attempt to Provide for both Printed and Digital editions." In *Digital Philology and Medieval Texts*, ed. A. Ciula/F. Stella, pp. 7784. Pisa, 2007.
3. Kartre, S.M. *An Introduction to Indian Textual Criticism.* Mumbai: Karnataka Publishing House, 1941.

4. Poleman, Horace I. *A Census of Indic Manuscripts in the United States and Canada.* New Haven: American Oriental Society, 1938.
5. Robinson, Peter. "Towards a Scholarly Editing System for the Next Decades". In *Sanskrit Computational Linguistics: First and Second International Symposia, Rocquencourt, France, October 2007; Providence, RI, USA, May 2008; Revised Selected and Invited Papers*, eds. Gérard Huet, Amba Kulkarni, and Peter Scharf. Lecture Notes in Artificial Intelligence 5402. Berlin-Heidelberg: Springer-Verlag, 2009.
6. Scharf, Peter M. et al. The Sanskrit Library Manuscript Catalogue. Providence, RI: The Sanskrit Library, 2012.
7. Thaker, Jayant P. *Manuscriptology and Text Criticism.* Oriental Institute, Maharaja Sayajirao University of Baroda, Vadodara, 2002.

Words in Metrical Milieux

A Computational Approach to a Neglected Field

Sven Sellmer

Adam Mickiewicz University, Department of Oriental Studies, Poznań, Poland

sven.sellmer@amu.edu.pl

Abstract. The paper explains how to build a metrical concordance, presents a number of new conceptions that can be developed on the basis of such data, and shows some possible applications for textual analysis, taking the *Mahābhārata* as an example. A quantification method for the phenomenon that many textual elements have a tendency to appear at the same metrical positions (called "polarization" after Ingalls) is given. This concept, in turn, is used to develop objective and quantifiable measures for the exceptionality, originality, and stereotypedness of both single expressions and larger textual units.

Keywords: Metrics, semantics, concordance, *Mahābhārata*

1 Introduction

The usual lexical resources show a complete lack of metrical information.[1] In the case of many texts this is a serious shortcoming, as I myself became acutely aware of when engaging in semantic studies of the *Mahābhārata [= Mbh]*, because, to put it simply, often the choice of words does not solely depend on their semantic, but also on their metrical properties. In order to tackle this problem in a systematic way it turned out to be necessary to develop a dynamic model of the traditional epic versification technique,[2] which

---

[1] I would like to thank three anonymous assessors for their helpful remarks and suggestions.

[2] This approach has been inspired by research on the Homeric epics. See esp. Visser (1987) for an exemplary piece of scholarship and further bibliographical information.

is obviously impossible without comprehensive information about the metrical structure of all the words, their frequencies, metrical positions and the like. In the following, it is not my goal to propose such a versification model - this is a much larger project I am planning to address in a book-length publication - but to do two other things instead: first, to present the databases I constructed for the purpose of that project and to briefly explain the technical details of their construction; second, to point, by way of examples drawn from the *Mbh*, to other possible usages of metrical data, especially for the internal and historical analysis of epical and similar texts.

To date, only very little attention has been paid to the importance of metrical aspects for the usage of words. This may partly be due to a lack of awareness for the crucial significance these data can have, especially for the understanding of texts that are products of oral poetry[3] or are at least strongly influenced by this kind of literature; but the most important reason for the present state of research in this field certainly is technical limitations: Without computer-aided methods it is nearly impossible to make any progress. Therefore the ways of collecting data described in the following section open up new perspectives for the research on metrical texts.

2 Construction of a Metrical Concordance

I used the R language (see R Development Core Team, 2010) for the construction of my databases, but the steps are so unspecific that it seems best to formulate them in general terms, so that they can easily be reproduced in any suitable computer language.

2.1 String List

Once we have an electronic text[4] and are content to stay on its surface level it is an easy task to prepare a list of basic elements,

---

[3] Oral poetry is taken here in the strong sense of texts that are the result of improvised production by traditionally trained specialists (bards).

[4] In the case of the *Mbh*, that will be the focus of the present paper, only the text of the Critical Edition is available in electronic form. The serious philological problems connected with this edition cannot be tackled here. For the following statistics I have only used the main text, i.e. no appendices and star passages.

i.e. character strings between blank spaces. These elements will be the main material of the following analyses; for the sake of simplicity I will refer to them just as "strings" e.g. the line *nārāyaṇaṁ namaskr̥tya naraṁ caiva narottamam* contains five strings: *nārāyaṇaṁ, namaskr̥tya, naraṁ, caiva,* and*narottamam.* As can be seen, this approach is rather primitive and purely technical, but it nevertheless leads to some interesting results, as I hope to be able to show. At the same time, it is important to clarify some things at the outset. First, strings do not always represent single word forms (cf. *caiva*). Second, they are the result of the specific orthographical conventions used in the transliteration of the electronic text of the CE, that strongly differ from other conventions based more closely on the usual orthography of printed Devanāgarī texts. Finally, every string is taken strictly "as is", so *naraṁ* and *naram* are two different strings.

The effect of *sandhi* is a major obstacle for normal concordances that, however, will be hopefully removed in the near future by tools like the Sanskrit Tagger (see Hellwig (2009)). In the case of a metrical concordance these difficulties are less pressing because here the items of primary interest are the concrete forms with their concrete metrical shape as they appear in the text. Nevertheless, it remains unsatisfactory that in the present concordance there is no easy way to locate, for instance, all *sandhi* versions of all inflected forms of a single lemma. This can only be done on a case-by-case basis with the help of especially constructed regular expressions [= regex]. Another problem to distinguish between, say, te_1 (pers. pronoun, 2. pers., gen. sg.) and te_2 (dem. pronoun, masc. nom. pl.) cannot be resolved at present. It is, however, to be hoped that information about specific metrical distributions of the members of such pairs (or groups) of words may contribute to the perfection of POS-tagging and semantic disambiguation tools.[5]

The crucial information for a metrical concordance, namely at which metrical position a given string is located, can be derived by counting the vowels (= syllables) preceding it, starting at the beginning of a line. In R this can most simply be done by removing the non-vowels and then counting the remaining characters. (One

[5] It is planned to make publicly available the data described in the following via Oliver Hellwig's Digital Corpus of Sanskrit (see Hellwig (2010-12).

only has to make sure that the diphthongs *ai* and *au* are treated as one vowel each – I therefore prefer to work with a modified version of the Harvard-Kyoto transliteration where they are represented by capital *E* and *O*, respectively.)

2.2 Metrical Structure

Luckily, Sanskrit is transliterated in such a manner that it is possible not only to count the number of syllables, but to directly derive the complete metrical structure of a piece of text from its surface appearance. Perhaps the easiest way to do this is by applying regex-based replacement operations. The following four steps are enough:[6]

1. Replace all long vowels and diphthongs by _
2. Replace all short vowels followed by more than one consonant (ignoring blank spaces)[7] by _
3. Replace all short vowels by ◡
4. Remove all characters other than _ and ◡

Thus, e.g. the first line of the *Mbh*,

nārāyaṇaṁ namaskr̥tya naraṁ caiva narottamam,

takes the following shape:

_ _ ◡ _ ◡ _ _ ◡ ◡ _ _ ◡ ◡ _ ◡ ◡

Combining the information obtained by the operations described so far we can construct a string list like in Table 1 where some information is added to the strings: their metrical structure, their position, i.e. their starting syllable, counted from the beginning of the line, and the running number of the line they appear in.

[6] In the case of whole lines it is useful to also record the "cæsuræ", understood in the technical sense of blank spaces between strings. As with strings their position can be established by counting the preceding vowels.

[7] While identifying syllables that are long by position one must be careful that the program treats aspirated consonants as single consonants.

Table 1: Word list with metrical information; running line numbers

String	Metrical Structure	Position	Line
nārāyaṇaṁ	– – ⏑ –	1	1
namaskṛtya	⏑ – – ⏑	5	1
naraṁ	⏑ –	9	1
caiva	– ⏑	11	1
narottamam	⏑ – ⏑ ⏑	13	1

2.3 Frequencies and Metrical Positions

On the basis of the string list, three additional types of information can be obtained: the overall frequency of a given string, its frequency at the different verse positions where it occurs, and the number of these positions. Taking the string *rājan* as an example, part of the data can be presented as in Table 2. Here it is clearly visible that one string may appear at different positions of the line with very different frequencies. As we shall see later it is sometimes useful to refer to these "strings-at-positions" individually. Coining a new technical term, I call them "heterotopes" because they appear at different places (*en hetérois tópois*) in a verse. In order to conveniently refer to heterotopes I add to the base string an upper index that signifies the number of the syllable in the hemistich where the heterotope starts. So ^{0}*bhava*, for example, is the heterotope of the string *bhava* that starts at the ninth syllable of a verse. Now we can, as a final step, add up all the attested positions of a string and the single frequencies of the heterotopes; we then get a list like in Table 3.

2.4 Formulæ

It is a well-known fact that, especially in epic texts, there is a considerable number of repetitions consisting of two or more words. In order to investigate these "formulæ" (to use the word in a purely technical sense) I prepared for them the same kinds of tables as described above, containing information about the metrical structure, positions in the verse, and frequency.

As it turned out to be the case that many of these "formulæ" have one or more elements in common I additionally divided them

Position	Frequency
1	60
2	12
3	109
4	43
5	0
6	0
7	1875
8	0
9	138
10	23
11	169
12	0
13	0
14	0
15	0
16	0

Table 2: Occurrences of *rājan* at different verse positions (two occurrences in hypermetrical lines have been omitted)

String	Number of Positions	Frequency
kaunteya	7	284
kaunteyas	3	17
kaunteyasya	2	11
kaunteyaḥ	2	86

Table 3: Overall frequency and number of verse positions

Table 4: "Formula" family related to ancestor [1]*anyeṣāṁ*

"Formulæ"	**Frequency**
anyeṣāṁ kṣatriyāṇāṁ ca	2
anyeṣāṁ kṣatriyāṇāṁ ca bhūridraviṇatejasām	2
anyeṣāṁ ca	5
anyeṣāṁ caiva	7
anyeṣāṁ caiva bhūtānāṁ	2
anyeṣāṁ caiva vṛddhānāṁ	2

into "families", with the heterotope appearing in all members of a given family as the common "ancestor". The structure of these families in the *Mbh*, where we find more than 18,000 of them, is a highly interesting, but complex topic that I am planning to address in a larger study.[8] May it suffice here to present as an illustration one small family of this kind (see Table 4).

3 Applications

The possible usages of the kind of data contained in the tables above may not be immediately obvious to all readers. As I said above, my personal main interest lies in a deeper understanding of the epic mechanisms of versification, but this is too broad a theme to be addressed here. A much more direct application of metrical data consists in using them in a straightforward statistical way: The frequency of certain metrical patterns, the appearance of words at unusual metrical positions and the like can be specific properties of text passages and may therefore be used as tools for textual analysis. Their special importance lies in the fact that they are completely objective; one can compare them to the features of old paintings that appear under X-ray examination. Some examples for this will be given in the present section though a deeper discussion of the initial results is beyond the scope of this paper.

[8] There are very valuable studies of formulaic language from the pre-computational era, cf. above all Grimer (1974) and Brockington (1999).

But it should be obvious that objective features of the kind mentioned may, among others things, play a crucial role in discussions of textual history. In the case of the *Mbh*, for example, where many scholars believe that the text grew over a considerable period of time and was composed by multiple authors in different intellectual milieus the discussion might be greatly furthered if it was possible to identify objective features that are characteristic of certain passages, strata, etc. And, in so far as some of these features display typical traces of oral poetry, also the discussion about possible oral origins of the great epic may advance beyond the present, rather unsatisfactory state.[9]

The following examples are all drawn from my *Mbh* studies, but they can directly be applied to the *Rāmāyaṇa* and, with some necessary modifications and precautions, to many other metrical texts as well.

3.1 Metrical Patterns

Because metrical patterns as such are not the topic of this paper, but rather their interaction with the choice and usage of words, I will restrict myself to only a few remarks that, at the same time, may serve to remind the reader of some basic facts about the *anuṣṭubh*.[10]

The study of the different metres occurring in the *Mbh* and of the implications of their distribution for questions of textual history, etc. goes back to the nineteenth century.[11] As pointed out already, here I am only dealing with the *anuṣṭubh* that makes up about 94 per cent of all lines. For statistical analyses the epic *śloka* is of special interest because of its flexibility. Its structure can be summarized in the following simplified scheme containing two lines

[9] The kind of futile clinch proponents of orality and written composition often find themselves in, can be studied on examples like Hiltebeitel (2011), ch. 1: "Weighting Orality and Writing in the Sanskrit Epics". This state of affairs is largely due to the lack of objectively verifiable arguments, I believe.

[10] In the following I will only deal with the *anuṣṭubh* and leave other metres out of the picture.

[11] May it suffice here to mention the classical work of E.Ẇ. Hopkins (1993).

with two *pādas* of eight syllables each:

⏓⏓⏓⏓⏑––⏓ | ⏓⏓⏓⏓⏑–⏑⏓
⏓⏓⏓⏓⏑––⏓ | ⏓⏓⏓⏓⏑–⏑⏓

As the structure of the first and second hemistich is identical, in statistical analyses usually the halves of a single line, i.e. two *pādas* of eight syllables each, serve as the basis of relevant data. Two places are of special interest, because they are liable to variation: the first four syllables of both odd and even *pādas* and syllables 5–7 in odd *pādas*. The opening sequence is represented here by four longum above breve symbols which suggests complete freedom, but this is indeed a simplification. Actually all of the sixteen possible patterns occur in the *Mbh*, but with a quite uneven distribution ranging from 20.1 per cent (–––– in odd *pādas*) to utter sporadicity. A somewhat similar picture emerges in relation to the metrical sequence of syllables 5–7 in odd *pādas*. The pattern ⏑–– given above is only the most often occurring variant, traditionally referred to as *pathyā*. The remaining so-called *vipulās* occur much more seldom; the exact figures are given in Table 5. The situation is made even more complex by the fact that the shape of the initial sequence is, to a certain extent, correlated to the variant occurring in syllables 5–7 (but only in odd *pādas*, because the pattern for syllables 5–7 in even *pādas* is almost always ⏑–⏑).

It is a rather obvious idea to look for the exact distribution of these patterns across the text.[12] The first scholar to have approached this question with the help of a computer was Muneo Tokunaga in 1995 (see Tokunaga, 1995). Unfortunately the figures collected by him were for whole books only (*parvans* XVI–XVIII being treated as one book), with the exception of the *Bhagavad Gītā* and the *Nalopākhyāna* that were used for the purpose of comparison. As Tokunaga himself remarks, "the metrical patterns of the books look fairly levelled" (1995, p. 6). For some reason he did not pursue this approach further in the logical direction–collecting data for suitably chosen smaller parts of the text. Mention must also be made at this point of M.R. Yardi's statistical studies collected in Yardi (1986). Yardi's work is statistically more sophisticated than

[12] In addition to Hopkins one should mention Jacobi here (cf. e.g. 1896(1970)).

Tokunaga's - he does a proper analysis of variance – but unfortunately his data are less differentiated. He manually (!) counted the heavy syllables in standard (i.e. *pathyā*) lines that occur at the ten flexible positions 1–4, 8, 9–12, and 16, thus obtaining only the number of these syllables per line, not their sequence. But luckily the times have changed. Having now at our disposal all the data and instruments necessary to doing fine-tuned statistical analysis of metrical phenomena it certainly would be worthwhile to continue what Yardi and Tokunaga have started. So far I have done only initial research in this direction, but the results are already quite promising.

Table 5: Metrical patterns of syllables 5–7 in odd *pādas*

Pattern	Frequency	Percentage
⏑––	122,293	86.30
⏑⏑⏑	7,351	5.19
–––	5,513	3.89
–⏑⏑	4,479	3.16
–⏑–	1,893	1.34
⏑–⏑	110	0.08
⏑⏑–	56	0.04
––⏑	11	0.01

3.2 Polarization

Most people with some experience in reading epic texts will have noticed that many words have a tendency to appear in some metrical positions much more frequently than in others, but the first to have given a name to this phenomenon is probably Ingalls in his path-breaking paper "The *Mahābhārata:* Stylistic Study, Computer Analysis, and Concordance" (1991). Using the terminology of natural sciences he calls it "polarization" and I will adopt this usage of the word. Intuitively it should be quite clear what is meant by it, Table 2 shows a typical example. In most occurrences of *rājan* it occupies the seventh syllable in the verse, at others it appears much less often, at some not at all. Let us now consider the three strings *rājan*, *rājā*, and *ca* whose metrical distribution, marked by the starting syllable, can be seen in the diagrams below (Fig. 1). It is obvious that *rājan* is almost completely polarized, *rājā* to a great extent, and *ca* only to a much smaller degree.

Now it certainly would be a useful thing to be able to quantify the degree of polarization, i.e. the inequality of distribution among the different metrical positions. There are several ways to measure inequality, but having tried some of the most popular methods developed in different sciences it seems to me that the best results for our problem can be obtained by using the so-called Gini coefficient that is normally used to measure the inequality among the levels of income in a society. The general idea is to construct two Lorenz curves (see Fig. 2): one representing a completely even distribution of income (a), the other showing the actual state in a given society (b). The Gini coefficient then is obtained by dividing the surface A between the line of equality and the Lorenz curve representing the actual state by the whole surface of the triangle formed by the axes and the line of equality.

It is not necessary to give a general method of calculation here because in our special case we always have some important pieces of information, namely the number of syllables among which the occurrences of a word are distributed and the frequencies for every syllable. This makes it possible to use a simplified and rescaled formula that was proposed by the development economist Angus Deaton (1997, p. 139):

$$\gamma = \frac{N+1}{N-1} - \frac{2}{N(N-1)\mu} \sum_{i=1}^{N} \rho_i x_i \tag{1}$$

where N is the number of people, μ the mean income, and ρ_i the income rank of the person with income x_i, the persons being ranked in decreasing order.

By inserting the known values in the case of a calculation of polarization *(P)*, we get:

$$P = \frac{17}{15} - \frac{2}{15f} \sum_{i=1}^{16} Pos_i x_i \tag{2}$$

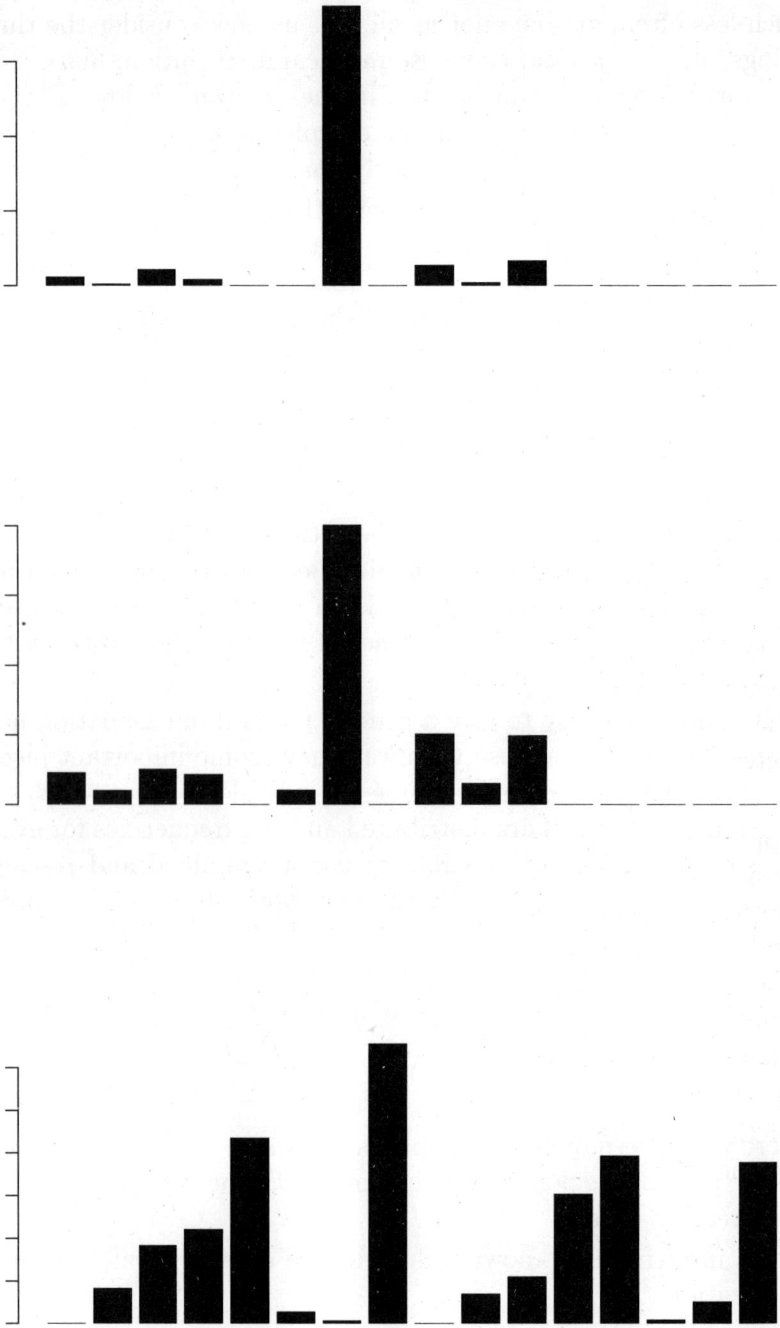

Fig. 1: Metrical distribution of the strings *rājan* (top), *rājā* (middle), and *ca* (bottom)

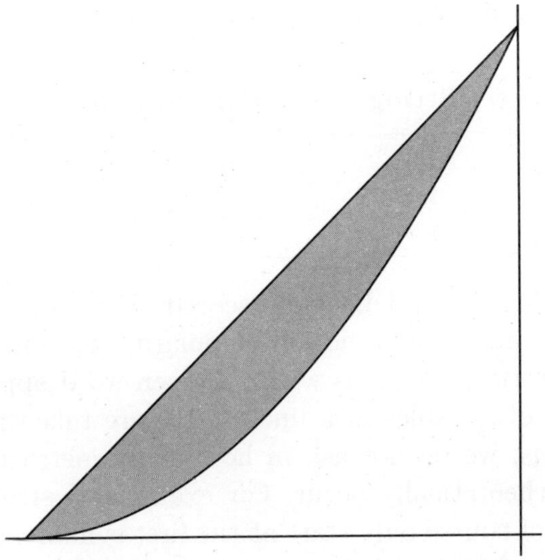

Fig. 2: Gini coefficient: graphical representation

with f symbolizing the overall frequency[13], Pos_i the rank of metrical position i (in decreasing order according to the frequencies of the heterotopes starting there) and x_i the frequency of the given heterotope.

As all of the values must lie between 0 (= no polarization, i.e. appearing at all sixteen metrical positions with the same frequency) and 1 (= complete polarization, i.e. appearing only at one metrical position), this formula can be used to calculate a measure of polarization. I propose, only half-jokingly, to name this new unit after the mythical author of the *Mbh*, Vyāsa (symbol: Vy). When we apply formula (2) to our three examples, the following polarization values are obtained (see Table 6).

The phenomenon of polarization is crucial for the understanding of the epic language, and the possibility to treat it in a precise, quantifiable way will hopefully advance our understanding of how epic verses were constructed. Here I must restrict myself to a few basic statistics and general remarks.

[13] $15f$ is the result of a simplification of $16(16-1)\mu$ because $\mu = \frac{f}{16}$.

Table 6: Polarization values

String	**Polarization**
rājan	0.921 Vy
rājā	0.731 Vy
ca	0.594 Vy

First of all it should be underscored that what is being discussed here is an *absolute* notion of polarity, i.e. only the factual number of metrical positions where a given word appears and the total number of syllables in a line (= 16) are taken into account. In other words, we do not ask in how many metrical positions a string could theoretically occur. For example, a string of sixteen syllables can of course only start at the first syllable, but this does not change the fact that its polarization value equals 1, just as in the case of a monosyllabic string (with sixteen possible positions) or an octosyllabic string (with nine possible positions) that happen to occur at only one position. In principle, one might also think of calculating a relative polarization where only the number of positions that are actually possible would be taken into account, but this is not the way pursued here.

In view of these facts it is to be expected that the polarization value should feature a strong statistical correlation to the number of syllables. And this is indeed the case as the following boxplots show (Fig. 3).[14] Here we can clearly see the mean rising with the number of syllables, but at the same time it should be noted that the ranges are rather big, and there are also some potentially interesting outliers. These observations point to the fact that the polarization value is partially a function of the metrical structure of a string, but that in many cases it must be treated as a feature of the epic language. As such, the phenomenon of polarization should be studied in a broader context, especially in connection with the structure and usage of "formulæ" (Section 2.4 above).

[14] Only strings with a frequency higher than 50 have been selected because polarization values for rarely occurring strings, which obviously tend to be rather high, are less telling.

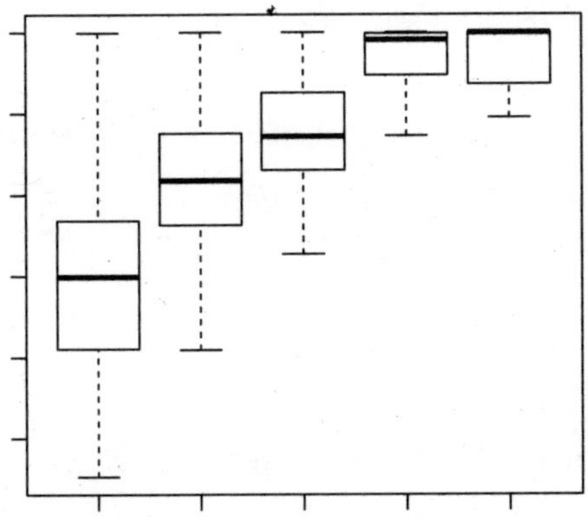

Fig. 3: Polarization values of strings consisting of 1–5 syllables (freq. > 50)

3.3 Exceptionality

Now it is possible to introduce a further important phenomenon, which is, in a certain sense, complementary to polarization: exceptionality (taken here, of course, only in the technical sense I am about to explain). In cases of strongly polarized frequent strings one metrical position is privileged, as it were, i.e. one heterotope of a given string is much more common than the others. This means, in turn, that the others are more or less exceptional. While it can be understood quite easily why strong polarization facilitates versification, the reasons for the appearance of rare heterotopes are not so obvious, therefore, every case of that kind is potentially interesting. (There is a certain analogy to the world of material things, where ^{14}C is much more important to historians than the usual isotope ^{12}C.)

But before it can be attempted to explain the occurrence of exceptional heterotopes one should try to quantify this phenomenon. In order to calculate exceptionality I use a formula that yields values between 0 (no exceptionality, i.e. the standard heterotope) and near 100 (very high exceptionality):

$$E_h = (1 - \frac{f_h}{f_{\max}})100 \tag{3}$$

Here f_h stands for the frequency of a given heterotope, $f_{\max}$ for the frequency of the most often occurring heterotope. To give an example, table 7 displays the exceptionality indices for all occurring heterotopes of *rājñā*.

Table 7: Exceptionality index of the heterotopes of *rājñā*

Position	Frequency	Exceptionality
1	20	59.18
2	3	93.88
3	16	67.35
4	8	83.67
6	14	71.43
7	46	6.12
9	49	0.00
10	1	97.96
11	25	48.98

It must be added at this point, however, that the values yielded by formula (3) are less useful in two cases: when a string has a low overall frequency and when a given heterotope, though relatively rare in comparison to the standard heterotope, is nevertheless frequent in absolute terms, i.e. it would rather be called "common" than "exceptional" in normal parlance. It is therefore advisable to restrict the notion of exceptionality to heterotopes that are both rare and belong to often occurring strings. These conditions are not clearly defined, so the decision must be taken for every text and every heterotope individually. For the following examples I have chosen to include only exceptionality values of heterotopes that occur less than twenty times, whereas the respective base string features a frequency higher than 50.

As already hinted at, every occurrence of a highly exceptional heterotope is potentially interesting, and this feature is inherited by larger parts of text. It yields quite promising results, therefore, to compute the mean of the exceptionality index of all strings of a line, excluding only seemingly exceptional heterotopes, as just explained (let us call this "line exceptionality"). In this way it is possible to identify both single hemistichs and whole passages that stick out because of their exceptionality. This procedure is certainly no end in itself, but it may significantly add to the understanding of the structure of a text, point to potential interpolations and the like. Such further results, however, may only be achieved by a detailed analysis of each particular case, which cannot be done here. So, by way of example, let me just present, with only a short commentary:

(1) one of the most exceptional lines of the *Mbh* according to this calculation method and (2) a moving average curve representing the exceptionality level over the whole text, thus showing two different applications of exceptionality values.

The line is part of a short passage in which Nārada introduces Mātali to Āryaka and consists only in an enumeration of virtues:

05,102.001cd *śuciḥ śīlaguṇopetas tejasvī vīryavān balī*

The exceptionality virtues for the single words can be seen in Table 8:

Table 8: One highly exceptional hemistich
(f_w = overall frequency of the base string)

Heterotope	E	f_h	f_w
[1]*śuciḥ*	96.39	3	101
[3]*śīlaguṇopetas*	0.00	1	1
[9]*tejasvī*	93.48	6	102
[12]*vīryavān*	99.65	1	299
[15]*balī*	0.00	164	175

The line exceptionality of this hemistich equals 57.90. This value is very high, which would be rather hard to guess for the human reader because the words as such are quite common, as can be seen from the last column. But if we have a closer look at the whole Mātali episode, we notice that it contains quite a few rather exceptional lines. How this fact is to be interpreted has to be left to the future, but even now one can say that the passage will probably warrant some closer investigation.

Taking now a look at the whole text let us consider the plot in Fig. 4 that displays the moving average of line exceptionality in such a way that the deviation from the mean becomes clearly visible. This rather ragged graph shows several long stretches of text that markedly deviate, in one direction or the other, from the mean exceptionality, as well as some remarkable peaks. The picture is surely too rough to immediately allow the drawing of any conclusions, but clear enough to underscore the importance of data of that kind for the analysis of the *Mbh*.

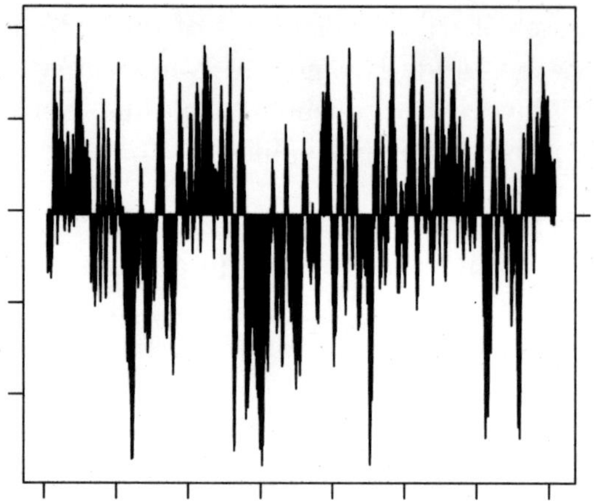

Fig. 4: Moving average of line exceptionality ($n = 1000$)

Finally, a factor must be mentioned that tends to obscure the picture as far as the exceptionality not of single lines but of whole passages is concerned. Also heterotopes of strings that occur only a couple of times in the whole *Mbh* are in a way exceptional, but in order to distinguish them from exceptional heterotopes as defined above I prefer to call them "original". If we take originality into account, we may modify the last diagram in a fruitful way. Instead of looking for exceptionality let us now, on the contrary, try to find the most stereotyped passages; this is possible by plotting the density of hemistichs that are neither exceptional ($E = 0$) nor original (i.e. to make a strong condition, contain no heterotope occurring only once) — the result can be seen in Fig. 5.

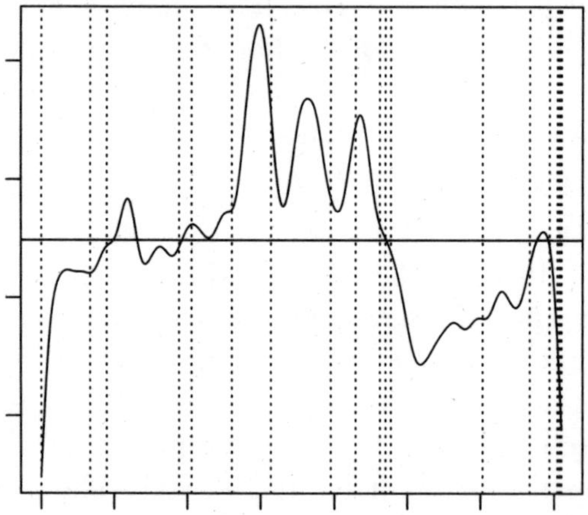

Fig. 5: Density of highly stereotyped verses (bandwidth = 2000). Dotted lines represent *parvan* boundaries.

Here the battle books emerge very clearly as the most stereotyped part of the *Mbh*, though with quite marked internal variations. This seems to be in accordance with the widely held theory that the battle books contain some of the oldest and most traditional material. But, as among others the detailed analyses of V. Simson (1974) have shown, these books are far from monolithic, and it certainly would be worthwhile to investigate the minima at the beginning of Books VII and VIII more closely. But this also has to be left for another publication.

4 Outlook

It hopefully has been shown in this paper that data concerning the usage of words in metrically regulated milieux throw an additional light on otherwise well-known and thoroughly analyzed texts. It is difficult to foresee in each particular case to which new insights this might lead, but even the few examples from the *Mbh* that have been given show clear enough some of the possible applications. As the technical problems that have hampered this kind of research for a very long time no longer exist, the proposed methodology should be applied to all kinds of metrical texts, which will not only contribute to the understanding of these works, but will also help to deepen our knowledge about Sanskrit verse making in general.

References

1. Brockington, John: 'Formulae in the Rāmāyaṇa: An Index of Orality?' In: Brockington et.al. (eds.): *Composing a Tradition: Concepts, Techniques and Relationships.* Proceedings of the First Dubrovnik International Conference on the Sanskrit Epics and Purāṇas, pp. 121–30. Croatian Academy of Sciences and Arts, Zagreb 1999.
2. Deaton, Angus: *Analysis of Household Surveys.* The Johns Hopkins University Press, Baltimore/London 1997.
3. Grincer, P.A.: 'Drevneindijskij ėpos. Genesis i tipologia.' *Gl. Red. vostočnoj literatury*, Moscow 1974.
4. Hellwig, Oliver: *DCS – The Digital Corpus of Sanskrit.* Heidelberg 2010–12. URL `http://kjc-fs-cluster.kjc.uni-heidelberg.de/dcs`
5. Hellwig, Oliver: 'SanskritTagger, A Stochastic Lexical and POS Tagger for Sanskrit.' In: Huet et. al. (eds.) *Sanskrit Computational Linguistics.* First and Second International Symposia, pp. 266–77. Springer, Berlin, 2009.
6. Hiltebeitel, Alfred: *Reading the Fifth Veda.* Brill, Leiden/Boston, 2011
7. Hopkins, E. Washburn: *The Great Epic of India. Character and Origin of the Mahabharata.* Reprint. Motilal Banarsidass, Delhi, 1993.
8. Ingalls, David: 'The Mahābhārata: Stylistic Study, Computer Analysis, and Concordance.' In: Arvind Sharma (ed.): *Essays on the Mahābhārata*, pp. 19-56. Brill, Leiden, 1991.
9. Jacobi, Hermann: 'Über den Śloka im Mahābhārata.' In: *Gurupūjākaumudī.* Festgabe A. Weber, pp. 50-53, Harrassowitz, Leipzig, 1896 [= Kölver, B. (ed.) H. Jacobi, Kleine Schriften, vol. 1, pp. 185-88. Harrassowitz, Wiesbaden (1970)].
10. R Development Core Team: R: A language and environment for statistical computing. R Foundation for Statistical Computing, Vienna (2010). URL `http://www.R-project.org/`
11. v. Simson, Georg: 'Altindische epische Schlachtbeschreibung.' Unpublished habilitation thesis. Göttingen, 1974.
12. Tokunaga, Muneo: 'Statistic Survey of the Śloka in the Mahābhārata.' *Memoirs of the Faculty of Letters*, Kyoto University 34, 1-37, 1995.
13. Visser, Edzard: Homerische Versifikationstechnik. Versuch einer Rekonstruktion. Peter Lang, Frankfurt am Main, 1987.
14. Yardi, M.R.: *The Mahābhārata. Its Genesis and Growth. A Statistical Study.* BORI, Poona, 1986.